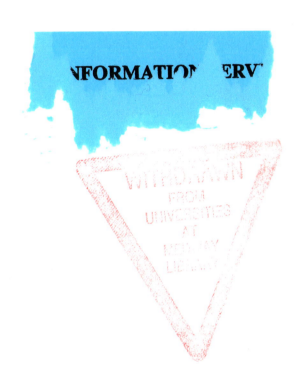

Social Judgments
Implicit and Explicit Processes

Social judgments are critically important in everyday life. It is through social judgments that a shared sense of reality is created and maintained, and coordinated interaction becomes possible. The objective of this book is to provide an informative, scholarly, yet readable overview of recent advances in judgmental research and to offer a closer integration between implicit, subconscious and explicit, conscious judgmental mechanisms. The chapters draw on the latest research on social cognition, evolutionary psychology, neuropsychology, and personality dynamics to achieve this objective. The contributions offer important new insights into the way everyday judgmental processes operate, and they are organized into three sections dealing with (1) fundamental influences on judgmental processes, (2) the role of cognitive and intrapsychic mechanisms in social judgments, and (3) the role of social and interpersonal variables in judgments. The book is written in a readable yet scholarly style, and researchers, practitioners, and students at both the undergraduate and graduate levels should find it an engaging overview of the field.

Joseph P. Forgas is Scientia Professor of Psychology at the University of New South Wales, Sydney, Australia.

Kipling D. Williams is Professor of Psychology at Macquarie University, Sydney, Australia.

William von Hippel is Senior Lecturer in Psychology at the University of New South Wales, Sydney, Australia.

The Sydney Symposium of Social Psychology series

This book is Volume 5 in the Sydney Symposium of Social Psychology series. The aim of the *Sydney Symposia of Social Psychology* is to provide new, integrative insights into key areas of contemporary research. Held every year at the University of New South Wales, Sydney, the symposia deal with important integrative themes in social psychology, and the invited participants are leading researchers from around the world. For further details see the Web site at *www.sydneysymposium.unsw.edu.au*

Previous books in the Sydney Symposium of Social Psychology series:

SSSP 1. FEELING AND THINKING: THE ROLE OF AFFECT IN SOCIAL COGNITION (Edited by Joseph P. Forgas). Contributors: Robert Zajonc (*Stanford*), Jim Blascovich and Wendy Mendes (*UC Santa Barbara*), Craig Smith and Leslie Kirby (*Vanderbilt*), Eric Eich and Dawn Macauley (*UBC*), Len Berkowitz et al. (*Wisconsin*), Leonard Martin (*Georgia*), Dan Gilbert (*Harvard*), Herbert Bless (*Mannheim*), Klaus Fiedler (*Heidelberg*), Joseph P. Forgas (*UNSW*), Carolin Showers (*Wisconsin*), Tony Greenwald, Marzu Banaji et al. (*U. Washington/Yale*), Mark Leary (*Wake Forest*), Paula Niedenthal and Jamin Halberstadt (*Indiana*). Cambridge University Press, New York, 2000; ISBN 0-521-64223-X (hardback), 0-521-01189-2 (paperback).

SSSP 2. THE SOCIAL MIND: COGNITIVE AND MOTIVATIONAL ASPECTS OF INTERPERSONAL BEHAVIOR (Edited by Joseph P. Forgas, Kipling D. Williams, and Ladd Wheeler). Contributors: Bill and Claire McGuire (*Yale*), Susan Andersen (*NYU*), Roy Baumeister (*Case Western*), Joel Cooper (*Princeton*), Bill Crano (*Claremont*), Garth Fletcher (*Canterbury*), Joseph P. Forgas (*UNSW*), Pascal Huguet (*Clermont*), Mike Hogg (*Queensland*), Martin Kaplan (*N. Illinois*), Norb Kerr (*Michigan State*), John Nezlek (*William & Mary*), Fred Rhodewalt (*Utah*), Astrid Schuetz (*Chemnitz*), Constantine Sedikides (*Southampton*), Jeffrey Simpson (*Texas A&M*), Richard Sorrentino (*Western Ontario*), Dianne Tice (*Case Western*), Kip Williams and Ladd Wheeler (*UNSW*). Cambridge University Press, New York, 2001; ISBN 0-521-77092-0 (hardback).

Continued following the Subject Index.

Social Judgments

Implicit and Explicit Processes

Edited by

JOSEPH P. FORGAS
University of New South Wales, Sydney, Australia

KIPLING D. WILLIAMS
Macquarie University, Sydney, Australia

WILLIAM VON HIPPEL
University of New South Wales, Sydney, Australia

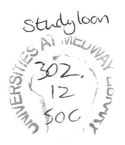

CAMBRIDGE
UNIVERSITY PRESS

PUBLISHED BY THE PRESS SYNDICATE OF THE UNIVERSITY OF CAMBRIDGE
The Pitt Building, Trumpington Street, Cambridge, United Kingdom

CAMBRIDGE UNIVERSITY PRESS
The Edinburgh Building, Cambridge CB2 2RU, UK
40 West 20th Street, New York, NY 10011-4211, USA
477 Williamstown Road, Port Melbourne, VIC 3207, Australia
Ruiz de Alarcón 13, 28014 Madrid, Spain
Dock House, The Waterfront, Cape Town 8001, South Africa

http://www.cambridge.org

First published 2003

Printed in the United Kingdom at the University Press, Cambridge

Typeface Palatino 10/12 pt.   *System* LATEX 2$_\varepsilon$ [TB]

A catalog record for this book is available from the British Library.

Library of Congress Cataloging in Publication Data
Social judgments : implicit and explicit processes / edited by Joseph P. Forgas,
Kipling D. Williams, William von Hippel.
p.   cm. – (Sydney Symposium of Social Psychology series ; v. 5)
A collection of 19 papers presented at the Symposium held annually at the University of New
South Wales in Sydney.
Includes bibliographical references and index.
ISBN 0-521-82248-3
1. Social perception – Congresses.   2. Social interaction – Congresses. 3. Affect (Psychology) –
Congresses.   4. Attitude (Psychology) – Congresses.   I. Forgas, Joseph P.   II. Williams,
Kipling D.   III. Hippel, William von.   IV. Series.
HM1041 .S63   2003
302′.12 – dc21   2002041239

ISBN 0 521 82248 3 hardback

Contents

About the Editors

Joseph P. Forgas received his DPhil and subsequently a DSc from the University of Oxford. He is currently Scientia Professor of Psychology at the University of New South Wales, Sydney, Australia. He has also spent various periods of time working at the Universities of Giessen, Heidelberg, Stanford, Mannheim, and Oxford. His enduring interest is in studying the role of cognitive and affective processes in interpersonal behavior. His current project investigates how mood states can influence everyday social judgments and social interaction strategies. He has published some 14 books and more than 130 articles and chapters in this area. He has been elected Fellow of the Academy of Social Science in Australia, the American Psychological Society, and the Society of Personality and Social Psychology, and he is recipient of the Alexander von Humboldt Research Prize (Germany) and a Special Investigator Award from the Australian Research Council.

Kipling D. Williams received his BS at the University of Washington. He then received his MA and PhD in social psychology at The Ohio State University. There he began his collaboration with Bibb Latané and Stephen Harkins, working on the causes and consequences of social loafing. Before coming to Macquarie University, Professor Williams taught at Drake University, the University of Washington, Purdue University, the University of Toledo, and the University of New South Wales. His recent research focus is on ostracism – being excluded and ignored, on which his book *Ostracism – The Power of Silence* was published in 2001. He also has interests in psychology and law, including research on the tactic of stealing thunder, eyewitness accuracy, and the impact of crime heinousness on jury verdicts.

William von Hippel received his BA from Yale University and his PhD from the University of Michigan. He taught at The Ohio State University for 11 years prior to coming to the University of New South Wales in 2001.

He has published some 30 papers and is currently Associate Editor of *Psychological Science* and *Personality and Social Psychology Bulletin*. His main research areas include stereotyping and prejudice, the self-concept, information processing styles, and social cognitive aging. His most recent work focuses on the cognitive underpinnings and consequences of stereotyping and prejudice, and he is currently investigating the role of inhibitory decline in the increased tendency to rely on stereotypes among elderly adults.

Contributors

Herbert Bless Faculty of Social Sciences, University of Mannheim, Germany

Marilynn B. Brewer Department of Psychology, The Ohio State University

David M. Buss Department of Psychology, University of Texas, Austin

Trevor I. Case Department of Psychology, Macquarie University, Sydney, Australia

Tanya L. Chartrand Department of Psychology, The Ohio State University

Woo Young Chun Department of Psychology, University of Maryland

Rebekah East School of Psychology, University of New South Wales, Sydney, Australia

Hans Peter Erb Department of Psychology, University of Halle, Wittenberg, Germany

Klaus Fiedler Department of Psychology, University of Heidelberg, Germany

Joseph P. Forgas School of Psychology, University of New South Wales, Sydney, Australia

Peter Freytag Department of Psychology, University of Heidelberg, Germany

David C. Funder Department of Psychology, University of California, Riverside

Adam D. Galinsky Department of Management and Organizations, Kellogg School of Management, Northwestern University

Cassandra L. Govan Department of Psychology, Macquarie University, Sydney, Australia

Martie G. Haselton Communication Studies Program and Department of Psychology, University of California, Los Angeles

Denis J. Hilton Department of Psychology, University of Toulouse II, France

Valerie E. Jefferis Department of Psychology, The Ohio State University

Lucy Johnston Department of Psychology, University of Canterbury, Christchurch, New Zealand

Arie W. Kruglanski Department of Psychology, University of Maryland

Gillian Ku Department of Management and Organizations, Kellogg School of Management, Northwestern University

Matthew D. Lieberman Department of Psychology, University of California, Los Angeles

Lucia Mannetti Department of Psychology, University of Rome, Italy

René Martin Department of Psychology, University of Iowa

Paul V. Martorana Department of Management and Organizations, Kellogg School of Management, Northwestern University

John L. McClure School of Psychology, Victoria University of Wellington, New Zealand

Mario Mikulincer Department of Psychology, Bar-Ilan University, Ramat Gan, Israel

Lynden Miles Department of Psychology, University of Canterbury, Christchurch, New Zealand

Antonio Pierro Department of Psychology, University of Rome, Italy

Norbert Schwarz Department of Psychology, University of Michigan

Denise Sekaquaptewa Department of Psychology, University of Michigan

Philip R. Shaver Department of Psychology, University of California, Davis

Scott Spiegel Department of Psychology, Columbia University

Diederik A. Stapel Heymans Institute, Department of Behavioral and Social Sciences, University of Groningen, The Netherlands

Colby J. Stoever Department of Psychology, University of Texas at El Paso

Jerry Suls Department of Psychology, University of Iowa

Robbie M. Sutton Department of Psychology, University of Keele, United Kingdom

Patrick Vargas Department of Marketing, University of Illinois

William von Hippel School of Psychology, University of New South Wales, Sydney, Australia

Michaela Wänke Department of Psychology, University of Basel, Switzerland

Ladd Wheeler Department of Psychology, Macquarie University, Sydney, Australia

Kipling D. Williams Department of Psychology, Macquarie University, Sydney, Australia

Michael A. Zárate Department of Psychology, University of Texas at El Paso

Preface

Social judgments are critically important in everyday life. To be human is to be social, and to be social requires a sophisticated ability to perceive, interpret, and predict the behavior of others. Social judgments are thus a key prerequisite for coordinated social life, and the ability to deal with complex social information is one of the most demanding cognitive tasks we undertake. It is through social judgments that a shared sense of reality is created and maintained, and sophisticated and coordinated interaction becomes possible. Social psychologists have traditionally relied on either mechanistic arithmetic models or constructive Gestalt principles to understand judgmental processes. More recently, the ascendant social cognition paradigm has highlighted the cognitive, information processing mechanisms that underlie many judgments. It is increasingly recognized, however, that not all judgments can be explained in terms of explicit information processing strategies. Many judgments are performed as the result of far more rapid, automatic, subconscious, and implicit judgmental processes.

These two judgmental systems, fast, "deep," primary processing and more elaborate systematic processing, frequently interact in determining a particular judgmental outcome. The main objective of this book is to provide an informative, scholarly, yet readable overview of recent advances in judgmental research and to offer a closer integration between implicit, subconscious and explicit, conscious judgmental mechanisms. The chapters included here argue that a proper understanding of social judgments requires a dynamic, interactive conceptualization that simultaneously focuses on both the cognitive, information processing strategies used and the more fundamental subconscious mechanisms that inform judgments. In other words, the book proposes a new, expanded conceptualization of social judgments that seeks to draw on the latest developments in research on social cognition, evolutionary psychology, neuropsychology, and personality dynamics. Given recent advances in these fields, we believe that this is a particularly fortuitous time to seek such an integration.

The chapters offer important new insights into the way everyday judgmental processes operate and address a variety of intriguing questions, such as: Are there evolutionary differences between the judgmental strategies of men and women? Can we identify brain structures linked to particular judgmental processes? How do early attachment experiences and personality dynamics shape judgmental strategies and the development of self-knowledge? How can we best model the fundamental cognitive processes involved in judgments, and what role do observed contingencies, contextual information, and affective states play in judgmental outcomes? What role do social comparison strategies, social goals, and other social variables such as social exclusion play in judgments? What sorts of strategies are likely to be most effective in reducing stereotyping in judgments?

Naturally, no single book could possibly include everything that is interesting and exciting in contemporary social judgment research. In selecting and inviting our contributors, we aimed to achieve a comprehensive and representative coverage, but, of course, we cannot claim to have fully sampled all of the relevant areas. The chapters are arranged into three parts dealing with (1) fundamental influences on judgmental processes, (2) the role of cognitive and intrapsychic mechanisms in social judgments, and (3) the role of social and interpersonal variables in judgments. The first, introductory chapter presents a historical overview of judgment research and outlines the case for a more comprehensive and integrative conceptualization of the field (Forgas, Williams, & von Hippel).

The chapters in Part I demonstrate the role of evolutionary influences (Haselton & Buss), neuropsychological mechanisms (Lieberman; Zárate & Stoever), and dynamic personality variables (Shaver & Mikulincer; Funder) in social judgments. In Part II, Kruglanski et al. propose an integrative unimodel of judgmental processes, Fiedler and Freytag look at the role of pseudocontingencies in producing judgmental errors, and Bless et al. discuss how contextual variables can induce assimilation or contrast effects. The influence of affective states in judgmental outcomes is considered (Forgas & East; Stapel), and the role of attitude-related processing differences in judgments is discussed (von Hippel et al.). In Part III, contributors look at the use of social comparison strategies (Suls et al.) and the effects of automatic goal pursuit on judgments (Chartrand & Jefferis). The judgmental consequences of social exclusion or ostracism are discussed by Williams et al., and the way various explicit strategies may influence the spontaneous, implicit use of stereotypes in social judgments is also considered (Galinsky et al.; Johnston & Miles). The final, integrative chapter by Marilynn Brewer identifies common themes across the chapters and offers a comprehensive theoretical analysis of the chapters presented here.

THE GENESIS OF THIS BOOK: THE SYDNEY SYMPOSIUM OF SOCIAL PSYCHOLOGY SERIES

This book is the fifth volume in the Sydney Symposium of Social Psychology series, held every year at the University of New South Wales, Sydney. Perhaps a few words are in order about the origins of this volume and the Sydney Symposium of Social Psychology series in general. First, we should emphasize that this is not simply an edited book in the usual sense. The objective of the Sydney Symposia is to provide new, integrative understanding in important areas of social psychology by inviting leading researchers in a particular field to a 3-day residential symposium in Sydney. This symposium has received generous financial support from the University of New South Wales as well as Macquarie University, allowing the careful selection and funding of a small group of leading researchers as contributors. Draft papers by all contributors are prepared and circulated well in advance of the symposium and are placed on a dedicated Web site. Thus, participants had an opportunity to review and revise their papers in the light of everyone else's draft contribution even before they arrived in Sydney.

The critical part of the preparation of this book has been the intensive 3-day face-to-face meeting between all invited contributors. Sydney Symposia are characterized by open, free-ranging, intensive, and critical discussion among all participants, with the objective of exploring points of integration and contrast among the proposed papers. A further revision of each chapter was prepared soon after the symposium, incorporating many of the shared points that emerged in our discussions. Thanks to these collaborative procedures, the book does not simply consist of a set of chapters prepared in isolation. Rather, this Sydney Symposium volume represents a collaborative effort by a leading group of international researchers intent on producing a comprehensive and up-to-date review of research on the social self. We hope that the published papers will succeed in conveying some of the sense of fun and excitement we all shared during the symposium. For more information on the Sydney Symposium series and details of our past and future projects, please see our website www.sydneysymposium.unsw.edu.au.

Four previous volumes of the Sydney Symposium series have been published. The first, *Feeling and Thinking: The Role of Affect in Social Cognition*, was edited by Joseph Forgas and published by Cambridge University Press, New York (2000). This book explored the role that affective states play in social cognition and social behavior, with contributions by Robert Zajonc, Jim Blascovich, Craig Smith, Eric Eich, Len Berkowitz, Leonard Martin, Daniel Gilbert, Herbert Bless, Klaus Fiedler, Joseph Forgas, Carolin Showers, Tony Greenwald, Mahzarin Banaji, Mark Leary, Paula Niedenthal, and Jamin Halberstadt, among others. The second volume, *The Social Mind: Cognitive and Motivational Aspects of Interpersonal Behavior*, was also published by Cambridge University Press (2001) and featured chapters by William McGuire and Claire McGuire, Susan Andersen, Roy Baumeister, Joel Cooper, Bill Crano, Garth Fletcher, Joseph Forgas, Pascal Huguet, Michael Hogg, Martin Kaplan, Norb Kerr, John Nezlek, Fred Rhodewalt, Astrid Schuetz, Constantine Sedikides, Jeffrey Simpson, Richard Sorrentino, Dianne Tice, Kip Williams, Ladd Wheeler, and others.

The third Sydney Symposium volume, *Social Influence: Direct and Indirect Processes*, edited by Joseph Forgas and Kip Williams, was published by Psychology Press (2001), with contributions by Bob Cialdini, Bibb Latané, Martin Bourgeois, Mark Schaller, Ap Disjksterhuis, Jim Tedeschi, Richard Petty, Joseph Forgas, Herbert Bless, Fritz Strack, Sik Hung Ng, Kip Williams, Charles Stangor, Debbie Terry, Michael Hogg, Stephen Harkins, John Turner, Barbara David, Russell Spears, and others. The fourth, most recent volume, edited by Joseph Forgas, Kip Williams, and William von Hippel, was entitled *The Social Self: Cognitive, Interpersonal and Intergroup Perspectives* (published by Psychology Press, 2002) and featured contributions by Eliot Smith, Tom Gilovich, Monica Biernat, Joseph Forgas, Ed Hirt, Fred Rhodewalt, Mark Leary, Roy Baumeister, Dianne Tice, Bertram Malle, William Ickes, Marianne LaFrance, Yoshi Kashima, Marilynn Brewer, Sabine Otten, Chris Crandall, Diane Mackie, Joel Cooper, Michael Hogg, Steve Wright, Art Aron, and Constantine Sedikides.

Given its comprehensive coverage, this book should be useful both as a basic reference book and as an informative textbook to be used in advanced courses dealing with social judgments. The main target audience for this volume comprises researchers, students, and professionals in all areas of the social and behavioral sciences, such as social, cognitive, clinical, counseling, personality, organizational, and applied psychology, as well as sociology, communication studies, and cognitive science. The book is written in a readable yet scholarly style, and students at both the undergraduate and graduate levels should find it an engaging overview of the field and thus useful as a textbook in courses dealing with the self. The book should also be of particular interest to people working in applied areas where using and understanding judgmental processes is important, such as clinical, counseling, educational, forensic, marketing, advertising and organizational psychology, and health psychology.

We want to express our thanks to the people and organizations who helped to make the Sydney Symposium of Social Psychology, and this fifth volume in particular, a reality. Producing a complex multiauthored book such as this is a lengthy and sometimes challenging task. We have been very fortunate to work with such an excellent and cooperative group of contributors.

Our first thanks must go to them. Because of their help and professionalism, we were able to finish this project on schedule. Past friendships have not frayed, and we are all still on speaking terms; indeed, we hope that working together on this book has been as positive an experience for them as it has been for us.

The idea of organizing the Sydney Symposia owes much to discussions with and encouragement by Kevin McConkey, and subsequent support by Chris Fell, Sally Andrews, Peter Lovibond, and numerous others at the University of New South Wales. We want to express our gratitude to Philip Laughlin and the production team at Cambridge University Press, who have been consistently helpful, efficient, and supportive throughout all the stages of producing this book. Our colleagues at the School of Psychology at the University of New South Wales and at Macquarie University, Simon Laham, Rebekah East, Norman Chan, Cassandra Govan, Bradley Hill, Karen Lau, Vee Scott, Vera Thomson, and others, have helped with advice, support, and sheer hard work to share the burden of preparing and organizing the symposium and the ensuing book. We also wish to acknowledge the financial support of the Australian Research Council, the University of New South Wales, and Macquarie University – support that was, of course, essential to get this project off the ground. Most of all, we are grateful for the love and support of our families, who have put up with us during the many months of work that went into producing this book.

Joseph Forgas, Kipling Williams, and William von Hippel
Sydney, August 2002

1

Responding to the Social World

Explicit and Implicit Processes in Social Judgments

Joseph P. Forgas, Kipling D. Williams,
and William von Hippel

CONTENTS

INTRODUCTION

Social judgments are among the most important and demanding tasks people perform in everyday life. The ability to perceive and interpret the actions of others, to make reliable judgments about them and ourselves, and to anticipate and plan our future actions and responses are vitally important for successful interpersonal behavior, and for the development and maintenance of rewarding personal relationships in both our private and working lives. The objective of this book is to survey and integrate the most recent developments in research on social judgments. In particular, our objective is to explore how implicit, automatic, and heuristic judgment processes interact with explicit, deliberative, and elaborated processes in the way people judge themselves and others, and in the way mental representations about the social world are formed.

This work was supported by Australian Research Council grants to Joseph P. Forgas and Kipling Williams, and by contributions from the University of New South Wales and Macquarie University. The contributions of Norman Chan, Simon Laham, Rebekah East, Trevor Case, Carol Yap, and Cassandra Govan to this project are gratefully acknowledged. Please address all correspondence in connection with this chapter to Joseph P. Forgas at the School of Psychology, University of New South Wales, Sydney 2052, Australia; e-mail jp.forgas@unsw.edu.au

1

The book is organized into three major parts. Part I considers recent evidence for the important role that fundamental evolutionary, neuropsychological, and personality processes play in social judgments. Part II focuses on intrapsychic mechanisms of social judgments, including explicit and implicit cognitive and affective processes. Finally, Part III considers the role of social variables in judgmental strategies, such as social motivation, social comparison, social exclusion, and social stereotypes. Within each of these parts, leading international researchers present their most recent integrative theories and empirical research. Our hope as editors is that the ultimate contribution of this book will amount to more than the sum of its parts. A proper understanding of social judgments requires the integration of the evolutionary, biological, cognitive, and social influences that shape our judgmental strategies within a dynamic system. In this introductory chapter, we want to offer some general theoretical and historical comments about the psychology of judgments before outlining the structure and introducing the content of the book.

THE SIGNIFICANCE OF SOCIAL JUDGMENTS

Sociability and gregariousness are key characteristics of our species. Arguably, the ability to perform highly elaborate and sophisticated interpersonal judgments is one of the most important evolutionary achievements of human beings and an essential prerequisite for the efficient functioning of complex social systems. As phenomenological social psychologists such as Heider (1958) also observed, perhaps the most fundamental problem faced by human beings is to understand and predict the behaviors of others. This is largely accomplished by moving from observations of external behaviors to inferences about their internal causes and states, a task that requires extensive and elaborate computational resources. Much of the remarkable evolutionary success of *Homo sapiens* is attributable to our impressive ability to cooperate and interact with each other, achievements that presuppose the ability to carefully monitor, judge, and interpret the behavior of others (Buss, 1999). One view that is gaining popularity in recent psychological theorizing emphasizes the evolutionary origins of psychological phenomena (Buss, 1999). In evolutionary terms, we may think about the human mind as a complex, modular information processing device that was shaped by evolution to facilitate the solution of specific problems (Pinker, 1997).

In these terms, we may consider the ability to perform social judgments as one of the many *mind modules* that developed because they confer distinct survival advantages over evolutionary time (Buss, 1999). What were the evolutionary pressures most likely to have produced the universal human capacity to judge – infer, evaluate, and predict – social behavior? One likely explanation is that having the ability to judge others produced distinct evolutionary advantages because it made sophisticated interaction with other members of our species more predictable and manageable. Indeed, there are some suggestions that the evolution of that immensely powerful computational device, the human cortex, was itself a consequence of the need to manage ever more complex interaction processes within increasingly sophisticated human groups (Pinker, 1997). There is now good evidence that evolutionary influences may have shaped gender differences in how certain social judgments are computed (see Haselton & Buss, this volume), and evolutionary pressures may also have left their mark on the cognitive neuropsychology of many judgmental processes and brain structures (see Lieberman, and Zárate & Stoever, this volume).

It is thus hardly surprising that the study of social judgments has been one of the core concerns of social psychology ever since the inception of our discipline. Classic contributors to our discipline, such as Wundt, James, Allport, Asch, Lewin, Heider, Festinger, and countless others, share an enduring fascination with how social judgments are performed. In fact, a proper understanding of how people perceive and judge themselves and each other, and how their symbolic mental representations about other persons and groups are formed and maintained, has never been of greater importance than today. Throughout the millennia of our evolutionary history, our judgmental skills and strategies were honed by living in close, face-to-face groups, surrounded by intimately known family, relatives, and friends, where almost all interaction involved well-known others. Relying on preexisting knowledge, habits, and schemas was probably a highly efficient way to perform many, if not most, social judgments when permanently surrounded by familiar and predictable others in such relatively stable and intimate social environments characterized by organic solidarity between individuals (e.g., Durkheim, 1956).

Since the 18th century, social organization has undergone a revolutionary change as small, face-to-face *primary groups* gradually lost importance and massive, faceless, impersonal industrial societies emerged. The same implicit habits of mind that served us so well in our evolutionary past may be less well adapted to coping with life in the modern, impersonal mass societies that have evolved in most Western countries. This profound transformation of social life, and the changes it has brought with it in our interpersonal relationships, have preoccupied some of the most creative social scientists such as Durkheim (1956), Weber (1947), and others. These societal changes occurred within a very short period of time – less than 200 years. Indeed, the scope and speed of social change have been further accelerating rather than diminishing in recent decades. As a result, our interactions with others within modern societies have become increasingly complex and impersonal, imposing new and ever-increasing demands on our judgmental capabilities, as most of our encounters now involve people we know superficially at best, if at all (Durkheim, 1956; Goffman, 1972).

As a result, social judges now increasingly need to rely on explicit, controlled cognitive processes to supplement the implicit, automatic judgmental strategies they spontaneously deploy to make sense of the world (see also Brewer, this volume). One of the key integrative objectives of this book is to explore the subtle interplay between implicit, automatic and explicit, conscious processing strategies in the performance of social judgments (see especially Bless, Schwarz, & Wänke; Fielder & Freytag; Forgas & East; Funder; Kruglanski et al.; Shaver & Mikulincer; and Stapel, all this volume). A better understanding of the interaction between these mechanisms is essential to an appreciation of how people evaluate social stimuli, how they form and maintain mental representations, and how they plan and execute their interactions with others (see especially Chartrand & Jefferis; Galinsky, Martorana, & Ku; Johnston & Miles; Suls, Martin, & Wheeler; von Hippel, Vargas, & Seskaquaptewa; and Williams, Case, & Govan, all this volume).

THE NATURE OF SOCIAL JUDGMENTS

Perhaps the most fundamental feature of social judgments is that they require the use of high-level cognitive processes to interpret and infer the complex, ambiguous, and often latent characteristics of people and events that are not obvious or directly observable (Heider, 1958; Kelly, 1955). In other words, social judgments are highly constructive. At least since the seminal work of Bruner (1957), it has been well recognized that judgments also involve an act of categorization, in which the expectations and states of the judge often play a more important role than do the actual characteristics of the judgmental target. Because social judgments involve highly constructive information processing, the outcome of judgments can be very dependent on the information processing strategy people adopt, as well as the content of people's preexisting knowledge, memories, and ideas about the world. The history of research on social judgments demonstrates that there are a host of influences on the way social information about another person is attended to, selected, interpreted, learned, remembered, and evaluated in judgments.

Historical Background

There are several important theoretical frameworks within the history of social psychology that continue to exert an influence on the study of social judgments. Symbolic interactionism, and the work of George Herbert Mead in particular, represent a comprehensive attempt to link interpersonal behavior to mental representations and judgments. For Mead (1934), it is the uniquely human ability to construct enduring symbolic representations based on direct interpersonal experiences that is the fundamental feature of all social judgments. Mead believed that symbolic representations about the social world constructed in the course of social judgments – our mental models of how interpersonal behavior should be enacted – are both the *product* of past social experiences and the *source* of planned behaviors. Thus, social judgments are not just temporary interpretations of fleeting events, but also have an enduring long-term influence on the construction of consensual reality. It is through social judgments and symbolic processes that a stable view of the world is created, and this is the foundation on which both enduring social systems and a sense of stable personality rest. A person develops a sense of unique individuality "only by taking the attitudes of other individuals toward himself within a social environment" (Mead, 1934, p. 138). Along the same lines, James (1890/1950) also argued that it is judgments and reactions by others that determine our sense of personhood (Forgas & Williams, 2002). These themes continue to be important in contemporary research on social judgments, as some of the chapters included here clearly illustrate (e.g., Funder, Kruglanski et al.).

Despite its theoretical promise, symbolic interactionism failed to become a major theory within social psychology, probably because its emphasis on symbolic representations was not easily amenable to empirical research. The contemporary social cognitive paradigm often deals with exactly the same kinds of questions that were also of interest to Mead: How do people interpret and make sense of social experiences, how do they construct a coherent and stable symbolic representation of the social world, and how do these representations, in turn, influence their plans and responses to novel situations? However, whereas Mead always emphasized the social, interpersonal origins of symbolic representations (social cognition), contemporary social cognition researchers often adopt a far more individualistic, cognitive perspective (Forgas, 1981, 1983). It is only during the past few years that social cognition has embraced a far wider variety of affective, motivational, social, and cultural variables (Kunda, 1999).

In fact, Mead's influence on social psychology has been largely indirect, through his influence on writers such as Erving Goffmann (1972), whose dramaturgical account of interpersonal judgments and behavior has contributed important insight into the strategic aspects of social judgments. For Goffman, much public behavior has the quality of role playing or *pretending*, and the main task of social judges is thus to interpret such performances and infer the intended objectives and meanings of actors. Goffman's work neatly captures the fundamental dilemma of most social judgments: What we see is almost never what it seems. The meaning of social events has to be inferred and constructed from ambiguous and often inadequate information. Social psychological theories essentially attempt to explain the constructive, generative nature of social judgments, as the next section will show.

Constructivist versus Mechanistic Models

The constructive, top-down nature of social judgmental processes is now clearly recognized in the literature. It was classical theorists such as Heider (1958), Kelly (1955), Bruner (1957), and Asch (1946) who first argued that the expectations and ideas of the perceiver have a major impact on social judgments. Judgments of even the simplest kinds of social stimuli – such as, famously, the size of a coin – may be subject to constructive perceptual biases as judges seek to interpret and categorize the information in the light of their prior knowledge, feelings, and experience (Bruner, 1957) and attempt to impose meaning, shape, form, or *Gestalt* on complex and often indeterminate stimulus information (Asch, 1946).

This line of thinking owes much to various phenomenological theories in social psychology. A classic example is Fritz Heider's pioneering work (Heider, 1958) exploring the kinds of inferences social actors must rely on in order to judge and interpret strategic interpersonal behaviors successfully. Heider's phenomenological ideas became the foundation of such key areas of judgmental research as the study of person perception and causal attributions, balance and dissonance theories, and research on the dynamics of attitude organization (see, e.g., McClure, Sutton, & Hilton; von Hippel et al., both this volume). Kurt Lewin, like Heider, also believed that understanding the subjective mental representations, or the phenomenological *life space* of individuals, should be the focus of social psychological inquiry. Early research on *personal constructs* by Kelly (1955) provides another important insight into the critical role that enduring subjective differences between judges play in how identical people and events are perceived. Subsequent research on implicit personality theories provided hard empirical evidence for the important role that individual differences in mental representations and constructive processes play in social judgments (Rosenberg & Sedlak, 1972). Other studies have also shown that not only person judgments, but also judgments about common social events or *social episodes*, are fundamentally determined by each individual's implicit theory of events (Forgas, 1979, 1982). Several of the chapters included here also present strong evidence for the constructive role that subjective and often implicit mechanisms play in judgments (see, e.g., the chapters by Bless et al., Chartrand & Jefferies, Fiedler & Freytag, Forgas & East, Suls et al., von Hippel et al., and Williams et al.).

This strong tradition of constructivism in the study of social judgments was not universally accepted, however. Alternative, perhaps more atomistic and mechanistic approaches were also quite popular. *Cognitive algebra*, a field pioneered by Anderson (1974) and clearly based on the psychophysical measurement tradition, conceptualized social judgments as the predictable outcome of simple, arithmetically derived information integration processes. The individual expectations, states, and constructions of the perceiver were of little interest within this paradigm. It was only recently that some reformulations of the model did suggest that some internal states such as affect could be incorporated within the information integration equation (Abele & Petzold, 1994; Kaplan, 1991). Anderson's (1974) model essentially assumes that (1) social traits may be treated as "given" and (2) that such traits retain permanent, enduring meanings. Both of these assumptions have been open to serious doubts. It is now almost universally recognized that contrary to Anderson's (1974) model, in social judgments the information is hardly ever given but has to be constructed and selected from what are usually exceedingly complex and ambiguous information arrays (Forgas, 1981). Indeed, biases in determining exactly what the most relevant information is can have a potentially major impact on social judgments, as work by Asch (1946), Kelly (1955), and Heider (1958) showed (see also the chapters by Bless et al., Fiedler & Freytag, Galinsky et al., McClure et al., and von Hippel et al., this volume). Secondly, the meaning of social information, such as personality traits, is almost never constant or given (see, e.g., the chapter by Funder). As Asch (1946) suggested, personality traits do seem to live an intensely "social" life, their meanings forever shifting and changing, depending on their association with other traits. Being "intelligent" or "determined" can have quite different meanings, depending on whether the person in question is also described as "warm" or "cold." Ultimately, the mechanistic information integration approach and its metaphor of the social judge as a passive and predictable information processor may at best offer an incomplete account of how realistic social judgments are performed (Forgas, 1981, 1983).

The Social Cognition Approach

The conflicting assumptions embodied in the holistic, constructivist and the mechanistic, reductionist views of social judgments were ultimately reconciled in the currently dominant social cognitive paradigm. This approach focuses on the role of information processing strategies and memory structures in social perception. For example, the field of *person memory* was initially defined as the study of the cognitive processes involved in the encoding, retrieval, and combination of information about other people (Hastie et al., 1980; Wyer & Srull, 1989). In these terms, social judgments involve a process of cognitive categorization, requiring the translation of information about people and events into semantic representations, and the subsequent activation of prior experiences and knowledge structures (Wyer & Srull, 1989).

In line with Bruner's (1957) original suggestions, it is the process of categorization and the activation of representational structures that allow perceivers to rely on past knowledge and so "go beyond the information given" by engaging in top-down processing, making inferences and attributions about their target based on their prior knowledge and experiences with people. The contribution of the social cognition approach lies in linking social judgments, clearly involving high-level cognitive processes, with established information processing and memory paradigms from cognitive psychology. Research within this tradition has shown that principles of learning, attention, memory, and semantic and evaluative priming do play an important role in explaining how realistic social judgments are constructed (Kunda, 1999; Wyer & Srull, 1989; see also Bless et al., Forgas & East, Kruglanski et al., Stapel, and von Hippel et al., this volume).

However, as Forgas (1981, 1983) argued almost two decades ago, the original social cognition paradigm also suffered from some important shortcomings. Like most cognitive psychology models, it also assumed "cold" cognition on the part of the perceiver, whereas feelings, emotions, and preferences were relatively neglected (Forgas, 1981, 1983). The model's focus on the isolated, lonely perceiver, separated from the social and cultural context in which judgments are usually made, has been another recurring point of criticism. The past few years saw a major expansion of the social cognitive approach to include careful consideration of the social, cultural, and evolutionary influences that also influence the processing and content of social judgments (see Haselton & Buss, this volume). It is this revised and extended social cognitive framework that is probably responsible for informing the majority of contemporary investigations into social judgmental phenomena, as the contributions to this volume also illustrate.

Which Process? Cognitive information processing theories that initially informed judgmental research typically assumed robust, universal, and relatively context-independent cognitive mechanisms (Wyer & Srull, 1989). The implicit assumption was that information processing models capture fundamental properties of the human mind; as such, they should apply to all minds and to all situations. In fact, few if any cognitive theories achieve such universality. During the past 20 years, cognitive researchers had to settle increasingly for more circumscribed and more context-sensitive information processing models (Neisser, 1982). Social cognitive research has undergone a similar shift as the discovery of numerous boundary conditions, situational variations, and other moderating and mediating influences came to limit the applicability of our models.

One response to the context sensitivity of many social cognitive processes has been the creation of various dual-process and even multiprocess theories of social judgments (e.g., Brewer, 1988; Chaiken, 1980; Forgas, 1995, 2002). These models often distinguish between superficial, fast, heuristic processing styles, on the one hand, and slower, more effortful, systematic processing styles, on the other. Indeed, there is some evidence that these two processing styles may correspond to neural activity located at two distinct sites within the brain (see Lieberman, this volume). *Deep processing* is more automatic and reflexlike, occurs at the subcortical level, and reflects evolutionary developmental experiences (see also Brewer, Haselton & Buss, and Shaver & Mikulincer, this volume). In contrast, *high processing* is slower, more inferential and deliberative; it is localized at the prefrontal cortex, and it is often based on intentional, motivated mechanisms (see, e.g., Brewer, Chartrand & Jefferis, and Galinsky et al., this volume). These two processing styles serve different but often complementary functions, according to several of the authors represented here (see especially Brewer, this volume).

In line with the dominant rationalist assumptions of our age, most judgmental research focused on high-level, systematic processing in the past, and the influence of deep processes on social judgments has been relatively neglected. One objective of this book is to rectify this imbalance and to show that evolutionary, subcortical, and implicit mechanisms do play a critical role in judgments (see especially Haselton & Buss, Lieberman, and Stapel, this volume). In particular, Kruglanski et al. (this volume) outline a powerful new unified theory of social judgments that holds out the promise of reuniting and integrating the various dual-process and multi-process theories in our field within a comprehensive unimodal model of judgments.

The Question of Accuracy. A common issue in judgmental research has been a concern with the question of accuracy (see Funder, this volume). When is a judgment accurate, and when does it demonstrate errors and biases? This question has been extensively explored in early person perception research (Cronbach, 1955), with rather disappointing conclusions. In the absence of reliable yardsticks of what constitutes accurate judgment, the very concept of accuracy turned out to be rather nebulous. Further, as Cronbach's (1955) insightful analysis showed, accuracy is a multifaceted construct, and accuracy in perceiving features of a category to which a target belongs rarely goes hand in hand with accuracy in perceiving the unique differentiating features of an individual target of judgment.

More recently, the issue of judgmental accuracy reemerged following the work of Kahneman and Tversky (1996), who proposed a normative view and argued that the various heuristics, shortcuts, and simplifications that inevitably characterize most real-life judgments represent "errors" and "biases." Others, such as Gigerenzer (2000), questioned the epistemological validity of this claim, and argued that it is inappropriate and misleading to define judgmental accuracy in relation to absolute, normative standards, as Kahneman and Tversky have done. According to Gigerenzer, judgmental accuracy should be defined more functionally, in terms of the judge's prevailing goals and objectives at the time (see also Brewer, this volume). Thus, judgmental heuristics or shortcuts do serve a functional purpose, even if their operation can sometimes produce normatively questionable

outcomes, especially in the highly manipulated and impoverished experimental situations used by Kahneman and Tversky (1996). Gigerenzer's
functionalist perspective is also closely related to adaptive evolutionary
ideas. For example, as Haselton and Buss (this volume) argue, when dealing with inherently ambiguous social information, judges do not necessarily seek normatively optimal outcomes, but may have a built-in bias
toward judgments that optimize the balance between false-positive and
false-negative errors.

Of course, this does not mean that social judgments cannot be subject to
some genuine errors. An excessive reliance on stereotypes when judging
unique individuals is perhaps the most salient example of a judgmental
failure that has important real-life consequences. As several chapters here
illustrate, motivated attempts to control such judgmental tendencies do
not always yield desirable results (e.g., Galinsky et al., Johnston & Miles).
Affective responses constitute another, and particularly important, internal
source of potential judgmental distortions, as suggested by the work of
Forgas and East, Shaver and Mikulincer, and Stapel here.

Of course, this necessarily brief survey of the various theoretical antecedents of research on social judgments is far from complete. Social psychology has an extremely rich tradition of theorizing about the implicit and
explicit mechanisms involved in producing social judgments. The past few
decades in social psychology have been dominated by the growing influence of the social cognitive paradigm. Despite its early rigidities and exces-
sively individualistic approach, the social cognitive framework has now
developed into a much more flexible and comprehensive approach that
allows the investigations of how social judges combine their preexisting
mental representations, feelings, and intentions with the observed features
of people and events in constructing a social judgment. Many of the chapters included here offer impressive illustrations of how social cognitive
methods can be applied to study these processes (see, e.g., Bless et al.,
Fiedler & Freytag, Forgas & East, Kruglanski et al., and von Hippel et al.,
this volume).

OVERVIEW OF THE VOLUME

Contributions to this volume have been organized into three parts dealing with the role of (1) fundamental evolutionary, neuropsychological,
developmental, and personality influences on judgments, (2) cognitive,
affective, and other intrapersonal influences on social judgments, and
(3) interpersonal and social influences on social judgments. The chapters address many of the key issues in contemporary social judgment research, including the following: What are the evolutionary and neuropsychological influences on social judgments (Haselton & Buss, Lieberman,
Zárate & Stoever)? How do childhood experiences impact on preferred

judgmental strategies (Shaver & Mikulincer), and what is the dynamic relationship between personality and social judgments (Funder)? How can we conceptualize the cognitive mechanisms that produce social judgments (Fielder & Freytag, Kruglanski et al., von Hippel et al.), and what role do the judgmental context (Bless et al.) and affective states (Forgas & East, Stapel) play in judgments? To what extent do our judgments depend on social comparison information (Suls et al.), information about the goals of the actor (Chartrand & Jefferis, McClure et al.), stereotypes (Galinsky et al., Johnston & Miles), and acceptance or exclusion by social groups (Williams et al.)?

Part I. Fundamental Influences on Social Judgments

After this introductory chapter, Haselton and Buss (chapter 2) look at the role of evolutionary mechanisms in social judgments. They begin with the premise that humans evolved specific psychological mechanisms to solve specific problems rather than general mechanisms that are applied across domains. Consequently, Haselton and Buss suggest that it is inappropriate to expect human judgment to follow abstract, content-free principles of formal logic. Rather, judgments should provide a domain-specific solution to the relevant adaptive problems faced by our human ancestors. They develop an Error Management Theory, suggesting that evolution has molded social perceivers toward judgments that minimize the cost of possible errors. Thus, they provide evidence that men are more likely to be biased toward inferring sexual intent in women (i.e., men are biased in this domain toward false positives), because a missed sexual opportunity is more costly for men than for women. Conversely, women are more likely to be biased toward judging a lack of commitment on the part of men (i.e., women are biased in this domain toward false negatives). In this case, because a relationship with a man who won't commit is reproductively costly, a bias away from the perception of commitment is adaptive for women. A variety of other judgmental biases are identified and explained within this evolutionary framework, such as risk of aggression and violence, snake fears, and food preferences and disgust.

In chapter 3, Lieberman distinguishes between automatic and controlled processes, using a cognitive neuroscience approach to social judgments. Specifically, he contrasts the traditional view of automatic versus controlled processes in social psychology – in which the same processes are either effortful or effortless, depending on practice – with a neuroscience model of automatic processes – in which different brain regions are responsible for automatic and controlled processes. This model provides an excellent example of why social psychologists should care about the brain. As Lieberman demonstrates, the possibility that automatic and controlled processes in judgments are identified with different brain systems suggests that (1) automatic and controlled processes should differ in qualitative ways, (2) they should interact with one another, and (3) the absolute contribution of both to a judgmental outcome should be assessable. All three of these predictions are inconsistent with the current social cognitive understanding of what it means for processes to be automatic and controlled. The author then reports imaging and traditional social cognitive experiments that support his model. He shows that automatic judgmental processes can be inhibited by controlled processes, and that the interaction of these processes plays a role in both social judgments and a variety of personality processes. The chapter suggests that neurological mechanisms and brain imaging studies can contribute much to our understanding of social judgments.

A somewhat similar theme is addressed in chapter 4 by Zárate and Stoever, who discuss the role of left–right hemispheric differences in the tendency to individuate or stereotype others. Empirical evidence suggests reliable hemispheric differences in using (individuating) and group (stereotyping) perception across a number of tasks. Zárate and Stoever propose that these two processes are typically competing, and that each process works to inhibit the alternative response. They suggest that many social psychological processes related to stereotyping may be understood from this neurocognitive perspective, and that similar mechanisms may also account for various dissociations between implicit and explicit measures of memory. The right hemisphere identifies the unique features of a stimulus, which makes for efficient person identification. The left hemisphere, however, responds well to the similarities across stimuli, which affords efficient group perception and stereotyping. There is a growing tendency among judgment theorists to recognize the role that such fundamental neurocognitive influences play in many everyday social judgments.

In chapter 5, Shaver and Mikulincer examine the influence of early parent–child attachment patterns on the judgmental strategies of adult perceivers. They offer a review and integration between the judgmental literature and the large body of research and theory on attachment styles. Attachment patterns may influence individual differences in many social judgments, including how people view themselves, how they react to new information, and how they respond to out-groups, others' needs, and fleeting affective states. Shaver and Mikulincer make use of several innovative methods to explore the links between attachment and social judgment, including the implicit priming of attachment themes. They assume that the monitoring of unfolding events results in activation of the attachment system, especially when a potential or actual threat is perceived. This activation evolves into automatic goal pursuits (similar to those discussed by Chartrand & Jefferis, this volume) to increase proximity to attachment figures. Shaver and Mikulincer present a comprehensive model that explains the judgmental implications of a variety of attachment styles formed in early childhood.

Funder's insightful chapter (chapter 6) explores the dynamic judgmental strategies that underlie accurate evaluations of personality and the construction of self-knowledge in particular. His Realistic Accuracy Model (RAM) suggests that accurate personality judgment is promoted through the greater availability, detection, and utilization of relevant behavioral cues. The author argues that in the case of personality judgments, judges can increase information availability and relevance by seeking out numerous interaction opportunities and contexts in which the targets feel free to express themselves. Individual differences in how a judge achieves these goals have important implications for judgmental ability. Similar mechanisms also influence judgments in the construction of self-knowledge. The RAM predicts that people may increase their self-knowledge by finding opportunities to display relevant behaviors (e.g., travel, meeting new kinds of people, attempting difficult tasks) and decrease self-knowledge by creating situations in which their behaviors are not diagnostic of their personality (e.g., self-handicapping; see also Forgas & Williams, 2002). The chapter also predicts that people in family environments or cultures that inhibit self-expression tend to lack self-knowledge and may describe themselves inaccurately or even be unaware of their own personality dispositions.

Part II. Cognitive and Intrapsychic Mechanisms of Social Judgments

In the first chapter in this part (chapter 7), Kruglanski, Chun, Erb, Pierro, Mannetti, and Spiegel propose a unified model of human judgment that integrates and simplifies previous dual-process models. The multiplicity of models and processes previously advanced are reduced to six simple parameters that guide all judgment and can be applied across domains. The model is highly parsimonious, and it generates a variety of novel hypotheses. So, for example, in the domain of persuasion, the authors show that both source cues and argument quality can have their impact under either a high or a low cognitive load, depending on the complexity and serial position of the information (parameters of the unimodel). These findings provide an alternative account to the Elaboration Likelihood Model of Petty and Cacioppo and the Heuristic/Systematic Model of Chaiken and colleagues. Similarly, in the domain of attribution, the authors show that the processes of behavioral identification and dispositional inference can both be made to be sensitive to cognitive load, depending on relative information complexity. Finally, in the domain of heuristics and biases, the authors show that base-rate neglect is sensitive to the complexity of the base-rate information and the amount of processing resources available. These findings offer an alternative account to the approach of Kahneman and Tversky, and suggest that Kruglanski et al.'s unified information processing theory of social judgments offers an integrative framework that can account for a wide range of empirical findings in the judgmental literature.

In chapter 8, Fiedler and Freytag examine what appears to be a universal tendency in social judgment: to infer not only correlation, but also causation, between two traits or behaviors when those traits or behaviors are extreme. If a group is known to be high (or low) in one tendency, say aggression, and high (or low) in another, say frequency in engaging in sexual fantasies, then observers of this information are likely to jump to the conclusion that the two behavioral tendencies are correlated and even causally linked. Fiedler and Freytag refers to this automatic judgmental error in logic as the *pseudocontingency bias*. The chapter provides logical and empirical evidence that such causal links are apparent rather than real, and argues that the pseudocontingency bias is an important and so far overlooked source of error in human judgment. They provide an explanation for its ubiquity, and show that the likelihood of generating pseudocontingencies is a function of highly skewed distributions, proximity to the groups in question, and artifacts relating to numerical experiences.

Bless, Schwarz, and Wänke, in chapter 9, look at context effects in social judgments and suggest that the context-dependent inclusion or exclusion of comparison information can selectively produce assimilation and contrast effects. It is for this reason that the *same* task (e.g., judging a stereotype-inconsistent target person) can result in either assimilation effects (when the stereotyped information is implicitly included in the temporary representation of the judgmental target) or contrast effects (when the stereotyped information is explicitly excluded from the representation of the target and is used instead as a standard of comparison). The chapter reviews several series of studies testing the model, exploring both the *direction* and the *size* of such context effects. For example, judgments of a specific product were assimilated toward a newly introduced top-of-the-line product when a joint representation was elicited, but contrast effects emerged when separate representations were elicited. The inclusion/exclusion model holds, and research confirms, that both assimilation and contrast effects are weaker as more information becomes accessible relative to the context information. Thus, assimilation and contrast effects in judgments seem to depend on the subtle interplay of implicit and explicit processing strategies cued by the judgmental context.

Forgas and East (chapter 10) discuss the role of affect in the way people select, learn, recall, and interpret information when making a social judgment or decision. A multiprocess theory of social judgments, the Affect Infusion Model (AIM) is presented as an integrated explanation of such effects (Forgas, 2002), suggesting that the influence of affective states on judgments and decisions depends on what information processing strategies people adopt in different situations. The model predicts that affect can influence both the content and the process of cognition in judgmental tasks, and that affect congruence occurs only in tasks that call for open, constructive processing strategies. The chapter presents a series of laboratory and field experiments demonstrating the process dependence of affective influences on social judgments about interpersonal behaviors, impression formation judgments, attribution judgments, relationship judgments, decisions about bargaining and negotiating strategies, and decisions about interpersonal behaviors. The relevance of these results for a better understanding of the implicit and explicit mechanisms of social judgments is discussed, and the implications of the findings for applied areas and professional practice in applied areas are also considered.

Stapel (chapter 11) suggests that the quick detection of affective stimulus features is most important for survival, and therefore that the processing of affective features should occur prior to the processing of nonaffective information. The question is, however, whether knowing that something is positive or negative provides sufficient information to respond adequately. Although valence detection is necessary, the chapter suggests that it is not always sufficient for an adequate judgment. Following and extending earlier theorizing on the function of emotions, the chapter proposes that to function successfully, people need to be more flexible in their immediate, spontaneous, and automatic judgments about their environment. It is descriptive processing, rather than mere valence detection, that allows for such flexibility. If this is the case, there should not only be automatic evaluation but also automatic description effects to ensure rapid responding. Automatic descriptive processing allows for the constant evaluation and reevaluation of complex stimuli, situations, and events without much time delay. The chapter presents a number of recent experiments illustrating the ubiquity, functionality, and automaticity of spontaneous descriptive processing in social judgments. It is concluded that automatic descriptive processing adds specificity and flexibility to affective processing and allows rapid, adaptive judgments and responses.

In the final chapter in this part, von Hippel, Vargas, and Sekaquaptewa (chapter 12) propose that attitudes might be considered to have both *process* and *content* components. According to this view, the process component of an attitude consists of the information processing biases that a person shows with regard to an attitude object. The content component of the attitude consists of the evaluative beliefs about the attitude object. The authors suggest that the process and content components of the attitude should be dissociated from one another, and their experiments support this prediction. Further, because the process component of the attitude directly influences how the attitude object is understood, the process component should predict judgments and behavior independently of the content component. Across the judgmental domains of politics, religion, gender and racial stereotypes, and the self, process measures of attitudes predicted variance in judgments and behaviors beyond that predicted by traditional content measures. These results were independent of social desirability concerns and occurred across a variety of different processing measures. These results suggest that it might be advantageous to expand our understanding of attitudes to account for the distinct role of attitude-related information processing styles in behaviors and judgments.

Part III. Interpersonal and Social Influences on Social Judgments

Suls, Martin, and Wheeler (chapter 13) note that little progress has been made in accomplishing one of social comparison theory's original aims – to understand how people actually use social comparisons to obtain accurate judgments of their abilities. The chapter describes two models, the Proxy Model of ability self-evaluation and the Triadic Model of opinion comparison. Experiments show that in answering questions like "Can I pass this course?", individuals rely on the experience of others who attempted this course (i.e., a proxy) if they have performed similarly to the proxy individual on prior related courses and are similar to the proxy on related attributes. The Triadic Model of opinion comparisons identifies three categories: preference assessment ("Do I like X?"), preference prediction ("Will I like X?"), and belief assessment ("Is X true or correct?"). Experiments showed that preference assessment is best addressed through comparison with others similar on related attributes; preference prediction is addressed through comparison with a person who has already experienced the stimulus (proxy) and who shows a pattern of consistent past preferences; and belief assessment is efficiently accomplished by comparison with someone who is more advantaged on related attributes but who also shares similar values. The chapter demonstrates how subtle contextual influences can determine the way social comparison information is used in social judgments.

In their chapter on nonconscious mimicry, Chartrand and Jefferis (chapter 14) propose an innovative model of the behavioral and judgmental consequences of nonconscious goals. According to their model, goals can become automatically associated with certain situations and then automatically pursued, with "downstream" consequences of success and failure that also remain outside of awareness. Evidence for this model is provided in a series of experiments on mimicry, in which various situations led to automatic mimicry of incidental motor movements. In addition, success and failure in achieving nonconsciously pursued goals also had an impact on behavior and judgments: Those who failed at their affiliation goals were more likely to mimic their partners' incidental behaviors in a subsequent interaction and were more liked in return. These experiments suggest that nonconscious goal pursuit can be initiated and completed automatically, with behavioral and judgmental consequences in response to the success or failure of the goal pursuit. The model of human behavior that emerges from these experiments is one in which nonconscious processes are sophisticated, sensitive to feedback, and largely successful in serving the broader goals of the individual.

Some of the most important social judgments concern the causal origins of human actions. McClure, Sutton, and Hilton (chapter 15) discuss why people explain most human actions in terms of goals, despite the fact that many actions are influenced by environmental factors. The preference for goal-based explanations in judgments is consistent with action theories that suggest that intentions are seen as necessary and sufficient explanations for actions, whereas other causes are seen as contributory causes rather than sufficient explanations. Why do people judge many causes to be necessary to actions, yet are uninformative when it comes to explanations? One reason may be that explanations conform to Grice's maxim that people should only communicate information that they think the listener lacks. They judge that a goal is a sufficient cause and a good explanation for the action. This chapter distinguishes between explicit and implicit processes in such judgments and argues that preferences for goals in judgments correspond to explicit judgments about actions, whereas judgments about other causes constitute implicit beliefs about actions. The chapter offers empirical evidence to support this view, and discusses whether judgments about actions are sharpened when framed in terms of distinctions between explicit and implicit processes.

Williams, Case, and Govan (chapter 16) analyze some of the judgmental consequences of social exclusion and rejection. They note an intriguing divergence in the literature suggesting that individuals sometimes respond with positive behaviors and judgments to ostracism to make themselves appear more socially attractive, but in other circumstances, they react with anger and hostility. The authors suggest that the inconsistencies may lie in whether the judgmental measures taken are transparent and explicit or disguised and implicit. The results of several studies indicate that when responses can be evaluated by others as signs of social attractiveness, ostracized individuals will behave more positively to achieve inclusion. When ostracized individuals believe that their actions cannot be taken as indicators of social propriety, they are more likely to respond with anger and contempt. In several studies, the authors induced ostracism and then administered explicit or implicit measures of social judgments. As expected, the results showed that ostracized individuals make relatively positive social judgments when they are assessed with explicit measures but produce negative social judgments when assessed implicitly, suggesting that the anticipated social consequences of their judgments motivated their responses.

Galinsky, Martorana, and Ku (chapter 17) explore the methods people can use to decrease stereotyped judgments and prejudice, such as active suppression and perspective taking. They argue that both methods are limited by important boundary conditions that relate to implicit versus explicit processing. Under some conditions, stereotype suppression can produce paradoxical effects, increasing the accessibility of the stereotype. Additionally, the explicit production of counterstereotypic thoughts depletes cognitive resources. Thus, when individuals are faced with multiple or complex tasks that diminish their cognitive capacity, reliance on stereotypes increases. Although the cognitive load limits the efficacy of stereotype suppression, perspective taking can also backfire, especially if the individual has temporary or chronic low self-esteem. In this case, individuals may judge stereotyped groups in light of their own negative self-schemas. Given the general tendency (at least in Western cultures) for individuals to have relatively high self-esteem, but also to be constantly faced with the complexities of multitasking, perspective taking rather than active suppression may be the most useful strategy to reduce prejudice in judgments.

In their chapter on stereotype change (chapter 18), Johnston and Miles suggest that stereotype-consistent information may sometimes produce greater stereotype change than does stereotype-inconsistent information. Because inconsistent information is unlikely to be sought out, when stereotype-consistent information is attributed externally rather than internally, it may have greater potential to lead to moderation of the stereotype. Johnston and Miles propose that low-prejudiced individuals are most likely to make situational attributions for stereotype-consistent events, and that such attributions challenge the validity of the stereotype. In other words, rather than seeking to deny or invalidate a stereotype by communicating stereotype-inconsistent information to judges, a more effective way to reduce prejudice may be to allow stereotype-consistent information to be considered, but attributed to an external rather than an internal cause. This line of research again suggests that explicit judgmental strategies (such as attributing target information internally or externally) may significantly moderate the outcome of implicit, automatic judgmental processes such as stereotyping.

In the final chapter in the volume, Brewer reviews and integrates the contributions of these chapters. She identifies important underlying themes across the contributions. For example, she suggests that a number of the chapters share a distinction between what she terms *deep* and *high* judgmental processes. Deep processes are often fast, automatic, and reflect deeply embedded evolutionary and personal preferences, mostly located at the subcortical level. High processes occur within the cortex and are slower, more systematic, rational and deliberative, and open to motivational and intentional influences. Explicit judgmental processes are mostly high-level processes, whereas implicit judgmental processes can be either deep or high, according to her analysis.

CONCLUSIONS

Understanding how people perform social judgments is one of the most fascinating yet difficult tasks within social psychology. The history of our discipline offers a variety of theoretical frameworks for analyzing judgmental processes, ranging from mechanistic models of cognitive algebra, through Gestalt conceptualizations, to contemporary social cognitive paradigms. Most early social cognitive research focused on the mental processes of isolated social actors and tended to ignore affective, social, and cultural influences on judgments. Information processing theories also emphasized rational, systematic processing strategies to the relative exclusion of more basic, evolutionarily determined heuristic processes. Our main purpose in this volume is to offer a reintegration of research on social judgments that links the implicit and the explicit, the individual and the social, and the conscious and the unconscious aspects of social judgment. The chapters included here, in their various ways, all make the point that an adequate understanding of social judgments requires the joint analysis of these mechanisms. There have been impressive developments during the past two decades in our knowledge of social judgmental phenomena that makes such a reintegration of the field even more imperative. We hope that the contributions within each of the three parts of the book succeed in highlighting key integrative principles that might help us to accomplish this task, and so generate new interest in this exciting area of research.

References

Abele, A., & Petzold, P. (1994). How does mood operate in an impression formation task? An information integration approach. *European Journal of Social Psychology, 24,* 173–188.

Anderson, N. H. (1974). Cognitive algebra: Integration theory applied to social attribution. In L. Berkowitz (Ed.), *Advances in experimental social psychology* (Vol. 7, pp. 1–101). New York: Academic Press.

Asch, S. E. (1946). Forming impressions of personality. *Journal of Abnormal and Social Psychology, 41,* 258–290.

Brewer, M. (1988). A dual-process model of impression formation. In T. K. Srull & R. S. Wyer (Eds.), *Advances in social cognition* (Vol. 1, pp. 1–36). Hillsdale, NJ: Erlbaum.

Bruner, J. S. (1957). On perceptual readiness. *Psychological Review, 64,* 123–152.

Buss, D. M. (1999). *Evolutionary psychology.* Boston: Allyn and Bacon.

Chaiken, S. (1980). Heuristic versus systematic information processing and the use of source versus message cues in persuasion. *Journal of Personality and Social Psychology, 39,* 752–766.

Cronbach, L. J. (1955). Processes affecting scores on "understanding of others" and "assumed similarity." *Psychological Bulletin, 52,* 177–193.

Durkheim, E. (1956). *The division of labor in society.* New York: Free Press.

Forgas, J. P. (1979). *Social episodes: The study of interaction routines*. London and New York: Academic Press.

Forgas, J. P. (1981). *Social cognition: Perspectives on everyday understanding*. New York: Academic Press.

Forgas, J. P. (1982). *Episode cognition: Internal representations of interaction routines*. In L. Berkowitz (Ed.), *Advances in experimental social psychology* (pp. 54–103). New York: Academic Press.

Forgas, J. P. (1983). What is social about social cognition? *British Journal of Social Psychology, 22,* 129–144.

Forgas, J. P. (1995). Mood and judgment: The Affect Infusion Model (AIM). *Psychological Bulletin, 116,* 39–66.

Forgas, J. P. (2002). Feeling and doing: Mood effects on interpersonal behavior. *Psychological Inquiry, 13,* 1–28.

Forgas, J. P., & Williams, K. D. (Eds.). (2002). *The social self: Cognitive, interpersonal and intergroup perspectives* (Vol. 4 in the Sydney Symposium of Social Psychology Series). New York: Psychology Press.

Gigerenzer, G. (2000). *Adaptive thinking: Rationality in the real world*. New York: Oxford University Press.

Goffman, E. (1972). *Strategic interaction*. New York: Ballantine Books.

Hastie, R., Ostrom, T. M., Ebbesen, E. B., Wyer, R. S., Hamilton, D. L., & Carlston, D. E. (Eds.). (1980). *Person memory: The cognitive basis of social perception*. Hillsdale, NJ: Erlbaum.

Heider, F. (1958). *The psychology of interpersonal relations*. New York: Wiley.

James, W. (1890/1950). *The principles of psychology* (Vol. 1). New York: Dover Books.

Kahneman, D., & Tversky, A. (1996). On the reality of cognitive illusions. *Psychological Review, 103,* 582–591.

Kaplan, M. F. (1991). The joint effects of cognition and affect on social judgment. In J. P. Forgas (Ed.), *Emotion and social judgment* (pp. 73–83). Oxford: Pergamon Press.

Kelly, G. A. (1955). *The psychology of personal constructs*. New York: W. W. Norton.

Kunda, Z. (1999). *Social cognition: Making sense of people*. Cambridge, MA: MIT Press.

Mead, G. H. (1934/1970). *Mind, self and society*. Chicago: University of Chicago Press.

Neisser, U. (1982). *Memory observed*. San Francisco: W. H. Freeman.

Petty, R. E., & Cacioppo, J. T. (1986). *Communication and persuasion: Central and peripheral routes to attitude change*. New York: Springer-Verlag.

Pinker, S. (1997). *How the mind works*. London: Penguin Books.

Rosenberg, S., & Sedlak, A. (1972). Structural representations of implicit personality theory. In L. Berkowitz (Ed.), *Advances in experimental social psychology* (pp. 232–257). New York: Academic Press.

Weber, M. (1947). *The theory of social and economic organization* (T. Parsons, ed.). Glencoe, IL: Free Press.

Wyer, R. S., & Srull, T. K. (1989). *Memory and cognition in its social context*. Hillsdale, NJ: Erlbaum.

PART I

FUNDAMENTAL INFLUENCES ON SOCIAL JUDGMENTS

2

Biases in Social Judgment

Design Flaws or Design Features?

Martie G. Haselton and David M. Buss

CONTENTS

INTRODUCTION

Humans appear to fail miserably when it comes to rational decision making. They ignore base rates when estimating probabilities, commit the *sunk cost* fallacy, are biased toward confirming their theories, are naively optimistic, take undue credit for lucky accomplishments, and fail to recognize their self-inflicted failures. Moreover, they overestimate the number of others who share their beliefs, demonstrate the *hindsight bias*, have a poor conception of chance, perceive illusory relationships between noncontingent events, and have an exaggerated sense of control. Failures at rationality do not end there. Humans use external appearances as an erroneous gauge of internal character, falsely believe that their own desirable qualities are unique, can be induced to remember events that never occurred, and systematically misperceive the intentions of the opposite sex (for reviews, see Fiske & Taylor, 1991; Kahneman, Slovic, & Tversky, 1982; and Nisbett & Ross, 1980; for cross-sex misperceptions of intentions, see Haselton & Buss, 2000). These documented phenomena have led to the

We thank Paul Andrews and Julie Smurda for helpful comments on portions of this chapter. Please address correspondence to Martie Haselton: haselton@ucla.edu widespread conclusion that our cognitive machinery contains deep defects in design.

This conclusion has not gone unchallenged (also see Brewer, this volume, and Funder, this volume). Some suggest that certain documented irrationalities are artifacts of inappropriate experimental design (e.g., Cosmides & Tooby, 1996; Gigerenzer, 1996). Others argue that the normative standards against which human performance is compared are inappropriate (Cosmides & Tooby, 1994; Fox, 1992; Pinker, 1997). Recently, we have articulated Error Management Theory (EMT), which proposes that some biases in human information processing should not be viewed as flaws at all (Haselton & Buss, 2000). To understand why demonstrating *bias* does not logically entail *flaw* requires knowledge of the general causal process responsible for fashioning human cognitive mechanisms and the specific adaptive problems humans were designed to solve.

THE HEURISTICS AND BIASES APPROACH

The study of cognitive biases in social psychology can be traced to the creative and influential work of Kahneman and Tversky (1972, 1973; Tversky & Kahneman, 1971, 1973, 1974). In their studies, Kahneman and Tversky documented surprisingly flagrant violations of basic rules of probability. The famous "Linda problem" (Tversky & Kahneman, 1983) is illustrative. Subjects in the Linda studies were provided with a short personality description: "Linda is 31 years old, single, outspoken, and very bright. She majored in philosophy. As a student, she was deeply concerned with issues of discrimination and social justice, and also participated in antinuclear demonstrations." They were then asked to determine which of two options was more probable: (a) Linda is a bank teller or (b) Linda is a bank teller and active in the feminist movement. Although the conjunct proposition cannot be more likely than either of its constituent elements, between 80% and 90% of subjects tend to select (b) as the more probable option, committing what Tversky and Kahneman (1983) called the *conjunction fallacy*.

Kahneman, Tversky, and others following in the *heuristic-and-biases* tradition documented many such violations, including neglect of base rates, misconceptions of chance, illusory correlation, and anchoring bias (Tversky & Kahneman, 1974; see Shafir & LeBoeuf, 2002, for a recent review). Theoretically, these purported irrationalities have been explained as a necessary consequence of the mind's limited computational power and time. As Tversky and Kahneman explain, "people rely on a limited number of heuristic principles which reduce the complex tasks of assessing probabilities and predicting values to simpler judgmental operations" (1974, p. 1124).

THE EVOLUTIONARY FOUNDATIONS OF SOCIAL JUDGMENTS AND DECISIONS

There are no known scientific alternatives to evolutionary processes as causally responsible for shaping organic mechanisms. There are no compelling arguments that humans have been exempt from this causal process. Nor is there reason to believe that human cognitive mechanisms have been outside the purview of evolution by natural selection.

The premise that human cognitive mechanisms, at some fundamental level of description, are products of the evolutionary process, however, does not by itself provide the information required for knowing precisely what those mechanisms are. There is wide disagreement, even among evolutionary theorists, about the nature of the products of the evolutionary process, especially when it comes to humans (e.g., Alexander, 1987; Buss, 1995; Tooby & Cosmides, 1992).

The primary disagreement centers on the relative domain specificity versus domain generality of the evolved mechanisms (Kurzban & Haselton, in press). At one end of the conceptual spectrum, some have argued for versions of domain-general rationality – that human consciousness has the power to "figure out" what is in the individual's best fitness interest. At the other end are those who argue that evolution by selection has produced a large and complex array of specific psychological mechanisms, each designed to solve a particular adaptive problem (e.g., Buss, 1994; Symons, 1987; Tooby & Cosmides, 1992). According to this line of theorizing, highly domain-general mechanisms are unlikely to have evolved, in part because they lead to *combinatorial explosion* – the rapid multiplication of potential alternative ways of cleaving the perceptual environment and of selecting courses of action (Tooby & Cosmides, 1992).

Humans have evolved to solve specific adaptive problems – avoiding predators, keeping warm, eating food, choosing mates – in real time. What constitutes a successful solution in one domain differs from successful solutions in other domains. Criteria for successful food selection (e.g., rich in calories and nutrients, lacking in toxins), for example, differ radically from criteria for successful mate selection (e.g., healthy, not already mated). One all-purpose mechanism is generally inefficient, and sometimes massively maladaptive, for solving adaptive problems that differ widely in their criteria for successful solution. Because there are only small islands of successful adaptive solutions, selection tends to favor specialized mechanisms that prevent drowning in the vast sea of maladaptive ones (Tooby & Cosmides, 1992).

This theoretical orientation has important implications for conceptualizing human information processing machinery. It suggests that the appropriate criterion against which human judgment is evaluated should not be the abstract, content-free principles of formal logic (Cosmides,

1989). Rather, human rationality should be evaluated against a different criterion – whether the information processing mechanism succeeds, on average, in solving the relevant adaptive problem.[1] Because what constitutes a successful solution will differ across domains, no single standard can in principle be appropriate for evaluating human judgment. Indeed, the chapters in this volume provide much evidence of functionally distinct processes surrounding social ostracism (Williams, Case, & Govan, this volume), attachment (Shaver & Mikulincer), and intergroup stereotyping effects (Galinsky, Martorana, & Ku, this volume), to name a few. Perhaps most importantly, this theoretical perspective suggests that the most successful adaptive solutions, for some adaptive problems, are those that are systematically biased.

In the balance of this chapter, we will show how this principle applies to considerations of the appropriateness of research designs and the selection of normative standards in the heuristics-and-biases approach. In the section on normative standards, we highlight EMT (Haselton & Buss, 2000), a new perspective on the evolution of social biases.

THE FORMAT AND CONTENT OF ADAPTIVE PROBLEMS

Ecologically Relevant Problem Formats

Data from nonhuman organisms with neurological systems considerably simpler than those of humans adhere closely to the same rules of probability humans are proposed to violate (Cosmides & Tooby, 1996). Foraging behavior in bumblebees, for example, adheres to some rules of probability (Real, 1991), and similarly sophisticated statistical logic has been identified in birds (Real & Caraco, 1986). Moreover, evidence from the study of language (Pinker & Bloom, 1992), visual perception (Shepard, 1992), and many other areas within human psychology suggests that the human mind does indeed possess computationally sophisticated and complex information processing mechanisms. If neurologically and computationally modest brains can embody a calculus of probability, why not human brains too? If other computational systems within the human mind are functionally

---

[1] Other constraints suggested by the evolutionary approach may also apply to this evaluation. There may be considerable differences between the current and past conditions under which the mechanism evolved. Moreover, in addition to limits on information processing time and capacity (Tversky & Kahneman, 1974), there are constraints imposed by the operation of multiple information processing systems, some of which may have competing demands (e.g., Lieberman, this volume). Thus, *evolutionary rationality* should be based on whether the solution works, somehow, in both solving a problem and coordinating with other mechanisms, and given the alternatives available at the time, and given the material constraints, and eventually leading (in the past) to successful replication.

complex, why should we not expect reasonably good performance involving assessments of probabilities?[2]

One possibility is that the mismatch between human performance and Bayesian expectations is an artifact of inappropriate experimental design. On evolutionary-ecological grounds, Gigerenzer (e.g., 1991, 1997) proposed that tasks intended to assess whether human reasoning embodies laws of probability should present information in a frequency format rather than in probabilities, as is typical in heuristics-and-biases tasks.

He argues that if information was represented in a stable format over human evolutionary history, mental algorithms designed to use the information can be expected to operate properly only when presented with information in that format, even if an alternative format is logically equivalent. Although numerical information can be represented equally well in binary and base-10 form, for example, a pocket calculator will produce logical output only when the input is in base 10. Statistically formatted probabilities are an evolutionarily novel format for computing event likelihood. Some kinds of natural frequencies, on the other hand, are easily observed and have been recurrently available over evolutionary history. For example, one can easily note the number of occasions on which one has met John and he has behaved aggressively versus those occasions on which he did not. According to this logic, if we wish to see whether humans can use Bayesian logic (e.g., inferring the likelihood of events given certain cues), we should present information in frequency form.

As predicted by this account, frequency formats reliably improve performance in tasks like the Linda problem (for sample problems, see Table 2.1). Whereas the probability format produces violations of the conjunction rule in 50% to 90% of subjects (Fiedler, 1988; Hertwig & Gigerenzer, 1999; Tversky & Kahneman, 1983), frequency formats decrease the rate of error to between zero and 25% (Fiedler, 1988; Hertwig & Gigerenzer, 1999; Tversky & Kahneman, 1983). Cosmides and Tooby (1996) documented a similar effect by rewording the medical diagnosis problem (Casscells, Schoenberger, & Grayboys, 1978) to shift it toward the frequency format.

The literature preceding these challenges is vast, with a large constituency, so naturally, these startling results are controversial (Gigerenzer, 1996; Kahneman & Tversky, 1996; Mellers, Hertwig, & Kahneman, 2001). Nevertheless, the frequency effect appears to be reliable (see the preceding discussion), and it cannot be attributed to a simple clarification of the terms involved in the original problems (Cosmides & Tooby, 1996, Exp. 6) or to the addition of the extensional cues (Hertwig & Gigerenzer,

---

[2] See Cosmides and Tooby (1996) for further elaboration of arguments suggesting that a calculus of probability should be expected in human judgment if the relevant adaptive problems recurred over human evolutionary history.

TABLE 2.1. *Comparison of Frequency and Probability Formats in the Linda Problem*

Representation	Conjunction Violations
Probability Format	
Linda is 31 years old, single, outspoken, and very bright. She majored in philosophy. As a student, she was deeply concerned with issues of discrimination and social justice, and also participated in antinuclear demonstrations.	82–88% (across two studies)
Rank the following hypotheses according to their probability: Linda is a bank teller. Linda is a bank teller and active in the feminist movement.	
Frequency Representation	
Linda is 31 years old, single, outspoken, and very bright. She majored in philosophy. [...]	20%
Imagine 200 women who fit the description of Linda. Please estimate the frequency of the following events. How many of the 200 women are bank tellers? —— out of 200 How many of the 200 women are bank tellers and active in the feminist movement? —— out of 200	
Frequency Variant	
Linda is 31 years old, single, outspoken, and very bright. She majored in philosophy. [...]	16%
Imagine women who fit the description of Linda. Please estimate the frequency of the following events. How many of the women are bank tellers? —— out of —— How many of the women are bank tellers and active in the feminist movement? —— out of ——	

Source: Adapted from Hertwig and Gigerenzer (1999).

1999, Exp. 4) implicated when performance improved in earlier studies (Tversky & Kahneman, 1983).

On the other hand, even with greatly reduced rates of error in the frequency format, some evidence suggests a lingering bias toward conjunction errors over other sorts of errors for subjects who fail to solve the conjunction problem correctly (Tversky & Kahneman, 1983). Thus, the frequency studies do not rule out the possibility that people use systematically fallible heuristics in solving some problems. To argue this point is, however, to miss the critical insight to be gained from these studies. The key point is that the human mind can use a calculus of probability in forming judgments, but to observe this, one must present problems in evolutionarily valid forms.

Evolutionarily Relevant Problem Content

A similar conclusion emerges from evolutionary-ecological research on the Wason selection task (Cosmides, 1989; Cosmides & Tooby, 1992; Fiddick, Cosmides, & Tooby, 2000). Past studies with the task suggested that people are unable to use proper falsification logic (Wason, 1983). Revised versions of the studies in which falsification logic was required to detect cheating in social contracts (Cosmides, 1989) or avoid dangerous hazards (Pereya, 2000) caused performance to increase from rates lower than 25% correct (Wason, 1983) to over 75% correct (Cosmides, 1989). The researchers argued that performance increased so dramatically because past studies used highly abstract rules that failed to tap into evolutionarily relevant problem domains. The revised studies did so and thereby activated evolved problem-solving machinery that embodies proper falsification logic (Cosmides, 1989; Cosmides & Tooby, 1992; Pereya, 2000; Fiddick et al., 2000).

The conclusion to be drawn from these studies is *not* that humans actually are good at using abstract rules of logic. Rather, it is that humans have evolved problem-solving mechanisms tailored to problems recurrently present over evolutionary history. When problems are framed in ways congruent with these adaptive problems, human performance can be shown to improve greatly.

In summary, shifting the format or content of problems of social judgment toward greater adaptive relevance can sometimes greatly improve performance. In the context of this volume, these changes might be thought of as shifts from *high* processing to *deep* processing (Brewer, this volume). High processing may be susceptible to limitations imposed by processing ability (Stanovich & West, 2000), effort, and motivation (Kruglanski et al., this volume), whereas deep processing may be relatively more effortless and unintentional, and it may often be superior because it is that for which selection has created specific adaptive design.

WHAT COUNTS AS GOOD JUDGMENT?

Adaptive versus Truthful Inferences

An evolutionary perspective raises questions about what should count as a good judgment. It suggests that the human mind is designed to reason adaptively, not truthfully or even necessarily rationally (Cosmides & Tooby, 1994). The criterion for selection is the net fitness benefit of a design relative to others that happen to be visible to selection at the time. Sometimes this might produce reasonably truthful representations of reality, whereas at other times it might not.

As Pinker notes, "conflicts of interest are inherent to the human condition, and we are apt to want *our version* of the truth, rather than the truth itself to prevail" (1997, p. 305; emphasis in the original). Thus, it might be for good adaptive reasons that we tend to overestimate our contributions to joint tasks (Ross & Sicoly, 1979), have positively biased assessments of ourselves (Brown, 1986), and believe that our strongly positive qualities are unique but that our negative ones are widely shared by others (Marks, 1984).

Biased Trade-offs

Biases can also emerge as a consequence of trade-offs. All adaptations have costs as well as benefits. Cost–benefit trade-offs can produce reasoning strategies prone to err in systematic ways (Arkes, 1991; Tversky & Kahneman, 1974). Less often recognized is the proposal that trade-offs in the relative costs of errors can produce biases (Haselton & Buss, 2000). It is this potential insight to which we now turn.

ERROR MANAGEMENT THEORY

Errors and Bias in Social Signal Detection Problems

Understanding and predicting the behavior of others is a formidable social task. Human behavior is determined by multiple factors, people sometimes mislead others for their own strategic purposes, and many social problems require inferences about concealed events that have already occurred or future events that might occur. It is unavoidable, therefore, that social judgments will be susceptible to error. Given the necessary existence of errors, how should these systems best be designed?

At one level of abstraction, we can think of two general types of errors in judgment: false positives and false negatives. A decision maker cannot simultaneously minimize both errors because decreasing the likelihood of one error necessarily increases the likelihood of the other (Green & Swets, 1966). When the consequences of these two types of errors differ in their relative costliness, the optimal system will be biased toward committing the less costly error (also see Cosmides & Tooby, 1996; Friedrich, 1993; Nesse & Williams, 1998; Schlager, 1995; Searcy & Brenowitz, 1988; Tomarken, Mineka, & Cook, 1989; Wiley, 1994).

Consider a human-made device as an example. Smoke alarms are designed to be biased toward false-positive errors, because the costs of missing an actual fire are so much more severe than the relatively trivial costs of putting up with false alarms. Similarly, the systems of inference in scientific decision making are biased, but in the reverse direction, because many scientists regard false positives (type I errors) as more costly than false negatives (type II errors).

In the smoke alarm example, the designer's (and buyer's) intuitive evaluation of what constitutes cost and benefit guides the design of the system. (Or perhaps those smoke alarm makers who designed systems that produced an equal number of false positives and false negatives went out of business.) The evolutionary process, however, provides a more formal calculus by which competing decision-making mechanisms are selected – the criterion of relative fitness. If one type of error is more beneficial and less costly than the other type of error, in the currency of fitness, then selection will favor mechanisms that produce it over those that produce less beneficial and more costly errors, even if the end result is a larger absolute number of errors. One interesting conclusion from this line of reasoning is that a *bias*, in the sense of a systematic deviation from a system that produces the fewest overall errors, should properly be viewed as an *adaptive bias*.

In sum, when the following conditions are met, EMT predicts that human inference mechanisms will be adaptively biased: (1) when decision making poses a significant signal detection problem (i.e., when there is uncertainty); (2) when the solution to the decision-making problem had recurrent effects on fitness over evolutionary history; and (3) when the aggregate costs or benefits of each of the two possible errors or correct inferences were asymmetrical in their fitness consequences over evolutionary history.

In our research, we have used EMT to predict several social biases. To start with, we hypothesized that there might exist biases in men's and women's interpretation of courtship signals. Because of their ambiguity and susceptibility to attempts at deception, these signals are prone to errors in interpretation. Moreover, with their close tie to mating and reproduction, courtship inferences are a likely target for adaptive design. Based on EMT, we advanced two hypotheses: the sexual overperception hypothesis and the commitment skepticism hypothesis.

Sexual Overperception by Men

We proposed that men possess evolved inferential adaptations designed to minimize the cost of missed sexual opportunities by overinferring women's sexual intent (Haselton & Buss, 2000). One primary factor limiting men's reproductive success over evolutionary history was their ability to gain sexual access to fertile women (Symons, 1979). Ancestral men who tended to infer falsely a prospective mate's sexual intent paid the relatively low costs of failed sexual pursuit – perhaps only some lost time and wasted courtship effort. In contrast, men who tended to infer falsely that a woman lacked sexual interest paid the costs of losing a reproductive opportunity. Given that sexual access to fertile women was one of the most important limiting resources for men, and a missed sexual opportunity could have meant some likelihood of missing a direct opportunity to reproduce, it is reasonable to hypothesize that the social inference errors that resulted in missed sexual opportunities were more costly than the social awkwardness associated with overestimating sexual interest.

Many studies, using a variety of different methods, are consistent with and have supported predictions based on this hypothesis. In laboratory studies, when male partners in previously unacquainted male–female dyads are asked to infer their partner's sexual interest, they consistently rate it as higher than the female partner's report suggests and higher than the ratings provided by female third-party viewers of the interaction (Abbey, 1982; Saal, Johnson, & Weber, 1989). A similar effect occurs in studies using photographic stimuli (Abbey & Melby, 1986), videos (Johnson, Stockdale, & Saal, 1991), short vignettes (Abbey & Harnish, 1995), ratings of courtship signals (Haselton & Buss, 2000), and in surveys of naturally occurring misperception events (Haselton, 2003). Importantly, evidence of sexual overperception does not appear in women (Haselton & Buss, 2000; Haselton, in press). (Figure 2.1 presents a representative effect.)[3]

Commitment Underperception by Women

We proposed an opposing inferential bias in women (Haselton & Buss, 2000). For women, the costs of falsely inferring a prospective mate's commitment when little or none exists were probably greater than the costs of failing to infer commitment that does exist. An ancestral woman who consented to sex with a man she intended to be her long-term mate, but who subsequently failed to invest in her and her offspring, could have suffered the costs of an unwanted or untimely pregnancy, raising a child without an investing mate, and possibly a reduction in her mate value (Buss, 1994). These were substantial costs given the lowered survival of the child (Hurtado & Hill, 1992) and impairment of future reproductive potential. An ancestral woman who erred by underestimating a man's commitment, in contrast, may have merely evoked more numerous and more frequent displays of commitment by the man who truly was committed. If, as we

---

[3] For nonhuman animal examples consistent with this proposal, see Alcock (1993) on *sexually indiscriminant behavior*.

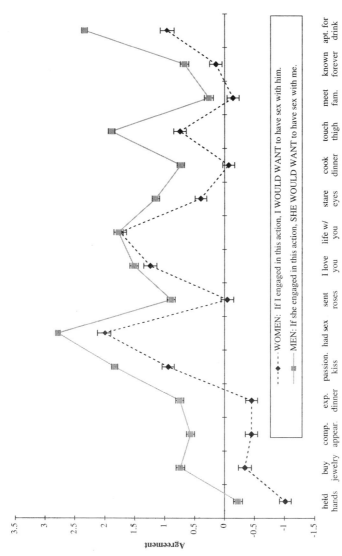

Figure 2.1. Comparison of women's and men's assessments of the degree to which courtship signals indicate sexual interest in women. Women ($n = 168$) provided ratings of their own likely sexual intent, and men ($n = 121$) provided ratings of a female dating partner's likely sexual intent, as determined by each dating behavior. All differences are significant at the $\alpha = .05$ level except "saying she [I] would like to spend her [my] life with me [him] ("life w/you] life with me [him]" in figure above)." Men's ratings of women's sexual interest also exceed women's ratings of other women's sexual interest (see Haselton & Buss, 2000, Study 1 and Study 2, Part 2); thus, the difference does not appear to be a simple self–other difference attributable to self-serving biases. In the same studies, women's ratings of men's sexual interest did not deviate systematically from men's ratings (Haselton & Buss, 2000), suggesting that the sexual overperception effect is limited to male perceivers. Error bars represent standard errors. (Adapted from Haselton & Buss, 2000.)

propose, false-positive errors in inferring commitment were more costly than false-negative errors for ancestral women, selection should have favored commitment-inference mechanisms in women biased toward underinferring men's commitment.

In our studies, we have found evidence of the predicted effect. In the context of courtship, women infer that potential indicators of men's desire for a committed relationship (e.g., verbal displays of commitment and resource investment) indicate less commitment than men report that they intend them to indicate (Haselton & Buss, 2000; see Figure 2.2). The same result appears when comparing women's and men's ratings of a third-party man's commitment signals (Haselton & Buss, 2000). Importantly, evidence of commitment bias does not appear in men's assessments of women's signals (Haselton & Buss, 2000).

Overperception of the Risk of Aggression and Homicide

We have also hypothesized that recurrent cost asymmetries have produced a bias toward overinferring aggressive intentions in others (Haselton & Buss, 2000). Duntley and Buss (2001) tested this hypothesis in the context of homicide. They asked men and women to estimate their own likelihood of committing homicide under certain conditions (e.g., if given a million dollars to do so). They also asked them how likely they were to be victims of homicide under the same conditions (if someone else was given a million dollars to kill them). There was a large and significant difference between these assessments; people estimated that their own likelihood of killing was far lower (10%) than their likelihood of being killed (80%). Although the possibility of a self-serving response bias cannot be ruled out by these data alone, these results are consistent with the error management prediction that we may overestimate the aggressive intentions of others to avoid the high costs of injury or death (Haselton & Buss, 2000).

Other Error Management Effects

Snake Fear. It is likely that the costs of different errors in inferring danger about snakes were asymmetrical over human evolutionary history, with failures to flee clearly being the more costly error (Tomarken et al., 1989). Many studies support the expectations of this hypothesis. Snake fears are easily acquired relative to other fears, they are notoriously difficult to extinguish, and even when successful, discrimination training quickly tends to revert back to a generalized snake fear (Mineka, 1992). Subjects in studies using a covariation paradigm tend to overestimate the association of negative outcomes such as shock and ancestrally dangerous stimuli (snakes or spiders), but do not overestimate the association of shock and innocuous stimuli (mushrooms or flowers; Tomarken et al., 1989), nor do

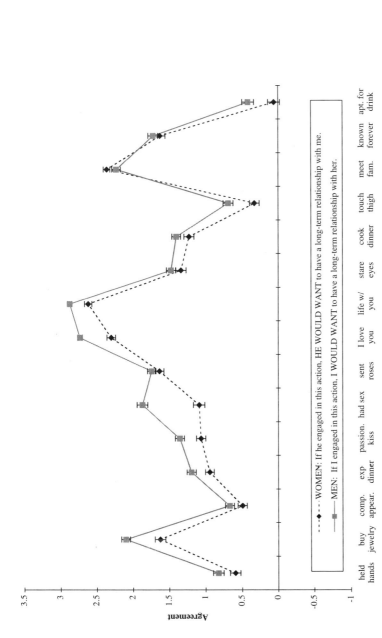

Figure 2.2. Comparison of men's and women's assessments of the degree to which courtship signals indicate commitment intent in men. Men ($n = 121$) provided ratings of their own likely commitment, and women ($n = 168$) provided ratings of a male dating partner's likely commitment, as determined by each dating behavior. All differences are significant at the $\alpha = .05$ level except "stared deeply into her [eyes]," "cooked her [me] a gourmet dinner," and "told her [me] I [he] would like to meet her [my] family." Women's ratings of men's commitment also exceed men's ratings of other men's commitment (see Haselton & Buss, 2000, Study 1 and Study 2, Part 2); thus, the difference does not appear to be a simple self-other difference attributable to self-serving biases. In the same studies, men's ratings of women's commitment did not deviate systematically from women's ratings (Haselton & Buss, 2000), suggesting that the commitment skepticism effect is limited to female perceivers. Error bars represent standard errors. (Adapted from Haselton & Buss, 2000.)

they overestimate the association of shock and presently dangerous stimuli with strong semantic associations with shock, such as electrical outlets (Tomarken et al., 1989).

Food Preferences and Disgust. Humans are finicky about what comes into contact with their food and are not willing to take many chances when deciding whether to consume something. Even though very young children are proposed to lack the cognitive prerequisites for understanding invisible contaminants, most 3- and 4-year-olds refuse to drink juice into which a sterilized cockroach has been dipped (Siegal & Share, 1990). Adults will not drink from a brand new urine-collection cup, even if the researcher takes it from a box of brand-new cups from the factory (Rozin & Fallon, 1987). People are even reluctant to sweeten a beverage with sugar taken from a bottle that says "not poison" or "not sodium cyanide," which suggests that the mere mention of contamination is sufficient to render a food inedible (Rozin, Markwith, & Ross, 1990). In ancestral conditions, in times when food was relatively abundant, the costs of failing to infer correctly that something was contaminated or poisonous were undoubtedly higher than the costs of inferring that a safe food was dangerous. Our present-day conditions typically represent such abundance and, as error management logic suggests, people appear to be biased against consuming foods that might be contaminated, even if the possibility is remote.

Application of EMT to Known Social Biases

Might EMT also help to explain some of the classic effects social psychologists have been interested in, such as the fundamental attribution error, illusory correlation, and the like? We suggest two particularly intriguing possibilities.

Paranoid Social Cognition. Paranoid social cognition occurs when people feel a misplaced or exaggerated sense of distrust and suspicion that often leads to inferences that others are negatively evaluating or conspiring against them (Kramer, 1998). A particular form of social paranoia is the *sinister attribution error* (Kramer, 1994). For example, if a colleague were to pass by in the hallway without saying hello, her coworker could assume that (1) she was simply busy and did not see him or (2) she disliked him or thought he was unimportant. The sinister attribution error occurs if construals of potentially negative events are biased toward personalistic interpretations like the latter.

From an error management perspective, this bias makes sense if it helped people to avoid missing highly costly situations in which they actually were the potential victims of vengeful, disdainful, or conspiratorial others. Of course, the vigilance that such a disposition would promote might distract too much attention from other important activities and prove too costly to maintain if it characterized all social inferences. As one might expect from this additional line of logic, the bias does not occur in all contexts. It is exhibited more by individuals who are under intense scrutiny, new to social organizations (e.g., first-year graduate students), or lower in status than others (e.g., assistant professors) (Kramer, 1994, 1998). These may be analogous to the ancestral conditions in which individuals may have incurred the greatest level of social risk, such as when immigrating into a new village or tribe with apprehensive inhabitants or when joining a new coalition.

The Fundamental Attribution Error. The fundamental attribution error (FAE) occurs when people assume that the behaviors of others and their mental contents (attitudes, dispositions) correspond to a greater degree than is logically warranted (Andrews, 2001; Gilbert & Malone, 1995; Ross, 1977). There are many potential causes of this effect (e.g., Andrews, 2001; Gilbert & Malone, 1995). One possibility is that the nature of the two causal categories under consideration (correspondent vs. noncorrespondent causes) yields different levels of prediction for the perceiver.

Correspondent causes, such as the fact that an aggressor's behavior was caused by his aggressive disposition or intense dislike of a person, are relatively limited in number. Noncorrespondent causes for the aggressor's behavior, such as the fact that the aggressor was provided money by an external source or was otherwise coerced to aggress, are potentially infinite in number (Andrews, 2001). Moreover, correspondent causes of behavior are easy to locate (they reside within the individual), whereas noncorrespondent causes will often be linked to situational factors that can vary, in principle, in an infinite number of ways (Funder, 2001). All else equal, it might simply pay off more for a perceiver to assume that the cause of behavior is the target's disposition or attitude (and that the person will behave aggressively again) than to attribute the behavior to any given element of a situation, even if 95% of the variance in behavior is due to situational determinants.

From an error management perspective, the FAE could evolve if underattribution of behaviors to corresponding mental states leads to more costly errors than overattribution (Andrews, 2001). This proposal is particularly compelling when the behavior in question could have highly negative consequences for a perceiver who failed to protect her- or himself from its perpetrator. Prime examples are aggressive, jealous, uncooperative, or politically distasteful behaviors. As Andrews (2001) suggests, it may be for precisely this reason that past histories of criminal convictions are inadmissible as evidence in court proceedings – they bias jurors too much. "In the hunter-gatherer groups that we evolved in, an individual with a history of uncooperative behavior was likely to pose a stable threat to the interests of other group members. If such a person was under suspicion for committing another offense, other group members might have had an interest in biasing their assessments toward guilt because the costs of erroneous inference of guilt were low and the costs of an erroneous inference of innocence were potentially high" (Andrews, 2001, p. 25).

CONCLUSIONS

The social world is filled with uncertainty. Was that sound in the dark a random accident or was it produced by a lurking intruder? Does this smile indicate sexual interest or mere friendliness? Who can I trust? Who will betray me? Amid the chaos of social cues, humans must render judgments, generate inferences, make decisions, and solve tangible problems in real time. Social psychology has taken on the important scientific task of identifying, describing, and explaining the information processing machinery responsible for producing social solutions to these problems.

Evaluating the performance of cognitive mechanisms requires the specification of standards against which performance is compared. Much work in the field has used content-free principles of formal logic as the crucial criteria and has found human performance wanting. This work, in the aggregate, has illuminated something important – that human judgment and inference can be shown to deviate, sometimes dramatically, from the optimal solutions that would be produced by formal logical systems (but see Funder, this volume, for a discussion of the *error paradigm*).

An evolutionary perspective suggests an alternative set of evaluative criteria – those anchored in successful solutions to specific and delimited adaptive problems. Evolution by selection does not favor information processing machinery according to whether it follows formal logic or even whether it maximizes truthful inferences (Cosmides & Tooby, 1994; Haselton & Buss, 2000). Nor does it favor content-general rules of information processing over content-specific ones (Symons, 1992). It favors mechanisms that minimize overall costs and maximize overall benefits, in the currency of evolutionary fitness, relative to the analogous costs and benefits generated by alternative designs present at the time.

There are several implications of this perspective that we believe have important consequences for the interpretation of biases. First, deviations from normative standards can be produced when problems are not presented in evolutionarily valid formats such as natural frequencies. Toasters should not be found deficient for failing to brown food presented in the shape of potatoes. Analogously, human cognition should not be found deficient for failing at tasks presented in forms that have no evolutionary precedent and for which the mind is not designed.

Deviations can also be produced when subjects are asked to solve abstract problems with evolutionarily novel content far removed from the adaptive problems human mechanisms were designed to solve. Thus, whether human reasoning is good or bad, and whether it adheres to formal standards or not, often cannot be known from studies that have simply demonstrated bias. The format of the input conditions and the problem content also must be scrutinized. Moreover, as Funder (1987, this volume) notes, bias in laboratory studies may or may not correspond to real-world mistakes, particularly when a subject's performance is deemed erroneous unless it lands squarely at the predicted point of optimal performance – a performance standard that should be missed due to measurement error alone.

Second, demonstrations of bias should not necessarily be explained by invoking notions of information processing constraints, cognitive short-cuts, or corner-cutting heuristics. Error management theory points to an alternative explanation – that cognitive biases are sometimes favored by natural selection because of the net benefit they produce relative to alternative designs. These biases, far from being mere by-products of constraints, are adaptive features of good design.

In summary, many have concluded that documented irrationalities suggest widespread flaws in human psychological design. These biases have been called *fallacies* (Kahneman & Tversky, 1972), *illusions*, and *sins* (Piatelli-Palmarini, 1994) and have been described as "ludicrous" and "indefensible" (Tversky & Kahneman, 1971). An evolutionary perspective suggests alternative criteria for evaluating the information processing machinery that drives social inference.

EMT, as a recent approach, has been explored in only a few domains – the sexual overperception bias displayed by men, the commitment skepticism bias displayed by women, and the aggressive intent bias exhibited by both sexes. It is too early to assess whether EMT can help to explain a wider array of biases that psychologists have discovered, from the hindsight bias to the FAE. But it does suggest a principled way in which these biases can be reexamined in a new conceptual light. And it provides a theoretical tool with which new biases can be discovered.

References

Abbey, A. (1982). Sex differences in attributions for friendly behavior: Do males misperceive females' friendliness? *Journal of Personality and Social Psychology, 42,* 830–838.

Abbey, A., & Harnish, R. J. (1995). Perception of sexual intent: The role of gender, alcohol consumption, and rape supportive attitudes. *Sex Roles, 32,* 297–313.

Abbey, A., & Melby, C. (1986). The effects of nonverbal cues on gender differences in perceptions of sexual intent. *Sex Roles, 15,* 283–289.

Alcock, J. (1993). *Animal behavior: An evolutionary approach* (5th ed.). Sunderland, MA: Basic Books.

Alexander, R. D. (1987). *The biology of moral systems.* Hawthorne, NY: Aldine.

Andrews, P. W. (2001). The psychology of social chess and the evolution of attribution mechanisms: Explaining the fundamental attribution error. *Evolution and Human Behavior, 22,* 11–29.

Arkes, H. R. (1991). Costs and benefits of judgment errors: Implications for debiasing. *Psychological Bulletin, 110,* 486–498.

Brown, J. D. (1986). Evaluations of self and others: Self enhancement biases in social judgments. *Social Cognition, 4,* 353–376.

Buss, D. M. (1994). *The evolution of desire: Strategies of human mating.* New York: Basic Books.

Buss, D. M. (1995). Evolutionary psychology: A new paradigm for psychological science. *Psychological Inquiry, 6,* 1–30.

Casscells, W., Schoenberger, A., & Grayboys, T. B. (1978). Interpretation by physicians of clinical laboratory results. *New England Journal of Medicine, 299,* 999–1001.

Cosmides, L. (1989). The logic of social exchange: Has natural selection shaped how humans reason? Studies with the Wason selection task. *Cognition, 31,* 187–276.

Cosmides, L., & Tooby, J. (1992). Cognitive adaptations for social exchange. In J. Barkow, L. Cosmides, & J. Tooby (Eds.), *The adapted mind* (pp. 163–228). New York: Oxford University Press.

Cosmides, L., & Tooby, J. (1994). Better than rational: Evolutionary psychology and the invisible hand. *American Economic Review, 84,* 327–332.

Cosmides, L., & Tooby, J . (1996). Are humans good intuitive statisticians after all? Rethinking some conclusions from the literature on judgment under uncertainty. *Cognition, 58,* 1–73.

Duntley, J. D., & Buss, D. M. (2001, June). *Anti-Homicide Design: Adaptations to prevent homicide victimization.* Paper presented to the Annual Meeting of the Human Behavior and Evolution Society, London, U.K.

Fiddick, L., Cosmides, L., & Tooby, J. (2000). No interpretation without representation: The role of domain specific representations and inferences in the Wason selection task. *Cognition, 77,* 1–79.

Fiedler, K. (1988). The dependence of the conjunction fallacy on subtle linguistic factors. *Psychological Research, 50,* 123–129.

Fiske, S. T., & Taylor, S. E. (1991). *Social cognition* (2nd ed.). New York: McGraw-Hill.

Fox, R. (1992). Prejudice and the unfinished mind: A new look at an old failing. *Psychological Inquiry, 3,* 137–152.

Friedrich, J. (1993). Primary error detection and minimization (PEDMIN) strategies in social cognition: A reinterpretation of confirmation bias phenomena. *Psychological Review, 100,* 298–319.

Funder, D. C. (1987). Errors and mistakes: Evaluating the accuracy of social judgment. *Psychological Bulletin, 101,* 75–90.

Funder, D. C. (2001). The really, really fundamental attribution error. *Psychological Inquiry, 12,* 21–23.

Gigerenzer, G. (1991). How to make cognitive illusions disappear: Beyond heuristics and biases. In W. Stroebe & M. Hewstone (Eds.), *European review of social psychology* (Vol. 2, pp. 129–162). New York: Wiley.

Gigerenzer, G. (1996). On narrow norms and vague heuristics: A reply to Kahneman & Tversky (1996). *Psychological Review, 103,* 592–596.

Gigerenzer, G. (1997). Ecological intelligence: An adaptation for frequencies. *Psychologische Beitrage, 39,* 107–129.

Gilbert, D. T., & Malone, P. S. (1995). The correspondence bias. *Psychological Bulletin, 117,* 21–38.

Green, D. M., & Swets, J. A. (1966). *Signal detection and psychophysics.* New York: Wiley.

Haselton, M. G. (2003). The sexual overperception bias: Evidence of a systematic bias in men from a survey of naturally occurring events. *Journal of Research in Personality, 37,* 43–47.

Haselton, M. G., & Buss, D. M. (2000). Error management theory: A new perspective on biases in cross-sex mind reading. *Journal of Personality and Social Psychology, 78,* 81–91.

Hertwig, R., & Gigerenzer, G. (1999). The "conjunction fallacy" revisited: How intelligent inferences look like reasoning errors. *Journal of Behavioral Decision Making, 12,* 275–305.

Hurtado, A. M., & Hill, K. R. (1992). Paternal effect on offspring survivorship among Ache and Hiwi hunter-gatherers. In B. S. Hewlett (Ed.), *Father–child relations: Cultural and biosocial contexts* (pp. 31–55). New York: Aldine De Gruyter.

Johnson, C. B., Stockdale, M. S., & Saal, F. E. (1991). Persistence of men's misperceptions of friendly cues across a variety of interpersonal encounters. *Psychology of Women Quarterly, 15,* 463–475.

Kahneman, D., Slovic, P., & Tversky, A. (1982). *Judgment under uncertainty: Heuristics and biases.* New York: Cambridge University Press.

Kahneman, D., & Tversky, A. (1972). Subjective probability: A judgment of representativeness. *Cognitive Psychology, 3,* 430–454.

Kahneman, D., & Tversky, A. (1973). On the psychology of prediction. *Psychological Review, 80,* 237–251.

Kahneman, D., & Tversky, A. (1996). On the reality of cognitive illusions. *Psychological Review, 103,* 582–591.

Kramer, R. M. (1994). The sinister attribution error: Paranoid cognition and collective distrust in organizations. *Motivation and Emotion, 18,* 199–230.

Kramer, R. M. (1998). Paranoid cognition in social systems: Thinking and acting in the shadow of doubt. *Personality and Social Psychology Review, 2,* 251–275.

Kurzban, R. O., & Haselton, M. G. (in press). Making hay out of straw: Real and imagined controversies in evolutionary psychology. In J. Barkow (Ed.), *Missing the revolution: Darwinism for social scientists.* New York: Oxford University Press.

Marks, G. (1984). Thinking one's abilities are unique and one's opinions are common. *Personality and Social Psychology Bulletin, 10,* 203–208.

Mellers, B., Hertwig, R., & Kahneman, D. (2001). Do frequency representations eliminate conjunction effects? An exercise in adversarial collaboration. *Psychological Science, 12,* 269–275.

Mineka, S. (1992). Evolutionary memories, emotional processing, and the emotional disorders. *The Psychology of Learning and Motivation, 28,* 161–206.

Nesse, R. M., & Williams, G. C. (1998). Evolution and the origins of disease. *Scientific American, 11,* 86–93.

Nisbett, R. E., & Ross, L. (1980). *Human inference: Strategies and shortcomings of social judgment.* Englewood Cliffs, NJ: Prentice Hall.

Pereya, L. (2000, June). *Function variation of the hazard management algorithm.* Paper presented at the Human Behavior and Evolution Society Conference, Amherst, MA.

Piatelli-Palmarini, M. (1994). *Inevitable illusions*. New York: Wiley.

Pinker, S. (1997). *How the mind works*. New York: W. W. Norton.

Pinker, S., & Bloom, P. (1992). Natural language and natural selection. In J. Barkow, L. Cosmides, & J. Tooby (Eds.), *The adapted mind* (pp. 451–493). New York: Oxford University Press.

Real, L. (1991). Animal choice and the evolution of cognitive architecture. *Science, 253*, 980–986.

Real, L., & Caraco, T. (1986). Risk and foraging in stochastic environments: Theory and evidence. *Annual Review of Ecology and Systematics, 17*, 371–390.

Ross, L. (1977). The intuitive psychologist and his shortcomings: Distortions in the attribution process. In L. Berkowitz (Ed.), *Advances in experimental social psychology* (Vol. 10, pp. 173–220). New York: Academic Press.

Ross, M., & Sicoly, F. (1979). Egocentric biases in availability and attribution. *Journal of Personality and Social Psychology, 37*, 322–336.

Rozin, P., & Fallon, A. E. (1987). A perspective on disgust. *Psychological Review, 94*, 23–41.

Rozin, P., Markwith, M., & Ross, B. (1990). The sympathetic magical law of similarity, nominal realism, and neglect of negatives in response to negative labels. *Psychological Science, 1*, 383–384.

Saal, F. E., Johnson, C. B., & Weber, N. (1989). Friendly or sexy? It may depend on whom you ask. *Psychology of Women Quarterly, 13*, 263–276.

Schlager, D. (1995). Evolutionary perspectives on paranoid disorder. *Delusional Disorders, 18*, 263–279.

Searcy, W. A., & Brenowitz, E. A. (1988, March 10). Sex differences in species recognition of avian song. *Nature, 332*, 152–154.

Shafir, E., & LeBoeuf, R. A. (2002). Rationality. *Annual Review of Psychology, 53*, 491–517.

Shepard, R. N. (1992). The three-dimensionality of color: An evolutionary accommodation to an enduring property of the natural world? In J. Barkow, L. Cosmides, & J. Tooby (Eds.), *The adapted mind* (pp. 495–532). New York: Oxford University Press.

Siegal, M., & Share, D. L. (1990). Contamination sensitivity in young children. *Developmental Psychology, 26*, 455–458.

Stanovich, K. E., & West, R. F. (2000). Individual differences in reasoning: Implications for the rationality debate. *Behavioral and Brain Sciences, 23*, 645–726.

Symons, D. (1979). *The evolution of human sexuality*. New York: Oxford University Press.

Symons, D. (1987). If we're all Darwinians, what's all the fuss about? In C. B. Crawford, M. F. Smith, & D. L. Krebs (Eds.), *Sociobiology and psychology: Ideas, issues, and applications* (pp. 121–146). Hillsdale, NJ: Erlbaum.

Symons, D. (1992). On the use and misuse of Darwinism. In J. Barkow, L. Cosmides, & J. Tooby (Eds.), *The adapted mind* (pp. 137–159) New York: Oxford University Press.

Tomarken, A. J., Mineka, S., & Cook, M. (1989). Fear-relevant selective associations and co-variation bias. *Journal of Abnormal Psychology, 98*, 381–394.

Tooby, J., & Cosmides, L. (1992). The psychological foundations of culture. In J. Barkow, L. Cosmides, & J. Tooby (Eds.), *The adapted mind* (pp. 19–136). New York: Oxford University Press.

Tversky, A., & Kahneman, D. (1971). Belief in the law of small numbers. *Psychological Bulletin, 76,* 105–110.

Tversky, A., & Kahneman, D. (1973). Availability: A heuristic for judging frequency and probability. *Cognitive Psychology, 5,* 207–232.

Tversky, A., & Kahneman, D. (1974). Judgment under uncertainty: Heuristics and biases. *Science, 185,* 1121–1131.

Tversky, A., & Kahneman, D. (1983). Extensional versus intuitive reasoning: The conjunction fallacy in probability judgment. *Psychological Review, 90,* 293–315.

Wason, P. C. (1983). Realism and rationality in the selection task. In J. Evans (Ed.), *Thinking and reasoning: Psychological approaches* (pp. 44–75). London: Routeledge & Kegan Paul.

Wiley, R. H. (1994). Errors, exaggeration, and deception in animal communication. In L. A. Real (Ed.), *Behavioral mechanisms in evolutionary ecology* (pp. 157–189). Chicago: University of Chicago Press.

3

Reflexive and Reflective Judgment Processes

A Social Cognitive Neuroscience Approach

Matthew D. Lieberman

INTRODUCTION

One of the driving forces in social cognition has been the goal of understanding the mental mechanisms that can produce the large array of paradoxical findings that have excited social psychology students for half a century. From persuasion to person perception, decision making to dissonance, and judgment to job descrimination, the distinction between automatic and controlled processes has provided tremendous empirical leverage in the crusade to divide and conquer mental phenomena (in this volume, see Brewer; Chartrand & Jefferis; Galinsky, Martorana, & Ku; Johnston & Miles; cf. Kruglanski et al.). Controlled processes (sometimes referred to as *explicit, conscious,* or *rational processes*) typically involve some combination of effort, intention, and awareness, tend to interfere with one another, and are usually experienced as self-generated thoughts. Automatic processes (sometimes referred to as *implicit, nonconscious,* or *intuitive processes*) typically lack effort, intention, or awareness, tend not to interfere with one another, and are usually experienced as perceptions or feelings. Deciding how to budget one's finances effectively to cover

Please address correspondence to Matthew Lieberman, Department of Psychology, Franz Hall, University of California, Los Angeles, Los Angeles, CA 90095-1563; e-mail: lieber@ucla.edu

44

necessary expenses in both the short and the long term is a controlled process that will likely require effort, intention, and awareness. Deciding to see the new movie starring one's favorite actor is more automatic, with the decision simply appearing in the form of an impulse.

Although progress has been made in terms of determining many of the behavioral and cognitive consequences of automatic and controlled processing, the theoretical utility of this progress has been hampered because automaticity and control refer to the processing phenomenology rather than to the qualitatively distinct representations that are utilized in the two kinds of processing. There is a tendency for us to believe that the same kinds of underlying symbolic representations are used regardless of the automaticity of their use in terms of effort, intention, and awareness (Smith, 1996). This view would suggest that as the processing of certain representations becomes increasingly automatic, the internal structure of the representations remains qualitatively the same but the individual's ability to initiate, prevent, and consciously guide the process changes. There is an increasing volume of work in the cognitive neurosciences that conflicts with this view, instead offering up distinct neural bases for automatic and controlled processes.

A second limitation of current models is that automaticity and control are often viewed as the anchors for two ends of a continuum. Controlled processes are those that involve effort, awareness, and intention. But what are automatic processes? It seems somewhat incomplete to answer that automatic processes are the ones that lack the qualities that controlled processes possess. Rather than defining automatic processes negatively, in terms of which components of controlled processes are lacking, a cognitive neuroscience approach allows us to examine automatic and controlled processes positively in terms of the qualitatively distinct computational properties that emerge from the neurophysiology and connectivity to other neural systems.

Additionally, traditional measures of automaticity and control cannot assess interactions between automatic and controlled processes. No matter how automatic and controlled processes are interacting, the resulting judgment or behavioral response will reflect a unified product that will look more or less automatic overall (Cacioppo & Gardner, 1999). Imagine a process that is two parts controlled and two parts automatic. A shift in processing that adds one part controlled process will be difficult to discriminate from a shift that instead subtracts one part automatic process if the test of automaticity measures the linear summation or relative contributions of the automatic and controlled components. Using neuroimaging techniques, the independent changes in automatic and controlled processes can be assessed prior to the output stage of behavior.

The goal of this chapter is to provide a simple model of the distinct neural correlates of automatic and controlled processes as they relate to social

and affective judgment. Once presented, a new way to understand the negative consequences of introspection in judgment will be presented, comple-
menting existing models (Wilson & Schooler, 1991). Finally, a connection
will be made between the neurocognitive systems involved in automatic
and controlled judgment processes and the personality-related reactivity
of these systems. Because the efficiency and sensitivity of these brain structures vary, these individual differences should be associated with different
judgment and decision-making styles. The field of social cognitive neuroscience is in its infancy (Lieberman, 2000a; Ochsner & Lieberman, 2001),
and thus a disclaimer is necessary: Some of the arguments made in this
chapter are bound to appear simplistic or flat-out mistaken in the clear
light of history. Nevertheless, some theorizing and speculating are in order if we are ever to pull the edges of the separate disciplines close enough
to overlap with one another. This chapter will, it is hoped, serve as an invitation to social psychologists to take a cognitive neuroscientist to lunch
and start exploring the ways that collaborations bringing the disciplines
closer can lead to progress on both new and old problems in judgment and
decision making.

REFLECTION-REFLEXION MODEL OF JUDGMENT

At every turn and at each moment in our daily lives, we are making countless implicit judgments and decisions that allow us seamlessly to make
sense of and navigate our social world. We intuitively make sense of the
nonverbal messages in the environment and often reciprocate appropriately without any effort (Ambady & Rosenthal, 1993; Chartrand & Jefferis,
this volume; Chen & Bargh, 1997; Word, Zanna, & Cooper, 1974); automatically judge objects as more likeable based on previous exposure or their
position in a display (Nisbett & Wilson, 1977; Zajonc, 1968); spontaneously
make sense of behavior in terms of intentions and traits (Gilbert, 1989;
Heider & Simmel, 1944; Winter & Uleman, 1984); and decide whether to
help strangers based merely on the syntax of the request, without careful
consideration (Langer, Blank, & Chanowitz, 1978).

As long as the judgments to be made address familiar stimuli that
are functioning in the way we are accustomed, our judgments can usually proceed automatically without ever becoming a focus of attention.
However, when our expectations are violated, doubt and ambiguity ensue, followed quickly by more explicit decision-making processes (Dewey,
1910; Whitehead, 1911). For instance, when we turn a doorknob to open a
door, we are making a number of assumptions about the nature of the doorknob in terms of structure and function. As long as the doorknob works
as expected, these assumptions remain tacit, allowing us to focus on other
thoughts, and most of the time we are not even reflectively aware of door-
knobs at all (i.e., aware of the doorknob as "a doorknob"). Doorknobs

recruit controlled processing only when they cease to function as door-knobs because broken doorknobs are anomalous and cannot be assimi-lated by our more automatic processes (Dreyfus, 1991; Heidegger, 1927). A broken doorknob that stands between us and where we want to be creates an expectancy violation that requires effort, attention, and reasoning to re-solve. In these cases, controlled decision-making processes occur primarily when automatic processes have failed to achieve our goals.

Previously, my collaborators and I have termed those processes that spontaneously link our goals to behavior *reflexive* (Lieberman, Gaunt, Gilbert, & Trope, 2002b). When reflexive processes fail, *reflective* processes are recruited to deal with circumstances that are exceptions to our implicit expectations. Although these terms may seem like yet another name for the same old dual-process dichotomy, reflexive and reflective processes are de-fined functionally and neurally, not just in terms of resistance to cognitive load and other standard measures of automaticity. Dual-process theories typically propose that the occurrence of controlled processing depends on the availability of cognitive resources and the motivation to be accu-rate. The reflection-reflexion model, taking its cue from cybernetic control models (Carver & Scheier, 1981; Miller, Galanter, & Pribram, 1960; Wiener, 1948), suggests that in addition to motivation and resources, the occurrence of reflective processes is determined by the success or failure of reflexive processes. In other words, reflective processes can be functionally defined as those designed for and recruited to handle situations that prove too difficult for reflexive processes. Additionally, the word *control* has come under increasing scrutiny for its association with free will and the implied homunculus that creates a philosophical regress (Dennett, 1984; Wegner & Bargh, 1998). *Reflexive* and *reflective* indicate the phenomenological expe-rience associated with these processes, without sneaking in a reified self through the backdoor (James, 1913).

The X-System

The neural correlates associated with these two types of processes are the X-system (for the *X* in reflexive) and the C-system (for the *C* in reflective). Functionally, the X-system is responsible for linking affect and social mean-ing to currently represented stimuli, regardless of whether those stimuli are activated bottom-up as a result of ongoing perception or top-down as the contents of working memory in the form of goals, explicit thoughts, or retrieved memories. These links usually reflect conditioning between the various features of a stimulus or between the stimulus and the outcomes for which the stimulus is a cue. The former (*stimulus–stimulus* associa-tions) might include implicit personality theories, stereotypes, and other forms of categorical cognition in which various characteristics, traits, or at-tributes are believed to co-occur. The latter (*stimulus–outcome* associations) generally refer to affective processes, in which one cue (e.g., an angry expression) indicates that one's goals are about to be advanced or thwarted. These affective processes have long been thought to prepare the individual to act on the basis of affective judgment, and thus these processes are assumed to link directly to motor systems in the brain (Frijda, 1986; LeDoux, 1996; Rolls, 1999).

The three neural structures associated with the X-system are the amygdala, basal ganglia, and lateral temporal cortex. There is strong evidence that the amygdala learns about and spontaneously reacts to threat cues as varied as snakes, fear expressions, and out-group race faces (LeDoux, 1996; Phelps et al., 2000); responds to even subliminal presentations of these threat cues (Morris, Ohman, & Dolan, 1999; Whalen et al., 1998); and has direct projections to various motor systems that mediate the *fight-or-flight* response, implicating the amygdala as part of an automatic avoidance system. Alternatively, the basal ganglia seem to serve as part of an automatic approach system, responding to various predictors of reward (Depue & Collins, 1999; Lieberman, 2000a; Schultz, 1998). Neuroimaging studies of implicit learning have shown that the basal ganglia is activated by sequences of cues that predict a desired outcome (Berns, Cohen, & Mintun, 1997; Lieberman, Chang, Chiao, Bookheimer, & Knowlton, 2002a) and in response to cues that elicit positive affect ranging from pictures of loved ones (Bartels & Zeki, 2000) to cocaine administration (Breiter, Gollub, & Weisskoff, 1997). Like the amygdala, the basal ganglia also have numerous projections that can initiate behavior; indeed, the first symptoms of basal ganglia–related neurodegenerative diseases like Parkinson's disease and Huntington's disease are impairments in habitual action patterns (Grant & Adams, 1996). There is evidence to suggest that the basal ganglia and amygdala each participate to some degree in reflexive responses to positive and negative cues; however, they do appear to be selectively more involved in one valenced affect than the other (Tabibnia, 2002).

Lateral temporal cortex is involved in recognizing the identity, attributes, and behavior of social (and nonsocial) objects. The lower (or *ventral*) part of temporal cortex is part of the "what" system in the visual processing stream (Mishkin, Ungerleider, & Macko, 1983). The contiguous regions that make up the ventral visual stream make progressively more abstract inferences about the identity and category membership of the underlying stimulus. In early stages (toward the back of the brain), visual attributes are constructed from lines, colors, and textures. In later stages (toward the front of the temporal lobes), the overall identity and category memberships are activated such that attributes that are missing or occluded are activated in addition to those that are strictly visible. Thus, just seeing part of a familiar face or the color of a stranger's skin will lead people to fill in all sorts of other characteristics associated with individual or group identity. This ability to "go beyond the information given" is a major component of most theories hoping to explain the strengths and weaknesses of human social cognition (Bruner, 1957; Fiske & Taylor, 1991; Griffin & Ross, 1991).

The upper part of lateral temporal cortex, referred to as *superior temporal sulcus*, is specialized for behavior identification (Allison, Puce, & McCarthy, 2000; Decety & Grezes, 1999; Haxby, Hoffman, & Gobbini, 2000; Lieberman et al., 2002b). This region is largely involved in extracting the intentions behind particular behaviors and has been theorized to be critical to the *Theory of Mind* lacking in children with autism (Baron-Cohen, 1995). Neurons in this region fire in conjunction with very different behaviors as long as the underlying intention associated with each behavior is the same (Jellema & Perrett, 2001). Moreover, accidental behaviors such as tripping and dropping an object do not activate these neurons (Perrett, Jellema, Frigerio, & Burt, 2001). Ventral temporal cortex and superior temporal cortex "talk" with one another to allow inferences about individual and group traits based on observed behaviors and inferences about the implications of behaviors based on who performed them.

To summarize, the X-system is composed of the amygdala, basal ganglia, and lateral temporal cortex to form a very efficient knowledge base about the social and affective characteristics of social phenomena that often sets into motion behaviors based on extensive learning histories that have accumulated slowly over time. The X-system contains our implicit theories and expectations that allow us to interface smoothly with the world, seamlessly promoting our goals and avoiding our foes.

The C-System

Sometimes our existing expectations in the X-system fail us. The failure can occur in one of two ways, but the result is the same in both cases: Another mechanism besides the X-system is needed to guide behavior. Sometimes the task or stimulus is novel, and consequently the X-system has no preexisting well-learned representations that can assimilate the incoming information. At other times the task or stimulus is familiar, but one's goal or the constraints of the current context render the X-system's habitual response inappropriate. For instance, egalitarian individuals may have negative racial stereotypes activated in the X-system in response to a member of that race. Given egalitarian motives, the X-system's response to the target is undesirable, leading to the involvement of controlled processing in order to override or suppress the X-system's response (Galinsky, Martorana & Ku, this volume; Monteith, 1993; cf. Moskowitz, Gollwitzer, Wasel, & Schaal, 1999). In each case, the X-system's generalities are not prepared to deal with the specific situation at hand.

In contrast to the X-system's efficiency with social phenomena that conform to its generalities, the C-system is critical for handling the exceptions to the rules (McClelland, McNaughton, & O'Reilly, 1995). The C-system is composed of three neurocognitive mechanisms that work closely together: anterior cingulate cortex, lateral prefrontal cortex, and the medial temporal lobe (including the hippocampus). The first two regions are responsible for detecting the need for top-down control and for implementing control, respectively. The medial temporal lobe stores information about past episodes to the extent that they required controlled processing (Brewer, Zhao, Desmond, Glover, & Gabrieli, 1998; Craik & Tulving, 1975; Otten, Henson, & Rugg, 2001; Wagner et al., 1998), presumably so that this information can facilitate processing the next time the special circumstances arise. The details of how these structures perform their functions have been described at length elsewhere (Lieberman et al., 2002b). Consequently, I will limit myself to some of the conclusions posited by the reflection-reflexion model.

First, the anterior cingulate cortex is sensitive to many forms of conflict and error in the X-system that generally indicate that the X-system is unable to advance one's current goals (Botvinick, Braver, Barch, Carter, & Cohen, 2000) and thus serves as an *alarm system* that alerts prefrontal cortex that control is needed. The anterior cingulate is sensitive to a variety of conflict and error signals including pain (Baciu et al., 1999; Ladabaum, Minoshima, & Owyang, 2000; Rainville, Duncan, Price, Carrier, & Bushnell, 1997), distress vocalizations (Lorberbaum et al., 1999; see Shaver & Mikulincer, this volume, for relevant attachment work), cognitive errors (Bush, Luu, & Posner, 2000), and tasks that require the overriding of a habitual response based on current goals (Barch, Braver, Sabb, & Noll, 2000; Carter et al., 2000). Although the anterior cingulate is clearly involved in recruiting controlled processes, it would be inaccurate to rigidly classify the computations of the anterior cingulate as controlled (or automatic). Instead, the anterior cingulate serves as an example of why the existing automaticity–control dichotomy is in need of revision. On the one hand, like a typical alarm clock, the anterior cingulate is a "set it and forget it" alarm. The anterior cingulate is sensitive to numerous kinds of errors simultaneously without requiring conscious intent or effort (Benedict et al., 2002). On the other hand, the sensitivity of the cingulate can be weighted more heavily toward some discrepancies than others based on current goals (Carter et al., 1998, 2000; Kropotov, Crawford, & Polyakov, 1997; Sawamoto et al., 2000), and its sensitivity can be undermined by cognitive load (Frankenstein, Richter, McIntyre, & Remy, 2001; Petrovic, Petersson, Ghatan, Stone-Elander, & Ingvar, 2000). This last finding, that the sensitivity of the anterior cingulate can be blunted by cognitive load, is of particular interest because it suggests that the standard account of cognitive load effects or controlled processing is only half of the story. Typically, cognitive load is thought to undermine the use of controlled processing resources, but the reflection-reflexion model suggests that much of the time cognitive load has its impact by making the anterior cingulate less likely to sound the alarm that controlled processing resources are needed. In other words, under cognitive load, maladaptive decisions constructed in the X-system will often go unchecked.

When the anterior cingulate does sound the alarm, it is usually for the benefit of lateral prefrontal cortex, which is activated during numerous processes that are associated with controlled processing including working memory load (Braver et al., 1997), propositional reasoning (Goel & Dolan, 2000; Waltz et al., 1999), causal inference (Lieberman et al., 2002c), linguistic constructions (Bookheimer, in press), goal generation (Milner, 1963), and hypothesis formation (Christoff & Gabrieli, 2000). Cohen and colleagues have posited that many of these prefrontal processes function to override the X-system or bias it to function temporarily in more contextually appropriate ways (MacDonald, Cohen, Stenger, & Carter, 2000; Miller & Cohen, 2001).

In summary, the C-system is designed to sense the floundering of the X-system and to intervene when appropriate. Of course, in the modern world the C-system is activated much of the time, regardless of the X-system's preparedness. That is to say, although the C-system may have evolved to come to the X-system's rescue, the C-system has clearly taken on a life of its own in a world in which nearly every external cue is designed to evoke some degree of C-system processing (Deacon, 1997). Moreover, the rationalist tradition of Western society looks down upon the use of intuition (Bruner, 1957; Haidt, 2001; Hogarth, 2001; Lieberman, 2000a), and consequently, people may tend to rely on C-system processing even when X-system processing would suffice.

HOW THE X- AND C-SYSTEMS MAKE DECISIONS

To this point, it is clear that the reflection-reflexion model posits that the brain is designed to give the X-system first crack at making most judgments and decisions. Quite literally, the structures of the X-system receive incoming information before the structures of the C-system (Fabre-Thorpe, Delorme, Marlot, & Thorpe, 2001; Iwata, LeDoux, Meeley, Arneric, & Reis, 1986; LeDoux, Ruggiero, & Reis, 1986). If the X-system is unable to generate a useful solution, the C-system is activated so that its arsenal of decision-making tools can be used. It is still unclear from this discussion how decision making actually differs in the two systems. One major difference that has long been accepted is that X-system processes operate in parallel, whereas C-system processes are exclusionary, operating one at a time (McClelland, Rumelhart, & Hinton, 1988; Posner & Snyder, 1975; Schneider & Shiffrin, 1977; Wegner & Bargh, 1998). Although this difference has usually been thought of in terms of processing speed, it also has enormous consequences for the nature of processing itself (Sloman, 1996; Smith &

DeCoster, 1999). Because X-system processes operate in parallel, and because many of the neurons in the X-system project to and receive projections from the same neurons, neurons are simultaneously influenced by the neurons they are influencing. In other words, neurons in the X-system are highly interdependent, acting much like people do according to balance theory (Heider, 1958; Read, Vanman, & Miller, 1997). This process of parallel constraint satisfaction in the X-system, described in detail elsewhere (Kunda & Thagard, 1996; Lieberman et al., 2002b; Read et al., 1997; Shultz & Lepper, 1995; Spellman & Holyoak, 1992), creates a pattern-matching function that yields both judgment shifts related to cognitive dissonance reduction and similarity-based decision making that is contextually inappropriate (Donovan & Epstein, 1997; Sloman, 1996).

Reflexive Judgment Shifts in Dissonance Reduction

Shultz and Lepper (1995) gave a radical reinterpretation of standard cognitive dissonance effects. Their computational model suggests that cognitions are interdependently represented; thus, changes in any one cognition in a network of cognitions or the introduction of a new cognition can have a ripple effect on others. Importantly, these ripple effects occur simply because of the distributed representational structure of the mind, rather than as a result of conscious awareness of a conflict between cognitions combined with effortful attempts to make the cognitions more consonant with one another, as other formulations have suggested (Brehm & Cohen, 1962; Elliot & Devine, 1994; Festinger, 1964).

Two recent studies (Lieberman, Ochsner, Gilbert, & Schacter, 2001b) have provided empirical support for the notion that this sort of judgment shift does not depend on C-system processes. In one study, patients with anterograde amnesia performed a variation of Brehm's (1956) free-choice paradigm. In this task, individuals rank 15 postcard-sized art prints and then are asked to choose whether they would prefer to have full-sized reproductions of the pair of prints they ranked 4th and 10th or the pair of prints they ranked 6th and 12th (participants are shown the pairs without any reminder of their previous rankings). In either case, participants are choosing one print they do not like very much (the 10th or 12th) and rejecting one print that they presumably do like (the 4th or 6th). At the end of the experiment, participants are asked to rerank the 15 prints based on how they are currently feeling. Normal healthy participants tend to rank the chosen prints higher and the rejected prints lower than they did originally. By "spreading the difference" between the accepted and rejected prints, the earlier choice becomes more consonant. Amnesics, in contrast to healthy adults, cannot form new episodic memories. Thus, when amnesics are distracted as soon as they choose between the 4/10 and 6/12 pairs, they cannot explicitly recall that they have just made a dissonance-inducing

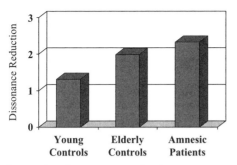

Figure 3.1. Dissonance reduction.

decision. Consequently, even if they feel physiological dissonance, amnesics will not have the counterattitudinal decision consciously accessible to which to attribute their physiological discomfort. Thus, if dissonance-based judgment changes require awareness of the conflict and the conscious effort to resolve the conflict, amnesic patients should not show any dissonance reduction. In fact, the amnesic patients showed just as much dissonance reduction as healthy elderly controls with natural declines in memory and twice as much dissonance reduction as college-age controls (see Figure 3.1), even though they evidenced no memory for having made a counterattitudinal decision moments earlier. In a second study, healthy college-age participants under cognitive load showed just as much dissonance reduction as participants who were not under cognitive load. These studies suggest, along with Shultz and Lepper (1995), that the C-system is not always involved in cognitive dissonance reduction.

Causal Inference in the X- and C-Systems

When the X-system is presented with a causal inference problem or any problem that requires propositional logic, the X-system transforms the problem into a similarity problem. That is, the X-system tends to resolve propositions by estimating the similarity between the antecedent and the consequent (Sloman, 1996). Thus, in the famous "Linda problem" (Donovan & Epstein, 1997; Tversky & Kahneman, 1983), individuals are given a description of Linda that is highly consistent with her being a feminist without actually specifying that she is one. Participants are then asked whether it is more likely that Linda is (a) a bank teller or (b) a bank teller and a feminist. The correct answer is *a* because of the principle of conjunction (i.e., the conjunction of any two events is less or equally likely than either event alone); however, most people choose *b*. This choice makes sense if the individuals are engaged in similarity-based pattern-matching because the description of Linda *is* more similar to *b* than *a*. The overall structure of the question can be formed as "If someone has background *x*, is she then more likely to be *a* or to be *b*?" Computing the similarity of the antecedent to each of the two possible consequents will yield the conjunction fallacy.

Unlike the X-system, the C-system is capable of testing for various kinds of asymmetric and unidirectional relationships between variables rather than just for bidirectional association. The C-system can represent statements such as "If *p* then *q*" without concluding *p* from the presentation of *q*, but the X-system cannot. This qualitative difference was previously used to explain why the X-system, but not the C-system, would be prone to the correspondence bias (Lieberman et al., 2002b). For though it may be true that "If a person is dispositionally friendly, that person is more likely to smile," it is an inferential error to infer that a person is dispositionally friendly because he or she has smiled. Nevertheless, the X-system presented with a smile will activate the representation for the corresponding trait of friendliness and draw this inference.

Whereas the X-system is designed to learn and use social and affective generalities, the C-system evolved to handle those *situations* in which the X-system fails (McClelland et al., 1995). Thus, the C-system needs to be able to represent individual situations that are exceptions to the rules and characterize how the same objective stimulus should be processed differently, depending on the situation. To facilitate this, the neural structure of prefrontal cortex is quite different from that of the X-system. Whereas representations in the X-system are massively distributed such that similar representations blur into one another, prefrontal and hippocampal representations are relatively sparse and separated from one another such that the activation of any one representation does not automatically activate semantically related representations (O'Reilly, Braver, & Cohen, 1999). Consequently, in the C-system, asymmetric relationships between representations can be produced and maintained without the interference of similarity effects (Holyoak & Hummel, 2000).

A recent functional magnetic resonance imaging (fMRI) study tested the reflection-reflexion hypothesis that asymmetric judgment processes depend on the C-system, whereas purely associative decision processes do not. In this study (Lieberman et al., 2002c), participants were shown word pairs one word at a time. Half of the time, participants judged whether there was a causal relation between the words (e.g., *fire → smoke*), and the other half of the time, participants judged whether there was an associative relation between the words (e.g., *bread → butter*). Even though the two trial types were equated for reaction time, suggesting that the two tasks were similarly difficult, the causal inference trials differentially activated prefrontal cortex. This suggests that the C-system is not just for more effortful decisions, but for qualitatively different kinds of decisions – in particular, those that require asymmetric processing of discrete symbols rather than computing similarity-based overlap between features.

REFLECTIVE PROCESSES DISRUPT REFLEXIVE PROCESSES

One of the basic principles of automaticity contends that genuinely automatic processes cannot be disrupted by controlled processes (Bargh, 1999). Controlled processes may frequently set automatic processes in motion, but the ability to run to completion once started is one of the hallmarks of automaticity theory dating back over a century (James, 1890). A number of judgment and decision-making studies conducted by Wilson and colleagues (Wilson, Dunn, Kraft, & Lisle, 1989; Wilson et al., 1993) highlight a possible exception to this rule. In Wilson's work, participants are required to generate careful introspective accounts of choices that would otherwise be made intuitively. Using a variety of outcome criteria, Wilson has found that introspection leads to poorer decisions. In one study (Wilson et al., 1993), participants were asked to provide ratings of five posters; some were artistic prints by Van Gogh and Monet, and others were humorous posters with captions. Only 5% of control participants preferred the humorous posters, whereas 36% of participants asked to introspect on the basis for their preference chose the humorous poster. Additionally, participants were allowed to take a copy of their preferred print home. When contacted weeks later, participants who had been in the introspection condition expressed less satisfaction with their earlier choice than did the control participants. Thus, introspecting on the reasons for our preferences changes our preferences temporarily, leading to outcomes that are less satisfactory in the long run.

Wilson and Schooler's (1991) explanation of these effects would suggest that introspective processes rely on the C-system and that the C-system sometimes generates less adaptive decision criteria than the X-system. In the poster study, most people probably have X-systems that prefer the artistic posters, but the X-system does not provide logical proofs for its output (Lieberman, 2000a). Thus, when people need to provide logical support for their preferences, they turn to the C-system, which allows for the development of logical arguments. Unfortunately, the C-system of individuals untrained in critiquing art is probably not sensitive to the same factors that drive the intuitive responses of the X-system. Instead, the C-system constructs relatively simplistic principles of preference based on those dimensions that can be easily articulated. This is easier to do for the humorous prints, which are quite simple and direct, if not of enduring aesthetic worth, compared with the complex appeal of real works of art.

This account is relatively agnostic as to whether the X-system continues to contribute its two cents to the preference judgments. Rather, this account seems to suggest that if the X-system processes do occur, they are passed over in favor of the C-system's conclusions. Here is a case, as described in the introduction to this chapter, in which the methods of social cognition cannot provide a full account of the relationship between the automatic and controlled processes. Introspection manipulations certainly increase the amount of C-system processing that occurs, but what is the consequence of C-system processing on the X-system processing that *would have occurred* had the C-system not been engaged? How can we distinguish between (a) the C-system outputs being selected over the ongoing X-system outputs and the possibility that (b) engaging the C-system prevents the X-system from producing its output in the first place (Gilbert, 1999)? Using fMRI, we can assess whether C-system processes merely override X-system processes, such that X-system activations are still present but do not covary with the resulting outputs, or whether the presence of C-system processes are associated with reduced X-system activity suggesting disruption.

In two fMRI studies of affective processing, an increase in prefrontal activity has been associated with diminished amygdala activity (Hariri, Bookheimer, & Mazziotta, 2000; Lieberman, Hariri, & Bookheimer, 2001a), suggesting that engaging the C-system can disrupt the X-system. In one of these studies (Lieberman et al., 2001a), African American and Caucasian participants were shown African American and Caucasian targets. In one task ("Match"), participants saw a pair of faces in addition to the target and had to choose which face of the pair was of the same race as the target face (e.g., choosing the African American face from the pair to match the African American target). In this condition, we replicated other fMRI studies of automatic stereotyping (Cunningham, Johnson, Gatenby, Gore, & Banaji, 2001; Hart et al., 2000; Phelps et al., 2000) and found amygdala activity to African American faces without any prefrontal activity. In the second task ("Label"), participants chose which of two race labels described the target. In the label condition, the minimal linguistic processing necessary to complete the task activated bilateral prefrontal cortex. Moreover, the amygdala activations were absent in this condition. Thus, when we activated the C-system ever so slightly, the X-system processing in the amygdala was disrupted. It is worth pointing out that although the linguistic labeling task presented the participants with fewer out-group faces than the perceptual matching task, there were still as many out-group faces presented in the linguistic task as in previous fMRI studies of automatic stereotyping. Moreover, we found a negative correlation between the responses of the prefrontal cortex and amygdala ($r = -.63$) during the Label condition. If the reduced amygdala activity was merely a consequence of not presenting a second African American face, there should not have been a strong negative correlation between prefrontal and amygdala activity (see Zárate & Stoever, this volume, for other neural approaches to stereotyping).

Although the results of this fMRI study may be somewhat provocative, this study is hardly a clean test of C-system processes disrupting X-system processing. Perceptual matching is certainly more reflexive than linguistic labeling, but neither comes from the standard arsenal of social cognition paradigms. To provide such a test, a subliminal mere exposure study was conducted in conjunction with a cognitive load manipulation (Lieberman & Jarcho, 2002). This provides a strong test of the hypothesis because subliminal processes are widely accepted as automatic or reflexive. Subliminal processes clearly do not involve effort, intention, or awareness, and because subliminal processes do not require controlled processing resources to operate, if cognitive load interrupts the subliminal mere exposure effect, the only sensible conclusion is that reflective processes can disrupt genuinely reflexive processes.

In this study, participants were shown a series of irregular polygons for very brief periods of time (80 ms), followed on each trial by a pattern mask (60 ms) and a second of a fixation cross alone. Each polygon was randomly presented in one of four locations on the screen, each parafoveal relative to the fixation cross in the middle of the screen. These methods were based on previously established techniques for ensuring subliminal exposure (Bargh & Chartrand, 2000). Each of 15 polygons was presented 1, 5, or 10 times. Half of the participants were also engaged in a cognitive load task during the presentation of the polygons. These participants were required to keep track of the number of tones at a particular pitch from among a series of tones. After the initial exposure period, participants were shown pairs of polygons and asked which they liked more. Unknown to the participants, in each pair, one polygon was new and the other had been presented subliminally during the prior exposure period. As shown in Figure 3.2, participants who were not under cognitive load replicated the standard mere exposure effect, preferring the previously exposed polygons to the new polygons two to one. Participants under cognitive load, however, showed no evidence of a mere exposure effect at all, instead expressing equal preference for the old and the new polygons.

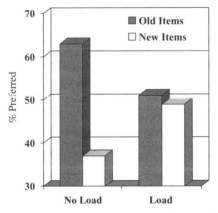

Figure 3.2. Mere exposure effects under conditions of cognitive load and no cognitive load.

If, as these data suggest, C-system processes can disrupt genuinely automatic X-system processes, then it would seem likely that inducing introspection would lead not only to the selection of C-system outputs over X-system outputs, but also to the disruption of the X-system processes that might have led to better decisions. This proposed mechanism complements, rather than supplants, that of Wilson and colleagues. People certainly do shift their bases of judgment as Wilson has described. I am merely pointing out that introspection, in addition to overriding our intuitive preferences, can disrupt the initial production of those intuitive preferences.

INDIVIDUAL DIFFERENCES IN REFLECTIVE JUDGMENT PROCESSES

If the X- and C-systems contribute to qualitatively different kinds of decision making, then individual differences in the reactivity of the neural bases of these systems should lead to personality differences in the likelihood that each kind of decision process occurs and is effective. In recent studies, extraversion has been associated with more efficient functioning in the executive components or working memory (Gray & Braver, 2002; Lieberman, 2000b; Lieberman & Rosenthal, 2001), which in turn is associated with prefrontal cortex functioning (Braver et al., 1997; Smith & Jonides, 1999). This difference in working memory efficiency predicted differences in social judgment under cognitive load, such that extraverts were more accurate under cognitive load than introverts, whereas there was no difference in the absence of cognitive load across three studies (Lieberman & Rosenthal, 2001). This finding contradicts the stereotype of the introvert as the more rational and precise decision maker, carefully weighing different options.

It is important here to differentiate the capacity of the C-system to contribute to decision making from the likelihood that the C-system will be called upon to contribute to decision making. A second personality variable, neuroticism, may be an important determinant of this latter aspect of decision making. Recall that in the reflection-reflexion model, the C-system evolved to deal with problems that the X-system fails to resolve. Whereas prefrontal cortex is essential to control exerted by the C-system, the anterior cingulate plays a major role in choosing when control will be called upon. Individual differences in the sensitivity of the anterior cingulate should determine the likelihood that a person will rely on the C-system in his or her decision making. Neurotics are hypothesized to have more sensitive anterior cingulates, and there is growing evidence that anxiety, a major component of neuroticism (Gray, 1991), is associated with the sensitivity of the anterior cingulate (Davidson, Abercrombie, Nitschke, & Putnam, 1999; Eisenberger & Lieberman, 2002). Thus, neuroticism and extraversion together should predict the likelihood and capacity of an individual to engage C-system processes in decision making.

This does not mean that questionnaire measures of extraversion and neuroticism will allow us to easily assess these decision-making differences across individuals. These questionnaires were initially meant to predict the peripheral consequences of individual differences in the central nervous system (Eysenck, 1967). That is, the questionnaires were constructed to predict skin conductance, which in turn was thought to be a consequence of cortical arousal. This has turned out to be like a game of telephone in which the original message was not entirely clear to begin with. The questionnaires predict psychophysiological responses imperfectly (Matthews & Gilliland, 1999), and the psychophysiological responses are affected by multiple processes in the brain in addition to cortical arousal. Furthermore, there is no simple neural equivalent to the concept of cortical arousal (Neiss, 1988; Robbins, 1997), upon which much of the original was based (Eysenck, 1967; Hebb, 1955).

Today, however, we can measure the sensitivity of different neural structures that are critical for self-regulation and problem solving relatively directly with neuroimaging. Given this access, attempting to find which structures in the brain have activation patterns that track existing questionnaire measures of personality would be one more bad link in the telephone chain. Instead, we would do well to build our personality theories around the capacities of different neurocognitive structures and the computational consequences of varying the sensitivity of these structures. From here, then, it would make sense to develop self-report and behavioral measures that predict the reactivity of one or more neural systems, because neuroimaging is still a very expensive and time-consuming way to measure these individual differences. Tasks that tap the central executive component of working memory can serve as a quick index of at least some aspects of prefrontal function (Lieberman & Rosenthal, 2001). Naomi Eisenberger and I (Eisenberger & Lieberman, 2002) are currently developing a behavioral task that measures anterior cingulate function. In our pilot fMRI work, we have presented participants with reversible illusions such as a Necker cube and have coded the rate of oscillation (i.e., flipping between the two views of the cube). Though this work is preliminary, thus far it appears that the oscillation rate is a good predictor of anterior cingulate activity. Incidentally, personality psychologists of the 1930s used this same measure but abandoned it because it did not correlate well with their questionnaire methods (Guilford & Braly, 1931; McDougall, 1933). Because the current approach allows researchers more direct access to the neurocognitive individual differences, it is possible that this time around, this task will provide us with better predictive power. With these better tools, psychologists should be able to reinvigorate the study of personality and its consequences for individuals in the tasks of everyday life.

CONCLUSION

In this chapter, I have laid out two neurocognitive systems involved in reflective and reflexive processing. On the one hand, these two systems correspond to cognitive processing dichotomies that have been around for a generation or more: automatic versus controlled and implicit versus explicit. At the same time, these old dichotomies are limited in their ability to provide adequate treatment to the positive contributions of each half of the dichotomy. Instead, these formulations define the dichotomy as one or more continua, and thus, both ends of the continua are defined as the presence or absence of particular characteristics (effort, intention, awareness). By focusing on the neural basis of these systems, links can be made to the known computational characteristics of these systems, and these characteristics provide us with important clues as to why the two systems produce the outputs they do. Furthermore, current operationalizations of automaticity and control make it difficult to identify anything but the relative contributions of each system, rather than the absolute contributions of each. Finally, this operationalization assumes that the effects of automatic and controlled processes add and subtract linearly, without interaction effects. Neuroimaging allows the study of the ongoing interactions between the two systems.

The reflective-reflexive model based in neurocognitive systems and the techniques of neuroimaging can make great contributions to the understanding of judgment and decision making. The findings from this chapter, as well as the other existing findings in social cognitive neuroscience, are undoubtedly just the tip of the iceberg. If we are ever going to size up the entire iceberg, we will need an army of scientists who are bilingual in social cognition and cognitive neuroscience, in terms of both theory and methods. As it stands, Berlitz does not have a crash course in either language, so let me end where I began by recommending that you take a cognitive neuroscientist to lunch.

References

Allison, T., Puce, A., & McCarthy, G. (2000). Social perception from visual cues: Role of the STS region. *Trends in Cognitive Sciences, 4*, 267–278.
Ambady, N., & Rosenthal, R. (1993). Half a minute: Predicting teacher evaluations from thin slices of nonverbal behavior and physical attractiveness. *Journal of Personality and Social Psychology, 64*, 431–441.
Baciu, M. V., Bonaz, B. L., Papillon, E., Bost, R. A., Le Bas, J. F., Fournet, J., & Segebarth, C. (1999). Central processing of rectal pain: A functional MR imaging study. *American Journal of Neuroradiology, 20*, 1920–1924.
Barch, D. M., Braver, T. S., Sabb, F. W., & Noll, D. C. (2000). Anterior cingulate and the monitoring of response conflict: Evidence from an fMRI study of overt verb generation. *Journal of Cognitive Neuroscience, 12*, 298–309.

Bargh, J. A. (1999). The cognitive monster: The case against the controllability of automatic stereotype effects. In S. Chaiken & Y. Trope (Eds.), *Dual-process theories in social psychology* (pp. 361–382). New York: Guilford Press.

Bargh, J. A., & Chartrand, T. L. (2000). The mind in the middle: A practical guide to priming and automaticity research. In H. T. Reis & C. M. Judd (Eds.), *Handbook of research methods in social and personality psychology* (pp. 253–285). New York: Cambridge University Press.

Baron-Cohen, S. (1995). *Mindblindness: An essay on autism and theory of mind.* Cambridge, MA: MIT Press.

Bartels, A., & Zeki, S. (2000). The neural basis of romantic love. *NeuroReport, 17,* 3829–3834.

Benedict, R. H. B., Shucard, D. W., Santa Maria, M. P., Shucard, J. L., Abara, J. P., Coad, M. L., Wack, D., Sawusch, J., & Lockwood, A. (2002). Covert auditory attention generates activation in the rostral/dorsal anterior cingulate cortex. *Journal of Cognitive Neuroscience, 14,* 637–645.

Berns, G. S., Cohen, J. D., & Mintun, M. A. (1997). Brain regions responsive to novelty in the absence of awareness. *Science, 276,* 1272–1275.

Bookheimer, S. Y. (in press). fMRI of language. *Annual Review of Neuroscience, 25.*

Botvinick, M. M., Braver, T. S., Barch, D. M., Carter, C. S., & Cohen, J. D. (2000). Conflict monitoring and cognitive control. *Psychological Review, 108,* 624–652.

Braver, T. S., Cohen, J. D., Nystrom, L. E., Jonides, J., Smith, E. E., & Noll, D. C. (1997). A parametric study of prefrontal cortex involvement in human working memory. *NeuroImage, 5,* 49–62.

Brehm, J. W. (1956). Post-decision changes in the desirability of alternatives. *Journal of Abnormal and Social Psychology, 52,* 384–389.

Brehm, J. W., & Cohen, A. R. (1962). *Explorations in cognitive dissonance.* New York: Wiley.

Breiter, H. C., Gollub, R. L., & Weisskoff, R. M. (1997). Acute effects of cocaine on human brain activity and emotion. *Neuron, 19,* 591–611.

Brewer, J. B., Zhao, Z., Desmond, J. E., Glover, G. H., & Gabrieli, J. D. E. (1998). Making memories: Brain activity that predicts how well visual experience will be remembered. *Science, 281,* 1185–1187.

Bruner, J. S. (1957). On perceptual readiness. *Psychological Review, 64,* 123–152.

Bush, G., Luu, P., & Posner, M. I. (2000). Cognitive and emotional influences in anterior cingulate cortex. *Trends in Cognitive Sciences, 4,* 215–222.

Cacioppo, J. T., & Gardner, W. L. (1999). Emotions. *Annual Review of Psychology, 50,* 191–214.

Carter, C. S., Braver, T. S., Barch, D. M., Botvinick, M. M., Noll, D., & Cohen, J. D. (1998). Anterior cingulate cortex, error detection, and the online monitoring of performance. *Science, 280,* 747–749.

Carter, C. S, MacDonald, A. M., Botvinick, M., Ross, L. L., Stenger, V. A., Noll, D., & Cohen, J. D. (2000). Parsing executive processes: Strategic vs. evaluative functions of the anterior cingulate cortex. *Proceedings of the National Academy of Science, 97,* 1944–1948.

Carver, C. S., & Scheier, M. F. (1981). *Attention and self-regulation: A control theory approach to human behavior.* New York: Springer-Verlag.

Chen, M., & Bargh, J. A. (1997). Nonconscious behavioral confirmation processes: The self-fulfilling consequences of automatic stereotype activation. *Journal of Experimental Social Psychology, 33,* 541–560.

Christoff, K., & Gabrieli, J. D. E. (2000). The frontopolar cortex and human cognition: Evidence for a rostrocaudal hierarchical organization within human prefrontal cortex. *Psychobiology, 28,* 168–186.

Craik, F. I. M., & Tulving, E. (1975). Depth of processing and retention of words in episodic memory. *Journal of Experimental Psychology: General, 104,* 268–294.

Cunningham, W. A., Johnson, M. K., Gatenby, J. C., Gore, J. C., & Banaji, M. R. (2001). *An fMRI study on the conscious and unconscious evaluations of social groups.* Paper presented at the UCLA Conference on Social Cognitive Neuroscience, Los Angeles.

Davidson, R. J., Abercrombie, H., Nitschke, J. B., & Putnam, K. (1999). Regional brain function, emotion and disorders of emotion. *Current Opinion in Neurobiology, 9,* 228–234.

Deacon, T. W. (1997). *The symbolic species: The co-evolution of language and the brain.* New York: W. W. Norton.

Decety, J., & Grezes, J. (1999). Neural mechanisms subserving the perception of human actions. *Trends in Cognitive Sciences, 3,* 172–178.

Dennett, D. C. (1984). *Elbow room: The varieties of free will worth wanting.* Cambridge, MA: MIT Press.

Depue, R. A., & Collins, P. F. (1999). Neurobiology of the structure of personality: Dopamine, facilitation of incentive motivation, and extraversion. *Behavioral and Brain Sciences, 22,* 491–569.

Dewey, J. (1910). *How we think.* Boston: D. C. Heath.

Donovan, S., & Epstein, S. (1997). Conjunction problem can be attributed to its simultaneous concrete and unnatural representation, and not to conversational implicature. *Journal of Experimental Social Psychology, 33,* 1–20.

Dreyfus, H. L. (1991). *Being-in-the-world: A commentary on Heidegger's being and time, division I.* Cambridge, MA: MIT Press.

Eisenberger, N. I., & Lieberman, M. D. (2002). The role of the anterior cingulate in neuroticism and social cognition. Unpublished raw data. University of California, Los Angeles.

Elliot, A. J., & Devine, P. G. (1994). On the motivational nature of cognitive dissonance: Dissonance as psychological discomfort. *Journal of Personality and Social Psychology, 67,* 382–394.

Eysenck, H. J. (1967). *The biological basis of personality.* Springfield, IL: Charles C. Thomas.

Fabre-Thorpe, M., Delorme, A., Marlot, C., & Thorpe, S. (2001). A limit to the speed of processing in ultra-rapid visual categorization of novel natural scenes. *Journal of Cognitive Neuroscience, 13,* 171–180.

Festinger, L. (1964). *Conflict, decision, and dissonance.* Stanford, CA: Stanford University Press.

Fiske, S. T., & Taylor, S. E. (1991). *Social cognition.* New York: McGraw-Hill.

Frankenstein, U. N., Richter, W., McIntyre, M. C., & Remy, F. (2001). Distraction modulates anterior cingulate gyrus activations during the cold pressure test. *NeuroImage, 14,* 827–836.

Frijda, N. H. (1986). *The emotions.* New York: Cambridge University Press.

Gilbert, D. T. (1989). Thinking lightly about others. Automatic components of the social inference process. In J. S. Uleman & J. A. Bargh (Eds.), *Unintended thought* (pp. 189–211). New York: Guilford Press.

Gilbert, D. T. (1999). What the mind's not. In S. Chaiken & Y. Trope (Eds.), *Dual-process theories in social psychology* (pp. 3–11). New York: Guilford Press.

Goel, V., & Dolan, R. J. (2000). Anatomical segregation of component processes in an inductive inference task. *Journal of Cognitive Neuroscience, 12*, 110–119.

Grant, I., & Adams, K. M. (1996). *Neuropsychological assessment of neuropsychiatric disorders.* New York: Oxford University Press.

Gray, J. A. (1991). Neural systems, emotion and personality. In J. Madden (Ed.), *Neurobiology of learning, emotion, and affect* (pp. 273–366). New York: Raven Press.

Gray, J. R., & Braver, T. S. (2002). Personality predicts working-memory-related activation in the caudal anterior cingulate cortex. *Cognitive, Affective & Behavioral Neuroscience, 2,* 64–75.

Griffin, D. W., & Ross, L. (1991). Subject construal, social inference, and human misunderstanding. In M. Zanna (Ed.), *Advances in experimental social psychology* (Vol. 24, pp. 319–359). San Diego: Academic Press.

Guilford, J. P., & Braly, K. W. (1931). An experimental test of McDougall's theory of extroversion-introversion. *Journal of Abnormal and Social Psychology, 25,* 382–389.

Haidt, J. (2001). The emotional dog and its rational tail: A social intuitionist approach to moral judgment. *Psychological Review, 108,* 814–834.

Hariri, A. R., Bookheimer, S. Y., & Mazziotta, J. C. (2000). Modulating emotional responses: Effects of a neocortical network on the limbic system. *NeuroReport, 11,* 43–48.

Hart, A. J., Whalen, P. J., Shin, L. M., McInerney, S. C., Fischer, H., & Rauch, S. L. (2000). Differential response in the human amygdala to racial outgroup vs. ingroup face stimuli. *NeuroReport, 11,* 2351–2355.

Haxby, J. V., Hoffman, E. A., & Gobbini, M. I. (2000). The distributed human neural system for face perception. *Trends in Cognitive Sciences, 4,* 223–233.

Hebb, D. O. (1955). Drives and the CNS (conceptual nervous system). *Psychological Review, 62,* 243–254.

Heidegger, M. (1927/1962). *Being and time.* New York: Harper & Row.

Heider, F. (1958). *The psychology of interpersonal relations.* New York: Wiley.

Heider, F., & Simmel, M. (1944). An experimental study of apparent behavior. *American Journal of Psychology, 57,* 243–259.

Hogarth, R. H. (2001). *Educating intuition.* Chicago: University of Chicago Press.

Holyoak, K. J., & Hummel, J. E. (2000). The proper treatment of symbols in a connectionist architecture. In E. Dietrich & A. B. Markman (Eds.), *Cognitive dynamics: Conceptual and representational change in humans and machines* (pp. 229–263). Mahwah, NJ: Erlbaum.

Iwata, J., LeDoux, J. E., Meeley, M. P., Arneric, S., & Reis, D. J. (1986). Intrinsic neurons in the amygdaloid field projected to by the medial geniculate body mediate emotional responses conditioned to acoustic stimuli. *Brain Research, 383,* 195–214.

James, W. (1890/1950). *The principles of psychology.* New York: Dover.

James, W. (1913). *Essays in radical empiricism.* New York: Longman, Green.

Jellema, T., & Perrett, D. I. (2001). *Coding of visible and hidden actions: A tutorial.* Manuscript in preparation.

Kropotov, J. D., Crawford, H. J., & Polyakov, Y. I. (1997). Somatosensory event-related potential changes to painful stimuli during hypnotic analgesia: Anterior cingulate cortex and anterior temporal cortex intracranial recordings. *International Journal of Psychophysiology, 27,* 1–8.

Kunda, Z., & Thagard, P. (1996). Forming impressions from stereotypes, traits, and behaviors: A parallel constraint satisfaction theory. *Psychological Review, 103,* 284–308.

Ladabaum, U., Minoshima, S., & Owyang, C. (2000). Pathobiology of visceral pain: Molecular mechanisms and therapeutic implications v. central nervous system processing of somatic and visceral sensory signal. *American Journal of Physiology: Gastrointestinal and Liver Physiology, 279,* G1–G6.

Langer, E. J., Blank, A., & Chanowitz, B. (1978). The mindlessness of ostensibly thoughtful action: The role of "placebic" information in interpersonal interaction. *Journal of Personality and Social Psychology, 36,* 635–642.

LeDoux, J. E. (1996). *The emotional brain: The mysterious underpinnings of emotional life.* New York: Simon & Schuster.

LeDoux, J. E., Ruggiero, D. A., & Reis, R. J. (1986). Projections to the subcortical forebrain from anatomically defined regions of the medial geniculate body in the rat. *Journal of Comparative Neurology, 242,* 182–213.

Lieberman, M. D. (2000a). Intuition: A social cognitive neuroscience approach. *Psychological Bulletin, 126,* 109–137.

Lieberman, M. D. (2000b). Introversion and working memory: Central executive differences. *Personality and Individual Differences, 28,* 479–486.

Lieberman, M. D., Chang, G. Y., Chiao, J., Bookheimer, S. Y., & Knowlton, B. J. (2002a). *An event-related fMRI study of artificial grammar learning in a balanced chunk strength design.* Unpublished manuscript. University of California, Los Angeles.

Lieberman, M. D., Gaunt, R., Gilbert, D. T., & Trope, Y. (2002b). Reflection and reflexion: A social cognitive neuroscience approach to attributional inference. In M. Zanna (Ed.), *Advances in experimental social psychology* (Vol. 34, pp. 199–249). New York: Academic Press.

Lieberman, M. D., Hariri, A., & Bookheimer, S. (2001a). *Controlling automatic stereotype activation. An fMRI study.* Paper presented at the second annual meeting of the Society for Personality and Social Psychology, February 4, San Antonio, TX.

Lieberman, M. D., Hariri, A., Jarcho, J. J., & Bookheimer, S. Y. (2002a). Two captains, one ship: A social cognitive neuroscience approach to disrupting automatic affective processes. Unpublished manuscript. University of California, Los Angeles.

Lieberman, M. D., & Jarcho, J. M. (2002). *When controlled processing disrupts genuinely automatic processes: Cognitive load and subliminal mere exposure effects.* Manuscript in preparation.

Lieberman, M. D., Ochsner, K. N., Gilbert, D. T., & Schacter, D. L. (2001b). Do amnesics exhibit cognitive dissonance reduction? The role of explicit memory and attention in attitude change. *Psychological Science, 12,* 135–140.

Lieberman, M. D., & Rosenthal, R. (2001). Why introverts can't always tell who likes them: Multi-tasking and nonverbal decoding. *Journal of Personality and Social Psychology, 80,* 294–310.

Lieberman, M. D., Sellner, D., Waldman, M. D., Satpute, A. B., Tabibnia, G., Bookheimer, S. Y., & Holyoak, K. J. (2002c). *Asymmetric decision making: An fMRI study of causal vs. associative inference.* Manuscript in preparation.

Lorberbaum, J. P., Newman, J. D., Dubno, J. R., Horwitz, A. R., Nahas, Z., Teneback, C. C., Bloomer, C. W., Bohning, D. E., Vincent, D., Johnson, M. R., Emmanuel, N., Brawman-Mintzer, O., Book, S. W., Lydiard, R. B., Ballenger, J., & George, M. S. (1999). Feasibility of using fMRI to study mothers responding to infant cries. *Depression and Anxiety, 10,* 99–104.

MacDonald, A. W., Cohen, J. D., Stenger, V. A., & Carter, C. S. (2000). Dissociating the role of the dorsolateral prefrontal and anterior cingulate cortex in cognitive control. *Science, 288,* 1835–1838.

Matthews, G., & Gilliland, K. (1999). The personality theories of H. J. Eysenck and J. A. Gray: A comparative review. *Personality and Individual Differences, 26,* 583–626.

McClelland, J. L., McNaughton, B. L., & O'Reilly, R. C. (1995). Why there are complementary learning systems in the hippocampus and neocortex: Insights from the successes and failures of connectionist models of learning and memory. *Psychological Review, 102,* 419–457.

McClelland, J. L., Rumelhart, D. E., & Hinton, G. E. (1988). The appeal of parallel distributed processing. In A. M. Collins & E. E. Smith (Eds.), *Readings in cognitive science: A perspective from psychology and artificial intelligence* (pp. 52–72). San Mateo, CA: Morgan Kaufmann.

McDougall, W. (1933). *Energies of men.* New York: Scribner's.

Miller, E. K., & Cohen, J. D. (2001). An integrative theory of prefrontal cortex function. *Annual Review of Neuroscience, 24,* 167–202.

Miller, G. A., Galanter, E., & Pribram, K. (1960). *Plans and the structure of behavior.* New York: Holt, Rinehart, & Winston.

Milner, B. (1963). Effects of different brain lesions on card sorting. *Archives of Neurology, 9,* 90–100.

Mishkin, M., Ungerleider, L. G., & Macko, K. A. (1983). Object vision and spatial vision: Two cortical pathways. *Trends in Neuroscience, 6,* 414–417.

Monteith, M. J. (1993). Self-regulation of prejudiced responses: Implications for progress in prejudice reduction efforts. *Journal of Personality and Social Psychology, 65,* 469–485.

Morris, J. S., Ohman, A., & Dolan, R. J. (1999). A subcortical pathway to the right amygdala mediating "unseen" fear. *Proceedings of the National Academy of Science, 96,* 1680–1685.

Moskowitz, G. B., Gollwitzer, P. M., Wasel, W., & Schaal, B. (1999). Preconscious control of stereotype activation through chronic egalitarian goals. *Journal of Personality and Social Psychology, 77,* 167–184.

Neiss, R. (1988). Reconceptualizing arousal: Psychobiological states in motor performance. *Psychological Bulletin, 103,* 345–366.

Nisbett, R. E., & Wilson, T. D. (1977). Telling more than we can know: Verbal reports on mental processes. *Psychological Review, 84,* 231–259.

Ochsner, K. N., & Lieberman, M. D. (2001). The emergence of social cognitive neuroscience. *American Psychologist, 56,* 717–734.

O'Reilly, R., Braver, T. S., & Cohen, J. D. (1999). A biologically-based computational model of working memory. In A. Maykae & P. Shah (Eds.), *Models of working memory* (pp. 375–411). New York: Oxford University Press.

Otten, L. J., Henson, R. N. A., & Rugg, M. D. (2001). Depth of processing effects on neural correlates of memory encoding: Relationship between findings from across- and within-task comparisons. *Brain, 124*, 399–412.

Perrett, D. I., Jellema, T., Frigerio, E., & Burt, M. (2001, April). *Using "social attention" cues (where others are attending) to interpret actions, intentions and emotions of others.* Paper presented at the UCLA Conference on Social Cognitive Neuroscience, Los Angeles.

Petrovic, P., Petersson, K. M., Ghatan, P. H., Stone-Elander, S., & Ingvar, M. (2000). Pain-related cerebral activation is altered by a distracting cognitive task. *Pain, 85*, 19–30.

Phelps, E. A., O'Connor, K. J., Cunningham, W. A., Funayama, E. S., Gatenby, J. C., Gore, J. C., & Banaji, M. R. (2000). Performance on indirect measures of race evaluation predicts amygdala activation. *Journal of Cognitive Neuroscience, 12*, 729–738.

Posner, M. I., & Snyder, C. R. R. (1975). Attention and cognitive control. In R. L. Solso (Ed.), *Information processing and cognition: The Loyola symposium* (pp. 550–585). Hillsdale, NJ: Erlbaum.

Rainville, P., Duncan, G. H., Price, D. D., Carrier, B., & Bushnell, M. D. (1997). Pain affect encoded in human anterior cingulate but not somatosensory cortex. *Science, 277*, 968–971.

Read, S. J., Vanman, E. J., & Miller, L. C. (1997). Connectionism, parallel constraint satisfaction processes, and gestalt principles: (Re)Introducing cognitive dynamics to social psychology. *Personality and Social Psychology Review, 1*, 26–53.

Robbins, T. W. (1997). Arousal systems and attentional processes. *Biological Psychology, 45*, 57–71.

Rolls, E. T. (1999). *The brain and emotion.* New York: Oxford University Press.

Sawamoto, N., Honda, M., Okada, T., Hanakawa, T., Kanda, M., Fukuyama, H., Konishi, J., & Shibasaki, H. (2000). Expectation of pain enhances responses to non-painful somatosensory stimulation in the anterior cingulate cortex and parietal operculum/posterior insula: An event-related functional magnetic resonance imaging study. *Journal of Neuroscience, 20*, 7438–7445.

Schneider, W., & Shiffrin, R. M. (1977). Controlled and automatic human information processing: I. Detection, search, and attention. *Psychological Review, 84*, 1–66.

Shultz, T. R., & Lepper, M. R. (1995). Cognitive dissonance reduction as constraint satisfaction. *Psychological Review, 103*, 219–240.

Schultz, W. (1998). Predictive reward signal of dopamine neurons. *Journal of Neurophysiology, 80*, 1–27.

Sloman, S. A. (1996). The empirical case for two systems of reasoning. *Psychological Bulletin, 119*, 3–22.

Smith, E. R. (1996). What do connectionist and social psychology offer each other? *Journal of Personality and Social Psychology, 70*, 893–912.

Smith, E. R., & DeCoster, J. (1999). Associative and rule-based processing: A connectionist interpretation of dual-process models. In S. Chaiken & Y. Trope (Eds.), *Dual-process theories in social psychology* (pp. 323–336). New York: Guilford Press.

Smith, E. R., & Jonides, J. (1999). Storage and executive processes in the frontal lobes. *Science, 283*, 1657–1661.

Spellman, B. A., & Holyoak, K. J. (1992). If Saddam is Hitler then who is George Bush? Analogical mapping between systems of social roles. *Journal of Personality and Social Psychology, 62*, 913–933.

Tabibnia, G. (2002). *Appetitive and aversive (e)motive systems: Contribution of functional neuroimaging studies.* University of California, Los Angeles.

Tversky, A., & Kahneman, D. (1983). Extensional versus intuitive reasoning: The conjunction fallacy in probability judgment. *Psychological Review, 90*, 293–315.

Wagner, A. D., Schacter, D. L., Rotte, M., Kootstaal, W., Maril, A., Dale, A. M., Rosen, B. R., & Buckner, R. L. (1998). Building memories: Remembering and forgetting of verbal experiences as predicted by brain activity. *Science, 281*, 1188–1191.

Waltz, J. A., Knowlton, B. J., Holyoak, K. J., Boone, K. B., Mishkin, F. S., Santos, M. M., Thomas, C. R., & Miller, B. L. (1999). A system for relational reasoning in human prefrontal cortex. *Psychological Science, 10*, 119–125.

Wegner, D. M., & Bargh, J. A. (1998). Control and automaticity in social life. In D. T. Gilbert, S. T. Fiske, & G. Lindzey (Eds.), *The handbook of social psychology* (4th ed., pp. 446–496). New York: Oxford University Press.

Whalen, P. J., Rauch, S. L., Etcoff, N. L., McInerney, S. C., Lee, M. B., & Jenike, M. A. (1998). Masked presentations of emotional facial expressions modulate amygdala activity without explicit knowledge. *Journal of Neuroscience, 18*, 411–418.

Whitehead, A. N. (1911). *An introduction to mathematics.* London: Williams and Norgate.

Wiener, N. (1948). *Cybernetics: Control and communication in the animal and the machine.* Cambridge, MA: MIT Press.

Wilson, T. D., Dunn, D. S., Kraft, D., & Lisle, D. J. (1989). Introspection, attitude change, and attitude–behavior consistency: The disruptive effects of explaining why we feel the way we do. In L. Berkowitz (Ed.), *Advances in experimental social psychology* (Vol. 22, pp. 287–343). New York: Academic Press.

Wilson, T. D., Lisle, D. J., Schooler, J. W., Hodges, S. D., Klaaren, K. J., & LaFleur, S. J. (1993). Introspecting about reasons can reduce post-choice satisfaction. *Personality and Social Psychology Bulletin, 19*, 331–339.

Wilson, T. D., & Schooler, J. W. (1991). Thinking too much: Introspection can reduce the quality of preferences and decisions. *Journal of Personality and Social Psychology, 60*, 181–192.

Winter, L., & Uleman, J. S. (1984). When are social judgments made? Evidence for the spontaneousness of trait inferences. *Journal of Personality and Social Psychology, 47*, 237–252.

Word, C. O., Zanna, M. P., & Cooper, J. (1974). The nonverbal mediation of self-fulfilling prophecies in interracial interaction. *Journal of Experimental Social Psychology, 10*, 109–120.

Zajonc, R. B. (1968). Attitudinal effects of mere exposure. *Journal of Personality and Social Psychology, 9*, 1–28.

4

Decomposing the Person Perception Process
Cerebral Hemispheric Asymmetries in Social Perception

Michael A. Zárate and Colby J. Stoever

CONTENTS

INTRODUCTION

How is it that with one quick glance, one can identify many things about others? A person's gender is almost always clearly identifiable. With very good accuracy, one can categorize others by their ethnicity, age, hair length, height, weight, attractiveness, and a host of other characteristics. Each of these characteristics may carry with it various associated stereotypes. Thus, people are referred to as "long-haired hippies," "fat pigs," "dumb blondes," "old fogies," and so on, and, of course, there are many ethnic and gender-related slurs. One can also scour the literature to find evidence supportive of the hypotheses that each of the previously cited characteristics is automatically encoded and used within a social perception task. At the same time, if one knows the person, most of the social features become less salient. Rather, the person is effortlessly identified by name. Similarly, with person identification, one often effortlessly makes various inferences

Please address correspondence to Michael A. Zárate, Department of Psychology, University of Texas at El Paso, El Paso, TX 79968; e-mail: mzarate@utep.edu about the person. "There is my friend Joe. I don't owe Joe a review, so I don't have to avoid him." Thus, on an experiential level, group categorization and person perception produce different outputs. Here, it is argued that on a perceptual level, person and group perception entail distinct processes, with divergent inferences. It is further argued that they are mediated by distinct neurological components. The goal of this chapter is to present a model of social perception based on these neurological components. The model will be extended to discuss how stereotyping and person-based inferences are evoked by these systems, and how various implicit and explicit processes might be further mediated by the cerebral hemispheres. The long-term goal is to further integrate the social and neurological literatures to advance both areas of study, consistent with other recent work within social psychology (see Brewer, Lieberman, this volume).

Person and group perception processes seem distinct enough to suggest that they rely on different perceptual and inferential mechanisms. Research on race categorization and recognition goes one step further and suggests that categorization and person identification actually work against each other. It is well established that out-group members are categorized quickly by race (Stroessner, 1996). It is also well established that out-group members are recognized more poorly than in-group members (Malpass, 1974). Thus, the encoding of out-group race appears to inhibit the person identification process. Recent research investigating cerebral hemispheric asymmetries in person perception processes provides further evidence for dual encoding mechanisms for nonsocial stimuli. Our own data (Zárate, Sanders, & Garza, 2000) demonstrate clear differences in person and group perception across a number of tasks. Here, person and group perception processes will be distinguished. The associated data derive from recent models of neurocognitive science and from data within the social psychological literature. The model further suggests that each process works to inhibit the alternative responses. These inhibitory mechanisms serve to dissociate various person and group measures. The long-term goal of the model is to use these neurological distinctions to address various dissociations between stereotypic and nonstereotypic process (see Galinsky, Martorana, & Ku, this volume). It is argued that many dissociations in the social psychological literature might be best described as neurological asymmetries. The model is presented and then extended to account for various dissociations regarding implicit and explicit measures of memory.

CEREBRAL PROCESSING ASYMMETRIES

Research within the neurocognitive domain reveals consistent cerebral hemispheric asymmetries in word and object perception. Traditionally, the right hemisphere was characterized as being more perceptual, and the left hemisphere was considered more verbal. Most recently, however, it has become evident that any cerebral asymmetries are far more complex than that (cf. Banich, 1998). Most current treatments of neurological asymmetries develop the notion that both hemispheres process all incoming information. The hemispheres differ, however, both in how they process information and in the efficiency with which they do so.

Multiple research programs demonstrate cerebral asymmetries in visual encoding processes. Navon (1977) first argued that visual encoding entails two distinct types of processes, referred to as *local* and *global* processing. Local processing entails the identification of particular features, whereas global processing refers to the perception and integration of multiple features. Within an array of features, local encoding involves perceiving the small items that are independent of the larger perceptual field. Global processing involves ignoring small details and integrating the entire set of features to identify one larger feature. To test these processes, Navon developed hierarchical stimuli, which are large stimuli produced by conflicting smaller stimuli. For example, many small *T*'s can be arranged to make a much larger letter *H*. Local processing would entail the perception of the small letters (e.g., *T*), whereas global processing would entail perceiving the larger letter *H*. In general, the smaller local features are perceived more efficiently by the left hemisphere (cf. Weissman & Banich, 1999). In contrast, identifying the larger letter *H* is performed more efficiently by the right hemisphere. The social psychological ramifications are clear. Most if not all models of face identification entail the integration of multiple features (Farah, Wilson, Drain, & Tanaka, 1998), whereas most group categorization tasks can be accomplished by the identification of a single feature. This model suggests that visual processing mechanisms are geared toward perceiving different aspects of any given stimulus. The right hemisphere perceives features in a manner that leads to person perception, whereas the left hemisphere perceives features in a manner that leads to group perception.

Marsolek and colleagues have developed a slightly different model, though the ramifications for social perception are similar. According to Marsolek, Kosslyn, and Squire (1992), visual encoding is served by two processing subsystems, which they label *abstract visual form* and *form specific processes*. The abstract form subsystem, which operates more efficiently in the left hemisphere, is particularly adept at identifying the semantic nature of stimuli. It identifies the feature that is consistent across multiple exemplars. In contrast, the right hemisphere is more adept at processing the form-specific features of stimuli. These features are specific to each individual stimulus. Within a word reading task, for instance, one can find the explicit form of semantic priming for previously presented words in the left hemisphere. For example, a previous presentation of a word will facilitate the perception of that word when it is presented to the left hemisphere. Further, the form of the word, be it in italics, normal font, or capital letters, has little impact on the ability of the left hemisphere to perceive the word (Marsolek et al., 1992). Thus, the left hemisphere responds to the semantic meaning of the word. The right hemisphere, however, responds to the specific visual shape of the word. One can find repetition priming for previously presented words in a word fragment completion task, but only when the words are presented to the right hemisphere. This effect, however, is contingent upon the font or form of the word staying the same across presentation and test. Thus, the right hemisphere responds to the physical quality of the stimulus and how that stimulus differs from other stimuli.

The ramifications for social perception are clear. The left hemisphere appears to respond to the features that are consistent across a number of stimuli, whereas the right hemisphere responds to the features that are unique to that stimulus. The social psychological consequences are similar to those of the previous model. The right hemisphere identifies the unique features of a stimulus, which leads well to person identification. The left hemisphere, however, responds well to the similarities across stimuli, which leads well to group perception.

Further support comes from the Hemispheric Encoding and Retrieval Asymmetries (HERA) model of memory retrieval (Cabeza & Nyberg, 2000; Nyberg, Cabeza, & Tulving, 1996; Tulving, 1999). The data consistently demonstrate that the left prefrontal cortex is more fully involved in semantic tasks, whereas the right prefrontal cortex is more fully involved in episodic retrieval. Nyberg et al. (1996) also show that these asymmetries are derived from studies using multiple methodologies, including functional magnetic resonance imaging (fMRI), hemifield studies, and studies of brain-damaged patients. That methodological diversity provides some degree of confidence in their conclusions. Thus, using mostly nonsocial stimuli, one can identify clear neurological processing differences between the right and left cerebral hemispheres. Across a number of research programs, one finds a consistent effect. The left hemisphere is superior at identifying local or specific features. The right hemisphere is superior at identifying the global features or the entire feature array. All three models discussed produce the types of mental representations proposed here. One can distinguish the models, though that is not the current intent. Following is an outline of the model and supportive data for these dual-processing mechanisms.

SOCIAL PSYCHOLOGICAL EXTENSIONS

One recent goal has been to extend the neurocognitive research to the social psychological domain. The main goal is to identify perceptual systems that influence social perception processes. It is hoped that this type of approach can help disentangle various social phenomena and can assist in the theoretical development of basic social psychological theories. It is also consistent with a growing body of research integrating the two literatures (Bourgeois, Christman, & Horowitz, 1998; Crites & Cacioppo, 1996; Klein & Kihlstrom, 1998; Klein, Loftus, & Kihlstrom, 1996; Lieberman, this volume). The immediate goal of our particular program is to identify the various perceptual systems and test their relevance for social psychological phenomena. It is not our goal to develop a clear understanding of the neuroanatomy of the brain and how that influences social judgments. The fact that these systems correspond to the cerebral hemispheres merely provides us with another tool to investigate social perception processes.

Across multiple studies, we have demonstrated a number of dissociations between group and person perception. Zárate et al. (2000) reported three studies testing for these dissociations. The mere exposure effect, which is mediated by the implicit memory trace of a previously presented person (Jacoby, 1983; Jacoby, Kelly, Brown, & Jasechko, 1989; Mandler, Nakamura, & Van Zandt, 1987), was demonstrated only in the right hemisphere. To test that hypothesis, target faces were presented for a later judgment task. During the first presentation, items were presented normally (i.e., centrally). At test, items were presented to either the left or the right visual field. Items presented to the right visual field are perceived first by the left hemisphere, and items presented to the left visual field are perceived first by the right hemisphere. The target items were paired with control items that had not previously been seen. For items presented to the right hemisphere, previously seen photos were liked better than never-before-seen targets. This did not occur for items presented to the left hemisphere.

In Experiment 2 of Zárate et al. (2000), stereotype priming, which is a semantic decision regarding a group, was demonstrated only in the left hemisphere. There was no evidence of stereotype priming in the right hemisphere despite the fact that word recognition latencies were similar across the hemispheres. In that experiment, in-group and out-group faces were presented to participants. The faces acted as primes for later positively and negatively valenced words. Positive words were responded to more quickly when primed by in-group faces, and negative words were responded to more quickly when primed by out-group faces, but only when presented to the left hemisphere. In Experiment 3, an on-line priming methodology (Malt, 1989) was used to test for exemplar- versus prototype-like processing. The right hemisphere demonstrated exemplar-like processing, whereas the left hemisphere demonstrated prototype-like processing. The studies demonstrated that the right hemisphere was superior in processing person- or instance-based information, and the left hemisphere was superior at processing group-level information.

In a later set of studies, Sanders, McClure, and Zárate (2001) tested for hemispheric asymmetries in person and gender identification. Participants were presented sequentially with a series of photo pairs for either a gender identification or a person identification task. The first photo acted as a prime for the second. During the same-person task, the goal of the participant was to determine if the second photo depicted the same person as the first. During the same-gender task, the goal was to determine if the second photo depicted a person of the same gender. Experiment 1 confirmed that the right hemisphere is more efficient at evaluating photos of individuals in different poses and recognizing that these photos are of the same person. Experiment 1 also demonstrated superior left hemisphere performance in the gender identification task.

In the second study, participants were classically conditioned to respond to a particular bearded man. Participants were taught to respond to a target; later, learning was tested for galvanic skin responses to the same target and for stimulus generalization. In the learning phase, participants heard an obnoxious tone when presented with a particular bearded man. Other faces were not presented with the tone. Later, skin conductance was measured to a new set of faces, including the conditioned bearded man and new bearded men (along with new and old nonbearded men). At test, the targets were presented to either the left or the right hemisphere. Regarding the conditioned target, both hemispheres responded with elevated skin conductance responses. Regarding the new bearded men, however, only the left hemisphere responded with elevated responses. Apparently, the left hemisphere responded to the category of "bearded men," whereas the right hemisphere responded only to the specific bearded man. The results support the conclusion that the hemispheres form unique associations and that conditional learning is represented differentially in the right and left hemispheres.

Across the multiple studies, we find consistent person perception effects in the right hemisphere and group perception effects in the left hemisphere. The left hemisphere processes, *which are mediated by the identification of salient or single features*, produce group-level representations of a social stimulus. In addition to the identification of single features, the left hemisphere attends to features that are consistent or invariant across a number of exemplars (Marsolek, 1999). For example, because race perception often entails the perception of a single feature (Levin, 1996), the left hemisphere is more efficient at this than the right. The attention to salient features produces an abstraction or a semantic representation for the items, commonly referred to as a *stereotypic inference*. Thus, stereotypic trait inferences, which are group based, are exhibited more efficiently in the left hemisphere (Zárate et al., 2000, Exp. 2).

It is further argued that the perceptual processing that occurs in the right hemisphere is conceptually similar to instance-based or exemplar-like processing (Medin & Schaffer, 1978; Smith & Zárate, 1992). Right hemispheric processes, *which are mediated by the identification of combinations of features or configurations*, support the representation of person-based outputs. Feature integration processes allow for person identification, memory for specific persons, and other individual-based processes. Thus, right hemispheric processing produces specific memory traces.

The dissociations just described are robust. Multiple measures have been used, and many of the effects have been replicated. It is also the case, however, that either process (feature identification or feature integration) can probably produce both types of outputs, meaning that the asymmetries are best described as biases rather than as distinctions. Further research, however, will have to determine the exact nature of the produced representations. We have argued that the feature identification and feature integration processes produce group- and person-based representations. It is equally plausible that those processes produce prototypic- and exemplar-based representations (Smith & Zárate, 1992). It is also possible that these dissociations are better accounted for by the episodic versus semantic nature of the memory trace (Schacter, 1995). Carlesimo (1999), however, argues against the episodic versus semantic distinction regarding these forms of repetition priming. No doubt other dimensions can also account for the associated findings. More importantly, these asymmetries are posited to rely on feature identification and feature integration processes, though that hypothesis has not been explicitly tested within a social psychological framework. Nevertheless, this approach offers one further tool to investigate why and how many of the various measures of person perception fail to correlate strongly with each other.

DISTINCT PROCESSES BUT ONE DECISION

Despite the robustness of the previously described processes, little is known about how these processes merge and impact each other. "Merging" models suggest that any output is a combination of both processes. This is possible and no doubt probable under many circumstances. It is also believed, however, that under many circumstances, the two outputs "compete." Under these circumstances, the two processes work in a horserace fashion, and once one hemisphere produces an output, it serves to inhibit the alternative output. These inhibitory mechanisms can produce many of the dissociations identified previously. It is further argued that this model can account for many of the reported distinctions between explicit and implicit memory processes. It is also the case, however, that the implicit processes can be further decomposed into perceptual and conceptual implicit processes, which may be further differentiated by the cerebral hemispheres. The following section presents a short discussion of how the hemispheres might influence each other (see Luh & Levy, 1995, for an extended discussion of various models of hemispheric cooperation and co-ordination). That is followed by some preliminary data investigating those processes.

THE HORSE-RACE MODEL OF COMPETITION

It is our hypothesis that these hemispheric asymmetries work somewhat independently of each other and work in parallel. A horse-race model predicts that upon initial perception of a social stimulus, dual encoding mechanisms are initiated. One process, working more efficiently in the right cerebral hemisphere, is particularly adept at person perception processes. The other process, working more efficiently in the left cerebral hemisphere, encodes the group categorization of the encountered targets. Dependent on multiple social factors such as experience with the targets, target proto-typicality, perceiver goals, feature relevance, and a number of other factors (see Kruglanski et al., this volume, for a discussion of factors influencing social judgments), either the right or left hemispheric process "wins the race" and produces the accordant output.

If a stimulus is presented that closely matches an abstracted concept, the semantic system produces the appropriate response more quickly and that becomes the overt response. If the presented stimulus more closely resembles stored specific memory traces, then the perceptual system produces the faster response, which becomes the overt response. Once a particular response by either system reaches a necessary threshold, that response is produced and the alternative response is inhibited (Shevtsova & Reggia, 1999). Thus, one response acts to inhibit the alternative response. This inhibition factor is important in developing multiple hypotheses regarding social perception.

The proposed horse-race model can potentially account for the para-doxical effects of extended contact with out-group members. If the group membership of a person and the individuating feature for a person are stored differently, then the associated response to that person may differ from the associated response to the group. This model predicts that learning about one person should inhibit race classification processes of that individual. Most models of social perception predict that experience with a target facilitates future perception. This model, however, predicts that experience with a person and his or her individuating features may actually inhibit the perception of group-based features. Just as the right hemisphere person perception processes can inhibit the left hemisphere processes, it is also possible that the left hemisphere group categorization processes can inhibit right hemisphere encoding. For instance, fast group categorizations, which occur for out-group members, should inhibit the encoding of the individuating facial features of that person (Levin, 1996). One can also identify multiple other forms of social perception in which group perception appears to inhibit person perception processes.

This basic logic was followed to investigate how experience with out-group members influences later race categorization processes. In two studies, we (Zárate, MacLin, & Stoever, 2002) tested how person and group representations work against each other to produce the described response representation. In both studies, participants were asked to learn about eight persons, four in-group and four out-group targets. Participants were presented with photos of target persons and given personalized information about each target person. In a later categorization task, participants were asked to categorize by race the learned and new targets. Across both studies, old targets were responded to more slowly than new targets. Thus, experience with an out-group member that personalizes the target inhibits the ability to identify the target by the group label. Importantly, Experiment 1 reveals that this inhibition is limited to the left cerebral hemisphere. Items were presented first to either the right or left cerebral hemisphere through visual field bilateral presentations. For items presented to the left cerebral hemisphere, old targets were responded to much more slowly by race. There was no difference for old and new targets for items presented to the right cerebral hemisphere. Experiment 2 demonstrates the same inhibition effects for centrally presented items. Thus, once one gets personalized information about a target person, it inhibits the ability of the left hemisphere to respond to the target using race-based labels. These data support a horse-race type of model whereby one representation inhibits the alternative forms of inhibition. These data also show how basic motives to encode persons using one dimension are exhibited differently across the cerebral hemispheres. Thus, just as neurocognitive mechanisms influence social perception, basic social psychological mechanisms influence neurocognitive processes.

Research within the neurocognitive domain provides further evidence for this type of horse-race model. Chee, Sriram, Soon, and Lee (2000) investigated the types of inhibition that occur within an Implicit Association Test (IAT; Greenwald, McGhee, & Schwartz, 1998). Using a nonsocial task (the association of flowers and pleasant versus insects and unpleasant), participants were scanned using fMRI technology. The main goal was to investigate how undesired responses were inhibited. Consistent with our results, they demonstrated that inhibition of the IAT responses was limited to the prefrontal cortex areas in the left hemisphere. It is important to point out, however, that the race categorization task (the association of the face with a label) and the IAT are conceptual implicit measures. Thus, across two distinct types of studies, conceptual implicit measures were strongly inhibited by the left cerebral hemisphere. It is unknown if left hemisphere processes mediate all forms of inhibition or if particular types of implicit processes are inhibited by the left cerebral hemisphere. This remains a particularly important line of research.

DIVIDE AND CONQUER

One alternative model entails a process Weissman and Banich refer to as a *divide-and-conquer* model of hemispheric communication (Banich & Karol, 1992; Weissman & Banich, 1999). Given the complexity of many encoding tasks, Weissman and Banich propose that interhemispheric communication is necessary with many difficult tasks. They further argue, however, that interhemispheric communication has costs. Encoding and communicating the information is beneficial only when the cost of communicating the information is less than the benefits incurred. Previous dissociations between the hemispheres, for instance, can be accounted for by their relatively simple tasks. Many previous studies have used comparatively simple tasks, so it would make sense that interhemispheric communication hurt performance more than helped it. In fact, the more difficult the task, the greater the task benefits from the use of both hemispheres and the greater the cooperation. Many social perception tasks, however, even "simple" gender categorization tasks, are far more complex than identification of the block letters used in the local–global paradigm (Navon, 1977), which suggests that cooperation processes will prevail. It may also be that social perception tasks are very well practiced, which serves to make them easy. As such, it is difficult to determine how difficult or easy social perception tasks are relative to other types of processes. It is anticipated that as with most dichotomies, the distinctions between divide-and-conquer and competition models will become blurred, and the goal will be to determine the conditions that promote one type of process or the other. Thus, it is probably the case that with many social perception tasks, "both hemispheres contribute to and collaborate in producing" the output (Luh & Levy, 1995, p. 1243).

Hemispheric Specialization

As previously stated, it is well recognized that the right hemisphere dominates face recognition processes. In particular, the fusiform gyrus of the right hemisphere is strongly involved in face perception (McCarthy, Puce, Gore, & Allison, 1997). It is stressed, however, that most previous studies have used face recognition tasks almost to the exclusion of gender or race categorization or almost any other form of social perception. Social perception can entail person recognition, group categorization, emotion perception, and a number of other tasks, so it is premature to contend that all face perception tasks are right hemisphere dominated. Furthermore, hemispheric specialization processes are rejected on multiple grounds. As previously stated, it is simplistic to believe that all relevant processing is accomplished by only one hemisphere. Rather, the hemispheres probably differ more in process than in content (von Hippel, Vargas, & Sekaquaptewa, this volume). More importantly, we demonstrate clearly that in a gender categorization task, the left hemisphere is more efficient at processing faces than the right (Sanders et al., 2001). In this task, participants were presented with a series of photos. The purpose was to determine if the second of two photos showed either the same gender as the first photo, or the same person as the first photo. The first photo was always presented centrally. The second photo was always presented to either the right or the left visual field. For the same-person task, the right hemisphere was always more efficient than the left hemisphere. This finding was expected. For the same-gender task, however, the left hemisphere was more efficient than the right hemisphere. This effect is important. This is one of the first studies to demonstrate left hemisphere superiority in a face perception task. It also demonstrates that the task is just as important as the stimuli in determining cerebral processing efficiency.

TASK AND PERSON VARIABILITY

Luh and Levy (1995) also highlight a number of other models of interhemispheric coordination. In particular, they suggest that there are individual difference variables impacting these processes. For example, some individuals, despite being right-handed, may be right hemisphere dominant, which will impact all further processing. Similarly, and possibly more important, one must keep in mind that these processing asymmetries, by definition, suggest that hemisphere dominance patterns differ for each task. Depending on task demands and available stimuli, one might find distinct left versus right hemisphere dominance. These types of asymmetries are difficult to determine a priori, and careful systematic research will be needed to understand fully how each task and each individual difference variable impacts cerebral asymmetries.

Summary

There are consistent findings demonstrating cerebral hemispheric asymmetries in social perception that appear to produce person- or group-based representations. It is also the case, however, that the ways in which the hemispheres work together to produce one conscious output are far more ambiguous. Nevertheless, there is clear evidence that at least under some conditions, the hemispheres work in parallel and "against" each other to inhibit the alternative response. In the process, they appear to produce multiple person versus group judgment dissociations. In the following section, the basic constructs of this model are applied to the implicit versus explicit memory distinction.

DECOMPOSING THE IMPLICIT PROCESS PHENOMENA

It is tempting to argue that many of the right hemisphere effects are implicit, whereas the left hemisphere effects are explicit (Schacter, 1995), but that distinction fails to account for all the relevant findings. It is argued, however, that the label *implicit process* is too broad to be derived from one particular process. Rather, research suggests that there are multiple types of implicit processes and that these processes are further delineated by the hemispheres. In particular, we wish to highlight the distinction between data-driven perceptual implicit processes and semantic or conceptual implicit processes (Carlesimo, 1999; Toth & Reingold, 1996). Perceptual processes rely on the physical characteristics of the presented items, whereas conceptual processes rely on the semantic meaning of the presented items. Repetition priming, picture fragment completion, and priming based on physical similarity between two target persons are classic forms of perceptual priming. Stereotype priming, in which a face can prime the activation of a stereotypic associate, is a classic form of social psychological conceptual priming. The IAT, in which participants pair positive and negative words with group labels (Greenwald et al., 1998), would be considered a conceptual implicit test. The distinction between perceptual and conceptual processes, however, entails some degree of overlap. For instance, most measures use multiple items to test the underlying construct. As items are repeated (e.g., the pairing of a particular type of face with a particular term), the process may become more perceptual due to the repetitive nature of the task. Nevertheless, this distinction has important ramifications for neurological asymmetries in social perception.

Most, if not all, of the right hemisphere processes studied so far in our lab are data-driven implicit processes. For example, the mere exposure effect, which relies on perceptual fluency for previously presented items, and exemplar-based similarity priming are data-driven processes. In contrast, all of the left hemisphere processes are conceptual, though the measures are sometimes explicit and sometimes implicit (cf. Richardson-Klavehn, Gardiner, & Java, 1996). For instance, in Zárate et al. (2000, Exp. 3), participants were presented with a gender categorization task. Photos were presented in one continuous stream for seemingly independent decisions. In reality, photos were placed such that some of them acted as primes for those that followed. Some prime photos were either similar or dissimilar in appearance to the target photos. Further, other primes tested the distinction between conceptual and perceptual processing. To do that, a prime was selected that was of the same sex as the target but from a different conceptual category (i.e., different ethnicity), providing a different group prime condition, or was from the same conceptual category but was dissimilar in appearance to the target.

For items presented to the right hemisphere, the perceptually similar prime facilitated performance better than the conceptual prime. This supports the hypothesis that the episodic/perceptual system is operating more efficiently in the right hemisphere than in the left hemisphere. For items presented to the left hemisphere, however, the similar and dissimilar primes produced equivalent levels of response facilitation. More importantly, whereas the different-group prime produced priming in the right hemisphere, it failed to produce any response facilitation in the left hemisphere. When the target differed on an important social categorization dimension (Brewer, 1988), no priming occurred. Thus, the left hemisphere produces a conceptual priming effect by responding only to items that are semantically related to the primes. The physical similarity between the target and prime had no impact on left hemisphere performance. Using response time as an implicit measure of category activation, one finds distinct cerebral asymmetries in social perception.

This dissociation in cerebral hemispheric asymmetries in response patterns to perceptual and conceptual primes was replicated using an entirely different procedure. In the previously described classical conditioning study, participants produced a heightened galvanic skin response based on previously learned negative associations. Classical conditioning reflects one form of implicit learning (Hugdahl, 1995). In fact, Hugdahl presents a short history of the classical conditioning literature to argue that the behavioristic dominance of the classical conditioning literature has obfuscated Pavlov's original hypothesis that classical conditioning should prove to be a valuable tool in understanding brain functioning. Classical conditioning fits nicely with any definition of implicit responses in that participants are not asked to use any past memory trace, learning is not necessarily intentional, and awareness of the prior learning experiences is not necessary.

In this study, the hemispheres differed markedly in how they generalized previously learned responses. At training, a target photo (one bearded man among four other nonbearded men) was always presented with an obnoxious tone. Later, galvanic skin responses were measured in reaction to the presentation of the same learned targets and new bearded and nonbearded control targets. The right hemisphere responded only to the same target. This form of perceptual priming is consistent with the exemplar priming in the gender categorization task. For items presented to the left hemisphere, however, participants responded with a heightened galvanic skin response to all bearded men. Thus, once again, the left hemisphere responded to the items in a conceptual manner. Any item from the group "bearded men" produced the same response.

Within the cognitive neuroscience literature, findings of cerebral hemisphere asymmetries in implicit and explicit memory are controversial (Hugdahl, 1995). Several studies show a right hemisphere advantage on implicit tasks (Berti & Rizzolatti, 1992; Tranel & Damasio, 1985), though only recently have neurocognitive researchers begun to disentangle conceptual from perceptual implicit processes. There has been some systematic attempt to identify the various neuroanatomical components of implicit memory, though some of the findings are still very preliminary. For instance, Rovee-Collier, Hayne, and Colombo (2001) claim that the neural substrates of implicit priming "are said to be dependent on the neocortex – a term only slightly more informative than saying that they depend on the brain" (p. 56). There is clearer evidence for the neural substrates of habit (the striatum) and emotion-based (amygdala) memory than for most forms of implicit memory (Rovee-Collier et al., 2001). One problem is that many studies test only amnesic patients, and some important studies provide conflicting results (see Carlesimo, 1999, pp. 221–223, for a short summary). Further, most distinctions between perceptual and conceptual implicit priming are difficult given the simple fact that "pure" tests of either form of priming are difficult to develop (see Maki, Bylsma, & Brandt, 2000, for one recent attempt). The recent use of the IAT by neurocognitive researchers, however, demonstrates how both areas should benefit from a merging of the literatures. Most implicit tasks favored by social psychologists (IAT, stereotype priming) are conceptual in nature, though many are more perceptual (repetition priming, mere exposure effects). It seems that one can easily derive equivalent conceptual and perceptual tasks for testing more clearly and explicitly the distinctions between these processes. Thus, experimental dissociations produced by social psychologists can be utilized by neurocognitive researchers to map out how those processes relate to specific brain regions.

The model presented here identifies still unstudied aspects of explicit and implicit processes. If there are distinct neurological systems operating in distinct brain regions, do they cooperate on most tasks or, as with our preliminary data, do they tend to compete to inhibit each other? How independent are these systems? The neurological asymmetries reported correlate well (though not perfectly) with the implicit versus explicit distinction. The social perception asymmetries identified previously are also consistent with other studies demonstrating dissociations between various explicit and implicit processes (e.g., Dovidio, Kawakami, Johnson, Johnson, & Howard, 1997; Galinsky et al., this volume; Johnston & Miles, this volume). Dovidio et al. (1997) demonstrate an important point. It is inaccurate to say that implicit measures merely reduce the social desirability factor and are thus better measures. They demonstrated that explicit self-report measures predicted well more conscious jury-based decisions. Implicit measures, however, predicted well other nonverbal measures such as eye blinking.

The preceding analysis demonstrates that distinct neurological components produce distinct types of mental representations. Depending on the stimuli and the task, one type of process will dominate the decision-making outcome. Once a decision is reached, it may even inhibit the alternative responses. Thus, one should find multiple person versus group dissociations and possibly implicit versus explicit dissociations. The preceding analyses also identify clear new directions for research. The neurocognitive literature demonstrates that there are distinct perceptual mechanisms for many particular tasks. As such, there is less reason to believe that various social psychological tasks should relate to each other. One will probably have to do more than merely label a task implicit or explicit. One must have some understanding of the processes involved and make finer distinctions before one can adequately encode the targets.

CONCLUSIONS

Social perception is not a serial process. One does not move from broad social categories to specific person memories. Rather, it appears that any social encounter initiates a number of processes. Those processes include person perception and social perception processes. Those processes are dependent on the degree to which they demand perceptual or conceptual processing. They appear to work independently to produce distinct mental representations. Once a representation is produced, it appears to inhibit the alternative response. Thus, one can easily identify most social characteristics of strangers, but friends are categorized by name. Details regarding friends, however, become lost in the gestalt. Thus, new hairstyles, facial hair, weight loss, and so on change the appearance but often go unnoticed. The dissociation between person and group perception suggests multiple identifying processes. It is believed that this approach can inform the field regarding how to decompose further the implicit perception phenomena to produce a more coherent model of social perception.

References

Banich, M. T. (1998). Integration of information between the cerebral hemispheres. *Current Directions in Psychological Science, 7*(1), 32–37.
Banich, M. T., & Karol, D. (1992). The sum of the parts does not equal the whole: Evidence from bihemispheric processing. *Journal of Experimental Psychology: Human Perception and Performance, 18*, 63–84.
Berti, A., & Rizzolatti, G. (1992). Visual processing without awareness: Evidence from unilateral neglect. *Journal of Cognitive Neuroscience, 4*, 345–351.
Bourgeois, M. J., Christman, S., & Horowitz, I. A. (1998). The role of hemispheric activation in person perception: Evidence for an attentional focus model. *Brain and Cognition, 38*, 202–219.
Brewer, M. B. (1988). A dual process model of impression formation. In R. S. Wyer & T. K. Scrull (Eds.), *Advances in social cognition* (Vol. 1., pp. 1–36). Hillsdale, NJ: Erlbaum.
Cabeza, R., & Nyberg, L. (2000). Imaging cognition II: An empirical review of 275 PET and fMRI studies. *Journal of Cognitive Neuroscience, 12*(1), 1–47.

Carlesimo, G. A. (1999). Perceptual and conceptual components of repetition priming in anterograde amnesia. In L. Nilsson & H. J. Markowitsch (Eds.), *Cognitive neuroscience of memory* (pp. 213–237). Seattle: Hogrefe & Huber.

Chee, M. W. L., Sriram, N., Sooon, C. S., & Lee, K. M. (2000). Dorsolateral prefrontal cortex and the implicit association of concepts and attributes. *Brain Imaging: NeuroReport, 17,* 135–140.

Crites, S. L., & Cacioppo, J. T. (1996). Electrocortical differentiation of evaluative and nonevaluative categorizations. *Psychological Science, 7,* 318–321.

Dovidio, J. F., Kawakami, K., Johnson, C., Johnson, B., & Howard, A. (1997). On the nature of prejudice: Automatic and controlled processes. *Journal of Experimental Social Psychology, 33,* 510–540.

Farah, M. J., Wilson, K. D., Drain, M., & Tanaka, J. N. (1998). What is "special" about face perception. *Psychological Review, 105,* 482–498.

Greenwald, A. G., McGhee, D. E., & Schwartz, J. L. K. (1998). Measuring individual differences in implicit cognition: The implicit association test. *Journal of Personality and Social Psychology, 74*(6), 1464–1480.

Hugdhal, K. (1995). Classical conditioning and implicit learning: The right hemisphere hypothesis. In R. J. Davidson & K. Hugdahl (Eds.), *Brain asymmetry* (pp. 235–267). Cambridge, MA: MIT Press.

Jacoby, L. L. (1983). Perceptual enhancement: Persistent effects of an experience. *Journal of Experimental Psychology: Learning, Memory, and Cognition, 9,* 21–38.

Jacoby, L. L., Kelly, C., Brown, J., & Jasechko, J. (1989). Becoming famous overnight: Limits on the ability to avoid unconscious influences of the past. *Journal of Personality and Social Psychology, 56,* 326–338.

Klein, S. B., & Kihlstrom, J. F. (1998). On bridging the gap between social-personality psychology and neuropsychology. *Personality and Social Psychology Review, 2,* 228–242.

Klein, S. B., Loftus, J., & Kihlstrom, J. F. (1996). Self-knowledge of an amnesic patient: Toward a neuropsychology of personality and social psychology. *Journal of Experimental Psychology: General, 125,* 250–260.

Levin, D. T. (1996). Classifying faces by race: The structure of race categories. *Journal of Experimental Psychology: Learning, Memory, and Cognition, 22,* 1364–1382.

Luh, K. E., & Levy, J. (1995). Interhemispheric cooperation: Left is left and right is right, but sometimes the twain shall meet. *Journal of Experimental Psychology: Human Perception and Performance, 21,* 1243–1258.

Maki, P. M., Bylsma, F. W., & Brandt, J. (2000). Conceptual and perceptual implicit memory in Huntington's disease. *Neuropsychology, 14*(3), 331–340.

Malpass, R. S. (1974). Racial bias in eyewitness identification? *Personality and Social Psychology Bulletin, 1,* 42–44.

Malt, B. C. (1989). An on-line investigation of prototype and exemplar strategies in classification. *Journal of Experimental Psychology: Learning, Memory, and Cognition, 15,* 539–555.

Mandler, G., Nakamura, Y., & Van Zandt, B. J. S. (1987). Nonspecific effects of exposure on stimuli that cannot be recognized. *Journal of Experimental Psychology: Learning, Memory, and Cognition, 13,* 646–648.

Marsolek, C. J. (1999). Dissociable neural subsystems underlie abstract and specific object recognition. *Psychological Science, 10*(2), 111–118.

Marsolek, C. J., Kosslyn, S. M., & Squire, L. R. (1992). Form-specific visual priming in the right cerebral hemisphere. *Journal of Experimental Psychology: Learning, Memory, and Cognition, 18*, 492–508.

McCarthy, G., Puce, A., Gore, J. C., & Allison T. (1997). Face-specific processing in the human fusiform gyrus. *Journal of Cognitive Neuroscience, 9*, 603–610.

Medin, D. L., & Schaffer, M. M. (1978). Context theory of classification learning. *Psychological Review, 85*, 207–238.

Navon, D. (1977). Forest before trees: The precedence of global features in visual perception. *Cognitive Psychology, 9*, 353–383.

Nyberg, L., Cabeza, R., & Tulving, E. (1996). PET studies of encoding and retrieval: The HERA model. *Psychonomic Bulletin and Review, 3*, 135–148.

Richardson-Klavehn, A., Gardiner, J. M., & Java, R. (1996). Memory: Task disassociations, process disassociations and dissociations of consciousness. In G. Underwood (Ed.), *Implicit Cognition* (pp. 85–158). New York: Oxford University Press.

Rovee-Collier, C., Hayne, H., & Colombo, M. (2001). *The development of implicit and explicit memory*. Philadelphia: Benjamins.

Sanders, J. D., McClure, K. A., & Zárate, M. A. (2001). *Cerebral hemispheric asymmetries in social perception: Perceiving and responding to the individual and the group*. Manuscript submitted for publication.

Schacter, D. L. (1995). Implicit memory: A new frontier for cognitive neuroscience. In M. S. Gazzaniga (Ed.), *The cognitive neurosciences* (pp. 815–824). Cambridge, MA: MIT Press.

Shevtsova, N., & Reggia, J. A. (1999). A neural network model of lateralization during letter identification. *Journal of Cognitive Neuroscience, 11*, 167–181.

Smith, E. R., & Zárate, M. A. (1992). Exemplar-based model of social judgment. *Psychological Review, 99*, 3–21.

Stroessner, S. J. (1996). Social categorization by race or sex: Effects of perceived nonnormalcy on response times. *Social Cognition, 14*, 247–276.

Tanaka, J. W., & Farah, M. J. (1993). Parts and wholes in face recognition. *The Quarterly Journal of Experimental Psychology, 46*, 225–245.

Toth, J. P., & Reingold, E. M. (1996). Beyond perception: Conceptual contributions to unconscious influences of memory. In G. Underwood (Ed.), *Implicit cognition* (pp. 41–84). New York: Oxford University Press.

Tranel, D., & Damasio, A. R. (1985). Knowledge without awareness: An autonomic index of face recognition by prosopagnosics. *Science, 228*, 1453–1454.

Tulving, E. (1999). On the uniqueness of episodic memory. In L. Nilsson & H. J. Markowitsch (Eds.), *Cognitive neuroscience of memory* (pp. 11–42). Seattle: Hogrefe & Huber.

Weissman, D. H., & Banich, M. T. (1999). Global–local inference modulated by communication between the hemispheres. *Journal of Experimental Psychology: General, 128*, 282–308.

Zárate, M. A., MacLin, K., & Stoever, C. J. (2002). *The neuropsychology of the contact hypothesis*. Unpublished manuscript.

Zárate, M. A., Sanders, J. D., & Garza, A. A. (2000). Neurological disassociations of social perception processes. *Social Cognition, 18*, 223–251.

5

The Psychodynamics of Social Judgments

An Attachment Theory Perspective

Phillip R. Shaver and Mario Mikulincer

CONTENTS

INTRODUCTION

In recent years, attachment theory (Bowlby, 1969/1982, 1973, 1980), designed originally to characterize infant–parent emotional bonding, has been applied first to the study of adolescent and adult romantic relationships and then to the study of broader social phenomena. In this chapter, we review and integrate this large and still growing body of work to demonstrate the usefulness and validity of attachment theory for explaining individual variations in a wide array of social judgments, including appraisals of self and others, appraisals of person–environment transactions, and cognitive reactions to new information, out-groups, others' needs, and transient affective states. We also provide an updated integrative model of the dynamics of the attachment system (Shaver & Mikulincer, 2002), which explains the effects of two major individual-difference dimensions, attachment-related *anxiety* and *avoidance*, on social

Preparation of this chapter was facilitated by a grant from the Fetzer Institute. Please address correspondence to Phillip R. Shaver, Department of Psychology, University of California, Davis, One Shields Avenue, Davis, CA 95616-8686; e-mail: prshaver@ucdavis.edu; Mario Mikulincer, Department of Psychology, Bar-Ilan University, Ramat Gan, 52900, Israel; e-mail: mikulm@mail.biu.ac.il judgments and identifies the implicit and explicit mechanisms that mediate these effects.

BASIC CONCEPTS IN ATTACHMENT THEORY AND RESEARCH

In his classic trilogy, Bowlby (1969/1982, 1973, 1980) developed a theoretical framework for explaining the nature of the affective ties we form with significant others and the relevance of these ties for socioemotional functioning. This theoretical framework can now be viewed as a part of evolutionary psychology (see Brewer and Haselton & Buss, this volume). Bowlby (1969/1982) argued that human infants are born with a repertoire of behaviors (*attachment behaviors*) aimed at attaining or maintaining proximity to supportive others (*attachment figures*) as a means of protecting themselves from physical and psychological threats. These proximity-seeking behaviors are organized around a psychoevolutionary adaptation (*attachment behavioral system*), which emerged over the course of evolution to increase the likelihood of survival and reproduction on the part of members of a species born with immature capacities for locomotion, feeding, and defense. Although the attachment system is most critical during the early years of life, Bowlby (1988) assumed that it is active over the entire life span and is manifested in thoughts and behaviors related to proximity seeking in times of need.

Beyond describing the universal aspects of the attachment system, Bowlby (1973) delineated possible individual differences in its functioning. In his view, these individual differences are derived from the reactions of significant others to attachment-system activation and from the internalization of these reactions in the form of *attachment working models* of self and others. On the one hand, interactions with significant others who are available and responsive to one's needs facilitate the optimal functioning of the attachment system and promote the formation of a sense of attachment security. This sense consists of positive expectations about others' availability in threatening situations, positive views of the self as competent and valued, a sense of optimism in dealing with threats, and increased confidence in support seeking as a primary distress-regulation strategy. The sense of attachment security also facilitates engagement in autonomy-promoting activities (e.g., exploration) and the ability to make risky decisions while feeling confident that support is available if needed (Bowlby, 1988).

On the other hand, interactions with significant others who are unresponsive to one's attachment needs foster insecurity regarding others' goodwill and doubts about the effectiveness of proximity seeking. During these painful interactions, distress is not properly managed, insecure attachment working models are formed, and strategies of affect regulation other than support seeking are developed. Attachment theorists (e.g., Cassidy & Kobak, 1988; Main, 1990) have delineated two major insecure strategies: *hyperactivation* and *deactivation* of the attachment system. Hyperactivation is characterized by recurrent attempts to minimize distance from attachment figures and elicit support by clinging and controlling responses. Deactivation consists of attempts to maximize distance from attachment figures while adopting a self-reliant stance (Bowlby, 1988; Cassidy & Kobak, 1988).

While testing these theoretical ideas in studies of adults, most researchers have focused on "styles" of attachment – systematic patterns of expectations, emotions, and behavior in close relationships that are viewed as the residue of particular kinds of attachment histories (Fraley & Shaver, 2000). These residues are thought to inhere in internal working models of self and others. Initially, individual-difference studies of attachment styles in adulthood were based on Ainsworth, Blehar, Waters, and Wall's (1978) tripartite typology of attachment styles in infancy – secure, anxious, and avoidant – and on Hazan and Shaver's (1987) conceptualization of adult parallels to these styles in the marital/romantic domain. Subsequent studies (e.g., Bartholomew & Horowitz, 1991; Brennan, Clark, & Shaver, 1998; Fraley & Waller, 1998) revealed that adult attachment styles are best conceptualized not as distinct types, but as regions in a continuous two-dimensional space. The dimensions defining this space, *attachment-related anxiety* and *attachment-related avoidance,* can be measured with reliable and valid self-report scales (Brennan et al., 1998), which are associated with a wide variety of cognitions and behaviors in close relationships (see Feeney, 1999, for a review) and feelings during daily social interactions (e.g., Pietromonaco & Feldman Barrett, 1997; Tidwell, Reis, & Shaver, 1996).

In this two-dimensional space, what was formerly called the *secure style* is a region in which both anxiety and avoidance are low. This region is defined by a positive history of interactions with significant others, a sense of attachment security, and comfort with closeness and interdependence. What was called the *anxious style* refers to a region in which anxiety is high and avoidance is low. Persons high in attachment anxiety are characterized by insecurity concerning others' goodwill and reliable support, a strong need for closeness, fear of being rejected, and reliance on hyperactivating affective strategies. What was called the *avoidant style* refers to a region in which avoidance is high. This region is defined by insecurity concerning others' goodwill, compulsive self-reliance, and the adoption of deactivating affect-regulation strategies. In Ainsworth et al.'s (1978) early two-dimensional analysis, based on a discriminant analysis that included all of these authors' continuous coding scales of infant behavior in a laboratory *strange situation*, avoidant infants occupied mainly the region where avoidance was high and anxiety was low. In adult attachment research, Bartholomew and Horowitz (1991) drew a distinction between *dismissing avoidants* (people who are high on avoidance and low on anxiety) and *fearful avoidants* (those high on both avoidance and anxiety).

Although attachment styles may initially be formed during early interactions with primary caregivers, Bowlby (1988) contended that meaningful interactions with significant others throughout life can update a person's attachment working models (and associated behavioral orientation). Moreover, although attachment style is often conceptualized as a global orientation toward close relationships, there are theoretical and empirical reasons for believing that working models of attachment are part of a hierarchical cognitive network that includes a complex, heterogeneous array of episodic, relationship-specific, and generalized attachment representations (Collins & Read, 1994). These representations can be viewed as existing at different levels along an implicit-to-explicit continuum of information processing, as discussed by Brewer and others in this volume. People possess multiple attachment schemas, and both congruent and incongruent attachment-related cognitions may coexist in the cognitive network with a global attachment style (Baldwin, Keelan, Fehr, Enns, & Koh Rangarajoo, 1996). In fact, research has shown that (a) people can hold relationship-specific attachment orientations organized around experiences with a specific partner (e.g., La Guardia, Ryan, Couchman, & Deci, 2000; Pierce & Lydon, 2001), and (b) actual or imagined encounters with supportive or nonsupportive others can contextually activate congruent attachment orientations (e.g., Mikulincer & Shaver, 2001; Mikulincer et al., 2001), even if these orientations do not fit with the global attachment style.

AN INTEGRATIVE MODEL OF THE DYNAMICS OF THE ATTACHMENT SYSTEM

Based on an extensive review of adult attachment studies, Shaver and Mikulincer (2002) proposed a model of the activation and dynamics of the attachment system. This model integrates recent findings with the earlier theoretical proposals of Bowlby (1969/1982, 1973), Ainsworth (1991), and Cassidy and Kobak (1988), and is a conceptual extension and refinement of previous control-system representations of the attachment system presented by Shaver, Hazan, and Bradshaw (1988) and Fraley and Shaver (2000).

The model (Figure 5.1) includes three major components. One component concerns the monitoring and appraisal of threatening events and is responsible for activation of the attachment system. The second component involves the monitoring and appraisal of the availability and responsiveness of attachment figures who might provide support and relief, satisfy attachment needs, build the individual's own inner resources, and broaden his or her thought-action repertoire. This component is responsible for

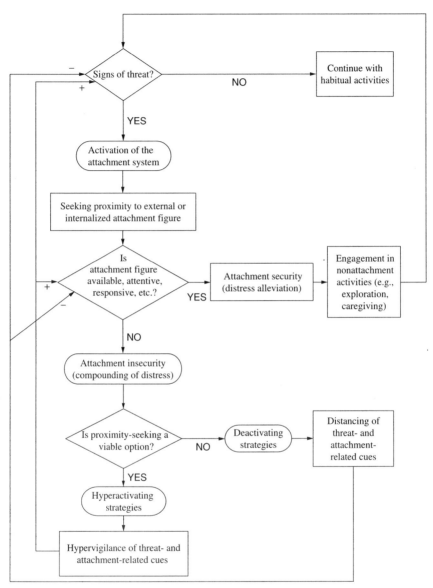

Figure 5.1. Shaver and Mikulincer's integrative model of the activation and dynamics of the attachment system.

variations in the sense of attachment security; it distinguishes between securely and insecurely attached persons, whether anxious or avoidant. The third component concerns monitoring and appraisal of the viability of proximity seeking as a means of coping with attachment insecurity and distress. This component is responsible for variations in the use of hyperactivating or deactivating strategies of affect regulation and distinguishes between anxious and avoidant people. The model also includes excitatory and inhibitory neural circuits (shown as arrows on the left side of the diagram) that result from the recurrent use of hyperactivating or deactivating strategies, which in turn affect the monitoring of threatening events and of attachment figures' availability.

Following Bowlby's (1969/1982) reasoning, Shaver and Mikulincer (2002) assume that the monitoring of unfolding events results in activation of the attachment system when a potential or actual threat is perceived. This activation can be viewed as part of what Chartrand and Jefferis (this volume) call *automatic goal pursuit*, manifested in efforts to seek and/or maintain proximity to attachment figures. Although this component of the model represents the normative operation of the attachment system, which occurs regardless of individual differences in attachment history and orientation, it is still affected by excitatory circuits resulting from the hyperactivating strategies of anxious persons and inhibitory circuits related to avoidant individuals' deactivating strategies.

Once the attachment system is activated, an affirmative answer to the question about attachment figures' availability results in a strong sense of attachment security and in what Shaver and Mikulincer (2002), following the lead of Fredrickson (2001), call a *broaden-and-build* cycle of attachment security. This cycle reflects optimal functioning of the attachment system and is characterized by distress alleviation and bolstered personal adjustment, as well as facilitation of other behavioral systems such as exploration and caregiving, which broaden a person's perspectives and capacities. Moreover, this cycle encourages a person to openly acknowledge future threats and to rely comfortably on proximity seeking as a primary coping strategy.

It is important to note that the answer to the question about attachment-figure availability depends on the subjective appraisal of this availability, and can be biased by a person's history of interactions with attachment figures and his or her attachment working models. Attachment research has consistently reported that securely attached persons are more likely to make a positive appraisal of attachment-figure availability than insecurely attached persons (Shaver & Hazan, 1993). Despite this cognitive bias, however, reality is still important in the appraisal of attachment-figure availability. In our view, the actual presence of an available attachment figure or contextual cues that activate representations of available attachment figures can lead people to give an affirmative answer to the question of attachment-figure availability. Recent findings have consistently shown that these contextual cues can activate the broaden-and-build cycle of attachment security even among chronically insecure persons (e.g., Mikulincer & Shaver, 2001; Mikulincer et al., 2001).

Perceived unavailability of an attachment figure results in attachment insecurity, which compounds the distress initiated by the appraisal of a threat. This state of insecurity forces a decision about the viability of proximity seeking as a protective strategy. When proximity seeking is appraised as a viable option – because of attachment history, temperamental factors, or contextual cues – people adopt hyperactivating strategies, which include intense approach to attachment figures and continued reliance on others as a source of comfort. Hyperactivation of the attachment system involves excitatory circuits that increase vigilance to threat-related cues and reduce the threshold for detecting cues of attachment figures' unavailability – the two kinds of cues that activate the attachment system (Bowlby, 1973). As a result, minimal threat-related cues are easily detected, the attachment system is chronically activated, pain related to the unavailability of attachment figures is exacerbated, and doubts about one's ability to achieve relief and attain a sense of security are heightened. These excitatory circuits account for the psychological correlates of attachment anxiety.

Appraising proximity seeking as not viable results in the adoption of deactivating strategies, manifested in distancing from cues that activate the attachment system – cues related to threats and attachment figures – and making attempts to handle distress alone. These strategies involve inhibitory circuits that lead to the dismissal of threat- and attachment-related cues and the suppression of threat- and attachment-related thoughts, memories, and emotions. These inhibitory circuits are further reinforced by the adoption of a self-reliant attitude that decreases dependence on others and acknowledgment of personal faults or weaknesses. These inhibitory circuits account for the psychological manifestations of attachment avoidance.

According to Shaver and Mikulincer (2002), the three major components of the model have both content and process aspects – a distinction analyzed by von Hippel, Vargas, and Sekaquaptewa (this volume). All components and circuits of the model can operate either consciously or unconsciously (see Brewer, this volume). Moreover, these components and circuits can operate either in parallel or in opposite ways at conscious and unconscious levels. This explains why some avoidant individuals experience conscious deactivation of threat-related cues while also exhibiting unconscious, including physiological, signs of distress (e.g., Dozier & Kobak, 1992; Mikulincer, 1998b; Mikulincer, Florian, & Tolmacz, 1990). It also explains why avoidant individuals exhibit heightened accessibility of attachment-related worries in cognitively demanding situations that prevent more controlled inhibition of these worries (Mikulincer, Birnbaum, Woddis, & Nachmias, 2000; see Lieberman, this volume, for a neuropsychological analysis of the effects of cognitive load).

THE DYNAMICS OF THE ATTACHMENT SYSTEM
AND SOCIAL JUDGMENTS

In our view, the formation of individual differences in attachment-system dynamics can be viewed as the prototypical precursor of variations in social judgments. These differences should play a role in theoretical models designed to explain accuracies and inaccuracies in social judgments (e.g., Funder, this volume; Kruglanski et al., this volume). According to Bowlby (1973), attachment-style differences are already present in the first year of life, in infants' interactions with their primary caregiver, and they form a foundation for the development of specific judgments about others (beliefs about others' availability), the self (beliefs about self-worth and self-efficacy), transactions with the environment (e.g., beliefs about the positivity of interactions with others, beliefs about the reversibility of threats), and ways of dealing with these transactions (e.g., beliefs about the efficacy of support seeking), as well as regulating cognitions in nonattachment areas (e.g., exploration). These mental products can be generalized across recurrent interactions with a relationship partner. Moreover, they can be generalized across relationships via top-down schematic processing of new partners and relationships, and then become the building blocks of a person's global social judgments.

Shaver and Mikulincer's (2002) model provides a guide for delineating attachment-related variations in social judgments. The module that monitors attachment-figure availability and creates a sense of attachment security is related to positive or negative working models of others, which can bias judgments of other people. Moreover, the sense of attachment security can regulate cognitions related to the exploration of new information and the provision of care for others who are in need. The module that monitors the viability of proximity seeking and determines the adoption of deactivating or hyperactivating strategies activates self-reliant or other-reliant attitudes and can therefore bias judgments about self-worth. In addition, because these strategies are defined by the regulation of threat cues (exaggeration vs. dismissal), proximity to others (maximization vs. minimization), and affective states (perpetuation of threat-related affect vs. distancing oneself from this affect), they can bias judgments of threatening events and self–other proximity as well as cognitive reactions to affective states. In the following sections, we review research findings concerning specific links between dynamics of the attachment system and social judgments.

Attachment-Figure Availability and Social Judgments

The perceived availability of attachment figures has direct implications for the appraisal of others. An affirmative answer to the question about attachment-figure availability activates positive models of others, which may spread to positive appraisals, expectations, and explanations of others' traits and behaviors. In contrast, a negative answer to this question activates negative models of others, which in turn may negatively bias judgments of other people. This reasoning implies that insecure attachment, either anxious or avoidant, which results from the perceived unavailability of attachment figures, should be associated with more negative judgments of others.

The perceived availability of attachment figures can also regulate attitudes related to exploration and caregiving, two of the other behavioral systems discussed by Bowlby (1969/1982). He claimed that the unavailability of attachment figures inhibits the activation of other behavioral systems, because a person without the protection and support of an attachment figure is likely to be so focused on attachment needs and feelings of distress that he or she lacks the attention and resources necessary to explore the environment and attend empathically to others' needs. This reasoning implies that attachment insecurity should reduce or prevent exploration of new information in making social judgments, favor the formation of rigid, stereotypic judgments, and inhibit the development of a prosocial orientation and a caring attitude toward needy others.

Appraisal of Others' Traits and Behaviors. Numerous studies have provided strong support for the hypothesis that attachment-related anxiety and avoidance are associated with negative appraisals of other people. Individuals who score high on the dimensions of attachment-related anxiety and/or avoidance have been found to hold a more negative view of human nature (Collins & Read, 1990), use more negative traits to describe relationship partners (e.g., Feeney & Noller, 1991; Levy, Blatt, & Shaver, 1998), perceive these partners as less supportive (e.g., Davis, Morris, & Kraus, 1998; Ognibene & Collins, 1998), be less satisfied with the support received from others (e.g., Collins & Read, 1990; Larose & Boivin, 1997), feel less trust toward partners (e.g., Collins & Read, 1990; Mikulincer, 1998a; Simpson, 1990), and believe that partners do not truly know them (Brennan & Bosson, 1998).

Both anxiety and attachment avoidance are also associated with negative expectations concerning partner behaviors (e.g., Baldwin, Fehr, Keedian, & Seidel, 1993; Baldwin et al., 1996; Mikulincer & Arad, 1999). For example, Baldwin et al. (1993) examined the cognitive accessibility of expectations concerning partners' behaviors in a lexical-decision task and found that for both anxious and avoidant persons, negative partner behaviors (e.g., partner being hurtful) were more accessible than they were among secure persons. These negative expectations have also been found in studies that assessed relationship-specific attachment orientations (e.g., Baldwin et al., 1996; Mikulincer & Arad, 1999).

Similar attachment-style differences have been found when research participants are asked to explain other people's behavior (e.g., Collins, 1996; McCarthy & Taylor, 1999; Mikulincer, 1998a, 1998b). For example, Collins (1996) asked participants to explain hypothetical negative behaviors of a romantic partner and found that more anxious and avoidant people were more likely to provide explanations that implied lack of confidence in the partner's love, attribute the partner's negative behaviors to stable and global causes, and view these behaviors as negatively motivated.

Exploration of New Information and the Rigidity of Social Judgments. The link between attachment security and exploration has been studied by adult-attachment researchers. Hazan and Shaver (1990) proposed that work serves as one form of exploration in adulthood, and found that more anxious and avoidant individuals reported more negative attitudes toward work and were less satisfied with work activities. Moreover, whereas secure people perceived work as an opportunity for learning and advancement, anxious individuals perceived it as an opportunity for social approval and avoidant individuals as an opportunity for evading close relationships (Hazan & Shaver, 1990). Additional studies reveal that more anxious and avoidant persons are less willing to explore the environment than secure persons (Green & Campbell, 2000), and avoidant persons report less curiosity about new information (Mikulincer, 1997, Study 1). Green and Campbell (2000, Study 2) found that the contextual priming of attachment security heightened people's willingness to explore novel stimuli.

There is also evidence that attachment insecurity, either anxious or avoidant, inhibits engagement in cognitive exploration, leads to rejection of new information, and fosters rigid, stereotypic judgments (e.g., Green-Hennessy & Reis, 1998; Mikulincer, 1997; Mikulincer & Arad, 1999). For example, Mikulincer (1997, Study 4) focused on the *primacy effect* – the tendency to make judgments on the basis of early information and to ignore later data – and found that both anxious and avoidant individuals were more likely than secure individuals to rate a target person based on the first information received. In a separate study, Mikulincer (1997, Study 5) examined stereotype-based judgments, that is, the tendency to judge a member of a group based on a generalized notion of the group rather than on exploration of new information about the member. More anxious and avoidant individuals tended to evaluate the quality of an essay based on the supposed ethnicity of the writer: The more positive the stereotype of the writer's ethnic group, the higher the grade assigned to the essay. In contrast, more secure individuals were less affected by ethnic stereotypes.

Mikulincer and Arad (1999) examined attachment-style differences in the revision of knowledge about a relationship partner following behavior on the part of the partner that seemed inconsistent with this knowledge. Compared to secure persons, both anxious and avoidant individuals showed fewer changes in their baseline perception of the partner after being exposed to expectation-incongruent information about the partner's behavior. They were also less capable of recalling this information. Importantly, this finding was replicated when relationship-specific attachment orientations were assessed: The higher the level of attachment anxiety or avoidance toward a specific partner, the fewer the revisions people made in their perception of this partner upon receiving expectation-incongruent information (Mikulincer & Arad, 1999, Study 2). Moreover, the contextual heightening of the sense of attachment security (visualizing a supportive other) increased cognitive openness and led even chronically anxious and avoidant people to revise their conception of a partner based on new information (Mikulincer & Arad, 1999, Study 3).

Attitudes Toward Others' Needs. Attachment studies have supported the hypothesis that attachment insecurity inhibits a caregiving orientation toward others who are in need. For example, attachment-related anxiety and avoidance are associated with low levels of reported responsiveness to a relationship partner's needs (e.g., Feeney, 1996; Kunce & Shaver, 1994) and fewer supportive behaviors toward a partner under threatening conditions (e.g., Fraley & Shaver, 1998; Simpson, Rholes, & Nelligan, 1992). Westmaas and Cohen Silver (2001) reported that whereas attachment avoidance was associated with a nonsupportive attitude toward a confederate who purportedly had been diagnosed with cancer, attachment anxiety was associated with the expression of high levels of distress during an interaction with this confederate. In addition, Mikulincer et al. (2001) found that both attachment anxiety and avoidance were associated with low levels of altruistic empathy with the plight of others. Moreover, whereas the contextual heightening of the sense of attachment security increased altruistic empathy, the contextual activation of attachment anxiety or avoidance reduced this prosocial attitude (Mikulincer et al., 2001).

There is also evidence that attachment insecurity inhibits the development of a prosocial orientation (e.g., Mikulincer et al., in press; Van Lange, De Bruin, Otten, & Joireman, 1997). For example, Mikulincer et al. (in press) reported that attachment avoidance was associated with low endorsement of two humanitarian values, universalism (concern for the welfare of all people) and benevolence (concern for the welfare of close persons). Moreover, contextual heightening of the sense of attachment security increased the endorsement of these values.

The Adoption of Hyperactivating or Deactivating Strategies and Social Judgments

The perceived viability of proximity seeking and the consequent adoption of hyperactivating or deactivating strategies have direct implications for self-appraisals, appraisals of person–environment transactions, judgments of self–other similarity, and cognitive reactions to affective states. With regard to attachment anxiety, the excitatory pathways running from hyperactivating strategies to the monitoring of threat-related cues cause attention to be directed to self-relevant sources of distress (personal weaknesses) and to threatening aspects of person–environment transactions. This process can foster chronic negative self-appraisals and exaggerated appraisals of external threats. These excitatory circuits also perpetuate and exacerbate negative affect, therefore encouraging judgments that are congruent with this affective state and inhibiting judgments that would be congruent with positive affect. In addition, chronic activation of the attachment system leads to recurrent attempts to minimize distance from others, which can promote a false consensus bias and overestimation of self–other similarity.

With regard to attachment avoidance, the inhibitory circuits running from deactivating strategies to monitoring of threat-related cues divert attention from self-relevant and external sources of distress, and can therefore inhibit the appraisal of negative aspects of the self as well as external threats. This cognitive bias is further reinforced by the adoption of a self-reliant attitude that requires protection and enhancement of self-worth. These inhibitory circuits also promote detachment from challenging and emotionally involving interactions that potentially constitute sources of threat. In this way, deactivating strategies favor the dismissal of the personal relevance and challenging aspects of person–environment transactions and the rejection of affective states as relevant inputs for making social judgments. In addition, deactivation of the attachment system and defensive attempts to maximize distance from others can promote a false distinctiveness bias and the overestimation of self–other dissimilarity.

Self-Appraisals. There is extensive evidence for the hypothesis that attachment anxiety is associated with negative self-appraisals. Compared to secure persons, anxiously attached persons report lower self-esteem (e.g., Bartholomew & Horowitz, 1991; Mickelson, Kessler, & Shaver, 1997), hold more negative perceptions of self-competence and more negative expectations of self-efficacy (e.g., Brennan & Morris, 1997; Cooper, Shaver, & Collins, 1998), incidentally recall more negative traits, and exhibit greater discrepancies between actual-self and self-standards (Mikulincer, 1995).

With regard to attachment avoidance, the findings are less consistent. Although some investigators have found that avoidant persons have higher self-esteem than anxiously attached persons (e.g., Bartholomew & Horowitz, 1991; Mikulincer, 1995), others have found that attachment avoidance is associated with low self-esteem (e.g., Brennan & Morris, 1997; Feeney & Noller, 1990). In addition, there is some evidence that attachment avoidance is related to negative appraisals of the self when these appraisals concern competence in social and interpersonal settings (e.g., Brennan & Bosson, 1998; Brennan & Morris, 1997).

These inconsistencies may be due to the fact that most of the reviewed studies have examined self-appraisals under neutral, nonthreatening conditions. This is a crucial feature of these studies with respect to avoidant individuals' self-appraisals, because avoidant individuals' deactivating strategies are hypothesized to be active mainly in threatening contexts (Shaver & Mikulincer, 2002). This feature is less important with regard to anxious individuals' self-appraisals, because anxious individuals' hyperactivating strategies have been found to be active even in neutral, nonthreatening contexts (e.g., Mikulincer, Gillath, & Shaver, 2002). In fact, in examinations of self-efficacy expectations for coping with threats, avoidant people have consistently reported more positive expectations than anxious people (e.g., Mikulincer & Florian, 1995, 1998). Accordingly, Mikulincer (1998c) reported that avoidant individuals exhibited a defensive self-enhancement reaction to threats. Specifically, Mikulincer (1998c) exposed participants to experimentally induced threatening or neutral situations and found that avoidant people made more positive self-appraisals following threatening than neutral situations.

Similar cognitive reactions have been observed in studies examining causal attribution for negative events (e.g., Kennedy, 1999; Kogot, 2001; Man & Hamid, 1998). For example, Kogot (2001) asked undergraduates to explain the reason for their failure in an academic examination and found that anxious persons displayed what Abramson, Metalsky, and Alloy (1989) called a *hopelessness-depressive* pattern of attributions. These people attributed failure to more internal, stable, global, and uncontrollable causes while attributing success to more external, unstable, specific, and uncontrollable causes. Avoidant people exhibited a defensive, self-protective pattern of causal attributions: They attributed failure to less internal causes, dismissed the diagnosticity of the failure, and blamed others for it.

Appraisals of Person–Environment Transactions. Attachment researchers have extensively documented an association between attachment anxiety and exaggerated appraisal of the threatening aspects of person–environment transactions. Compared to secure persons, anxious persons hold more pessimistic beliefs about close relationships (e.g., Carnelley & Janoff-Bulman, 1992; Whitaker, Beach, Etherton, Wakefield, & Anderson, 1999), use more threat/loss frames in thinking about relationships (Boon & Griffin, 1996; Pistole, Clark, & Tubbs, 1995), appraise relational outcomes as more negative (Feeney & Noller, 1992), and endorse more dysfunctional beliefs about relationships (Whisman & Allan, 1996). Anxious individuals' exaggerated threat appraisals have also been observed in daily social interactions (e.g., Pietromonaco & Feldman Barrett, 1997), in small group interactions (Rom & Mikulincer, 2001), and in response to stressful life events (e.g., Mikulincer & Florian, 1995, 1998, 2001).

Anxious threat exaggeration was also observed in a recent study on attitudes toward out-groups (Mikulincer & Shaver, 2001). Persons scoring high on attachment anxiety were more likely to appraise out-groups as psychologically threatening and to display more negative and hostile attitudes toward them than less anxious persons. Importantly, contextual heightening of the sense of attachment security reduced anxious individuals' negative appraisals and responses to out-groups. These findings may be relevant to researchers who study stereotypes, prejudice, and intergroup biases, such as Galinsky, Martorana, and Ku, Johnston and Miles, and von Hippel et al. (this volume).

With regard to attachment avoidance, studies have consistently found that avoidant persons perceive stressful events in less threatening terms than anxious persons (see Mikulincer & Florian, 2001, for a review). More important, there is some evidence that avoidant people minimize personal involvement in transactions with the environment. They dismiss the importance and relevance of close relationships, social interactions, and threatening events (e.g., Kogot, 2001; Miller, 2001; Pistole et al., 1995), and see fewer benefits and challenges in social interactions than do secure individuals (e.g., Horppu & Ikonen-Varila, 2001; Pietromonaco & Feldman Barrett, 1997; Rom & Mikulincer, 2001).

Cognitive Reactions to Affective States. Recent studies on the link between affect and cognition (see Forgas & East, this volume, for a review of this research area) provide strong evidence concerning anxious people's perpetuation of negative affect and avoidant people's distancing from affective states. Mikulincer and Sheffi (2000) exposed participants to positive or neutral affect inductions and then assessed their breadth of mental categorization and creative problem-solving performance. The beneficial effects of positive affect induction on problem solving and category breadth (reported by Isen & Daubman, 1984, and Isen, Daubman, & Nowicki, 1987) were observed only among secure people. For avoidant persons, no significant difference was found between positive and neutral affect conditions. For anxiously attached people, a reverse effect was found that resembled the typical effects of negative affect induction: They reacted to a positive affect induction with impaired creativity and a narrowing of mental categories.

In another study, Pereg (2001) exposed participants to a negative or neutral affect induction and then assessed recall of positive and negative information. A negative mood induction led to better recall of negative information and worse recall of positive information than a neutral condition (mood-congruent recall pattern) mainly among anxiously attached people. A negative mood induction had no effect on the recall pattern of avoidant people. Pereg (2001) conceptually replicated this finding while studying causal attributions for negative relationship events. A negative mood induction led to more stable/global attributions than a neutral condition (mood-congruent attribution pattern) among anxiously attached people. A negative mood induction had no effect on avoidant individuals' causal attributions. Importantly, persons scoring low on both attachment anxiety and avoidance (secure style) exhibited mood-*incongruent* patterns of recall and attribution following negative mood induction. (Such differences in patterns of affect infusion are extensively discussed by Forgas and East, this volume.)

In integrating Mikulincer and Sheffi's (2000) with Pereg's (2001) findings, one can delineate the following patterns of cognitive reactions. Anxiously attached people exhibit cognitive reactions that maintain and even exacerbate negative mood – mood-incongruent cognitions following positive affect induction and mood-congruent cognitions following negative affect induction. Avoidant individuals tend to distance themselves from both positive and negative affect and to inhibit the cognitive impact of any affective state.

Appraisals of Self–Other Similarity. In a series of studies, Mikulincer, Orbach, and Iavnieli (1998) provided direct evidence concerning the links between attachment insecurity and false-consensus and false-distinctiveness biases in social judgment. Whereas anxious people were more likely than secure people to perceive others as similar to themselves, and to show a false-consensus bias in both trait and opinion descriptions, avoidant individuals were more likely to perceive other people as dissimilar to them and to exhibit a false-distinctiveness bias. Mikulincer et al. (1998) also found that anxious individuals reacted to threats by generating a self-description that was more similar to a partner's description and by recalling more partner traits that were shared by themselves and the partner. In contrast, avoidant persons reacted to the same threats by generating a self-description that was more dissimilar to a partner's description and by forgetting more traits that were shared by themselves and the partner.

Summary

Taken as whole, there is extensive evidence that the dynamics of the attachment system can explain variations in a wide variety of cognitions and social judgments. Figure 5.2 provides a schematic summary of the reviewed findings. In the next section, we discuss the possible mediational processes by which the dynamics of the attachment system affect social judgments.

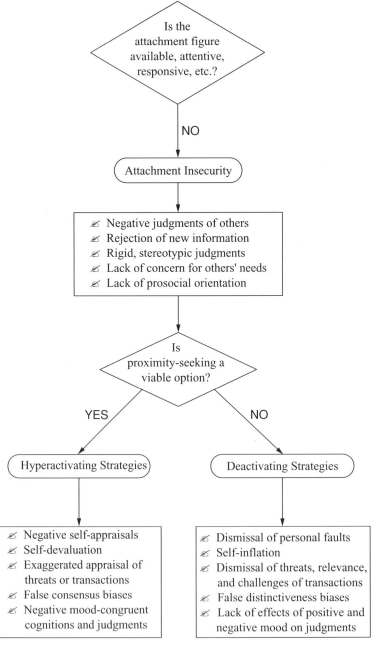

Figure 5.2. Flowchart illustrating the contribution of attachment-system dynamics to social judgments.

EXPLICIT AND IMPLICIT PROCESSES THAT LINK
ATTACHMENT PROCESSES AND SOCIAL JUDGMENTS

In explaining attachment-style variations in social judgments, we invoke the principle of multiple causation and propose that multiple explicit and implicit processes underlie these effects (see Brewer, Chartrand & Jefferis, Galinsky et al., and Lieberman, this volume, for discussions of the explicit–implicit distinction). Shaver and Mikulincer (2002) assumed that attachment-related strategies and their excitatory and inhibitory circuits involve both explicit and implicit processes.

Explicit Processes

Interaction Goals and Motivational Orientations. One explicit component of attachment-related strategies is the specific goal that people pursue in their transactions with the environment. (See Chartrand & Jefferis, this volume, for a discussion of explicit and implicit goals.) Whereas the hyperactivating strategies of anxious individuals seem to be organized around the pursuit of closeness and security, the deactivating strategies of avoidant individuals seem to be constructed around the pursuit of self–reliance, control, and distance (Collins & Read, 1994). We propose that these goals underlie insecure people's distorted appraisals of self and others. On the one hand, the search for closeness, acceptance, and understanding can explain anxious people's false-consensus bias and overestimation of self-other similarity. On the other hand, the search for self-reliance and interpersonal distance can explain avoidant individuals' false-distinctiveness bias and overestimation of self–other dissimilarity. Furthermore, these goals may underlie insecure people's deficits in cognitive exploration and lack of caregiving attitudes. These people tend to be more focused on regulating cognitive and emotional distance from others than on exploring attachment-unrelated information or attending to others' needs.

Research provides support for these attachment-related goals in both social interactions and close relationships (e.g., Mikulincer, 1998a; Mikulincer & Nachshon, 1991; Rom & Mikulincer, 2001). For example, Mikulincer (1998a) assessed the goals that underlie the sense of trust in close relationships using both self-report scales and subtler measures of cognitive accessibility, such as reaction times for goal-related words. Whereas anxious people emphasized security seeking as the most important trust-related goal and showed high accessibility of thoughts about security in a trust-related context, avoidant people emphasized desire for control and exhibited high accessibility of thoughts about control in trust-related contexts.

Ways of Coping with Threatening Events. Another explicit component of attachment-related strategies is the coping strategy people overtly adopt when dealing with distress-eliciting life events. On the one hand, anxious people tend to adopt what Kuhl (1981) called *state focus* and Lazarus and Folkman (1984) called *emotion-focused coping* – directing attention toward the current emotional state without trying actively to solve the distress-eliciting problem (Mikulincer & Florian, 1998, 2001). Anxious individuals' excitatory circuits hyperactivate the monitoring of internal and external sources of threat, and then favor the activation of a wide array of explicit emotion-focused strategies, such as ruminating about the meaning and implications of the threat as well as focusing on threat-related feelings and thoughts, self-preoccupation, self-criticism, and overt display of distress. In the attachment realm, emotion-focused coping is part of anxious individuals' negative self-views and exaggerated appraisal of threats.

On the other hand, avoidant people tend to adopt what Lazarus and Folkman (1984) called *distancing coping* – cognitive maneuvers aimed at preventing both intrusion of threat-related thoughts into consciousness and confrontation with the meaning and implications of the threat (Mikulincer & Florian, 1998, 2001). Avoidant individuals' inhibitory circuits deactivate the monitoring of, and confrontation with, internal and external sources of threat and favor a wide array of explicit distancing strategies, such as suppression of threat-related thoughts and feelings, inhibition of self-related worries, diversion of attention away from the threatening situation, behavioral disengagement and withdrawal of problem-focused efforts, and engagement in other distracting activities. These distancing coping strategies are part of avoidant individuals' dismissal of the importance and personal relevance of person–environment transactions, their dismissal of the threatening and challenging aspects of these transactions, and the maintenance of a positive self-appraisal.

Studies examining ways of coping with stressful events provide direct evidence concerning both the emotion-focused strategies of anxious people and the distancing strategies of their avoidant counterparts (see Mikulincer & Florian, 1998, 2001, for reviews). For example, Mikulincer and Florian (1998) exposed participants to repeated failures in a cognitive task and found that those who scored high on attachment anxiety displayed a heightened tendency to engage in rumination and to report having experienced task-related worries and mind wandering during task performance. Regarding avoidant persons, Fraley and Shaver (1997) provided strong evidence for the suppression of threat-related thoughts when dealing with separation reminders. When asked first to think vividly about a breakup with a romantic partner and then to stop thinking about that possibility, more avoidant individuals were better able than less avoidant individuals not only to stop thinking about it, but also to lower the level of their autonomic response to breaking up.

Impression Management and Intentional Affective Induction. Sometimes people make social judgments in order to manage the way an audience (self, others) perceives them as well as this audience's emotional and cognitive responses. These deliberate attempts to manipulate the responses of an audience seem to be another explicit component of attachment-related strategies and may explain anxious and avoidant persons' appraisals of the self and others. According to Mikulincer (1998c), anxious individuals' heightened appraisals of personal deficiencies and helplessness may be, in part, attempts to convince an audience that they need urgent help to deal with life problems and to elicit others' compassion and support. Mikulincer (1998c) also claimed that avoidant individuals' positive self-image and self-inflation responses may be, in part, attempts to convince an audience that they can rely on their strong and efficacious self. These two strategies – ingratiation as a route to acceptance and self-inflation as a route to angry separation – have parallels in research on reactions to social ostracism (see Williams, Case, & Govan, this volume).

Mikulincer (1998c) provided evidence regarding this explicit component of attachment-related strategies. Findings revealed that avoidant individuals' tendency to endorse a more positive self-view in threatening than in neutral contexts was inhibited by a message that broke the link between a positive self-view and self-reliance ("People who hold a balanced self-view and acknowledge both strong and weak self-aspects are better equipped to perform the experimental task and have been found to succeed in this task without a supervisor's help"). The findings also revealed that anxious individuals' tendency to endorse a less positive self-view in threatening than in neutral contexts was inhibited by a message that broke the link between self-devaluation and others' positive responses ("People who hold a balanced self-view and acknowledge both strong and weak self-aspects tend to elicit others' affection and support").

Implicit Processes: Spread of Activation, Information Encoding, and Mental Architecture

Attachment-related strategies can also affect social judgments automatically, without conscious deliberation, intentionality, or goal directedness. Attachment-style differences in spread of activation within the semantic associative network and the architecture of this network – the way information is encoded and organized, the level of differentiation between segments of the network, and the level of integration between these segments – may implicitly underlie attachment-style variations in social judgments.

With regard to anxiously attached persons, the excitatory circuits that hyperactivate appraisal and monitoring of threat- and attachment-related cues lead to chronic activation of the attachment system, exacerbation of worries about others' unavailability, and consequent pain and distress. This pattern of activation heightens the accessibility of distressing cognitions and makes it likely that new sources of distress will mingle and become confounded with old ones (Shaver & Mikulincer, 2002). That is, anxious individuals may have difficulty controlling the spread of activation from one cognition with a negative emotional tone to other, different negatively tinged cognitions, and their cognitive system may be overwhelmed by an uncontrollable flow of negative thoughts and feelings. This pattern of cognitive activation gives predominance to the affective nature of the information and then favors the organization of cognitive structures in terms of simple, undifferentiated features, such as the extent to which the information is threatening or implies rejection. As a result, hyperactivating strategies create a chaotic, undifferentiated mental architecture that is constantly pervaded by negative affect.

The heightened accessibility of threat- and attachment-related cognitions also creates a specific cognitive context that biases the encoding of incoming information. According to cognitive theories (e.g., Anderson, 1994), this context predisposes attentional processes to congruent information (e.g., threat- and attachment-related cues) and speeds up the encoding of this information while diverting attention away from the encoding of context-incongruent information. This cognitive context also facilitates the creation of excitatory links between threat- and attachment-related information and the large number of congruent cognitions that are highly accessible in the semantic network. As a result, this information is encoded at a deep level of processing, which seems to be further exacerbated by anxious persons' repetitive rumination on threat- and attachment-related material. In contrast, context-incongruent information may be encoded in a shallow way and then may easily be forgotten or recalled in a very inaccurate manner.

We propose that this pattern of cognitive organization is part of anxiously attached individuals' negative appraisals of self and others, their pessimistic and catastrophic appraisals of person–environment transactions, and their tendency to react to negative moods with cognitions and judgments that perpetuate these affective states. The undifferentiated, autonomous activation of negative cognitions and the deep-level encoding of negative information about the self, others, and transactions with the environment facilitate the retrieval of this information and make it highly accessible during the social judgment process. Furthermore, it can explain Mikulincer and Sheffi's (2000) finding that anxious persons react with paradoxical cognitive closure to positive affect induction. It is possible that the spread of activation across negative emotions can begin with positive affect. That is, an anxious person may at first experience a positive state but then be reminded of the down side of previous experiences that began positively and ended painfully. Once attuned to the negative memories and possibilities, the anxious mind may suffer from a spread of negative associations that interferes with creative and flexible cognitive processing.

Evidence is accumulating in support of the hypothesis that attachment anxiety is associated with heightened accessibility of negative cognitions and undifferentiated mental architecture. For example, Mikulincer and Orbach (1995) showed that anxiously attached individuals exhibited the highest accessibility (lowest recall time) of negative memories, and that this activation spread to both dominant emotions (e.g., sadness when asked to retrieve a sad memory) and nondominant emotions (e.g., anger when asked to retrieve a sad memory). In addition, Mikulincer (1995) found that anxious people sorted self-defining traits into a few undifferentiated categories based on simple affective criteria. This undifferentiated architecture has also been observed in the activation of attachment-related cognitions. Anxiously attached people show heightened accessibility of worries about separation even when no explicit or implicit threat is present (Mikulincer et al., 2000) and react to separation reminders with heightened accessibility of death-related thoughts (Mikulincer, Florian, Birnbaum, & Malishkewitz, 2002). With regard to the encoding of information, Miller and Noirot (1999) found that anxious attachment facilitates the encoding of negative friendship story events relative to positive ones.

With regard to attachment avoidance, the inhibitory circuits that deactivate appraisal and monitoring of threat- and attachment-related cues lead to the exclusion of this information from awareness and memory. This pattern of cognitive activation lowers the accessibility of threat- and attachment-related cognitions and inhibits the spread of activation from these cognitions to other, different cognitions and emotions (Shaver & Mikulincer, 2002). It can also create difficulties in the encoding of information that is congruent with the excluded cognitions. Attention is diverted from threat- and attachment-related information, and when encoded, this information is processed at a shallow level because it has no strong excitatory association with the accessible segments of the semantic network. As a result, this information is not fully integrated with other segments of the network. Instead, it is encapsulated into segregated structures and dissociated from other segments of the semantic network. Thus, deactivating strategies create a shallow cognitive context for the encoding of emotionally relevant information and a disintegrated, dissociated cognitive architecture.

This architecture may contribute to avoidant individuals' failure to recognize negative aspects of the self and threatening aspects of person–environment transactions (threat-related cues). It may also contribute to avoidant people's negative appraisals of others, which may reflect an inability to attend to and process others' positive traits, intentions, and behaviors (attachment-related information). This architecture can also explain Pereg's (2001) finding that a negative mood failed to affect avoidant individuals' judgments. In fact, information that is congruent with a negative mood can be excluded from awareness and memory, which may render it inaccessible when making social judgments.

The constricted and segregated mental architecture of avoidant individuals is well illustrated in several studies. Avoidant persons' relatively poor access to negative information has been documented with regard to autobiographical memories, negative self-aspects, and attachment-related worries (Fraley & Shaver, 1997; Mikulincer, 1995; Mikulincer & Orbach, 1995; Mikulincer et al., 2000). In the case of attachment-related worries, findings also revealed that avoidant people's poor access to negative material occurred even when they were subliminally primed with the word *death*, which is usually a potent activator of attachment-related fears (Mikulincer et al., 2000). Importantly, this pattern of accessibility is accompanied by the retrieval of relatively shallow emotions (Mikulincer & Orbach, 1995) and the projection of unwanted self-aspects onto representations of other persons (Mikulincer & Horesh, 1999).

Avoidant individuals' disintegrated cognitive structures have been documented in the case of the self-system. Specifically, these people scored low on measures of cognitive integration of self-defining traits: They failed to perceive the mutual influences, trade-offs, and joint interactions between different self-aspects (Mikulincer, 1995). Dissociative tendencies have also been documented with regard to painful experiences of attachment-related frustration, anger, and fear of death. In this case, attachment avoidance has been found to be associated with relatively large discrepancies between self-reports of negative experiences (e.g., frustration, anger, fear of death) and physiological and projective measures of those experiences (Dozier & Kobak, 1992; Mikulincer, 1998b; Mikulincer et al., 1990).

Avoidant individuals' shallow pattern of encoding was documented by Fraley, Garner, and Shaver (2000) in their analysis of forgetting curves for attachment- and loss-related information over time. The findings revealed that avoidant persons' forgetting of this material reflects diversion of attention and inhibition of a deep, elaborate encoding of the information. That is, avoidant people tend to hold distressing material out of awareness and memory right from the start. Along these lines, Miller (2001) found that attachment avoidance is associated with lack of attention to a confederate's remarks during a long conversation as well as subsequent poor recall of these remarks.

Summary

In this section, we reviewed evidence that both explicit and implicit processes mediate the links between dynamics of the attachment system and

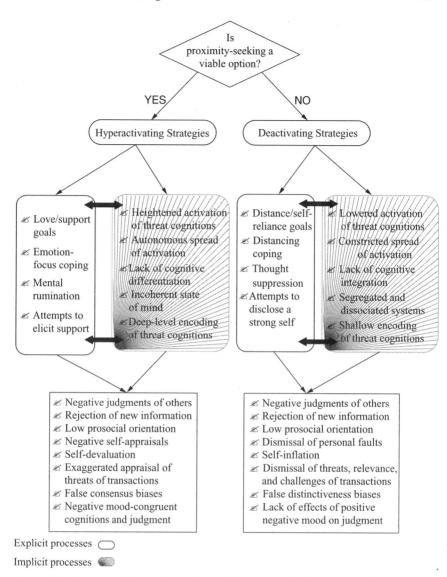

Figure 5.3. Flowchart illustrating the explicit and implicit processes that mediate the effects of attachment-related strategies on social judgments.

social judgments. Figure 5.3 provides a schematic summary of the possible mediational processes. There is already strong evidence for these processes at levels that can be assessed using self-report measures, behavioral observations, and information processing experiments. Future research linking these processes to their neural underpinnings should clarify their nature still further (see Lieberman and Zárate & Stoever, this volume).

CONCLUDING REMARKS

Our review of recent research demonstrates that attachment theory is a useful and generative framework for explaining individual variations in social judgments. Although attachment theory was not originally constructed to explain social judgments, our reading of Bowlby suggests that he intended the theory to be quite broad in its implications. We believe we have begun to map some of the important effects of the dynamics of the attachment system on social judgments. As shown in this chapter, individual differences in self-report measures of attachment anxiety and avoidance, as well as contextual activation of attachment-related representations, do relate coherently to a broad array of social judgments, including appraisals of self and others, appraisals of person–environment transactions, out-group hostility, cognitive closure, stereotypic thinking, empathic attitudes toward others' needs, value priorities, and mood–cognition congruence.

In our view, one of the most interesting features of our recent work is that similar effects can be obtained either as a function of chronic individual-difference dimensions, such as anxiety and avoidance, or as a function of contextual manipulations of attachment threats and attachment security. This parallelism not only supports the theoretical notion that individual differences in attachment style arise developmentally out of important transactions between the attachment behavioral system and its local social environment. It also suggests ways in which undesirable social judgments can be altered – at first momentarily and eventually in a more lasting way. Pursuing these leads may prove useful for change efforts ranging from individual and couples therapy to reduction of intergroup hostility and violence.

References

Abramson, L. Y., Metalsky, G. I., & Alloy, L. B. (1989). Hopelessness depression: A theory-based subtype of depression. *Psychological Review, 96*, 358–372.

Ainsworth, M. D. S. (1991). Attachment and other affectional bonds across the life cycle. In C. M. Parkes, J. Stevenson-Hinde, & P. Marris (Eds.), *Attachment across the life cycle* (pp. 33–51). New York: Routledge.

Ainsworth, M. D. S., Blehar, M. C., Waters, E., & Wall, S. (1978). *Patterns of attachment: Assessed in the strange situation and at home.* Hillsdale, NJ: Erlbaum.

Anderson, J. (1994). *Cognitive psychology.* New York: Academic Press.

Baldwin, M. W., Fehr, B., Keedian, E., & Seidel, M. (1993). An exploration of the relational schemata underlying attachment styles: Self-report and lexical decision approaches. *Personality and Social Psychology Bulletin, 19*, 746–754.

Baldwin, M. W., Keelan, J. P. R., Fehr, B., Enns, V., & Koh Rangarajoo, E. (1996). Social-cognitive conceptualization of attachment working models: Availability and accessibility effects. *Journal of Personality and Social Psychology, 71*, 94–109.

Bartholomew, K., & Horowitz, L. M. (1991). Attachment styles among young adults: A test of a four-category model. *Journal of Personality and Social Psychology, 61*, 226–244.

Boon, S. D., & Griffin, D. W. (1996). The construction of risk in relationships: The role of framing in decisions about relationships. *Personal Relationships, 3*, 293–306.

Bowlby, J. (1969/1982). *Attachment and loss: Vol. 1. Attachment* (2nd ed.). New York: Basic Books.

Bowlby, J. (1973). *Attachment and loss: Vol. 2. Separation: Anxiety and anger.* New York: Basic Books.

Bowlby, J. (1980). *Attachment and loss: Vol. 3. Sadness and depression.* New York: Basic Books.

Bowlby, J. (1988). *A secure base: Clinical applications of attachment theory.* London: Routledge.

Brennan, K. A., & Bosson, J. K. (1998). Attachment-style differences in attitudes toward and reactions to feedback from romantic partners: An exploration of the relational bases of self-esteem. *Personality and Social Psychology Bulletin, 24*, 699–714.

Brennan, K. A., Clark, C. L., & Shaver, P. R. (1998). Self-report measurement of adult attachment: An integrative overview. In J. A. Simpson & W. S. Rholes (Eds.), *Attachment theory and close relationships* (pp. 46–76). New York: Guilford Press.

Brennan, K. A., & Morris, K. A. (1997). Attachment styles, self-esteem, and patterns of seeking feedback from romantic partners. *Personality and Social Psychology Bulletin, 23*, 23–31.

Carnelley, K. B., & Janoff-Bulman, R. (1992). Optimism about love relationships: General vs. specific lessons from one's personal experiences. *Journal of Social and Personal Relationships, 9*, 5–20.

Cassidy, J., & Kobak, R. R. (1988). Avoidance and its relationship with other defensive processes. In J. Belsky & T. Nezworski (Eds.), *Clinical implications of attachment* (pp. 300–323). Hillsdale, NJ: Erlbaum.

Collins, N. L. (1996). Working models of attachment: Implications for explanation, emotion, and behavior. *Journal of Personality and Social Psychology, 71*, 810–832.

Collins, N. L., & Read, S. J. (1990). Adult attachment, working models, and relationship quality in dating couples. *Journal of Personality and Social Psychology, 58*, 644–663.

Collins, N. L., & Read, S. J. (1994). Cognitive representations of attachment: The structure and function of working models. In K. Bartholomew & D. Perlman (Eds.), *Attachment processes in adulthood: Advances in personal relationships* (Vol. 5, pp. 53–92). London: Jessica Kingsley.

Cooper, M. L., Shaver, P. R., & Collins, N. L. (1998). Attachment styles, emotion regulation, and adjustment in adolescence. *Journal of Personality and Social Psychology, 74*, 1380–1397.

Davis, M. H., Morris, M. M., & Kraus, L. A. (1998). Relationship-specific and global perceptions of social support: Associations with well-being and attachment. *Journal of Personality and Social Psychology, 74*, 468–481.

Dozier, M., & Kobak, R. R. (1992). Psychophysiology in attachment interviews: Converging evidence for deactivating strategies. *Child Development, 63*, 1473–1480.

Feeney, J. A. (1996). Attachment, caregiving, and marital satisfaction. *Personal Relationships, 3*, 401–416.

Feeney, J. A. (1999). Adult romantic attachment and couple relationships. In J. Cassidy & P. R. Shaver (Eds.), *Handbook of attachment: Theory, research, and clinical applications* (pp. 355–377). New York: Guilford Press.

Feeney, J. A., & Noller, P. (1990). Attachment style as a predictor of adult romantic relationships. *Journal of Personality and Social Psychology, 2*, 281–291.

Feeney, J. A., & Noller, P. (1991). Attachment style and verbal descriptions of romantic partners. *Journal of Social and Personal Relationships, 8*, 187–215.

Feeney, J. A., & Noller, P. (1992). Attachment style and romantic love: Relationship dissolution. *Australian Journal of Psychology, 44*, 69–74.

Fraley, R. C., Garner, J. P., & Shaver, P. R. (2000). Adult attachment and the defensive regulation of attention and memory: Examining the role of preemptive and postemptive defensive processes. *Journal of Personality and Social Psychology, 79*, 816–826.

Fraley, R. C., & Shaver, P. R. (1997). Adult attachment and the suppression of unwanted thoughts. *Journal of Personality and Social Psychology, 73*, 1080–1091.

Fraley, R. C., & Shaver, P. R. (1998). Airport separations: A naturalistic study of adult attachment dynamics in separating couples. *Journal of Personality and Social Psychology, 75*, 1198–1212.

Fraley, R. C., & Shaver, P. R. (2000). Adult romantic attachment: Theoretical developments, emerging controversies, and unanswered questions. *Review of General Psychology, 4*, 132–154.

Fraley, R. C., & Waller, N. G. (1998). Adult attachment patterns: A test of the typological model. In J. A. Simpson & W. S. Rholes (Eds.), *Attachment theory and close relationships* (pp. 77–114). New York: Guilford Press.

Fredrickson, B. L. (2001). The role of positive emotions in positive psychology: The broaden-and-build theory of positive emotions. *American Psychologist, 56*, 218–226.

Green, J. D., & Campbell, W. K. (2000). Attachment and exploration in adults: Chronic and contextual accessibility. *Personality and Social Psychology Bulletin, 26*, 452–461.

Green-Hennessy, S., & Reis, H. T. (1998). Openness in processing social information among attachment types. *Personal Relationships, 5*, 449–466.

Hazan, C., & Shaver, P. R. (1987). Romantic love conceptualized as an attachment process. *Journal of Personality and Social Psychology, 52*, 511–524.

Hazan, C., & Shaver, P. R. (1990). Love and work: An attachment-theoretical perspective. *Journal of Personality and Social Psychology, 59*, 270–280.

Horppu, R., & Ikonen-Varila, M. (2001). Are attachment styles general interpersonal orientations? Applicants' perceptions and emotions in interaction with evaluators in a college entrance examination. *Journal of Social and Personal Relationships, 18*, 131–148.

Isen, A. M., & Daubman, K. A. (1984). The influence of affect on categorization. *Journal of Personality and Social Psychology, 47*, 1206–1217.

Isen, A. M., Daubman, K. A., & Nowicki, G. P. (1987). Positive affect facilitates creative problem solving. *Journal of Personality and Social Psychology, 52*, 1122–1131.

Kennedy, J. H. (1999). Romantic attachment style and ego identity, attributional style, and family of origin. *College Student Journal, 33,* 171–180.

Kogot, E. (2001). *The contribution of attachment style to cognitions, affect, and behavior in achievement settings.* Unpublished PhD dissertation, Bar-Ilan University.

Kuhl, J. (1981). Motivational and functional helplessness: The moderating effect of state versus action orientation. *Journal of Personality and Social Psychology, 19,* 448–468.

Kunce, L. J., & Shaver, P. R. (1994). An attachment-theoretical approach to caregiving in romantic relationships. In K. Bartholomew & D. Perlman (Eds.), *Attachment processes in adulthood: Advances in personal relationships* (Vol. 5, pp. 205–237). London: Jessica Kingsley.

La Guardia, J. G., Ryan, R. M., Couchman, C. E., & Deci, E. L. (2000). Within-person variation in security of attachment: A self-determination theory perspective on attachment, need fulfillment, and well-being. *Journal of Personality and Social Psychology, 79,* 367–384.

Larose, S., & Boivin, M. (1997). Structural relations among attachment working models of parents, general and specific support expectations, and personal adjustment in late adolescence. *Journal of Social and Personal Relationships, 14,* 579–601.

Lazarus, R. S., & Folkman, S. (1984). *Stress, appraisal and coping.* New York: Springer.

Levy, K. N., Blatt, S. J., & Shaver, P. R. (1998). Attachment styles and parental representations. *Journal of Personality and Social Psychology, 74,* 407–419.

Main, M. (1990). Cross-cultural studies of attachment organization: Recent studies, changing methodologies, and the concept of conditional strategies. *Human Development, 33,* 48–61.

Man, K., & Hamid, P. N. (1998). The relationship between attachment prototypes, self-esteem, loneliness, and causal attributions in Chinese trainee teachers. *Personality and Individual Differences, 24,* 357–371.

McCarthy, G., & Taylor, A. (1999). Avoidant/ambivalent attachment style as a mediator between abusive childhood experiences and adult relationship difficulties. *Journal of Child Psychology and Psychiatry and Allied Disciplines, 40,* 465–477.

Mickelson, K. D., Kessler, R. C., & Shaver, P. R. (1997). Adult attachment in a nationally representative sample. *Journal of Personality and Social Psychology, 73,* 1092–1106.

Mikulincer, M. (1995). Attachment style and the mental representation of the self. *Journal of Personality and Social Psychology, 69,* 1203–1215.

Mikulincer, M. (1997). Adult attachment style and information processing: Individual differences in curiosity and cognitive closure. *Journal of Personality and Social Psychology, 72,* 1217–1230.

Mikulincer, M. (1998a). Attachment working models and the sense of trust: An exploration of interaction goals and affect regulation. *Journal of Personality and Social Psychology, 74,* 1209–1224.

Mikulincer, M. (1998b). Adult attachment style and individual differences in functional versus dysfunctional experiences of anger. *Journal of Personality and Social Psychology, 74,* 513–524.

Mikulincer, M. (1998c). Adult attachment style and affect regulation: Strategic variations in self-appraisals. *Journal of Personality and Social Psychology, 75,* 420–435.

Mikulincer, M., & Arad, D. (1999). Attachment, working models, and cognitive openness in close relationships: A test of chronic and temporary accessibility effects. *Journal of Personality and Social Psychology, 77,* 710–725.

Mikulincer, M., Birnbaum, G., Woddis, D., & Nachmias, O. (2000). Stress and accessibility of proximity-related thoughts: Exploring the normative and intraindividual components of attachment theory. *Journal of Personality and Social Psychology, 78,* 509–523.

Mikulincer, M., & Florian, V. (1995). Appraisal and coping with a real-life stressful situation: The contribution of attachment styles. *Personality and Social Psychology Bulletin, 21,* 408–416.

Mikulincer, M., & Florian, V. (1998). The relationship between adult attachment styles and emotional and cognitive reactions to stressful events. In J. A. Simpson & W. S. Rholes (Eds.), *Attachment theory and close relationships* (pp. 143–165). New York: Guilford Press.

Mikulincer, M., & Florian, V. (2001). Attachment style and affect regulation: Implications for coping with stress and mental health. In G. Fletcher & M. Clark (Eds.), *Blackwell handbook of social psychology: Interpersonal processes* (pp. 537–557). Oxford: Blackwell.

Mikulincer, M., Florian, V., Birnbaum, G., & Malishkewitz, S. (2002). The death-anxiety buffering function of close relationships: Exploring the effects of separation reminders on death-thought accessibility. *Personality and Social Psychology Bulletin, 28,* 287–299.

Mikulincer, M., Florian, V., & Tolmacz, R. (1990). Attachment styles and fear of personal death: A case study of affect regulation. *Journal of Personality and Social Psychology, 58,* 273–280.

Mikulincer, M., Gillath, O., Halevy, V., Avihou, N., Avidan, S., & Eshkoli, N. (2001). Attachment theory and reactions to others' needs: Evidence that activation of the sense of attachment security promotes empathic responses. *Journal of Personality and Social Psychology, 81,* 1205–1224.

Mikulincer, M., Gillath, O., Sapir-Lavid, Y., Yaacovi, E., Arias, K., Tal-Aloni, A., & Bor, G. (in press). Attachment theory and concern for others' welfare: Evidence that activation of the sense of secure base promotes endorsement of self-transcendence values. *Basic and Applied Social Psychology.*

Mikulincer, M., Gillath, O., & Shaver, P. R. (2002). Activation of the attachment system in adulthood: Threat-related primes increase the accessibility of mental representations of attachment figures. *Journal of Personality and Social Psychology, 83,* 881–895.

Mikulincer, M., & Horesh, N. (1999). Adult attachment style and the perception of others: The role of projective mechanisms. *Journal of Personality and Social Psychology, 76,* 1022–1034.

Mikulincer, M., & Nachshon, O. (1991). Attachment styles and patterns of self-disclosure. *Journal of Personality and Social Psychology, 61,* 321–332.

Mikulincer, M., & Orbach, I. (1995). Attachment styles and repressive defensiveness: The accessibility and architecture of affective memories. *Journal of Personality and Social Psychology, 68,* 917–925.

Mikulincer, M., Orbach, I., & Iavnieli, D. (1998). Adult attachment style and affect regulation: Strategic variations in subjective self–other similarity. *Journal of Personality and Social Psychology, 75,* 436–448.

Mikulincer, M., & Shaver, P. R. (2001). Attachment theory and intergroup bias: Evidence that priming the secure base schema attenuates negative reactions to out-groups. *Journal of Personality and Social Psychology, 81,* 97–115.

Mikulincer, M., & Sheffi, E. (2000). Adult attachment style and cognitive reactions to positive affect: A test of mental categorization and creative problem solving. *Motivation and Emotion, 24,* 149–174.

Miller, J. B. (2001). Attachment models and memory for conversation. *Journal of Social and Personal Relationships, 18,* 404–422.

Miller, J. B., & Noirot, M. (1999). Attachment memories, models and information processing. *Journal of Social and Personal Relationships, 16,* 147–173.

Ognibene, T. C., & Collins, N. L. (1998). Adult attachment styles, perceived social support, and coping strategies. *Journal of Social and Personal Relationships, 15,* 323–345.

Pereg, D. (2001). *Mood and cognition: The moderating role of attachment style.* Unpublished PhD dissertation, Bar-Ilan University.

Pierce, T., & Lydon, J. (2001). Global and specific relational models in the experience of social interactions. *Journal of Personality and Social Psychology, 80,* 1441–1448.

Pietromonaco, P. R., & Feldman Barrett, L. (1997). Working models of attachment and daily social interactions. *Journal of Personality and Social Psychology, 73,* 1409–1423.

Pistole, M. C., Clark, E. M., & Tubbs, A. L. (1995). Love relationships: Attachment style and the investment model. *Journal of Mental Health Counseling, 17,* 199–209.

Rom, E., & Mikulincer, M. (2001). *Attachment theory and group processes: The association between attachment style and group-related representations, goals, memories, and functioning.* Unpublished manuscript, Bar-Ilan University.

Shaver, P. R., & Hazan, C. (1993). Adult romantic attachment: Theory and evidence. In D. Perlman & W. Jones (Eds.), *Advances in personal relationships* (Vol. 4, pp. 29–70). London: Jessica Kingsley.

Shaver, P. R., Hazan, C., & Bradshaw, D. (1988). Love as attachment: The integration of three behavioral systems. In R. J. Sternberg & M. Barnes (Eds.), *The psychology of love* (pp. 68–99). New Haven, CT: Yale University Press.

Shaver, P. R., & Mikulincer, M. (2002). Attachment-related psychodynamics. *Attachment and Human Development, 4,* 131–161.

Simpson, J. A. (1990). Influence of attachment styles on romantic relationships. *Journal of Personality and Social Psychology, 59,* 871–980.

Simpson, J. A., Rholes, W. S., & Nelligan, J. S. (1992). Support seeking and support giving within couples in an anxiety-provoking situation: The role of attachment styles. *Journal of Personality and Social Psychology, 62,* 434–446.

Tidwell, M. C. O., Reis, H. T., & Shaver, P. R. (1996). Attachment, attractiveness, and social interaction: A diary study. *Journal of Personality and Social Psychology, 71,* 729–745.

Van Lange, P. A. M., De Bruin, E. M. N., Otten, W., & Joireman, J. A. (1997). Development of prosocial, individualistic, and competitive orientations: Theory and preliminary evidence. *Journal of Personality and Social Psychology, 73,* 733–746.

Westmaas, J. L., & Cohen Silver, R. (2001). The role of attachment in responses to victims of life crises. *Journal of Personality and Social Psychology, 80,* 425–438.

Whisman, M. A., & Allan, L. E. (1996). Attachment and social cognition theories of romantic relationships: Convergent or complementary perspectives? *Journal of Social and Personal Relationships, 13*, 263–278.

Whitaker, D. J., Beach, S. R. H., Etherton, J., Wakefield, R., & Anderson, P. L. (1999). Attachment and expectations about future relationships: Moderation by accessibility. *Personal Relationships, 6*, 41–56.

6

Toward a Social Psychology of Person Judgments

Implications for Person Perception Accuracy and Self-Knowledge

David C. Funder

CONTENTS

INTRODUCTION

Person perception is a social process. It occurs when people meet, interact, observe each other, and begin to draw conclusions. These conclusions are often perceptions of personality traits such as sociability, reliability, kindness, or even dangerousness. Such perceptions are interesting, useful, and certainly important: They may determine further interaction. A person perceived as sociable will be approached, one perceived as reliable may be offered a job, and one perceived as dangerous may be avoided or even attacked. Because the judgments people make of each other have consequences, it matters whether they are accurate. An important task for psychology is to understand how accurate social judgment is achieved, the circumstances under which accuracy is more and less likely, and how accuracy might be improved.

The thesis of this chapter is that a social psychological approach to person perception can illuminate these issues. This may seem a strange thesis to have to make, but the currently dominant approach is *not* social psychological, it is cognitive, and although sometimes interpreted as having implications for accuracy, it actually has surprisingly few.

Please address correspondence to David C. Funder, University of California, Riverside, Riverside, CA 92521-0426; e-mail: funder@citrus.ucr.edu

A social psychological approach can address accuracy issues more directly because it goes beyond cognitive functioning by considering relevant interpersonal processes, contextual factors, and social psychological variables.

This chapter has three objectives. First, it considers the differences between cognitive and social psychological approaches to person perception and accuracy. Second, it outlines a particular social psychological approach, the Realistic Accuracy Model (RAM; Funder, 1995, 1999), and examines how it addresses the social psychological processes and contextual factors that affect accuracy. Third and finally, it develops some specific implications of RAM for the nature of the "good judge" of personality and the conditions under which self-knowledge may be possible.

TWO APPROACHES TO PERSON PERCEPTION

The Cognitive Approach

The cognitive approach to person perception can be traced to pioneers such as Solomon Asch (1946) and contributors to the seminal volume by Tagiuri and Petrullo (1958). The approach gained immediate and long-lasting success in part because of the creativity and persuasiveness of these investigators. Another reason is that the historical moment was right. The previously active research literature on social judgment was in shambles. To devastating effect, Cronbach (1955; also Gage & Cronbach, 1955) had recently pointed out that one of its major methods, the comparison of self-derived and judge-derived personality profiles, was complicated by several potential artifacts. The artifacts were avoidable, and indeed were not always artifacts (i.e., some were substantive phenomena in their own right), but the critical articles were complex and difficult to understand, and the statistical remedies they prescribed were difficult to implement in a precomputer age. It came to many as a huge relief, therefore, when, as related by Jones (1985, p. 87), Asch "solved the accuracy problem by bypassing it."

Asch's insight was that the process of interpersonal judgment could be studied in much the same way as any other cognitive process, by proposing and testing models that predict particular relations between stimuli and responses. In his pioneering studies, the stimuli were lists of trait words, the models described processes such as *primacy* (which predicted that the first words presented would be more influential), and the responses were judgmental outputs in which the relative influences of the stimulus words could be detected. These studies laid down the paradigm for most of the next 40 years of research on person perception and (as the field later came to be called) social cognition (see Fiske & Taylor, 1991; Kunda, 1999). The approach has been extraordinarily fruitful, demonstrating phenomena such as the primacy effect, the halo effect, illusory correlation, stereotype formation, effects of scripts on perception and recall, and the self-reference effect on memory, to name just a few.

Among the most prominent studies, especially in recent years, have been those demonstrating judgmental error (Funder, 1987, 1995). Studies of error vary the standard cognitive paradigm by proposing models of the judgmental outputs that would be produced if subjects were to process the stimulus inputs *perfectly*, and these studies are deemed successful when they *dis*confirm rather than confirm the models proposed. The definition of perfect processing may derive from abstract principles, formal logic, or even mathematical formulas. For example, a sizable subliterature presents subjects with inputs (such as categorical base rates) that can be processed by Bayesian calculations and finds that the subjects' subsequent judgments never quite equal what the formulas dictate.[1] Numerous studies following this basic design have shown that subjects incorrectly compute posterior probabilities, correlation coefficients, expected values, and confidence intervals, among other errors.

Although the popularity of such studies surely stems, in part, from their apparently counterintuitive nature, the findings are not really surprising. The research design almost preordains error because the normative standard is a point prediction, which the mean judgment of a sample can never match precisely (Krueger & Funder, in press). If measurement sensitivity and sample size are adequate, this deviation will be statistically significant, and the discovery of a new error will be proclaimed.

A sampling of the errors discovered through this route is shown in Table 6.1. Some are actually alternative labels for the same phenomenon, and others refer to several different phenomena (the *jingle-jangle* effect: Block, 1995). Several appear to be contradictory, as might be expected given that errors are identified by significant deviation on either side of the normative point prediction. For example, subjects have been observed to overestimate the effect of individual differences on behavior relative to the effect of the situation (fundamental attribution error) and to overestimate the effect of the situation relative to individual differences (false consensus effect, external agency illusion). They have been too prone to expect runs to end (gambler's fallacy) and to expect that they will last (hot-hand bias). They have given too little weight to beliefs about categorical frequencies (base rate neglect error) as well as too much weight (stereotyping bias). Positivity and negativity biases have been reported many times, as have undue optimism and pessimism. It may be possible to resolve such inconsistencies, such as exemplified by Shaver and Mikulincer's (this volume) delineation of the circumstances under which false consensus and false distinctiveness will be found, but such resolutions are rare, probably because

---

[1] According to some research, they use signal detection formulas instead (Birnbaum, 1983).

TABLE 6.1. *Some Errors in Social Judgment Identified by the Cognitive Paradigm*

Overconfidence bias	Correspondence bias
Fundamental attribution error	Halo effect
False consensus effect	False uniqueness effect
Positivity bias	Negativity bias
Confirmation bias	Disconfirmation bias
Justice bias	Male bias
Hot-hand fallacy	Gambler's fallacy
Self-protective similarity bias	Hindsight bias
Self-serving bias	"Ultimate" self-serving bias
Optimistic bias	Pessimistic bias
Sinister attribution error	Conjunction fallacy
In-group/out-group bias	Vulnerability bias
Hypothesis-testing bias	Positive outcome bias
Durability bias	Diagnosticity bias
Self-image bias	Egocentric bias
Observer bias	Labeling bias
Systematic distortion effect	External agency illusion
Asymmetric insight illusion	Intensity bias
Dispositional bias	Just world bias
Blind spot bias	

the balkanization of the literature causes such inconsistencies to be seldom noticed.

The errors form a long list but no particular pattern. Typically, they are studied one at a time; some are effectively the property of particular labs or investigators. Singly or together, they do not yield a general theory of judgment, nor do they explain how accurate judgment is ever achieved (Anderson, 1990; Funder, 1995; Krueger & Funder, in press). Moreover, the sheer number of errors – the list in Table 6.1 gets longer with every issue of the *Personality and Social Psychology Bulletin* and the *Journal of Personality and Social Psychology*[2] – can make it seem as if human inferential processes are so basically flawed that accurate judgment is rare or impossible (e.g., Shaklee, 1991).

Any such implication is false. Recall that the express purpose of the cognitive paradigm, upon which demonstrations of error are based, was to *bypass* accuracy considerations (Jones, 1985). The processes revealed by

---

[2] Additions to the corpus of knowledge while the first draft of this chapter was being written, just in these two journals, included the *intensity bias*, the *asymmetric insight illusion*, the *vulnerability bias*, and no fewer than nine articles on *automatic biases*. The discovery of the *blind spot bias* (people are biased not to realize that they are biased) was announced in March 2002, just before this conference opened.

the cognitive paradigm, including those that distort stimulus information, may lead to inaccurate judgments; then again, they may, like optical illusions, reveal adaptive processes that enhance accuracy in most real-life circumstances (Funder, 1987). As Haselton and Buss (2000, this volume) point out, the most reasonable explanation of the existence of so many judgmental biases is that they are adaptive in the long run and perhaps even promote accuracy. In a similar vein, Forgas and East (this volume) note that biases resulting from emotional influences on judgment are not necessarily disruptive but can lead to decisions that better serve personal goals. Discoveries of error per se, notwithstanding their (ever-increasing) number, do not speak to the accuracy issue one way or the other; they bypass it, just as Jones said. To address the degree to which, the circumstances under which, and the process by which judgmental accuracy is ever achieved, a fundamentally different approach is necessary.

The Social Psychology of Person Perception

If the cognitive psychology of person perception can be traced to the 1950s, the social psychology of this topic can be traced back even further, to the 1930s. Gordon Allport and several of his contemporaries examined connections between personality traits and behavior, and between behavioral observations and interpersonal perception. For example, Allport and Vernon (1933) showed that extraverts tend to walk with large steps and that lay observers regard people who walk with large steps as extraverts. Underlying the approach was the assumption that people are, by and large, accurate. Allport noted that usually we are able "to select gifts that our friends will like, to bring together a congenial group at dinner, to choose words that will have the desired effect upon an acquaintance, or to pick a satisfactory employee, tenant, or room-mate" (Allport, 1937, p. 353). He viewed the job of psychology as being to explain how this is possible.

The criterion for accuracy used in most of the early research was self–other agreement; a judgment was presumed accurate to the degree that it matched a target's self-description (e.g., Taft, 1955). The whole approach was undermined when the statistical issues entailed by using profile correlations to assess this match came under statistical scrutiny, as has already been mentioned. A further issue, never really considered by Cronbach and the other methodological critics, is that self-description is less than a sure criterion for truth. But the previous quote from Allport shows that he envisioned a much wider array of criteria (and he used them in some of his own work). The accuracy of a personality judgment resides not just in the degree to which it matches a target's self-perception, but also in the degree to which it predicts his or her social behavior (e.g., reaction to a gift, compatibility at a dinner party) and performance (e.g., as a tenant, employee, or roommate).

A critical difference between the cognitive and social psychological approaches to social judgment lies in the use of wide-ranging criteria such as these. The cognitive paradigm, as we have seen, entails assessment of whether subjects' judgments of artificial stimuli match the prescriptions of a normative model. The social paradigm uses *correspondence* criteria, the degree to which judgments match the actual properties of real stimuli, as best as those can be independently assessed (Hammond, 1996). Of course, there is no single gold standard for assessing what the actual personality properties of a target person are, but several silver standards (if you will) are available. Investigators can assess accuracy via interjudge agreement, either between judges (e.g., Kenny, 1994) or between judges and targets (self–other agreement, e.g., Funder, 1980; Kenny & DePaulo, 1993). Judgmental accuracy can also be assessed according to whether it can predict outcomes such as job performance (e.g., Mayfield, 1972; Waters & Waters, 1970) or directly observed social behavior (e.g., Kolar, Funder, & Colvin, 1996). Accuracy is indicated by convergence among these varied sources of data.

This shift in criterion is fundamental to the difference between the two approaches. From a cognitive perspective, judgmental accuracy is all about the stimulus information. Is it correctly recalled, processed without distortion, and combined according to normative formulas? These questions concern what happens between the ears. From a social perspective, judgmental accuracy is about social interaction. Does Jack agree with Bob about what kind of person Jill is? Do they both agree with Jill herself? If they invite Jill to a dinner party, will she make a congenial companion? If they rent her a room, will she trash the place? These questions concern what happens in the social world. Their answers have social consequences and, as was observed at the beginning of this chapter, it is these consequences that make the accuracy issue important.

THE REALISTIC ACCURACY MODEL

RAM (Funder, 1995, 1999) is a social psychological approach that describes the interpersonal process that allows accurate interpersonal judgment to occur in particular circumstances.

RAM begins with two assumptions. First, personality traits exist. Twenty years of debate notwithstanding (e.g., Kenrick & Funder, 1988), people really do have traits such as sociability, honesty, talkativeness, reliability, and so on. Their behavior relevant to these traits is consistent enough that it is worthwhile to characterize them in such terms, especially if you are intending to give them a gift, invite them to a dinner party, or rent them a room. The second assumption is that people sometimes manage to judge these traits accurately. As Allport might have put it, gifts are sometimes poorly received, dinner parties are disasters, and rented rooms

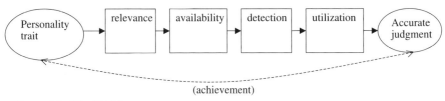

Figure 6.1. The RAM.

become uninhabitable, but outcomes like these are at least sometimes successfully avoided. If these two assumptions are granted, then a question immediately arises: How is this degree, or any degree, of accurate personality judgment possible?

According to RAM, accurate personality judgment is possible only to the degree that four things happen, as diagrammed in Figure 6.1. First, the person who is judged must do something *relevant* to the trait in question. Second, this relevant behavior must be *available* to the person who would judge the trait. Third, this relevant, available behavior must be *detected* by the judge – it must register, somehow, on his or her nervous system. Fourth and finally, the relevant, available, detected behavioral information must be correctly *utilized* – interpreted and judged.

The Four Steps to Accurate Judgment

An example may clarify the process. Imagine that a person has the trait of friendliness – he or she really does like to be with people and seeks out their company. How could someone else judge this trait accurately?

Only if, first, the friendly person does something friendly. All the friendly feelings and impulses in the world are no use, from a judgmental standpoint, if the person never acts on them. A *relevant* behavior, one produced by and therefore diagnostic of friendliness, is required. Notice that RAM already yields an important implication: that a person may have a trait that is never exhibited and therefore never becomes judgable. Consider the trait of courage. Most of us have no idea whether we possess this trait or not. In the film *Saving Private Ryan*, the character played by Tom Hanks clearly did have courage, which was exhibited in his clear thinking and ability to plan while under heavy fire on Omaha Beach. It was this extreme situation that elicited relevant behavior. Had he stayed home, the opportunity (or need) to exhibit such behavior might never have arisen, and neither he nor anyone else would have had any way of knowing he had the trait.

Getting back to the easier example of friendliness, the relevant friendly behavior, perhaps an approachable smile or a warm greeting, must next be *available* to the person who judges it. Work described by Lieberman (this volume) and by Zárate and Stoever (this volume) raises the interesting prospect that some traits may be manifested by brain processes detectable via neural imaging but not necessarily in overt behavior. In more ordinary cases, the availability step simply means that the judge must be present. People live in a variety of social contexts that influence or limit their behavior. A person may display competent behavior in a workplace, whereas family members, who see him or her only at home, may have no basis on which to judge this trait. Another person may display warm behavior at home to a degree his coworkers would never suspect. In our dramatic example, the wife of the Tom Hanks character, back in Pennsylvania, probably had no idea about some of the traits he was displaying in France, because the relevant behavior was unavailable to her.

The availability stage has two important implications. First, the more contexts one shares with the person one is trying to judge, the more likely one is to be able to make a judgment that is generally rather than narrowly accurate (e.g., Blackman & Funder, 1998). Second, the less context-dependent an individual's behavior is – the less he or she varies behavior from one situation to the next – the easier he or she will be to judge (e.g., Colvin, 1993).

At the third stage, once our friendly person has exhibited a relevant behavior in an available context, the judge must successfully *detect* it. RAM does not make a strong claim that this detection must be conscious – behavioral cues might be detected only implicitly – but it does seem obvious that the behavioral information must register somehow on the perceiver's nervous system before anything else can happen.

Detection can be problematic. An observer might be distracted by his or her own thoughts (including enhanced sexual fantasies; see other chapters in this volume) or unable to do the multitasking necessary to simultaneously generate behavior and observe the actions of his or her interaction partner (Lieberman & Rosenthal, 2001). For example, an extremely shy person might be so self-conscious that he or she has little attention to spare for noticing the informative behaviors of anyone else. Or relevant and available behaviors might be overlooked to the degree that other salient stimuli are present. It is easy to imagine that his companions under fire on Omaha Beach may have had other things on their minds besides assessing how much courage the Hanks character was demonstrating. Another possibility is that sensory deficits may interfere with detection. For example, older people who begin to lose their hearing may have problems in social relationships, including misperceiving the intentions of others, because they fail to detect informative social cues.

The final stage of accurate judgment begins only after a relevant behavior has become available to the judge and successfully detected. The judge must then correctly *utilize* this information. It must be matched with similar observations in memory, interpreted, perhaps even calculated. For example, the smile of our friendly person must be interpreted as a friendly smile and not as an indication of nervousness, manipulation, or rueful embarrassment. The Hanks character's fellow soldiers must realize that his decision to charge off of Omaha Beach came from a cool realization that no other move had any chance of success, not from narcissistic bravado or a failure to appreciate the risks – and that such good judgment under pressure is the definitive hallmark of courage.

The memory retrieval models, information combination formulas, and processing heuristics demonstrated by research on social cognition all occur within the utilization stage, and these processes have potential implications for accuracy. The cognitive and social approaches differ in two ways, however. First, from a social perspective, this stage is only the last of four important stages in accurate judgment rather than an exclusive focus. Second, from a social perspective, the success of the utilization stage is judged not by internal criteria, whether the information was processed correctly according to a normative model, but by external criteria in the social world. In the end, was the judgment correct? Did it agree with the target's self-judgment or correctly predict his or her future behavior?

This second difference is important because a utilization process that is incorrect from a purely cognitive perspective may be just right, or generally right, from a social perspective. For example, the *fundamental attribution error* is the putative tendency to see behavior as influenced by aspects of the person who performed it, even when information is ambiguous or suggests that the situation was more important. This error might lead to distortions in the literal information that the judge detected, but it will lead to correct judgments to the extent that behavior generally is a function of personality characteristics. In all its functions, the cognitive system typically goes beyond the information given; it augments, filters, amplifies, and even distorts stimulus inputs in accord with its general understanding of the world, past experience, and perhaps even evolutionary history (Haselton & Buss, this volume). In the cognitive paradigm as followed in the study of person perception, any alteration of the stimulus input is inevitably viewed as a source of error (see Table 6.1). The social psychology of person perception recognizes – along with mainstream cognitive psychology (e.g., Gardner, 1985) – that the augmentation of stimuli is precisely what makes adaptive perception and judgment possible.

Implications of RAM

The most fundamental implication of RAM is that the process of person perception is not exclusively cognitive. The stages of the model are not sensory buffers, memory registers, or perceptual matching processes. Rather, as we have seen, they are social processes that depend upon social variables such as context, behavior, acquaintance, and interaction.

The second implication of RAM is that accurate social judgment is difficult. RAM is optimistic – and contrasts strongly with the error paradigm – in that it describes how judgments may be made accurately. But it emphatically does *not* assume that accurate judgment is easy or even typical. As was shown in the examples concerning friendliness and courage, each stage of RAM identifies a set of possibilities for how judgment could go awry: A relevant behavior might never be performed; it might not be available; it might fail to be detected; it might be misinterpreted. Accuracy is difficult to achieve because it requires that all four steps of RAM be successfully traversed; imperfections at each stage will combine multiplicatively.

Third, RAM implies social rather than exclusively cognitive explanations for moderators of accurate judgment. Research has found that four kinds of moderators affect accuracy: properties of the judge, the target, the trait being judged, and the information on which the judgment is based (Funder, 1995, 1999). Explanations and predictions concerning each can be derived from RAM.

For example, some traits are easier to judge accurately than others (Funder & Dobroth, 1987). RAM explains this difference in terms of the availability and detection stages. Relatively easy-to-judge traits, such as extraversion, are manifested in many different situations (hence are widely available) through overt behaviors (hence are likely to be detected). Difficult-to-judge traits, such as a tendency to worry, have fewer visible signs. Other traits, such as the ability to organize small work groups, may have narrow implications and so may be observed only under specific circumstances. Still other difficult-to-judge traits, such as deceitfulness, may be deliberately concealed. A dishonest business partner may perform many behaviors relevant to his dishonesty but will try to limit their availability.

The insight that RAM can provide into moderators of accuracy may be its most important contribution. The final section of this chapter will consider two aspects in more detail: the good judge of personality and the problem of self-knowledge.

THE GOOD JUDGE OF OTHERS AND OF THE SELF

The Good Judge

The social psychological literature of the 1940s and 1950s focused on a search for the characteristics of the good judge of personality (e.g., Taft, 1955). The goal proved surprisingly elusive. In part this was because of the measurement problems that plagued much of the literature of the time (Funder, 1987) but also because the good judge did not seem to be a very robust creature (Schneider, Hastorf, & Ellsworth, 1979). The individual difference characteristics that predicted judgmental success in one context sometimes did not generalize to other contexts, and in general, findings tended to have a quality of "now you see it, now you don't."

To the extent that findings did emerge, they were generally interpreted as reflections of judgmental ability. In the terms used by RAM (which still lay 40 years in the future), they were assumed to arise at the utilization stage, an assumption still widely held. Because accuracy is implicitly assumed to be a matter of correct information processing, research often looks for and sometimes finds evidence that people who are intelligent or in some sense cognitively more able – for example, those who enjoy *social intelligence* or *emotional intelligence* (Cantor & Kihlstrom, 1987; Goleman, 1995) – tend to make more accurate interpersonal judgments. IQ is correlated with accuracy to some degree (Lippa & Dietz, 2000), as are more specific abilities such as *nonverbal sensitivity* (e.g., Ambady, LaPlante, & Johnson, 2001; Funder & Harris, 1986).

These assumptions and findings are certainly reasonable. The utilization stage is important, and it stands to reason that people better able to process information – in a word, smarter people – would do better at it. However, the surprisingly spotty findings might lead one to wonder whether this is the whole story, and the other stages of RAM may suggest where it might be incomplete.

The detection stage, which comes just prior to utilization, refers to the degree to which relevant and available stimulus information registers on the judge's nervous system. Most studies of social cognition simply bypass this stage, because the stimulus information is presented so blatantly (e.g., trait lists on a computer display) that it could scarcely be missed. In real life, however, detection is important. As was mentioned earlier, a judge might fail to detect cues to personality to the degree that he or she is self-conscious, distracted, unable to process multiple stimuli simultaneously, or beset by sensory deficits. To the extent that they are stable, any or all of these variables might produce individual differences in accuracy.

Implications of the other stages have received less research attention but may be even more important. The availability stage of RAM implies that judges who share many different contexts with their targets will become more likely to be accurate. This implies that knowing someone longer will tend to increase accuracy, the *acquaintance effect* (Blackman & Funder, 1998). It also implies that judgmental accuracy might be enhanced by efforts to share diverse experiences with the people one is getting to know – going out of one's way to socialize, perform tasks with, and otherwise observe people in a variety of different contexts. For example, a businessperson who puts the effort (and expense) into socializing with his or her clients or customers, as well as merely selling to or negotiating with them, may come to know them better and ultimately enjoy greater success. Psychologists at conferences have been known to do the same thing. Much of what one comes to know about one's colleagues arises from interactions in the hotel bar rather than in the symposium room, and those conferees who go straight to their rooms when the formal talks are over miss a good deal. As a result, individuals with personality traits such as extraversion that promote social interaction may have an advantage in making accurate interpersonal judgments.

The first, relevance stage of RAM may have implications for individual differences in judgmental accuracy as well. At first, this may not be obvious, because the performance of a personality-relevant behavior might seem to depend on the target, not the judge. But a judge can affect the relevance of the behavior of the judgmental target through his or her own actions, deliberate or not.

The simplest form of deliberate elicitation is questioning. The standard undergraduate greeting of "what's your major?" may be just the beginning of an extended interrogation. Questioning another person about behaviors, interests, experiences, and personal history is a common feature of dates, job interviews, and all sorts of casual encounters. Each question is designed, perhaps semideliberately and certainly with variable success, to elicit a response that will be a behavior relevant to a trait the questioner would like to know about.

Some people go even further and set little tests to appraise a friend's loyalty or an employee's conscientiousness. I once had a graduate student who recruited undergraduate research assistants by scheduling three consecutive 8 am meetings. Anyone who showed up for all three meetings was hired. (This turned out to be an excellent strategy.) In general, and intentionally or not, every behavior performed by a judge in a social interaction can be viewed as a gentle or not-so-gentle probe that will elicit some kind of response that may be relevant to, and therefore informative about, the target's personality.

Judges may vary in the degree to which their actions elicit relevant behavior. Some may be skilled questioners, and by displaying interest may elicit even more information. Some judges are the kinds of persons around whom others feel free to "be themselves." More obvious is the counterexample: the person, commonly described as "touchy," around whom other people feel inhibited. If a target feels that anything he or she might do has a possibility of infuriating, disgusting, irritating, or otherwise setting off the judge, he or she will become inhibited and as a result display fewer self-relevant behaviors. Some bosses know very little about their employees, teachers about their students, and even parents about their children for exactly this reason.

RAM's full description of the process of accurate judgment extends the picture of the good judge of personality beyond a view of him or her as merely smart or socially intelligent. The good judge of personality seeks out opportunities to interact with others, shows interest in what they say and do, and encourages rather than inhibits their self-expression. This conclusion, in turn, may offer predictions about how to identify the good judge of personality and, perhaps even more importantly, how to train judgmental ability. The prescription for better judgment offered by the standard cognitive paradigm is that the best judge of personality is the one who makes the fewest cognitive errors. But training a person to make fewer errors may be counterproductive. As Galinsky, Martorana, and Ku (this volume) note, attempts to suppress errors can actually lead them to be hyperaccessible. And at least some errors, such as the Müller–Lyer illusion in the domain of visual perception, are part of accurate judgment (Funder, 1987). RAM illuminates the further fact that successfully training a person to be a better judge of personality would entail much more than teaching him or her to think better, however that might be defined. Good judgment is a social process and is in large part the result of social behavior.

Self-Knowledge

RAM was developed to explain how one person might attain an accurate understanding of another. Bem's (1972) description of the parallels between the processes by which we know others and the processes by which we know ourselves suggests that it might be possible to extend RAM to the problem of self-knowledge. As Bem pointed out, among the people everyone knows is someone who shares his or her Social Security number, address, and name. How does one attain knowledge about this person? The four stages of RAM outline the beginning of an answer.

Starting with the last stage first, utilization implies that, similarly to the case of other-perception, the attainment of self-knowledge depends to some degree on cognitive ability and social intelligence. Every individual is complex, and integrating the vast array of information available in self-observation is no mean feat. Indeed, some people seek expert help – psychotherapy – in the quest for self-understanding. In a related vein, self-knowledge may be blocked at the utilization stage to the degree that an individual is defensive or otherwise avoids processing or distorts the processing of certain kinds of information about the self. Again, professional help may be useful, as may the insight of a trusted friend.

The detection stage also has implications for self-knowledge. An individual may have trouble detecting information about the self to the degree that he or she utilizes perceptual defenses. People may deliberately or at least effectively prevent themselves from noticing information that is obvious to others. A student may be oblivious to repeated indications that he or she is about to fail a course, a spouse to multiple signs that his or her partner is unhappy, an employer to indications that his or her employees are disgruntled. Such blindness prevents anxiety in the short run but leads in the not-so-long run not only to a failure to judge these other people accurately, but also a failure to begin to process the implications for the self. The student might not be aware of the causes of failure in his or her own work habits or motivation; the spouse of the way his or her own inconsiderate behavior is causing problems; the boss of the aspects of his or her management style that undermines employee morale. These observations yield a wider moral as well: Because every person lives immersed in a social world, shortcomings in the perception of others quickly redound to shortcomings in self-perception, and vice versa.

There are other reasons, besides defensiveness, that a person might be oblivious to self-relevant information. One is that during social interaction, people are so busy trying to respond to the constantly changing situation that they may fail to notice the characteristic aspects of their own behavior. Only later, staring at the ceiling, late at night, or on the therapist's couch, does the individual realize that "I always act that way" (this is the basis of the false consensus effect [Ross, Greene, & House, 1977] as well as of the dispositional shift in self-attribution over time [Moore, Sherrod, Liu, & Underwood, 1979]).

An even simpler reason for failing to detect self-relevant information is a phenomenon Kolar et al. (1996) dubbed the *fish and water effect*. Informative aspects of one's own behavior may become almost invisible to the person himself or herself for roughly the same reason that fish are said to be unaware that they are wet. People who are extraordinarily sociable, charming, or bright may find this aspect of themselves so routine that it fails to register, whereas others notice the trait almost immediately. On the darker side, some people are characteristically cheap, and may act this way so consistently that they have effectively forgotten that there is any other way to behave. Doesn't everybody suddenly have to go to the bathroom as soon as the group's dinner check arrives? Yet this kind of behavior may be the first thing a new acquaintance notices, and the (correct) conclusion will be quickly drawn. Nalini Ambady and her colleagues (2001) have found that a few seconds of observation are sufficient to identify the speech styles of physicians that predict the probability they will be sued for malpractice; the physicians themselves are almost certainly unaware of what these styles are!

Part of the problem may lie at the next earlier stage, availability. The patients of the physicians who are more likely to be sued probably could provide behavioral feedback that would warn them of problems ahead, but the physicians may not seek it or may even act as if to prevent it, such as by rushing through the appointment (itself one of the danger signs) or by using an intimidating manner (another of the danger signs). In general, a seeker of self-knowledge can make more relevant information available by garnering feedback from others. One becomes more likely to obtain this feedback to the extent that one asks "How am I doing?" and, even more importantly, to the extent that one is the kind of person others feel free to respond to openly. A boss who is about to make a bad business decision may or may not be warned by his employees; whether they do warn him will depend on whether he is the kind of person who can be corrected without incurring adverse consequences. Similarly, the person who wonders "Why does nobody like me?" may in fact be the last person on earth to whom anybody would dare to explain the reasons.

The most interesting implications of all for self-knowledge may arise at the first step of accurate judgment, which is relevance. As was mentioned during the discussion of other-judgment, the accurate judgment of personality begins to be possible to the degree that the person in question emits relevant behavior. By the same token, the accurate judgment of a trait is stymied at the very outset if the person being judged never emits a relevant behavior. This principle has several implications for self-knowledge.

The first implication is that to understand oneself better, one should seek out situations where behaviors relevant to heretofore unknown aspects of personality have a chance to emerge. This might involve experiences such as bungee jumping or mountain climbing, or simply striving to interact with a wide variety of people. New Zealand has a tradition of the "O.E." (overseas experience), in which young people take a year or two off from their studies to travel the world, moving from job to job. I suspect one reason for this custom is that otherwise, growing up in New Zealand could be a rather limiting experience – it is far from most of the rest of the world with which it is culturally attuned (and isolated from many of its woes as well). To give another example, people with experience serving in the military often report that they learned much about themselves that they might never have suspected otherwise.

The relevance stage also implies that self-knowledge will be prevented to the extent that one prevents relevant behaviors from being emitted. This could happen by severely limiting one's contexts and activities, such as living the life of the recluse or the hermit. Such individuals are likely to know very little about their own personalities. Another example is the well-known phenomenon of self-handicapping (Jones & Berglas, 1978). Some people avoid learning about their possible shortcomings by short-circuiting the relevance of their behavior. A student who goes on a drinking binge the night before a major exam has a ready-made excuse for why he flunked; his performance on the exam can plausibly be regarded as not relevant to his actual ability, and he is therefore prevented from learning what that ability is or is not. Of course, at the same time, he has guaranteed his own failure.

Other people might limit one's self-knowledge at this stage through restrictions on self-expression. A family environment that suppresses the expression of emotions and other impulses may produce children who grow up to be unsure who they are. Some students at my university have been pressed so hard to achieve high grades and a prestigious occupation (usually medicine) that they have no idea what they really want to do; the opportunity to question, let alone experiment, has never been afforded them. In another vivid but fictional example, the HBO series *Six Feet Under* dramatizes the very confused lives of a family of undertakers who grew up in a funeral home; their childhood was spent repressing emotion and other unseemly impulses, and the development of their self-knowledge was severely stunted.

Opportunities for self-expression may vary across cultures as well. Recent years have seen many studies of *collectivist* cultures (such as those of China, Japan, and India) in which, it is said, individual differences and personality traits are much less salient than they are in *individualist* cultures (such as those of the United States, Europe, or Australia). Indeed, it has even been argued that in India and other Eastern cultures there is no sense of the individual *self* as Westerners know it (e.g., Markus & Kitayama, 1991; Shweder & Bourne, 1982). To the extent that there is truth to any of this, part of the reason may be that collectivist cultures limit opportunities for individual self-expression. A culture that routinely chooses one's spouse, for example, would seem to be a culture that allows limited rein for individual proclivities. Persons who grow up and live in such a context may have fewer opportunities to learn about their own proclivities, develop a less individualized sense of self, and perhaps come to feel that their behavior is under the control of the social context rather than their own personalities (e.g., Morris & Peng, 1994).

CONCLUSION

Accurate social judgment, when it occurs, is the result of a social process that extends beyond the individual judge into the social world. According to RAM, it occurs only to the extent that relevant behaviors emitted by the person in question are available to, detected by, and correctly utilized by a social judge. Only the last of these stages is addressed by the currently dominant cognitive paradigm of person perception. A description of the entire process of accurate social judgment requires a return to *social* psychology.

References

Allport, G. W. (1937). *Personality: A psychological interpretation.* New York: Holt, Rinehart & Winston.
Allport, G. W., & Vernon, P. E. (1933). *Studies in expressive movement.* New York: Macmillan.

Ambady, N., LaPlante, D., & Johnson, E. (2001). Thin-slice judgments as a measure of interpersonal sensitivity. In J. A. Hall & F. J. Bernieri (Eds.), *Interpersonal sensitivity: Theory and measurement* (pp. 67–88). Mahwah, NJ: Erlbaum.

Ambady, N., LaPlante, D., Nguyen, T., Rosenthal, R., Chaumeton, N., & Levinson, W. (2001). Surgeons' tone of voice: A clue to malpractice history. *Surgery, 132,* 5–9.

Anderson, N. H. (1990). A cognitive theory of judgment and decision. In N. H. Anderson (Ed.), *Contributions to information integration theory* (pp. 105–142). Hillsdale, NJ: Erlbaum.

Asch, S. E. (1946). Forming impressions of personality. *Journal of Abnormal and Social Psychology, 9,* 258–290.

Bem, D. J. (1972). Self-perception theory. In L. Berkowitz (Ed.), *Advances in experimental social psychology* (Vol. 6, pp. 1–62). New York: Academic Press.

Birnbaum, M. H. (1983). Base rates in Bayesian inference: Signal detection analysis of the cab problem. *American Journal of Psychology, 96,* 85–94.

Blackman, M. C., & Funder, D. C. (1998). The effect of information on consensus and accuracy in personality judgment. *Journal of Experimental Social Psychology, 34,* 164–181.

Block, J. (1995). A contrarian view of the five-factor approach to personality description. *Psychological Bulletin, 117,* 187–215.

Cantor, N., & Kihlstrom, J. F. (1987). *Personality and social intelligence.* Englewood Cliffs, NJ: Prentice-Hall.

Colvin, C. R. (1993). Judgable people: Personality, behavior and competing explanations. *Journal of Personality and Social Psychology, 64,* 861–873.

Cronbach, L. J. (1955). Processes affecting scores on "understanding of others" and "assumed similarity." *Psychological Bulletin, 52,* 177–193.

Fiske, S. T., & Taylor, S. E. (1991). *Social cognition* (2nd ed.). New York: McGraw-Hill.

Funder, D. C. (1980). On seeing ourselves as others see us: Self–other agreement and discrepancy in personality ratings. *Journal of Personality, 48,* 473–493.

Funder, D. C. (1987). Errors and mistakes: Evaluating the accuracy of social judgment. *Psychological Bulletin, 101,* 75–90.

Funder, D. C. (1995). On the accuracy of personality judgment: A realistic approach. *Psychological Review, 102,* 652–670.

Funder, D. C. (1999). *Personality judgment: A realistic approach to person perception.* San Diego: Academic Press.

Funder, D. C., & Dobroth, K. M. (1987). Differences between traits: Properties associated with interjudge agreement. *Journal of Personality and Social Psychology, 52,* 409–418.

Funder, D. C., & Harris, M. J. (1986). On the several facets of personality assessment: The case of social acuity. *Journal of Personality, 54,* 528–550.

Gage, N. L., & Cronbach, L. J. (1955). Conceptual and methodological problems in interpersonal perception. *Psychological Review, 62,* 411–422.

Gardner, H. (1985). *The mind's new science: A history of the cognitive revolution.* New York: Basic Books.

Goleman, D. (1995). *Emotional intelligence.* New York: Bantam Books.

Hammond, K. R. (1996). *Human judgment and social policy.* New York and Oxford: Oxford University Press.

Haselton, M. G., & Buss, D. M. (2000). Error management theory: A new perspective on biases in cross-sex mind reading. *Journal of Personality and Social Psychology, 78*, 81–91.

Jones, E. E. (1985). Major developments in social psychology during the past five decades. In G. Lindzey & E. Aronson (Eds.), *The handbook of social psychology* (3rd ed., Vol. 1, pp. 47–107). New York: Random House.

Jones, E. E., & Berlgas, S. (1978). Control of attributions about the self through self-handicapping strategies: The appeal of alcohol and the role of underachievement. *Personality and Social Psychology Bulletin, 4*, 200–206.

Kenny, D. A. (1994). *Interpersonal perception: A social relations analysis.* New York: Guilford Press.

Kenny, D. A., & DePaulo, B. M. (1993). Do people know how others view them? An empirical and theoretical account. *Psychological Bulletin, 114*, 145–161.

Kenrick, D. T., & Funder, D. C. (1988). Profiting from controversy: Lessons from the person–situation debate. *American Psychologist, 43*, 23–34.

Kolar, D. W., Funder, D. C., & Colvin, C. R. (1996). Comparing the accuracy of personality judgments by the self and knowledgeable others. *Journal of Personality, 64*, 311–337.

Krueger, J., & Funder, D. C. (in press). Towards a balanced social psychology: Causes, consequences and cures for the problem-seeking approach to social behavior and cognition. *Behavioral and Brain Sciences.*

Kunda, Z. (1999). *Social cognition: Making sense of people.* Cambridge, MA: MIT Press.

Lieberman, M. D., & Rosenthal, R. (2001). Why introverts can't always tell who likes them: Multitasking and nonverbal decoding. *Journal of Personality and Social Psychology, 80*, 294–310.

Lippa, R. A., & Dietz, J. K. (2000). The relation of gender, personality and intelligence to judges' accuracy in judging strangers' personality from brief video segments. *Journal of Nonverbal Behavior, 24*, 25–43.

Markus, H. R., & Kitayama, S. (1991). Culture and the self: Implications for cognition, emotion, and motivation. *Psychological Review, 98*, 224–253.

Mayfield, E. C. (1972). Value of peer nominations in predicting life insurance sales performance. *Journal of Applied Psychology, 56*, 319–323.

Moore, B. S., Sherrod, D. R., Liu, T. J., & Underwood, B. (1979). The dispositional shift in attribution over time. *Journal of Experimental Social Psychology, 15*, 553–569.

Morris, M. W., & Peng, K. (1994). Culture and cause: American and Chinese attributions for social and physical events. *Journal of Personality and Social Psychology, 67*, 949–971.

Ross, L., Greene, D., & House, P. (1977). The false consensus phenomenon: An attribution bias in self-perception and social perception processes. *Journal of Experimental Social Psychology, 13*, 279–301.

Schneider, D. J., Hastorf, A. H., & Ellsworth, P. C. (1979). *Person perception* (2nd ed.). Reading, MA: Addison-Wesley.

Shaklee, H. (1991). An inviting invitation. *Contemporary Psychology, 36*, 940–941.

Shweder, R. A., & Bourne, E. J. (1982). Does the concept of the person vary cross-culturally? In R. A. Shweder & R. A. LeVine (Eds.), *Culture theory: Essays on mind, self, and emotion* (pp. 158–199). New York: Cambridge University Press.

Taft, R. (1955). The ability to judge people. *Psychological Bulletin, 52,* 1–23.

Tagiuri, R., & Petrullo, L. (Eds.). (1958). *Person perception and interpersonal behavior.* Palo Alto, CA: Consulting Psychologists Press.

Waters, L. K., & Waters, C. W. (1970). Peer nominations as predictors of short-term sales performance. *Journal of Applied Social Psychology, 54,* 42–44.

PART II

COGNITIVE AND INTRAPSYCHIC MECHANISMS OF SOCIAL JUDGMENTS

7

A Parametric Unimodel of Human Judgment

Integrating Dual-Process Frameworks in Social Cognition from a Single-Mode Perspective

Arie W. Kruglanski, Woo Young Chun,
Hans Peter Erb, Antonio Pierro, Lucia Mannetti,
and Scott Spiegel

CONTENTS

INTRODUCTION

Judging people and events is something we do a lot of, and about a great many topics. This diversity of judgmental topics is paralleled (if not exactly equaled) by a diversity of judgmental *models* proposed by social psychologists (see also Haselton & Buss, this volume). Typically, these are domain-specific frameworks that seemingly are quite unrelated to each other. Thus, major models of persuasion (Chaiken, Liberman, & Eagly, 1989; Petty & Cacioppo, 1986) seem unrelated to major attributional models (Jones & Davis, 1965; Kelley, 1967; McClure, Sutton, & Hilton, this volume; Trope & Gaunt, 1999), which in turn seem unrelated to models of stereotyping (Brewer, 1988; Fiske & Neuberg, 1990), of group perception (Hamilton

Please address correspondence to Arie W. Kruglanski, Department of Psychology, University of Maryland, College Park, College Park, MD 20742. This work was supported by a National Science Foundation Grant (SBR-9417422) to Arie W. Kruglanski, a National Institute of Mental Health predoctoral fellowship (1F31MH12053) to Scott Spiegel, and a Korea Research Foundation postdoctoral fellowship to Woo Young Chun.

& Sherman, 1999), or of statistical likelihood judgments (Kahneman & Tversky, 1982; Tversky & Kahneman, 1974).

As an apparent exception to this disjunctivity, most judgmental models distinguish between *two qualitatively distinct* modes of judgment. This seeming commonality, however, only compounds the fragmentation, because each dual-process model proposes its own pair of qualitatively distinct modes. Thus, a recent dual-process sourcebook edited by Shelly Chaiken and Yaacov Trope (1999) contains 31 chapters, most of which describe their own unique, dual modes of judgment. Consequently, the current literature features nearly 60 (!) distinct judgmental *modes*. The picture they paint of human judgment processes is quite *heterogeneous* and divergent.

For something completely different, we would like to describe an integrative model of human judgment. This model unifies the two judgmental modes *within* the separate dual-process models and effects a *unification across* models as well; accordingly, we call it the *unimodel* (see also Erb et al., in press).

The unimodel accomplishes its integration by highlighting elements that the dual modes within each model (and the various models across domains) have in common. Admittedly, merely identifying commonalities is easy. Even the most unlikely set of objects, people, and events have at least some characteristics in common. The trick is to identify *crucial commonalities* that explain the target phenomena productively and carry novel implications. As we hope to show, the commonalities addressed by the unimodel do just that.

THE JUDGMENTAL PARAMETERS

Our proposal at once differs radically from "business as usual" in the human judgment field and at the same time is strangely familiar. It differs radically because we propose to replace close to 60 divergent modes of human judgment by just 1. But we do not do it by invoking mysterious novel entities no one has ever heard of before. To the contrary, our fundamental constructs are readily recognizable. Yet, their essential role in the judgmental process may have been obscured by their inadvertent confounding with a plethora of content elements. These fundamental constructs concern the common parameters of human judgment.

By these we mean several dimensional continua represented at some of their values in every instance of judgment. We assume that these parameters are quasi-orthogonal (much like obliquely related factors in a factor analysis) and that they can *intersect* at different values. Informational contents can be attached to each of these intersections. At some intersections the information will affect judgments (i.e., it will be persuasive, convincing, and impactful, and it will produce judgmental change). At other intersections it will not. According to the unimodel, whether it will or not has *nothing to do* with the informational contents per se and has *everything to do* with the parametric intersections to which the contents were attached. But this is getting ahead of the story. Instead, let us now introduce the judgmental parameters, show how they account for prior results, and what novel predictions they afford.

The Concept of Evidence

As a general background, we assume that judgments constitute conclusions based upon pertinent evidence. Such evidence is roughly syllogistic in form. It consists of contextual information that serves as a *minor premise* in a syllogism, for instance, "Laura is a graduate of MIT." This may serve as evidence for a conclusion if it instantiates an antecedent of a major premise in which the individual happens to believe, for example, "All MIT graduates are engineers" or "If one is an MIT graduate, one is an engineer." Jointly, the major and minor premises yield the conclusion "Laura is an engineer."

Subjective Relevance. Viewed against this backdrop, our first parameter is that of *subjective relevance,* by which is meant the *degree to which the individual believes in a linkage between the antecedent and consequent terms in the major premise.* A strong belief renders the antecedent and the information that instantiates it (in our example, *knowledge* that "Laura is a graduate of MIT") highly relevant to the conclusion. A disbelief renders it irrelevant. Consider the statement "All persons weighing more than 150 lb are medical doctors." We all disbelieve this particular statement and hence consider the information that a target weighs 162 lb irrelevant to her being a doctor. We assume, not very surprisingly, that the greater the perceived relevance of the evidence, the greater its impact on judgments.[1]

---

[1] A comment is in order with regard to our assumption of "syllogistic" if-then reasoning on part of the lay knower. We are not proposing that human reasoning is rational in the sense of necessarily yielding a *correct* conclusion (for discussion, see Kruglanski, 1989a, 1989b), for the premises one departs from may be false, and the conclusion is constrained by the premises. Thus, one may depart from a premise such as "If the shaman executes the rain dance, it will rain" that others might dismiss as irrational, as they might the belief that it will rain given that a rain dance has been performed (see also Cole & Scribner, 1974; Weber, 1947). This does not vitiate the subjective syllogistic relevance for the believer of a rain dance to subsequent raining. Nor are we assuming that human beings are strictly logical, a proposition belied by 30 years of research on the Wason (1966) card problem. Thus, people may incorrectly treat an implicational "if a then b" relation as if it were an equivalence relation implying also that "if b then a." Furthermore, people may be more correct in recognizing the implicational properties of concrete statements in familiar domains rather than those of abstract, unfamiliar statements (Evans, 1989). None of this is inconsistent with the notion that persons generally reason from subjectively relevant rules of the if-then format (Mischel & Shoda, 1995) that may or may not coincide with what some third party (e.g., the experimenter) had intended.

The subjective-relevance parameter (see also Fiedler & Freytag, this volume) is the "jewel in the parametric crown," to which the remaining parameters are auxiliary. The latter concern various *enabling conditions* that afford the realization of the *relevance potential* of the information given. Let us consider what these auxiliary parameters might consist of.

Experienced Difficulty of the Judgmental Task. An important parameter in this category is experienced difficulty of the judgmental task. Its value may depend upon such factors as the *length and complexity* of the information confronted by the knower, the information's ordinal position in the informational sequence, its salience, accessibility from memory of the pertinent inference rules, and our evolutionarily evolved capacity to deal with various information types (such as frequencies versus ratios; cf. Cosmides & Tooby, 1996; Gigerenzer & Hoffrage, 1995; but see Evans, Handley, Perham, Over, & Thompson, 2000).

Within the *unimodel*, perceived difficulty is treated as a parameter ranging from great ease (e.g., when the information appears early, is simple, brief, salient, and fits a highly accessible inference rule) to considerable hardship (e.g., when the information appears late, is lengthy, complex, and nonsalient, and/or fits only a relatively inaccessible rule). Generally, the ease of information processing *enables* a quick and relatively effortless realization of its degree of judgmental relevance, whereas the difficulty of processing hinders such a realization.

Magnitude of Processing Motivation. The magnitude of the motivation to engage in extensive information processing en route to judgment is determined variously by the individual's information processing goals such as the goals of accuracy (Chaiken et al., 1989; Petty & Cacioppo, 1986), accountability (Tetlock, 1985), need for cognition (Cacioppo & Petty, 1982), need to evaluate (Jarvis & Petty, 1996), or need for cognitive closure (Kruglanski & Webster, 1996; Webster & Kruglanski, 1998). For instance, the higher the accuracy motivation or the need for cognition, the greater the processing motivation. By contrast, the higher the need for closure, the smaller the degree of such motivation.

Magnitude of processing motivation may be additionally determined by the desirability of initially formed beliefs. If such beliefs were desirable, the individual would be disinclined to engage in further information processing, lest the current conclusions be undermined by further data. On the other hand, if the individual's current beliefs were undesirable, he or she would be inclined to process further information that hopefully would serve to alter the initial undesirable notions (Ditto & Lopez, 1992).

We assume, again unsurprisingly, that the higher the degree of processing motivation, the greater the individual's readiness to invest efforts in information processing, and hence the greater her or his readiness to cope with difficult-to-process information. Thus, if some particularly relevant information was presented in a format that rendered it difficult to decipher, a considerable amount of processing motivation would be needed to *enable* the realization of its relevance.

Cognitive Capacity. Another factor assumed to affect individuals' processing efforts is their momentary cognitive capacity, determined by such factors as cognitive busyness (i.e., the other tasks they are attempting to execute in parallel), as well as by their degree of alertness and sense of energy versus feelings of exhaustion or mental fatigue (e.g., Webster, Richter, & Kruglanski, 1998) perhaps resulting from prior information processing. We assume that a recipient whose cognitive capacity is depleted would be less successful in decoding complex or lengthy information and, hence, less impacted by such information compared to an individual with full cognitive capacity at his or her disposal. Capacity drainage will also favor the use of highly accessible as well as simple decision rules (and related evidence) over less accessible and/or more complex rules that are more difficult to retrieve from background knowledge (e.g., Chaiken et al., 1989). In short, the less one's cognitive capacity at a given moment, the less one's ability be to process information, particularly if doing so appears difficult, complicated, and laborious.

Motivational Bias. Occasionally, individuals do not particularly care about the judgmental outcome, that is, the conclusion they may reach, or about the judgmental process by which it was reached. When they do care, we speak of *motivational bias* (see also Dunning, 1999; Kruglanski, 1989a, 1990, 1999; Kunda, 1990; Kunda & Sinclair, 1999). In principle, all possible goals may induce such bias under the appropriate circumstances, rendering conclusions (judgments) congruent with the goal desirable and those incongruent with the goal undesirable. Thus, the *ego-defensive, ego-enhancing,* and *impression management* goals discussed by Chaiken et al. (1989) may induce motivational biases, but so may other goals that would render the use of specific information (e.g., the use of specific, conversationally appropriate [Grice, 1975] inference rules) or specific conclusions particularly desirable to the individual (e.g., prevention and promotion goals [Higgins, 1997], goals of competence, autonomy, or relatedness [Ryan, Sheldon, Kasser, & Deci, 1996]), and so on. Motivational biases may enhance the realization (or use) of subjectively relevant information yielding such conclusions and hinder the realization of subjectively relevant information yielding the opposite conclusions (cf. Dunning, 1999; Kunda, 1990). Again, we view the degree of motivational bias as lying on a continuum ranging from an absence of bias to considerable bias with regard to a given judgmental topic.

Processing Sequence. Our final parameter concerns the sequence in which the information is considered by the knower. Specifically, conclusions derived from prior processing can serve as evidential input in terms of which subsequent inferences are made. Thus, for example, several prior conclusions can combine to form a subsequent aggregate judgment (Anderson, 1971; Fishbein & Ajzen, 1975). In addition, prior conclusions can affect the construction of specific inference rules whereby subsequent ambiguous information is interpreted. Given that a source has been classified as "intelligent," for example, her or his subsequent ambiguous pronouncements may be interpreted as "clever." Given that an actor has been classified as a "middle-class housewife," the epitaph "hostile" may be interpreted as referring to "verbal aggressiveness," whereas had she been classified as a "ghetto resident," "hostile" may be interpreted to mean "physical aggression" (cf. Duncan, 1976).[2]

PARAMETERS' PROPERTIES AND INTERRELATIONS:
CONTINUA VERSUS DICHOTOMIES

The present parametric approach is distinct in major ways from the prevalent dual-process paradigm. A critical difference is that the dual-process models assume *qualitative dichotomies* (e.g., between central and peripheral processes, heuristic and systematic processes, heuristic and extensional reasoning, or category-based and individuating processing), whereas all of our parameters represent *continua* (e.g., recipients may have differing degrees of processing motivation or of cognitive capacity; they may experience greater or lesser difficulty in addressing a given judgmental task, or they may perceive the information given as more or less relevant to the judgmental topic).

Admittedly, some dual-process models explicitly incorporate continua into their formulations. Most notably, Petty and Cacioppo (1986) discuss a continuum of elaboration likelihood that runs from brief elaboration to extensive and thorough elaboration "received by the message" (ibid., p. 129). However, as shown later, the "brief and shallow" processing at one end of the continuum targets peripheral cues, whereas the thorough and extensive elaboration targets issue and message arguments. Thus, the elaboration likelihood model blends together the degree of elaboration and the information being elaborated (cues versus message arguments).

---

[2] Are these parameters all the judgmental parameters there are? In other words, is this parameter set *exhaustive*? There can be no guarantee on that. Like all scientific endeavors, the unimodel constitutes a work in progress. All we can say, however, is that the present parameter set does a good job of accounting for previous judgmental data and of yielding new, testable predictions.

That is perhaps why Petty, Wheeler, and Bizer (1999) insist on the *qualitative* difference in modes of processing beyond mere *quantitative* variation inherent in the notion of a continuum. As they put it (ibid., p. 161), "the key question is whether all persuasion findings can be explained by this quantitative variation. If so, then the qualitative variation postulated by the elaboration likelihood model (and other dual-route models) would not be necessary." Of course, they conclude that it is necessary and that, *contrary to our present claims*, it is unrelated to differences in informational contents. To demonstrate this last point, Petty et al. (1999) cite research by Petty and Cacioppo (1984) wherein *counting* the arguments (three versus nine) constituted the *cue*, juxtaposed to the substance of the *message arguments*. But note that the *number of arguments* represents a *content* of information every bit as much as the substance of the arguments, whatever it may be. Just as the substance of arguments may indicate to the recipient that the conclusion is valid, so too can the number of arguments (many versus few) to someone subscribing to the appropriate premise (e.g., "If there are so many arguments, it must be good") (as Petty et al., 1999, p. 161, explicitly recognize). Indeed, Petty et al. (1999) acknowledge that the processing of both cues and message arguments "could reasonably ... [represent] ... some type of if-then reasoning" (interpolation ours). This is in accord with our present assumption that the if-then premises in the two cases contain different *informational contents* (i.e., cues or message arguments) than the antecedent terms in the appropriate if-then statements, defining what the persuasive evidence in each case consists of.

Similarly, Fiske and Neuberg (1990) propose a continuum model that extends from the early consideration of *one type of content* (i.e., *social categories*) to subsequent consideration of *another content* (*individuating* or *attribute* information), given sufficient motivation and capacity. Hence, once again, the quantitative continuum of processing sequences from early- to late-processed information is intimately bound up here with *contents* of the information processed (categories versus attributes), and it is the contents of information that lend the air of qualitative difference to Fiske and Neuberg's (1990) dual modes.

In short, whereas the dual-process models assume (content-laden) *qualitative* differences in the ways judgments are reached, the unimodel accounts for variability in judgments in thoroughly *quantitative* terms related to the parameter values.

(Quasi)-Orthogonality of the Parameters

The presently identified judgmental parameters are assumed to be quasi-orthogonal to each other, and hence to form a multidimensional space containing a vast number of points, each representing a parametric intersection at different values. By contrast, the dual-process models typically isolate two such intersections (e.g., high processing difficulty and high motivation and capacity versus low processing difficulty and low motivation and capacity), join them to two separate types of content (e.g., message-related versus message-unrelated contents or social category–based versus individuating contents), and treat them as qualitatively distinct modes of forming judgments.

We assume that the judgmental parameters are generally orthogonal to each other and that their values derive from largely independent determinants. Thus, the subjective relevance of information may derive from a prior forging of conditional if-then links between informational categories, the magnitude of processing motivation may derive from the goal of accuracy, and the difficulty of processing may depend on accessibility of inference rules or the salience of pertinent information, all representing clearly separate concerns. Nonetheless, the parameters may share some determinants and occasionally may affect one another, and in that sense, they are only roughly (or quasi) rather than "pristinely" orthogonal. For example, highly relevant information may be used more frequently than less relevant information, fostering greater accessibility, which in turn should lower the value of the processing difficulty parameter. Conversely, high accessibility of information may increase its perceived relevance in some contexts (e.g., Jacoby, Kelley, Brown, & Jasechko, 1989; Schwarz & Clore, 1996).

A similar case can be made for the influence of motivation on subjective relevance in that a given bit of information may be perceived as more relevant, the more desirable the conclusion it points to (e.g., Lord, Ross, & Lepper, 1979) or the more congruent its implications are with the knower's motivation. For instance, in order to justify their *freezing* on early information, persons with a strong need for closure may perceive it as more relevant to the judgment at hand than persons with little need for closure (Webster & Kruglanski, 1998); by contrast, persons with a strong need for cognition (Cacioppo & Petty, 1982) may perceive the early information as less relevant, so that they may carry on with their information processing activity. Finally, limited cognitive capacity may reduce processing motivation or induce a need for cognitive closure (cf. Kruglanski & Webster, 1996), and so on. Despite these interrelations, however, the judgmental parameters are relatively independent (quasi-orthogonal) because many of their determinants are in fact unique or nonoverlapping.

THE PARAMETERS' ROLE IN JUDGMENT FORMATION

What specific role do the foregoing parameters play in judgment formation? As already noted, our key parameter is subjective relevance. All the remaining parameters define conditions allowing the subjective-relevance parameter to take effect. Thus, where the information processing task is difficult, the information's (degree and type of) relevance may not be accurately realized unless the knower had an appropriately high degree of processing motivation and an appropriately ample degree of cognitive capacity to handle the difficulty. The more difficult the task, the more motivation and capacity would be required to discern the information's (subjective) relevance to the judgment. Similarly, the ordinal position parameter may supply grist for the "relevance mill" by yielding on-line conclusions serving as evidence for subsequent inferences, for example of a combinatorial (cf. Anderson, 1971; Fishbein & Ajzen, 1975) or interpretive nature. It is in the foregoing sense that the parameters of motivation, capacity, task difficulty, and ordinal position play an auxiliary or enabling role with respect to the crucial parameter of subjective relevance.

Over the years, different judgmental models have highlighted distinct judgmental parameters out of the present set. For example, the *probabilogical* models of McGuire (1960, 1968) or Wyer (1970) emphasized the syllogistic relation between evidence and conclusions related to the present relevance parameter. Motivational bias was highlighted in models of cognitive dissonance (Festinger, 1957) or motivated reasoning (Kunda, 1990; Kunda & Sinclair, 1999). It was also accorded some attention in contemporary dual-process models (e.g., Chaiken et al., 1989; Petty & Cacioppo, 1986), though these models emphasized in particular the factors of nondirectional motivation and cognitive capacity, to the relative neglect of evidential-relevance considerations. Most judgmental models in the social psychological literature paid relatively little attention to perceived difficulty of the judgmental task, and none of the prior models, to our knowledge, attempted to elucidate the full set of judgmentally relevant parameters. As a consequence, much judgmental research failed to control for some of these parameters, leaving the door open to rival alternative interpretations of the findings.

For instance, in research claiming support for a qualitative difference in the processing of heuristic or peripheral cues versus message arguments (Chaiken et al., 1989; Petty & Cacioppo, 1986), one would need to control for the difficulty of processing these two types of information, their degree of perceived relevance to the judgmental topic, the desirability of conclusions each may yield given the participants' momentary motivation, and so on. The same holds for research claiming support for a qualitative difference in the processing of social category versus individuating-attribute information (Fiske & Neuberg, 1990), statistical versus heuristic information (Tversky & Kahneman, 1974), or behavioral identity versus dispositional trait information (Trope & Alfieri, 1997). Such controls have been conspicuous by their absence from large bodies of judgmental work. Instead, such work typically confounded *informational contents* with *parameter values*; hence, the latter provide a general alternative interpretation of results often cited in support of various dual-process models.

WHAT ABOUT CONTENTS?

Contents are an inseparable aspect of any judgmental situation. They constitute an *input* into the judgmental process and its ultimate *output*. We assume that contents per se do not matter as far as judgmental impact is concerned. What matters are the parametric intersections to which they are attached. Admittedly, contents *may partially determine* the parameter values; for example, a given content may be perceived as more or less relevant or more or less difficult to process. However, what ultimately counts are the parametric intersections, not the contents, because diverse contents may be attached to the same parametric intersection and they will all exert or fail to exert an impact as a function of the intersection to which they are attached.

In what follows, we consider from the present perspective dual-process work in three major areas: (1) persuasion, (2) attribution, and (3) biases and heuristics. Other areas could be similarly analyzed; these, however, lie beyond the scope of the present chapter (for a fuller discussion see Erb et al., in press).

PERSUASION

In a typical persuasion study, peripheral or heuristic cues are presented up front, and message arguments are presented subsequently. Moreover, the message arguments are typically lengthier and more complex than the cues. All this may render the message arguments more difficult to process than the cues. Thus, past persuasion research may have confounded the contents of persuasive information (i.e., cues versus message arguments) with processing difficulty. That is perhaps why cues typically were persuasive under low processing motivation or capacity and message arguments under high motivation and capacity. If that is true, controlling for processing difficulty should *eliminate* these differences. And it does.

Processing Difficulty and Informational Contents

We find that when the *message* is presented briefly and up front, it *mimics* the prior effects of cues. It too has impact under low motivation or low capacity. Similarly, when the cues are lengthy/complex and appear late, they *mimic* the prior effects of message information. They too are persuasive only under high motivation and capacity conditions, and not when motivation and capacity are low.

In one study, brief source information (suggesting expertise or a lack of it via the prestige of the university affiliation) was followed by lengthy source information (suggesting expertise or inexpertise via a lengthy curriculum

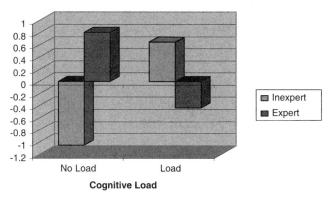

Figure 7.1a. Attitudes toward exams as a function of long source information and load.

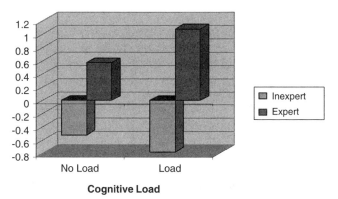

Figure 7.1b. Attitudes toward exams as a function of load and brief source information.

vitae); orthogonally, we manipulated cognitive load (Figures 7.1a and 7.1b). When the cue information was lengthy, its impact (the difference between expert and inexpert conditions) was wiped out by cognitive load (*mimicking* distraction effects on *message argument information* in prior research). When it was brief, however, its impact was greater under load versus no load (*replicating* the effects of cue information under low elaboration conditions).

In another study, we found that brief *initial arguments* had greater impact under low involvement, *mimicking* prior findings for peripheral or heuristic information, whereas *subsequent lengthy arguments* had greater impact under high involvement, replicating the typical message argument effect of prior research (Figures 7.2a and 7.2b).

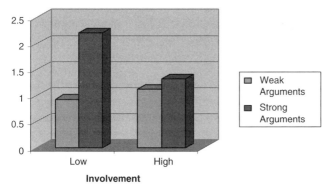

Figure 7.2a. Attitudes toward exams as a function of brief initial arguments and involvement.

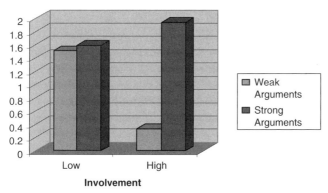

Figure 7.2b. Attitudes toward exams as a function of lengthy subsequent arguments and involvement.

Biasing Effects of One Information Type on Another

Within the dual-process models of persuasion, systematic or central processing can be biased by heuristic or peripheral cues (Bohner, Chaiken, & Hunyadi, 1994; Bohner, Ruder, & Erb, in press; Chaiken & Maheswaran, 1994; Darke et al., 1998; Mackie, 1987; Petty, Schumann, Richman, & Strathman, 1993). This biasing hypothesis is asymmetrical. It is the heuristic or peripheral cues that are presumed to bias systematic or central processing, not vice versa: Because heuristic or peripheral cues typically appear before the message arguments, it did not make much sense to ask whether *they* might be biased by processing message arguments. But the unimodel removes the constraint on presentation order and thus allows one to ask whether *any* information can yield conclusions that may serve as evidence for interpreting (and, in this sense, biasing the processing of) subsequent

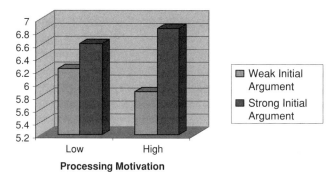

Figure 7.3. Attitudes toward subsequent message aspects as a function of initial argument quality and processing motivation.

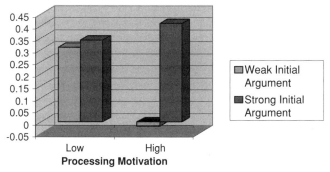

Figure 7.4. Valence of cognitive responses to subsequent arguments as a function of processing motivation and initial argument quality.

information, provided that one is sufficiently motivated to consider it. And the answer appears to be: *yes, it can*.

We presented participants with an initial argument of high or low quality. The subsequent five arguments were all of moderate quality. We found that under high (but not low) processing motivation, the attitude toward the subsequent arguments (those constant for all the participants) (Figure 7.3) and thoughts about these arguments (Figure 7.4) were biased by the initial message, and that under high (vs. low) motivation, final attitudes were mediated by those biased thoughts (Figure 7.5). Thus, not only can cues or heuristics bias the processing of message arguments, but also *prior* message arguments can bias the processing of *subsequent* message arguments.

In a different study we found that under high processing motivation, early message arguments can bias the processing of subsequent source information, thus standing the usual sequence on its head. The initial message biases attitudes toward the source (Figure 7.6) and thoughts about the source (Figure 7.7), which in turn mediate the final attitudes (Figure 7.8).

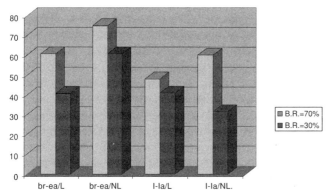

Figure 7.5. Likelihood of Dan's being a lawyer as a function of information presentation and load.

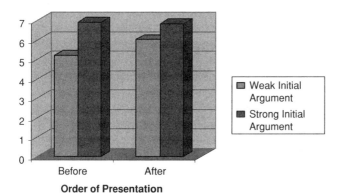

Figure 7.6. Perceived expertise of the communicator as a function of order of presentation and initial argument quality.

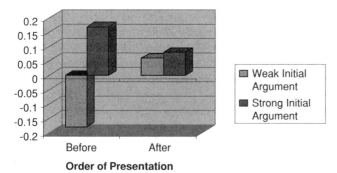

Figure 7.7. Valence of cognitive responses to communicator information as a function of initial argument quality and order of presentation.

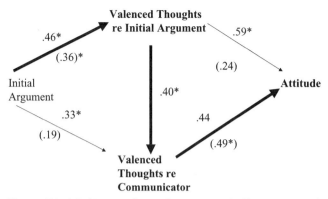

Figure 7.8. Mediation of initial arguments' effect on attitudes by biased thought about the communicator in the "before" condition.

In summary, the contents of persuasive information do not matter; what matters are the parameter values (e.g., on the processing difficulty parameter). When these are controlled for, differences between peripheral/ heuristic or central/systematic information types are eliminated.

DISPOSITIONAL ATTRIBUTIONS

Consider now the classic problem of dispositional attributions. In this area, Yaacov Trope and his colleagues (Trope, 1986; Trope & Alfieri, 1997; Trope & Liberman, 1996) outlined an influential dual-process model wherein the context information impacts *behavior identification* and *dispositional inference* in qualitatively different ways. In the *behavioral identification* phase, the effect of context is assumed to be assimilative or *automatic*, hence independent of cognitive resources, and *irreversible* by invalidating information. By contrast, the discounting of context in *inferring* an actor's *disposition* is assumed to be deliberative and resource-dependent. In support of these notions, Trope and Alfieri (1997) found that (1) cognitive load did not influence the effects of context upon *behavioral identification*, whereas it eliminated the discounting of context in *dispositional inference*, and (2) invalidating the contextual information had no effect on behavior identification, whereas it again eliminated the discounting effect on dispositional inference.

According to the unimodel, however, *behavioral identification* and dispositional inference differ only in the *contents* of the question asked. Behavior identification concerns the question "What is it?" (the behavior, that is), whereas dispositional inference concerns the question "What caused it?". But if content differences are all there is, how can one account for the differential effects of cognitive load on behavioral identification and dispositional inference? Once again, in terms of a confounding between

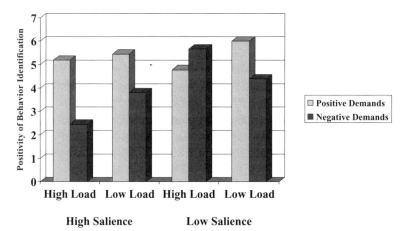

Figure 7.9. Positivity of behavioral identifications as a function of situational demands, salience, and load.

processing difficulty and question contents. Trope and Alfieri (1997) might have inadvertently selected a behavior identification task that was relatively easier to perform than the dispositional inference task, and that is why the former was performed more automatically than the latter and, independently of load.

Recent research supports this suggestion. First, Trope and Gaunt (2000) themselves found that the dispositional task can be made *easier* (by increasing the salience of the situational information), which totally eliminates the effects of load on *dispositional inferences*, that is, it renders dispositional inferences resource independent. More recent work by Chun, Spiegel, and Kruglanski (2002) demonstrates that the reverse is also true. The behavior identification task can be made *more difficult*, which renders it resource dependent; moreover, under these conditions, invalidating the contextual information does effect a revision of prior identifications.

As shown in Figure 7.9, when the contextual information is salient (as in the research of Trope & Alfieri, 1997), cognitive load does not make a difference, and the behavioral identification is assimilated to the context regardless of load. However, when the contextual information is less salient (hence, the information processing task is more difficult), the effects of context are eliminated by load.

We also find (Figure 7.10) that in the *high-salience* condition (where processing was easy and hence relatively automatic), participants' identification of the ambiguous behavior was independent of subsequent invalidation. This finding nicely replicates the work of Trope and Alfieri (1997). However, in the *low-salience* condition (where processing difficulty was greater, causing greater awareness of the process), behavior identifications

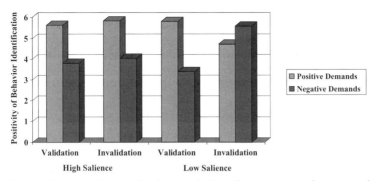

Figure 7.10. Positivity of behavioral identifications as a function of validation, situational demands, and salience.

significantly depended on validation. When the context was invalidated, it no longer had an effect on identification.

These data, together with Trope and Gaunt's (2000) findings, obviate the need to posit *qualitatively distinct* judgmental processes for *behavior identification* versus *dispositional inference*. Rather, we see that when the parameter of processing difficulty is controlled for (as it should be), the putative processing differences between these phases are eliminated.

BIASES AND HEURISTICS

One of the most influential research programs in judgment and decision making has been the *biases-and-heuristics* approach instigated by the seminal work of Amos Tversky and Danny Kahneman (see also Haselton & Buss, this volume). This view implies that there is something qualitatively distinct about the use of heuristics versus statistics. A different perspective is offered by the unimodel. According to this view, heuristics and statistics are two content categories of inferential rules. Other than that, their use and impact should be governed by the same by-now-familiar parameters.

Relevance

Consider the ubiquitous "lawyer and engineer" problem. In a typical study, participants are given individuating information about a target and about base rates of engineers and lawyers in the sample. In judging whether the target is an engineer, for example, the participant might use a *representativeness* rule whereby "if the target has characteristics a, b, and c, he/she is likely/unlikely to be an engineer." Alternatively, she might use a *base rate* rule whereby "if the base rate of engineers in the sample is X, the target is likely/unlikely to be an engineer." The original demonstrations by Tversky and Kahneman evidenced substantial base-rate neglect. The question is, why? Our analysis suggests that the constellation of parametric values in Tversky and Kahneman's studies might have favored the representativeness over the statistical rule. For instance, it could be that participants perceived the representativeness rule as *more relevant* to the judgment than the base-rate rule. But the relative relevance of rules can be altered or reversed, of course. Research conducted over the past two decades strongly supports this possibility. For instance, work on *conversational relevance* established that framing the lawyer-engineer problem as statistical or scientific significantly reduced the base-rate neglect (Schwarz, Strack, Hilton, & Naderer, 1991). In present terms, such framing may well have increased the *perceived relevance* of the statistical information to the judgment.

Another way to accomplish the same thing is to alter the "chronic" relevance of the statistical information by teaching statistical rules and hence strengthening participants' beliefs in if-then statements linking statistics to likelihood judgments. This too has been successfully accomplished. Thus, research by Nisbett, Cheng, Fong, and Lehman (1987) and more recently by Sedlmeier (1999) has established that statistical reasoning can be taught and that it can result in increased use of statistical information. As Seddlemeier recently summarized it (1999, p. 190), "The pessimistic outlook of the heuristics and biases approach cannot be maintained.... Training about statistical reasoning can be effective."

Accessibility

The psychological context of early base-rate neglect studies might have rendered the statistical rules not only *less subjectively relevant* but also *less accessible in memory*. In one study, prior to exposing participants to the lawyer-engineer problem, we primed them with words that call to mind statistical information such as *random*, *percentage*, and *ratio*. As Figure 7.11 shows, in the no-priming control condition, we robustly replicate the base-rate neglect. However, in the statistical priming condition, sensitivity to

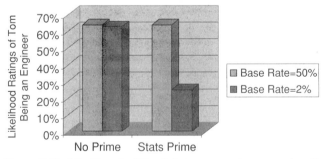

Figure 7.11. Likelihood of Tom's being an engineer as a function of base-rate information and statistical priming (in percentages).

base rates is greatly increased; participants distinguish significantly between the two base rates.

Processing Difficulty

As with the processing of message and cue information in persuasive contexts, the processing of statistical and representativeness information may be affected by its length and complexity. In the original demonstrations, the base-rate information was presented briefly, up front, in a single sentence. The case information followed and was presented in a relatively lengthy vignette. If we assume that participants in those studies had sufficient degrees of processing motivation and cognitive capacity, they may have been inclined to process the lengthier, more difficult-to-digest information and hence may have given it considerable weight, just as in classic persuasion studies the lengthier, later-appearing message information had the greater impact under high motivation or capacity.

But if processing difficulty is what matters, we should be able to vary the use of statistical information by varying its processing difficulty. To accomplish this, in one condition we presented the usual sequence of brief base-rate information followed by extensive case information. In the novel condition we presented *brief case information* followed by *more extensive base-rate information*. Participants in that condition read that "We collected data regarding a group of people. One member of the group is Dan. His hobbies are home carpentry, sailing and mathematical puzzles [this constituted the brief presentation condition]. He was drawn randomly from that group of people. The group included 14% criminal lawyers, 6% trade lawyers, 9% mechanical engineers, 4% patent lawyers, 10% human rights lawyers, 11% electrical engineers, 12% public defense lawyers, 8% divorce lawyers, 10% nuclear engineers, and 16% tax lawyers" [this constituted the lengthy and complex presentation condition]. The participants' task was to judge the likelihood that the target was an engineer.

As shown in Figure 7.12, when the base rate was presented briefly and up front, it had an advantage *under cognitive load* (just like peripheral cues under low-elaboration conditions), where participants in the 70% engineer condition ($M = 62.00$) differed significantly from participants in the 30% engineer condition ($M = 43.33$); in the *absence of load*, there was no significant difference between these two conditions ($M = 76.67$ and $M = 62.22$, respectively).

A very different pattern of results were obtained with the lengthy/complex base-rate information. Here the load constitutes a handicap, not an advantage. Specifically, base rates had no effect *under load* ($M = 50.00$ and $M = 42.86$, respectively). They did, however, have an effect in the *absence of load* (just like message arguments, typically, under high-elaboration conditions), where participants in the 70% engineer condition ($M = 61.25$)

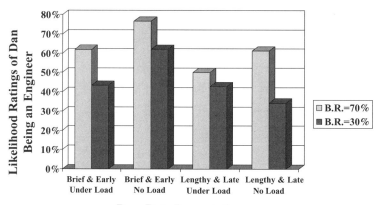

Figure 7.12. Likelihood of Dan's being an engineer as a function of information presentation and load.

were significantly more likely to estimate that the target was an engineer than participants in the 30% engineer condition ($M = 34.29$).

In short, it appears that the use of statistical and nonstatistical (i.e., heuristic) information is governed by the same parameters that determine persuasion or attribution. There seems to be nothing special or qualitatively different about the use of statistical versus nonstatistical information.

CONCLUSION

The theory and data presented in this chapter support the idea that human judgment is determined by an intersection of several dimensional parameters that are present at some of their values in every instance of judgment.[3] This notion offers a number of advantages.

1. It is simpler and more parsimonious than prior notions.
2. Its predictions are supported when pitted against the dual-mode predictions.

---

[3] The foregoing analysis focused on content confounds within major dual-process models. What about content-free dual-process models? Our analysis is not incompatible with the possibility that some dual-process models will prove to be valid, but it suggests that we should approach each such candidate model with caution. The most general content-free dual-process model available today rests on the distinction between associative and rule-based judgments (Sloman, 1996; Smith & DeCoster, 2000). However, as Sloman (1996) himself noted, *any* putatively associative effect can be reinterpreted in terms of a rule-following process. Furthermore, the fact that some inferences may occur very quickly, outside the individual's conscious awareness and with only minimal dependence on cognitive resources (as in the work of Uleman [1987] on spontaneous trait-inferences), does not imply a qualitatively separate cognitive process. Some if-then inferential rules may be *overlearned* to the point of automaticity (Bargh, 1996), and Uleman's spontaneous inferences are if-then

3. It is more flexible than prior notions (e.g., in suggesting that any information can appear anywhere in the sequence considered by the knower, that any information type can be processed effortfully or effortlessly, and that any information can be impactful or not under the appropriate conditions).

4. It suggests a novel research direction of refocusing theoretical and empirical work in the human judgment field from judgmental contents to judgmental parameters.

We would like to close with a note of appreciation for the dual-process models. Though we have proposed a general alternative to these formulations, we hardly think they should not have been proposed or that they did not make fundamental contributions. Quite to the contrary, we feel that they were extremely important, that they moved the science of human judgment a long way, and that they solved important problems and identified important phenomena. The unimodel has benefited immensely from concepts, findings, and methodological paradigms developed by the dual-process theorists, and its formulation would not have been possible otherwise. In that sense, it merely carries the work that they initiated one step further.

References

Anderson, N. H. (1971). Integration theory and attitude change. *Psychological Review, 78*, 171–206.

Bargh, J. A. (1996). Automaticity in social psychology. In E. T. Higgins & A. W. Kruglanski (Eds.), *Social psychology: Handbook of basic principles* (pp. 169–183). New York: Guilford Press.

Bohner, G., Chaiken, S., & Hunyadi, P. (1994). The role of mood and message ambiguity in the interplay of heuristic and systematic processing. *European Journal of Social Psychology, 24*, 207–221.

inferences after all. In terms of the unimodel, the relevant information in such automatized cases would be characterized by very low degrees of processing difficulty, and hence would require very low degrees of processing motivation and cognitive capacity. Also, according to the unimodel, semantic associations alone do not a judgment make, because not all associations that come to mind are relevant to the topic at hand. For instance, imagine that you observed John smile. This may evoke the association "friendly" and also the memory of a *teeth-bleaching ad* claiming to improve the quality of one's smile. Only the former association, of course, would affect the judgment that John is friendly because of the subjective relevance of smiling to friendliness. The moral of the story is that associations affect judgments only if they activate (subjectively) relevant if-then rules. According to this argument, associationistic processes need not be viewed as a qualitative alternative to a rule-following process assumed by the unimodel. Associations may activate certain constructs, hence making them accessible, but only those among the activated constructs that are also subjectively relevant would be used in judgment formation.

Bohner, G., Ruder, M., & Erb, H. P. (in press). When expertise backfires: Contrast and assimilation in persuasion. *British Journal of Social Psychology.*

Brewer, M. B. (1988). A dual process model of impression formation. In T. K. Srull & R. S. Wyer (Eds.), *Advances in social cognition* (Vol. 1, pp. 1–36). Hillsdale, NJ: Erlbaum.

Cacioppo, J. T., & Petty, R. E. (1982). The need for cognition. *Journal of Personality and Social Psychology, 42,* 116–131.

Chaiken, S., Liberman, A., & Eagly, A. H. (1989). Heuristic and systematic processing within and beyond the persuasion context. In J. S. Uleman & J. A. Bargh (Eds.), *Unintended thought* (pp. 212–252). New York: Guilford Press.

Chaiken, S., & Maheswaran, D. (1994). Heuristic processing can bias systematic processing: Effects of source credibility, argument ambiguity, and task importance on attitude judgments. *Journal of Personality and Social Psychology, 66,* 460–473.

Chaiken, S., & Trope, Y. (Eds.). (1999). *Dual-process theories in social psychology.* New York: Guilford Press.

Chun, W. Y., Spiegel, S., & Kruglanski, A. W. (2002). Assimilative behavior identification can also be resource-dependent: A unimodal-based analysis of dispositional attribution phases. *Journal of Personality and Social Psychology, 83,* 542–555.

Cole, M., & Scribner, S. (1974). *Culture and thought: A psychological introduction.* New York: Wiley.

Cosmides, L., & Tooby, J. (1996). Are humans good intuitive statisticians after all? Rethinking some conclusions from the literature on judgment under uncertainty. *Cognition, 58,* 1–73.

Darke, P. R., Chaiken, S., Bohner, G., Einwiller, S., Erb, H.-P., & Hazelwood, D. (1998). Accuracy motivation, consensus information, and the law of large numbers: Effects on attitude judgments in the absence of argumentation. *Personality and Social Psychology Bulletin, 24,* 1205–1215.

Ditto, P. H., & Lopez, D. F. (1992). Motivated skepticism: Use of differential decision criteria for preferred and nonpreferred conclusions. *Journal of Personality and Social Psychology, 63,* 568–584.

Duncan, B. L. (1976). Differential social perception and attribution of intergroup violence: Testing the lower limits of stereotyping of blacks. *Journal of Personality and Social Psychology, 34,* 590–598.

Dunning, D. (1999). A newer look: Motivated social cognition and the schematic representation of social concepts. *Psychological Inquiry, 10,* 1–11.

Erb, H-P., Kruglanski, A. W., Chun, W. Y., Pierro, A., Mannetti, L., & Spiegel, S. (in press). Beyond the trees and into the forest: On commonalities underlying differences in modes of human judgment. *European Review of Social Psychology.*

Evans, B. T., Jr. (1989). *Bias in human reasoning: Causes and consequences.* Hove, UK: Erlbaum.

Evans, B. T., Sr., Handley, S. J., Perham, N., Over, D. E., & Thompson, V. A. (2000). Frequency versus probability formats in statistical word problems. *Cognition, 77,* 197–213.

Festinger, L. (1957). *A theory of cognitive dissonance.* Evanston, IL: Row, Peterson.

Fishbein, M., & Ajzen, I. (1975). *Belief, attitude, intention, and behavior: An introduction to theory and research.* Reading, MA: Addison-Wesley.

Fiske, S. T., & Neuberg, S. L. (1990). A continuum model of impression formation, from category-based to individuating processes: Influences of information and motivation on attention and interpretation. In M. P. Zanna (Ed.), *Advances in experimental social psychology* (Vol. 23, pp. 1–74). New York: Academic Press.

Gigerenzer, G., & Hoffrage, U. (1995). How to improve Bayesian reasoning without instruction: Frequency formats. *Psychological Review, 102,* 684–704.

Grice, H. P. (1975). Logic and conversation. In P. Cole & J. L. Morgan (Eds.), *Syntax and semantics 3: Speech acts* (pp. 41–58). San Diego, CA: Academic Press.

Hamilton, D. L., & Sherman, S. J. (1999). Dualities and continua: Implications for understanding perceptions of persons and groups. In S. Chaiken & Y. Trope (Eds.), *Dual-process theories in social psychology* (pp. 606–626). New York: Guilford Press.

Higgins, E. T. (1997). Beyond pleasure and pain. *American Psychologist, 52,* 1280–1300.

Jacoby, L. L., Kelley, C. M., Brown, J., & Jasechko, J. (1989). Becoming famous overnight: Limits on the ability to avoid unconscious influences of the past. *Journal of Personality and Social Psychology, 56,* 326–338.

Jarvis, W. B. G., & Petty, R. E. (1996). The need to evaluate. *Journal of Personality and Social Psychology, 70,* 172–194.

Jones, E. E., & Davis, K. E. (1965). From acts to dispositions: The attribution process in person perception. In L. Berkowitz (Ed.), *Advances in experimental social psychology* (Vol. 2, pp. 219–266). San Diego, CA: Academic Press.

Kahneman, D., & Tversky, A. (1982). On the study of statistical intuitions. *Cognition, 11,* 123–141.

Kelley, H. H. (1967). Attribution theory in social psychology. In D. Levine (Ed.), *Nebraska symposium on motivation* (Vol. 15, pp. 192–240). Lincoln: University of Nebraska Press.

Kruglanski, A. W. (1989a). *Lay epistemics and human knowledge: Cognitive and motivational bases.* New York: Plenum Press.

Kruglanski, A. W. (1989b). The psychology of being "right": The problem of accuracy in social perception and cognition. *Psychological Review, 106,* 395–409.

Kruglanski, A. W. (1990). Lay epistemic theory in social cognitive psychology. *Psychological Inquiry, 1,* 181–197.

Kruglanski, A. W. (1999). Motivation, cognition, and reality: Three memos for the next generation of research. *Psychological Inquiry, 10,* 54–58.

Kruglanski, A. W., & Webster, D. M. (1996). Motivated closing of the mind: "Seizing" and "freezing." *Psychological Review, 103,* 263–283.

Kunda, Z. (1990). The case of motivated reasoning. *Psychological Review, 108,* 480–498.

Kunda, Z., & Sinclair, L. (1999). Motivated reasoning with stereotypes: Activation, application, and inhibition. *Psychological Inquiry, 10,* 12–22.

Lord, C. G., Ross, L., & Lepper, M. R. (1979). Biased assimilation and attitude polarization: The effects of prior theories on subsequently considered evidence. *Journal of Personality and Social Psychology, 37,* 2098–2109.

Mackie, D. M. (1987). Systematic and nonsystematic processing of majority and minority persuasive communications. *Journal of Personality and Social Psychology, 53,* 41–52.

McGuire, W. J. (1960). A syllogistic analysis of cognitive relationships. In C. I. Hovland & M. J. Rosenberg (Eds.), *Attitude organization and change: An analysis of consistency among attitude components* (pp. 65–111). New Haven, CT: Yale University Press.

McGuire, W. J. (1968). Personality and attitude change: An information processing theory. In A. G. Greenwald, T. C. Brock, & T. M. Ostrom (Eds.), *Psychological foundations of attitudes* (pp. 171–196). San Diego, CA: Academic Press.

Mischel, W., & Shoda, Y. (1995). A cognitive-affective system theory of personality: Reconceptualizing situations, dispositions, dynamics and invariance in personality structure. *Psychological Review, 102,* 246–268.

Nisbett, R. E., Cheng, P. W., Fong, G. T., & Lehman, D. (1987). *Teaching reasoning.* Unpublished manuscript, University of Michigan.

Petty, R. E., & Cacioppo, J. T. (1984). The effects of involvement on responses to argument quantity and quality: Central and peripheral routes to persuasion. *Journal of Personality and Social Psychology, 46,* 69–81.

Petty, R. E., & Cacioppo, J. T. (1986). The elaboration likelihood model of persuasion. In L. Berkowitz (Ed.), *Advances in experimental social psychology* (Vol. 19, pp. 123–205). San Diego, CA: Academic Press.

Petty, R. E., Schumann, D. W., Richman, S. A., & Strathman, A. J. (1993). Positive mood and persuasion: Different roles for affect under high- and low-elaboration conditions. *Journal of Personality and Social Psychology, 64,* 5–20.

Petty, R. E., Wheeler, S. C., & Bizer, G. Y. (1999). Is there one persuasion process or more? Lumping versus splitting in attitude change theories. *Psychological Inquiry, 10,* 156–163.

Ryan, R. M., Sheldon, K. M., Kasser, T., & Deci, E. L. (1996). All goals are not created equal: An organismic perspective on the nature of goals and their regulation. In P. M. Gollwitzer & J. A. Bargh (Eds.), *The psychology of action* (pp. 7–26). New York: Guilford Press.

Schwarz, N., & Clore, G. L. (1996). Feelings and phenomenal experiences. In E. T. Higgins & A. W. Kruglanski (Eds.), *Social psychology: A handbook of basic principles* (pp. 433–465). New York: Guilford Press.

Schwarz, N., Strack, F., Hilton, D., & Naderer, G. (1991). Base rates, representativeness, and the logic of conversation: The contextual relevance of "irrelevant" information. *Social Cognition, 9,* 67–84.

Sedlmeier, P. (1999). *Improving statistical reasoning: Theoretical models and practical implications.* Mahwah, NJ: Erlbaum.

Sloman, S. A. (1996). The empirical case for two systems of reasoning. *Psychological Bulletin, 119,* 3–22.

Smith, E. R., & DeCoster, J. (2000). Dual-process models in social and cognitive psychology: Conceptual integration and links to underlying memory systems. *Personality and Social Psychology Review, 4,* 108–131.

Tetlock, P. E. (1985). Accountability: A social check on the fundamental attribution error. *Social Psychology Quarterly, 48,* 227–236.

Trope, Y. (1986). Identification and inferential processes in dispositional attribution. *Psychological Review, 93,* 239–257.

Trope, Y., & Alfieri, T. (1997). Effortfulness and flexibility of dispositional judgment processes. *Journal of Personality and Social Psychology, 73,* 662–674.

Trope, Y., & Gaunt, R. (1999). A dual-process model of overconfident attributional inferences. In S. Chaiken & Y. Trope (Eds.), *Dual-process theories in social psychology* (pp. 161–179). New York: Guilford Press.

Trope, Y., & Gaunt, R. (2000). Processing alternative explanations of behavior: Correction or integration? *Journal of Personality and Social Psychology, 79*, 344–354.

Trope, Y., & Liberman, A. (1996). Social hypothesis testing: Cognitive and motivational mechanisms. In E. T. Higgins & A. W. Kruglanski (Eds.), *Social psychology: Handbook of basic principles* (pp. 239–270). New York: Guilford Press.

Tversky, A., & Kahneman, D. (1974). Judgment under uncertainty: Heuristics and biases. *Science, 185*, 1124–1130.

Uleman, J. S. (1987). Consciousness and control: The case of spontaneous trait inferences. *Personality and Social Psychology Bulletin, 13*, 337–354.

Wason, P. C. (1966). Reasoning. In B. M. Foss (Ed.), *New horizons in psychology* (pp. 113–135). Harmondsworth, Middlesex, UK: Penguin Books.

Weber, M. (1947). *The theory of social and economic organization.* Glencoe, IL: Free Press.

Webster, D. M., & Kruglanski, A. W. (1998). Cognitive and social consequences of the need for cognitive closure. In W. Stroebe & M. Hewstone (Eds.), *European review of social psychology* (Vol. 8, pp. 133–141). Chichester, UK: Wiley.

Webster, D. M., Richter, L., & Kruglanski, A. W. (1998). On leaping to conclusions when feeling tired: Mental fatigue effects on impression formation. *Journal of Experimental Social Psychology, 32*, 181–195.

Wyer, R. S., Jr. (1970). Quantitative prediction of belief and opinion change: A further test of a subjective probability model. *Personality and Social Psychology, 16*, 559–570.

8

Social Judgments Based on Pseudocontingencies

A Forgotten Phenomenon

Klaus Fiedler and Peter Freytag

CONTENTS

INTRODUCTION

Is it possible that in the industrious endeavor of contemporary experimental psychology a major phenomenon has simply been missed? To be sure, our startling question refers to a *major* phenomenon that can be expected to play an important role in everyday adaptive behavior. In this chapter, we present such a phenomenon in the area of implicit judgment and decision making. It will be illustrated with both anecdotal and experimental evidence, along with a discussion of its theoretical implications. We (Fiedler & Freytag, 2003) have named the phenomenon *pseudocontingencies* (PCs), which may sound a bit monstrous but precisely conveys its nature. PCs mimic contingencies but on closer inspection turn out to be essentially different. Although confusing PCs with genuine contingencies involves a serious category mistake, both laypeople and experts treat them alike, precisely because PCs often provide the only way to resolve high environmental uncertainty.

The research underlying this chapter was supported by various grants from the German Research Foundation (Deutsche Forschungsgemeinschaft). Correspondence concerning this chapter should be addressed to Klaus Fiedler or Peter Freytag, Department of Psychology, University of Heidelberg, Hauptstrasse 47-51, 69117 Heidelberg, FRG; e-mail: kf@psychologie.uni-heidelberg.de or pf@psychologie.uni-heidelberg.de

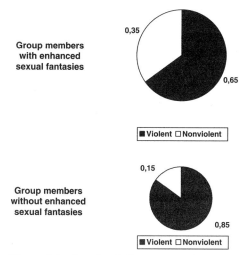

Figure 8.1. Graphical illustration of a PC based on enhanced base rates for sexual fantasies and violence.

Let us introduce the phenomenon by presenting a couple of examples, one referring to lay theories and the other referring to scientific reasoning. To begin, assume that in a minority group with a particular ethnic background, the base rate of, say, sexual fantasies is inflated relative to that of other groups. Assume further that in the same minority group, the base rate of another behavioral tendency, say violent aggression, is also conspicuously high. Such a coincidence of enhanced sexual fantasies and enhanced violence, especially when both tendencies are absent in relevant reference groups, will often give rise to the impression that the two attributes are mutually contingent. Sexual fantasies seem to correlate with violent aggression. One may even feel a sense of causality (e.g., sexual fantasies causing violent aggression). However, closer inspection may reveal the following (Figure 8.1). The proportion of individuals showing pronounced sexual fantasies in the minority group is 75%. Further, the proportion of individuals showing violent aggression is 65% among those who show increased sexual fantasies and 85% among those who do not, yielding an overall base rate of $(0.75 \cdot 65\%) + (0.25 \cdot 85\%) = 70\%$ violent aggression in the group. Note that the violence rate is lower among group members with pronounced sexual associations. Notwithstanding the fact that enhanced base rates for both attributes hold for the group as a whole, the actual contingency between the two is therefore *negative*.

Assuming the two attributes to be mutually contingent thus entails an obvious category mistake. As a matter of principle, the coincidence of two elevated base rates must not be confused with a contingency between the attributes involved. Indeed, given high base rates, evidence for a contingency is particularly hard to get. Empirically, a positive contingency not only requires that the violence rate in people with sexual associations is above average, but also that it exceeds a base rate that is already very high. Over a wide range of values, contingencies are independent of base rates. Holding base rates constant, the violence rate could increase, remain constant, or decrease with the frequency of sexual fantasies. Psychologically, however, lay observers will often fall prey to a PC illusion under these conditions and erroneously infer to have witnessed a relationship that in fact was not there.

Moving from laypeople to experts, consider the following analogy referring to a common scheme in psychological test validation studies. For instance, in an attempt to validate the Implicit Association Test (IAT; Greenwald, McGhee, & Schwartz, 1998) in an applied setting, one may report that members of a target group produce strong IAT effects for some sorts of sexual associations in a first step. Construct validity may then be "secured" in a second step by showing the base rate of various relevant criterion behaviors to be similarly elevated in the same target group, including violent aggression and other related constructs (e.g., perversion, neuroticism). Whenever test validation studies rely on group comparisons rather than interpersonal variation, PC illusions may exist.

DO PCs CONSTITUTE A DISTINCT PHENOMENON?

The question arises whether PCs really represent something new, distinct from other well-known phenomena. One interpretation that suggests itself is in terms of simple associative learning. After all, when two base rates are inflated in a target group, the most frequent event combination will probably refer to the joint occurrence of the most frequent variable levels (e.g., sexual fantasies and violent aggression). Theories of associative learning and conditioning would thus entail the same prediction without postulating a new phenomenon. However, the PC phenomenon is indeed different. It predicts an illusory contingency not only when both base rates are high but also when both base rates are low! For instance, given a low rate of sexual fantasies and a low rate of violent aggression, the two factors should appear to be correlated as well, even though the absolute frequency of the critical observations is particularly low in this case. PCs are therefore distinct from classical conditioning, frequency-based heuristic inference, or density bias (Allan, 1993).

In a similar vein, PCs are distinct from illusory correlations (Fiedler, 2000; Garcia-Marques & Hamilton, 1996), spurious correlations, Simpson's paradox, and other multivariate paradigms (Fiedler, Walther, Freytag, & Stryczek, 2002) that all presuppose that genuine contingency information is encoded in the first place. A premise for all these models and paradigms would be that observers actually receive information about the *joint occurrence* of both attributes in the same individuals. Unless information about the joint frequencies or conditional frequencies (of one attribute given different values of the other attribute) can be assessed directly, a contingency task cannot be performed. In contrast, PCs are not restricted to this (seemingly) necessary condition. One might observe sexual fantasies on one occasion and violent aggression on another, perhaps even years later, without having the slightest chance to coordinate these detached data with the same reference persons, and still infer a strong relationship between these separately encoded attributes.

That PCs are not confined to *inductive* learning is evident in the scientific community's readiness to accept PC-like theoretical explanations at the level of *deductive* reasoning. For example, the following explanation of the confirmation bias in social hypothesis testing was published by Zuckerman, Knee, Hodgins, and Miyake (1995) and accepted by expert reviewers and readers as logically sound. When the task in different experimental conditions is either to test the hypothesis that an interview partner is extraverted or that an interview partner is introverted, either hypothesis tends to be confirmed. Those focusing on extraversion tend to find their partners rather extraverted, whereas those focusing on introversion tend to find them rather introverted. The explanation offered by the authors involves the joint application of two well-established trends. First, it is well known that hypothesis testers engage in positive testing. When focusing on extraversion, they ask more extraversion questions (e.g., referring to time spent with friends). When focusing on introversion, they raise more introversion questions (e.g., referring to time spent on one's own). This tendency is complemented by an acquiescence response tendency. Respondents tend to provide more affirming than disconfirming responses, regardless of the question's focus. Both tendencies together, the questioner's question focus and the respondent's tendency to provide affirming answers, appear to provide a plausible account for the confirmation bias.

This account is based on a PC illusion, though, because acquiescence is by definition *noncontingent*; that is, regardless of whether the majority of questions refer to extraverted or introverted behavior, acquiescence means, say, 75% "yes" responses in general. Logically, then, the account offered by Zuckerman et al. (1995) cannot explain that conversation results in hypothesis confirmation, simply because the confirmation rate remains constant. Rather, an appropriate account must explain why the same confirmation rate is worth more when more data had been gathered on a specific hypothesis (Fiedler, Walther, & Nickel, 1999).

ORIGINS OF PC ILLUSIONS

Granting that PCs may intrude inductive as well as deductive reasoning and given that the underlying mistake can be readily understood, one

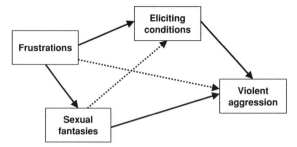

Figure 8.2. Schematic representation of contingencies among potential antecedents of violent aggression.

might speculate about the illusion's evolutionary origin (for related topics, see Haselton & Buss, this volume). Indeed, a closer inspection of our learning environment renders PCs quite plausible – and even indicative of adaptive intelligence. No doubt, assessing (multiple) contingencies between aggression and antecedent factors is of adaptive value. Figure 8.2 identifies three potentially relevant factors: frustrations, sexual fantasies, and eliciting stimuli. To assess the comprehensive relation between all variables, one would have to encode aggressive events contingent on all three factors at the same time. Each memory trace referring to aggressive behavior should not be stored in isolation, but instead should be conditionalized on a certain eliciting condition, a certain frustration level in the aggressor, and a certain level of sexual fantasies. Such a full three-factorial design is hardly ever available. Frustration is a hidden internal state, sexual fantasies may be kept secret, and eliciting conditions may be less apparent to observers than to actors. Even when the full design is available, acquiring systematic data would be a tedious and time-consuming task that would often exceed an observer's capacity or motivation. And even when we engage in complex multifactorial assessment, we may still regret the effort because, at some later time, we have to decide on completely different questions. For instance, having just encoded aggression as a function of frustration, sexual fantasies, and eliciting conditions, we may find ourselves in a situation that requires a decision on whether aggression increases with, say, heat or skin color.

As a matter of principle, it is impossible to gather simultaneously empirical data on all contingency problems that happen to become relevant at some later time. What can we do in the face of this dilemma? A useful heuristic – which is by no means irrational but which is in fact the heuristic used in empirical sciences – is to rely on approximations from less complex subordinate contingencies. To predict the risk of violent aggression in a particular target group, it would be important, first of all, to recognize the base rate of aggression. If the base rate is extreme enough, assessing contingencies between aggression and eliciting conditions may be dysfunctional; it may be more adaptive to avoid such a situation altogether, rather than trying to acquire contingency information in too dangerous an environment. As noted by Kareev (2000), the risks and information costs of contingency learning are justified only when the base rate is not too extreme.

In the latter case, however, more control might be achieved by a model that explains when aggression occurs. Lacking a full design of all relevant factors, a useful proxy might be to assess other relevant factors having enhanced (or reduced) base rates in the target group. When the sexual fantasy base rate is high, and the violent aggression base rate too, this coincidence could provide the basis for the inference that sexual fantasies and aggression are somehow related to each other. If another base rate is elevated, say the frustration base rate, this triple coincidence supports an explanation of aggression in terms of both factors; for example, both sexual fantasies and heightened frustration levels could reflect the same sort of deprivation that explains the target group's aggressiveness. Such an inference would be in line not only with common attribution theories (Jones & McGillis, 1976; Kelley, 1973) but also with reasoning schemes in politics and economics. In any case, taking PCs as a proxy is presumably the best strategy an organism can apply in a complex environment, for it helps to identify highly probable event combinations in the absence of covariation information.

EMPIRICAL EVIDENCE

Positive PCs

To demonstrate PC illusions experimentally, one ought to rule out prior knowledge and expectancies. Accordingly, the first series of PC experiments (cf. Fiedler & Freytag, 2003) referred to two unspecified personality tests, X and Y. The experimental cover story mentioned two groups of people, those in which psychotherapy is successful and those in which psychotherapy fails. For convenience, let us refer to groups A and B, respectively. In the first part of the stimulus presentation series, participants were informed about the outcomes on test X of various members of both groups. Rather than merely providing a numerical test score, each stimulus displayed the profile of a respondent's outcome on 12 items of the test. Aggregating over all 12 items, participants had to assess within a few seconds whether the overall (average) value of the respondent on a test was high (mean value about 1.0) or low (mean value about 3.0). To control how accurately participants had identified the test value in question, they were asked to provide online estimates of the mean test value they had just seen using a vertical graphical bar that could be adjusted on a scale ranging from 0 to 4.0. In this manner, participants learned over the course of 36 trials that high test X values prevailed in members of one group, whereas low test X values prevailed in members of the other group. Specifically, the stimulus distribution was 24 high and 12 low test scores in group A compared to 12 high and 24 low scores in group B. In a second run, participants learned about test Y scores of members of the same two groups. The group in which high test X scores had predominated (i.e., A) also had more high (24) than low (12) scores on test Y, and the group in which low X scores had prevailed (i.e., B) also had more low (24) than high (12) test Y scores. Again, graphical online ratings revealed that participants correctly encoded the base rate distributions.

In fact, the X and Y test scores assessed in the first and second parts of the stimulus series belonged to the same individuals from the two groups. However, as X and Y scores were presented in separate runs, participants had no chance to encode the actual contingency, which accorded to the distribution in Figure 8.3. However, the alignment of two skewed base rate distributions should create a PC illusion. Participants should come to believe that X and Y are correlated within both groups due to the co-occurrence of either high X and high Y values (group A) or low X and low Y values (group B).

For a suitable test, a simple prediction task was administered. In each of the 16 prediction task trials, a new member of either group A or group B was presented whose score on either test X or test Y was given in the same graphical format as in the online rating during the learning phase, and participants were asked to predict the new member's score on the other test using the same graphical adjustment device as before. A PC effect would be evident in a positive correlation between the given and

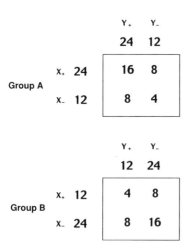

Figure 8.3. Stimulus distributions used to induce PC illusions for two-level variables characterized by skewed marginal distributions.

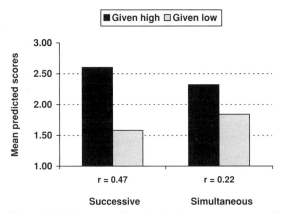

Figure 8.4. Mean predicted criterion test scores as a function of predictor test scores (high vs. low) and presentation mode (successive vs. simultaneous).

predicted values on this task. That is, given a high value on the predictor test, the values adjusted for the other test should be higher than when a low value was given on the predictor test – regardless of whether X was given and Y left open to be predicted or Y was given and X to be predicted. Moreover, the PC illusion should hold for (the high-scoring) group A as well as for (the low-scoring) group B.

In fact, the correlations between X and Y produced on the prediction test were fairly above zero for most of the participants (see the first pair of bars in Figure 8.4). There was a regular tendency to predict higher values on one test when the given values on the other test were high rather than low, and to predict lower values when the given values were low rather than high. Virtually the same trends held for predictions with test X (Y) as the predictor and test Y (X) as the criterion. The positive relation was not confined to those prediction task trials that involved the frequently paired test scores. When the most frequently paired test scores in a group were high X and high Y values, predictions from low Y and low X values yielded the same positive relation, emphasizing the independence of PCs from simple associative learning effects.

Thus, even though no contingency information was provided – observations of X and Y were presented in separate runs, making contingent encoding impossible – the alignment of two skewed base rate distributions created the illusion that X and Y were positively related, as evident in participants' predictions. To be sure, a manipulation check showed that judges did recognize the skewed base rates. That is, they ought to have known that a coincidence of high X and high Y scores in the one group (and of low X and low Y scores in the other) could be expected from the base rates alone.

Given the tendency to infer PCs from joint base-rate manipulations, the idea suggests itself that the same tendency might be at work in tasks that look like contingency tasks. Thus, when information about a person's X and Y scores is given simultaneously rather than in successive runs, making the contingent encoding of both variables possible, there is no guarantee that participants encode the contingency proper. Instead, they might still be sensitive to the alignment of X and Y base rates, which might actually override the genuine contingency information. To test this consideration empirically, we repeated the experiment described previously with simultaneous rather than successive presentation of X and Y test scores. Note that although the base rates of high (low) X and high (low) Y were aligned in the two target groups, the proportion of high versus low scores on one test were the same for high and low levels of the other test – yielding a zero correlation (Figure 8.3). Nevertheless, the participants' predictions yielded a PC pattern similar to that of successive presentation (see the second pair of bars in Figure 8.4).

One intriguing implication that suggests itself is that PC illusions – reflecting confusion of base rate and contingency information – may be involved in many other demonstrations of illusory correlations based on the joint infrequency of two attributes (e.g., minority group membership and undesirable behaviors in Hamilton & Gifford, 1976). Unlike previous explanations of illusory correlations, the PC effect suggests that joint base rates may be sufficient to explain the tendency to associate variables sharing high versus low base rates. Beyond previous accounts of illusory correlations (Fiedler, 1991, 2000; Hamilton & Sherman, 1989), the PC effect holds for individuating predictions from the frequent as well as the infrequent categories and, as we shall demonstrate later, also for predictions referring to event combinations for which no information was presented at all.

Negative PCs

Having demonstrated the basic phenomenon, we extended the current line of research in an attempt to address the scope of the PC illusion. Most obviously, the findings presented so far demonstrated only positive PCs. That is, the mere alignment of two similarly skewed distributions was shown to be sufficient to create the impression that increasing levels in one variable coincide with increasing levels in another variable. If our premise that the alignment of stimulus distributions via similarities in mean, skew, or variability is the driving force underlying PC illusions, then the effect should also show up when the characteristics of two distributions point in opposite directions. More specifically, a negative PC should be observed under these conditions.

This corollary was tested in an experiment designed to evoke positive *or* negative PCs for the same set of observations (Freytag, 2001, Exp. 1). Higher values for one attribute dimension were made to appear associated with higher or lower values for another attribute dimension by systematic variations in frame of reference. Specifically, verbal descriptions of the behavior performed by individual group members served to make participants familiar with a focal category of students showing intermediate degrees of commitment to their studies and low degrees of commitment to their social lives. For half of the participants, this category was contrasted with a context category whose members showed high degrees of commitment to either domain of life. Under these conditions, *relatively low* degrees of commitment to either domain of life should be associated with *relatively low* degrees of commitment to the other. That is, the pattern typical of a positive PC illusion should emerge. For the other half of the participants, however, the members of the context category showed high degrees of commitment to their social life only, whereas commitment to one's studies was extremely low. Under these conditions, *relatively low* degrees of commitment to either domain of life should be associated with *relatively high* degrees of commitment to the other. Pretests made sure that the commitment values associated with the verbal descriptions always constituted a zero contingency between the two domains of life within each type of student. Again, the prediction task served as the main dependent variable.

The results were clearly in line with a PC interpretation. When the context category scored above the focal category on either attribute dimension, higher (lower) given values for one domain of life evoked higher (lower) predicted values for the other domain of life, thus replicating the familiar pattern of a positive PC illusion. When the context category scored above the focal category on one dimension and lower on the other, however, higher (lower) given values for one domain of life evoked lower (higher) predicted values for the other. That is, a reliable negative PC illusion emerged. One may argue that the specific attributes selected in this study worked in favor of a negative PC, because folk wisdom has it that commitment to one's job and social life tend to be negatively correlated. However, such an expectation bias cannot account for the strong PC effects obtained in both the negative and the positive PC conditions of this experiment. A second alternative explanation that suggests itself is that participants may actively create positive or negative interattribute relations over the course of stimulus presentation. Once the clear and stable intercategory differences for the two domains of life have been noticed, processes of perceptual accentuation (Krueger, 1992; Tajfel & Wilkes, 1963) may turn the manipulated zero contingency within categories into subjectively experienced positive and negative contingencies in the respective conditions.

To rule out the latter alternative explanation, participants in a replication of the preceding experiment were asked to actively rate, rather than merely monitor, the perceived degree of commitment to the two domains of life for individual category members in a series of online ratings (Freytag, 2001, Exp. 2). In this manner, the contingencies produced in the prediction task could be analyzed as a function of both the intergroup context and the intragroup contingency produced in online ratings. The basic PC was replicated under these conditions and, what is more, mediational analyses revealed that the online ratings could account for only a small proportion of the reported PC effect.

Determinants of Effect Size

Thus far, we have shown that PCs generalize over different content domains (abstract personality tests vs. more concrete domains of life), presentation modes (successive vs. simultaneous), and alignment strategies (skew vs. frame of reference). However, the strength of the PC illusion can also be expected to vary with changes in the parameters of its inductive component. For example, if the skew in the underlying distributions plays a key role in the emergence of the PC illusion, one may expect that more extremely skewed distributions should yield more extreme PCs. This implication was tested in an experiment (Fiedler & Freytag, 2003) using three-level rather than two-level attributes in the personality test setting described previously. As depicted in Figure 8.5, the frequency distribution underlying stimulus presentation in this study was based on test scores that could take on low, intermediate, or high levels. The enhanced skew of the underlying distributions is manifest in marginal frequencies of 24 high, 6 intermediate, and 6 low test scores in either test in the group scoring

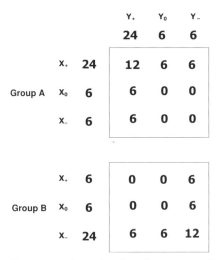

Figure 8.5. Stimulus distributions used to induce PC illusions for multilevel variables characterized by extremely skewed marginal distributions.

predominantly high, and 6 high, 6 intermediate, and 24 low test scores for either test in the group scoring predominantly low. Note that the resulting correlation between the two tests is actually negative ($r = -.43$ if only high and low values are considered). Note also that some of the cells in the 3×3 table remain empty, that is, some combinations of test values are absent from the stimulus list. Granting that participants accurately encode stimulus information, the crucial question was whether predictions would still follow the simple association of (in)frequently observed test scores. In other words, would participants continue to associate higher test scores in one test with higher test scores in another test, thereby turning an objectively negative contingency into a positive PC? And if so, would they even predict event combinations that had not been presented at all?

Both of these speculations received strong empirical support. The mere alignment of similarly skewed distributions induced a strong belief in a mutually contingent relationship between the two tests. Moreover, increasing the skew of the marginal distributions led to even more illusory predictions, yielding an average correlation between given and predicted values of $r = .69$. Thus, the substantial negative correlation encoded during stimulus presentation turned into a substantial positive correlation in the immediately administered prediction task. An even more intriguing aspect of these results is that the overwhelming majority of participants produced event combinations that had been completely absent during stimulus presentation. In the group scoring predominantly low, for example, predicting a relatively high score in the criterion test from a relatively high score in the predictor test means creating an event combination that refers to an empty cell in the lower part of Figure 8.5. These results are all the more remarkable as the present study used simultaneous presentation of stimulus information only, thus equipping participants with the information necessary for actual contingency assessment. Moreover, subsequent manipulation checks once more showed that participants had accurately encoded the skewed base rates within each group, making incorrect encoding and retrieval an unlikely candidate for an alternative explanation.

In view of the strength of the PC illusion observed when extremely skewed marginal distributions are learned in the presence of contrasting categories, we ran an additional experimental group using a singular target group in order to determine the relative contribution of skew. Using the stimulus series used for the group scoring predominantly high on both tests (see the upper half of Figure 8.5), a significant but reduced PC illusion was obtained. Specifically, the correlation between given and predicted test scores dropped to $r = .19$. Thus, participants continued to associate higher predictor test scores with higher criterion test scores, but this tendency was weaker in the absence of a contrasting category. Aside from possible reductions in cognitive load or biased recall, we see at least two plausible explanations for this discrepancy. First, the same tendency toward predominantly high test scores may be more apparent when a reverse relationship holds in a contrasting category.

Second, the enhanced magnitude of the effect observed for contrasting categories could be due in part to context-sensitive variation in the perceived prototypicality of frequently versus infrequently observed attribute levels in these conditions. Specifically, according to the metacontrast principle proposed in self-categorization theory (e.g., Oakes, Haslam, & Turner, 1998; Turner, 1987), the typicality of a stimulus is assumed to increase not only as differences from other exemplars in the same category decrease, but also as differences from stimuli in contrasting categories increase. In view of the fact that the frequently observed variable levels in those studies involving contrasting categories always pronounced differences from the contrasting category, our participants may simply have determined the typicality of the given attribute in a first step and then inferred a similarly (a)typical value for the to-be-predicted attribute in a second step. From this point of view, performance in the prediction task would be reminiscent of typicality-based judgment strategies known from the person perception literature (e.g., Fiske & Neuberg, 1990; Lambert & Wyer, 1990).

Extension to Natural Contexts

Having found a robust PC across several experiments with relatively abstract variables, in which prior expectancies were negligible, we finally report one experiment embedded in a more meaningful context. The twofold purpose here is to highlight the generality of the phenomenon and to suggest real-world analogies. The experiment took place within the simulated-classroom environment (Fiedler, Walther, Freytag, & Plessner, 2002) – a recently developed paradigm for studying social inference and hypothesis testing processes in a complex seminatural setting. The simulated classroom consists of 16 students, 8 boys and 8 girls, sitting in fixed positions in the classroom represented on the computer screen. Participants have to play the role of a teacher who is to teach the students in various disciplines or lessons. For each lesson, a list of knowledge questions is available in a pull-down menu from which the teacher can choose one on each trial. The chosen question is then inserted in the classroom display, and some of the students raise their hands, indicated graphically. The teacher must then call upon one student, whose answer turns out to be correct or incorrect. Across a large number of such trials, the teacher can figure out the performance differences between students in terms of ability (proportion correct) and motivation (rate of hand raising when a question is being asked). The actual ability and motivation parameters are specified in a students by lessons matrix. That is, the computer is programmed such that the probability with which a given student raises his or her hand in a given lesson is determined experimentally, just like the probability that the student will give a correct answer. Experiments in the simulated classroom are typically extended over several sessions and many hours. Teacher participants report developing personal relationships with the individual students that can be viewed on photographs and that have to be evaluated after each lesson.

Here we are concerned only with one experiment (Fiedler et al., 2002, Exp. 3) that involved a very simple manipulation of the ability base rate. In the high-ability condition, the ability parameter was constantly high (A = 0.7), whereas in the low-ability condition, the ability parameter was constantly low (A = 0.3). Whoever was asked, the likelihood of a correct answer was either uniformly high or uniformly low. The motivation parameter was held constant (for all students) at a medium level (M = 0.5) in both conditions. However, because it is impossible to monitor all 16 students' motivation rates at the same time, teachers' subjective estimates of motivation varied substantially. In particular, they believed that those students at whom they directed most questions had actually raised their hands more frequently than those students whom they had neglected. It is unimportant, for the present purpose, whether this subjective variation originates in sampling error or in teachers' preconceptions.

The major results of interest meet all criteria of the familiar PC effect, such that ability ratings should be contingent on motivation ratings in a characteristic way. First, the actual contingency was set to zero, because in both experimental conditions the latent parameters for motivation (M = 0.5) as well as ability (A = 0.3 or 0.7) in the population were held constant. Second, the perceived base rate of motivation and ability in the samples of stimulus observations came to match or to be opposite. Thus, in the high-ability environment (A = 0.7), a high base rate of raising hands coincided with a high base rate of correct responses, whereas in the low-ability environment (A = 0.3), a high base rate of raising hands coincided with a low base rate of incorrect responses. These base rate coincidences should produce a positive PC between motivation and ability in the high-ability environment (i.e., the impression that ability is higher in highly motivated students) but a negative PC in the low-ability environment (i.e., the impression that ability is reduced in highly motivated students). Exactly this pattern was corroborated by the findings. Students who appeared to raise their hands very often were rated as giving more correct answers than less motivated students in the high-ability condition. The opposite held in the low-ability condition, where ability ratings for students who raised their hands very often were reduced.

Thus, PC illusions can provide both an account of the naive theory that the smartest students are also the ones who cooperate most, as well as a specification of the conditions that would have to be met in the environment to trigger complementary beliefs. We believe that complex environments like the simulated classroom – and even more so the real world – afford a rich source of such PC illusions because the multitude of possible contingencies is too complex to be assessed and the only level at which observers could be sensitive realistically is the base rate of the salient variables.

DISCUSSION

At the beginning of this chapter we introduced PC illusions as a major phenomenon that can play a role in a variety of psychological processes. Did we promise too much? Can the contention be upheld that PCs are of general importance for adaptive behavior in an uncertain environment? We believe that PCs are as ubiquitous as attribute dimensions with skewed distributions, yielding high base rates at one pole and low base rates at the opposite pole. The social and physical stimulus world is basically skewed for several reasons. One generic source of skewed distributions is social norms. By definition, normative behavior is the rule and deviations from the norm are the exception; we would not refer to normative behavior if it were distributed normally or in a rectangular fashion. All kinds of norm violations like criminality, obscenity, neuroticism, abnormal appearance or sexuality, and many other variants give rise to skewed distributions, contrasting high versus low base rates. Another reason is proximity. From individual points of view, some persons and objects are nearby and easy to reach, whereas others are far away and hardly accessible. Therefore, neighbors, in-group members, and people from cultural, geographical, and professional backgrounds similar to one's own are typically more frequent than strangers, out-group members, or people with a different background. Third, the enumerative experience underlying many quantities creates skewed distributions. A good car driver is one who never causes an accident; decreasing driving skill can be defined in terms of a growing number of accidents. As nobody can cause fewer than zero accidents, whereas the distribution is open to the high-frequency side, the distribution of driving skill has to be skewed, with most people causing few, if any, accidents and very few people causing many accidents. For all these reasons – and several others – the conditions for PC illusions are met very often.

One may distinguish PCs between groups, between groups and attributes, or between attributes. For instance, membership in one minority group (e.g., homosexuals) may appear rather high within another minority group (e.g., some ethnic minority), or membership in an ethnic minority may appear related to an infrequent trait attribute (e.g., aggressiveness), or two infrequent attributes (e.g., aggressiveness and illiteracy) may appear related. However, as attributes are needed for defining groups, the distinction may be more apparent than real.

Despite our claim that PCs are probably very widespread, we are more cautious about their precise boundary conditions. Exactly because skewed stimulus distributions are so ubiquitous, one should not expect each and every high or low base rate event to be linked to a PC illusion. Thus, the coincidence of, say, many aggressive drivers on the highway and many cars with four wheels would hardly create the suspicion that four wheels are essential or causally related to aggression. It seems more reasonable to assume that PCs will only link attributes that somehow belong together in terms of domain-specific world knowledge. Thus, aggressiveness may be linked to drivers' personality, and four wheels may be linked to the difference of cars and trucks, but four wheels will be hardly related to aggression. However, admitting these soft constraints, we hasten to add that we do not expect strong constraints on PCs. A low–base rate attribute such as *mental illness* may be related to another low–base rate attribute such as *dangerous*, but it could as well be related to the opposite attribute, *extreme harmlessness*. We definitely refute the contention that PCs are contingent on prior expectancies, as the simulated-classroom experiment has shown: Depending on whether high or low ability was prevalent in the class, either a positive or a negative PC was induced between motivation (raising hands) and ability (correct answer).

Let us finally return to the issue of ecological rationality and the adaptive value of PCs as a proxy for genuine contingencies. Assessing base rate coincidences may be the best an organism can do in a complex environment in which the assessment of the entire covariation matrix is impossible. The adaptive potential is even more evident if one considers that environmental learning tasks often involve changes rather than stable attributes. A high absolute aggression base rate may have been the rule for a long time and may thus go unnoticed. However, when a sudden increase in the aggression rate occurs, and at the same time an increase in the base rate of, say, sexual fantasies, then base rates may become salient. However, in such a case, the question arises of why both base rates increase at the same moment. The temporal coincidence would render it rather unlikely that both changes reflect completely independent factors, although this possibility exists, of course. It would be much more likely that both base rate changes reflect either a common cause or that one base rate change immediately caused the other. In this regard, the PC paradigm may lie at the heart of a theory of causal inference that emphasizes temporal coincidence of base rate changes. In any case, we believe that PC illusions afford a challenge not only for the adaptive organism but also for the researcher who wants to understand and explain the assets and deficits of social cognition.

References

Allan, L. G. (1993). Human contingency judgments: Rule based or associative? *Psychological Bulletin, 114*, 435–448.

Fiedler, K. (1991). The tricky nature of skewed frequency tables: An information loss account of distinctiveness-based illusory correlations. *Journal of Personality and Social Psychology, 60*, 24–36.

Fiedler, K. (2000). Illusory correlations: A simple associative algorithm provides a convergent account of seemingly divergent paradigms. *Review of General Psychology, 4,* 25–58.

Fiedler, K., & Freytag, P. (2003). *Pseudo-contingencies.* Paper submitted for publication.

Fiedler, K., Walther, E., Freytag, P., & Plessner, H. (2002). Judgment biases and pragmatic confusion in a simulated classroom – A cognitive–environmental approach. *Organizational Behavior and Human Decision Processes, 88,* 527–561.

Fiedler, K., Walther, E., Freytag, P., & Stryczek, E. (2002). Playing mating games in foreign cultures: A conceptual framework and an experimental paradigm for trivariate statistical inference. *Journal of Experimental Social Psychology, 38,* 14–30.

Fiedler, K. Walther, E., & Nickel, S. (1999). The autoverification of social hypothesis. Stereotyping and the power of sample size. *Journal of Personality and Social Psychology, 77,* 5–18.

Fiske, S. T., & Neuberg, S. L. (1990). A continuum of impression formation, from category-based to individuating processes: Influences of information and motivation on attention and interpretation. In M. Zanna (Ed.), *Advances in experimental social psychology* (Vol. 23, pp. 1–74). New York: Academic Press.

Freytag, P. (2001). *Contextually determined typicality.* Unpublished dissertation, University of Heidelberg.

Garcia-Marques, L., & Hamilton, D. L. (1996). Resolving the apparent discrepancy between the incongruency effect and the expectancy-based illusory correlation effect: The TRAP model. *Journal of Personality and Social Psychology, 71,* 845–860.

Greenwald, A. G., McGhee, D. E., & Schwartz, J. L. K. (1998). Measuring individual differences in implicit cognition: The implicit association test. *Journal of Personality and Social Psychology, 74,* 1022–1038.

Hamilton, D. L., & Gifford, R. K. (1976). Illusory correlation in interpersonal perception: A cognitive basis of stereotypic judgments. *Journal of Experimental Social Psychology, 12,* 392–407.

Hamilton, D. L., & Sherman, S. J. (1989). Illusory correlations: Implications for stereotype theory and research. In D. Bar-Tal, C. F. Graumann, A. W. Kruglanski, & W. Stroebe (Eds.), *Stereotype and prejudice: Changing conceptions* (pp. 59–82). New York: Springer.

Jones, E. E., & McGillis, D. (1976). Correspondent inferences and the attribution cube: A comparative reappraisal. In J. H. Harvey, W. J. Ickes, & R. F. Kidd (Eds.), *New directions in attribution research* (pp. 389–420). Hillsdale, NJ: Erlbaum.

Kareev, Y. (2000). Seven (indeed, plus or minus two) and the detection of correlations. *Psychological Review, 107,* 397–402.

Kelley, H. H. (1973). The processes of causal attribution. *American Psychologist, 28,* 107–128.

Krueger, J. (1992). On the overestimation of between-group differences. In M. Hewstone & W. Stroebe (Eds.), *European Review of Social Psychology* (Vol. 3, pp. 31–56). Chichester, UK: Wiley.

Lambert, A. J., & Wyer, R. S. (1990). Stereotypes and social judgment: The effects of typicality and group homogeneity. *Journal of Personality and Social Psychology, 59,* 676–691.

Oakes, P. J., Haslam, S. A., & Turner, J. C. (1998). The role of prototypicality in group influence and cohesion: Contextual variation in the graded structure of social categories. In S. Worchel, J. F. Morales, D. Páez, & J. C. Deschamps (Eds.), *Social identity* (pp. 75–92). London: Sage.

Tajfel, H., & Wilkes, A. L. (1963). Classification and quantitative judgement. *British Journal of Psychology, 54,* 101–114.

Turner, J. C. (1987). A self-categorization theory. In J. C. Turner, M. A. Hogg, P. J. Oakes, S. D. Reicher, & M. D. Wetherell (Eds.), *Rediscovering the social group: A self-categorization theory* (pp. 42–67). Oxford: Blackwell.

Zuckerman, M., Knee, C. R., Hodgins, H. S., & Miyake, K. (1995). Hypothesis confirmation: The joint effect of positive test strategy and acquiescence response set. *Journal of Personality and Social Psychology, 68,* 52–60.

9

The Size of Context Effects in Social Judgment

Herbert Bless, Norbert Schwarz,
and Michaela Wänke

CONTENTS

INTRODUCTION

All of us have firsthand experience with the context dependency of social judgment. In one situation we consider ourselves assertive, a politician trustworthy, and the stock market full of potential. At other moments our assertiveness seems less compelling, the politician less trustworthy, and the stock market less enticing. In many cases the variation of judgments is due to a change of judgmental context. This context influences which information comes to mind or how the accessible information is used. So, simply by changing the judgmental context, we may come up with different evaluations about our assertiveness, the politician, or the stock market.

The context dependency of social judgment is one of the most fascinating phenomena in social psychology (see also Forgas & East; McClure, Sutton, & Hilton; and Stapel, this volume). Countless findings from experimental studies and natural observations indicate that the evaluation of a target stimulus may be either assimilated or contrasted to the context in which it is presented. We refer to *assimilation effects* whenever the judgment reflects a positive relation between the implications of some piece of

The reported research was supported by Grants Bl 289/5 from the Deutsche Forschungsgemeinschaft to H. Bless, N. Schwarz, and M. Wänke. Correspondence should be addressed to Herbert Bless, Fakultät für Sozialwissenschaften, Universität Mannheim, D-68131 Mannheim, Germany; e-mail hbless@sowi.uni-mannheim.de information and the judgment, and to *contrast effects* whenever the judgment reflects a negative (inverse) relationship between the judgment and the implications of some piece of information. There is wide agreement among researchers that assimilation and contrast effects may reflect the operation of a number of different processes, which have often been conceptualized in independent theories. One group of models focused on the distribution of the contextual stimuli, assuming that they influence the adaptation level (Helson, 1964), standard of comparison (e.g., Thibaut & Kelley, 1959), or scale anchor (Ostrom & Upshaw, 1968; Parducci, 1965) used in making a judgment. Another group of models focused on categorization processes (e.g., Herr, Sherman, & Fazio, 1983; Martin, 1986; Tajfel, 1981; Turner, 1987). According to these models, assimilation effects are likely to emerge when the target stimulus and the context stimuli are assigned to the same category, whereas contrast effects may emerge when they are assigned to different categories.

Emphasizing the role of information accessibility and categorization processes, we have proposed the inclusion/exclusion model (Schwarz & Bless, 1992a) as a general framework for conceptualizing assimilation and contrast effects in social judgment. Building on theorizing by Barsalou (1987), Herr et al. (1983), Kahneman and Miller (1986), and Martin (1986), the model offers predictions about the emergence, direction, and size of context effects. In this chapter we focus on the latter, often neglected, aspect: What determines the *size* of assimilation and contrast effects? We first review the core assumptions of the inclusion/exclusion model. Next, we elaborate on the model's predictions pertaining to the size of context effects and review supporting evidence. Finally, we highlight the simultaneous operation of direct and indirect context effects, which presents a rarely addressed complication in predicting the size of contextual influences.

THE INCLUSION/EXCLUSION MODEL

The inclusion/exclusion model (Schwarz & Bless, 1992a; see also Bless & Schwarz, 1998; Schwarz, Bless, Wänke, & Winkielman, in press) assumes that the influence of a given piece of information depends on how it is *used*. Evaluative judgments that are based on features of the target (rather than on the perceiver's affective response; see Schwarz & Clore, 1996; see also Forgas & East, this volume; Stapel, this volume) require two mental representations, namely, a representation of the target and a representation of a standard against which the target is evaluated. Both representations are formed on the spot, drawing on information that is chronically or temporarily accessible. Information that is used in forming a representation of the target results in assimilation effects; that is, the inclusion of positive (negative) information results in a more positive (negative) judgment. Conversely, information that is used in forming a representation of the comparison standard results in a contrast effect; that is, more positive (negative) information results in a more positive (negative) standard, against which the target is evaluated less (more) favorably. Hence, the *same* piece of accessible information can have opposite effects, depending on how it is used (see also von Hippel, Vargas, & Sekaquaptewa, this volume).

The inclusion/exclusion model holds that three filters channel information use. First, individuals will exclude accessible information when they believe that this information was brought to mind by some irrelevant influence (Lombardi, Higgins, & Bargh, 1987; Martin, 1986; Strack, Schwarz, Bless, Kübler, & Wänke, 1993; see also Brewer, this volume). Second, information is excluded when it is not considered representative of the target. This decision is driven by the numerous variables known to influence the categorization of information, including the information's extremity and typicality (e.g., Bless & Wänke, 2000; Bless, Schwarz, Bodenhausen, & Thiel, 2001), as well as the presentation format and related context variables (for reviews see Martin, Strack, & Stapel, 2001; Schwarz & Bless, 1992a). A third filter pertains to the norms of conversational conduct that govern information use in conversations. Information is likely to be excluded when its repeated use would violate conversational norms of nonredundancy (e.g., Schwarz, Strack, & Mai, 1991; for a review see Schwarz, 1996).

Information that passes all three filters is included in the representation formed of the target and results in assimilation effects. Information that fails any one of these tests is excluded from the representation formed of the target but may be used in forming a representation of the standard, resulting in contrast effects. In addition to specifying the direction of context effects, the model offers predictions about the size of context effects. In the remainder of this chapter we focus on this aspect.

SET-SIZE EFFECTS IN MENTAL CONSTRUAL

Determinants of the *size* of assimilation and contrast effects have often been neglected in psychological research. One of the more obvious variables is the *extremity* of the accessible context information: The more extreme the information included in the representation of the target or the representation of the standard, the larger the resulting assimilation or contrast effect (Schwarz & Bless, 1992a). Hence, a major political scandal would influence judgments of politicians' trustworthiness more than a minor scandal, for example. Although this logic seems straightforward, a potential caveat needs to be noted. Although more extreme exemplars should be more influential, extreme exemplars are also more likely to be perceived as atypical and may consequently trigger exclusion from, rather than inclusion in, the representation formed of the superordinate category (see Bless & Wänke, 2000; Schwarz & Bless, 1992a). This, in turn, results in contrast effects (e.g., Herr et al., 1983) rather than more pronounced assimilation effects. Moreover, it is worth noting that it is not the extremity of the context information per se but its relative difference from otherwise accessible information that influences the size of an effect: If the chronically accessible information is as extreme as the context information, including the context information in the temporary representation formed of the target has little additional impact.

Theoretically more interesting is a variable that may increase as well as decrease the size of context effects, namely, the *amount* of information used in forming a representation of the target or the standard. As many models of social judgment assume (e.g., Anderson, 1981; Wyer & Srull, 1989), the impact of a given piece of information decreases as the overall amount of information considered increases. We assume that this general *set-size principle* also holds when individuals construct mental representations of the target and the standard of comparison.

Suppose, for example, that an individual constructs a mental representation of a social category ("American politicians") and an extreme exemplar (Nixon) comes to mind due to contextual influences. Including this exemplar in the representation formed results in an assimilation effect. The size of this effect, however, should depend on the amount and extremity of other information used in forming this representation. This logic is depicted in the left panel of Figure 9.1, where either three or six exemplars (E) are used in forming a representation of a superordinate target category. Leaving aside potential differences in the weighing of the exemplars, adding Nixon would contribute either one-fourth or one-seventh to the representation of the social category. In the latter case, the impact of Nixon would hence be smaller than in the former case. These predictions are consistent with numerous studies that investigated information integration in social judgment (see Anderson, 1981). For example, Schwarz and colleagues

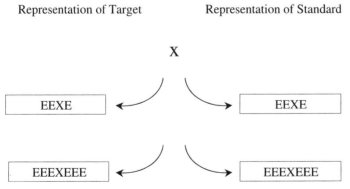

Figure 9.1. Context effects as a function of categorization and amount of competing information.

(1991) observed in a different content domain that inducing participants to think about the quality of their marriage affected subsequent judgments of general life satisfaction more when marriage was the only life domain brought to mind than when marriage was only one of four life domains addressed in preceding questions. As expected, the accessibility of a larger amount of competing information attenuated the impact of marriage-related information.

The inclusion/exclusion model assumes that the same set-size principle applies to the construction of standards of comparison, an issue that has not been addressed in information integration research. If standards of comparison are constructed on the basis of accessible information, the size of contrast effects should parallel the previous predictions. First, the impact of a given extreme piece of information should decrease as a function of the amount of other information used in constructing the standard (see the right panel of Figure 9.1), resulting in attenuated contrast effects. Conversely, contrast effects should increase, the more extreme is the information included in the representation of the standard.

In summary, the inclusion/exclusion model predicts that the size of context effects is a function of the amount and extremity of the information used in forming temporary representations of the target and the standard. On the one hand, the size of assimilation and contrast effects should increase, the larger the amount and the extremity of the information used in forming the respective representation. This prediction is consistent with numerous models of social judgment and will not be pursued further in this chapter. On the other hand, the impact of extreme context information should be attenuated, the more other information with different implications is used in forming the respective representation. Accordingly, including additional exemplars in the representation of the social category should attenuate the resulting assimilation effect on judgments of the social category, whereas including additional exemplars in the representation of the standard should attenuate the resulting contrast effect on judgments of other exemplars. The following discussion of set-size effects will focus primarily on this second set of predictions.

Temporary Accessibility: Reducing Context Effects by Adding Context Information

To test the implications of our set-size assumption, we built on prior research that addressed the categorical relationship of context information and target (Schwarz & Bless, 1992b). In this research, we did or did not bring to mind politicians who were involved in a major political scandal and assessed the impact of this context information on judgments of the political class in general or of specific politicians. The scandal-ridden politicians reduced the perceived trustworthiness of "politicians in general" (superordinate target category), presumably because the scandal-ridden politicians were included in the representation of this target. Other participants evaluated specific politicians (lateral target category) who were not involved in the scandal. Because lateral categories are mutually exclusive, the scandal-ridden politicians cannot be included in the representation formed of the other exemplars and may hence be used in forming a standard of comparison. Confirming this prediction, thinking about scandal-ridden politicians increased judgments of the trustworthiness of all other specific politicians assessed (Schwarz & Bless, 1992b; see also Stapel & Schwarz, 1998).

Building on this study, we tested the implications of our set-size assumption by varying the number of accessible exemplars (see Bless, Igou, Schwarz, & Wänke, 2000). We asked German participants to evaluate either the trustworthiness of "German politicians in general" (superordinate category) or the trustworthiness of specific well-known politicians (lateral categories). Prior to making these judgments, participants received a list of politicians who, either currently or in the recent past, held the office of prime minister in one of the states of the Federal Republic of Germany. Participants were asked to indicate the state each prime minister represented. As a context manipulation, this list either did or did not include a prime minister who was involved in a well-known scandal, namely, Max Streibl, the former prime minister of Bavaria. Consistent with our previous findings, we again observed that bringing a scandal-ridden politician (Max Streibl) to mind decreased judgments of the trustworthiness of German politicians in general but increased judgments of the trustworthiness of specific exemplars who were not involved in the scandal, as shown in the left-hand panel of Table 9.1.

To address the set-size predictions, we manipulated how many other prime ministers of German states were presented on the list, which included either three or six other prime ministers in addition to Max Streibl. In either case, Max Streibl was presented in the second to last position, thus ensuring that set size was not confounded with the temporal delay between thinking about Max Streibl and the target judgments. As shown in the right-hand panel of Table 9.1, bringing additional exemplars to mind decreased both the assimilation and the contrast effect. Specifically, activating additional prime ministers eliminated the negative impact of the scandal-ridden politician on the evaluation of politicians in general, reflecting a reduced assimilation effect that is consistent with many models of information integration. More important, the activation of additional prime ministers also attenuated the contrast effects observed on judgments of other exemplars, supporting a prediction that is unique to the inclusion/exclusion model.

This conclusion receives additional support from another look at the findings. The findings described so far pertain to the first three specific politicians evaluated. As can be seen in Table 9.1, these effects were attenuated for the evaluation of the second set of three politicians. This observation is consistent with the assumption that each exemplar that participants

TABLE 9.1. *Evaluation of the Trustworthiness of Politicians in General and Specifically as a Function of a Scandal Activation and Amount of Additional Information*

| | Additionally Activated Context Information | | | |
| | Three Other Exemplars | | Six Other Exemplars | |
Dependent Variable	Not Activated	Scandal Activated	Not Activated	Scandal Activated
Politicians in general				
M	5.5	3.9	4.6	4.7
SD	1.9	1.6	1.9	2.3
Specific known exemplars				
First three				
M	5.3	6.9	6.5	5.9
SD	1.6	1.9	1.6	1.7
Second three				
M	6.1	6.0	6.5	5.7
SD	1.5	2.2	1.2	1.7

Note: Evaluations were assessed on 11-point rating scales, with higher scores reflecting more trustworthiness.
Source: After Bless, Igou, Schwarz, and Wänke (2000).

evaluated served as additional context information, thus further attenuating the impact of the earlier context information.

In addition to illustrating the important role of category structure in the emergence of assimilation and contrast effects, these findings support a core postulate of the inclusion/exclusion model: The impact of any given piece of context information decreases with the amount and extremity of other information used in constructing a representation of the target or of the standard. The attenuation of the assimilation effect is consistent with numerous models of social judgment that assume that the judgment is based on an integration of the information accessible at the time (e.g., Anderson, 1981; Wyer & Srull, 1989). The more other information is accessible, the less the impact of any particular piece of information. More important, rendering additional information accessible also attenuates contrast effects. This finding is consistent with the assumption that individuals construct a standard of comparison based on the information accessible at the time – and the more relevant information is accessible, the less impact each piece of information has.

Chronic Accessibility: Expertise and the Size of Context Effects

Compared to novices, experts possess a rich and well-organized knowledge structure in their domain of expertise (Alba & Hutchinson, 1987), which renders a larger amount of relevant information chronically accessible. The inclusion/exclusion model treats chronically and temporarily accessible information as functionally equivalent. We therefore assume that the influence of high expertise parallels the influence of being exposed to a large amount of context information. Accordingly, the model specifies conditions under which expertise will increase as well as decrease the size of context effects. In fact, previous research observed increased (e.g., Herr, 1989) as well as decreased (e.g., Bettman & Sujan, 1987; Bickart, 1992; Rao & Monroe, 1988) context effects among experts. We address these apparently contradictory influences in turn.

Expertise May Increase Context Effects. Suppose that consumers are presented with a 20×20 letter matrix and are asked to identify the names of different cars. Depending on conditions, the cars are either inexpensive (e.g., Ford Fiesta) or expensive (e.g., Ferrari). Of interest is how exposure to the car names, hidden in the letter matrix, influences consumers' subsequent ratings of the price of other cars. Given the well-organized knowledge base of experts exposure to the car names may spontaneously bring price information to mind for experts but may not do so for novices (even though novices may be able to retrieve this information when asked to do so). If so, we may expect that consumers with high expertise in the domain of cars are more influenced by this task than consumers with low expertise. In the present case, the primed cars should result in contrast effects on judgments of the target cars, reflecting that both are lateral categories. Consistent with this analysis, Herr (1989), who conducted this and related experiments, observed that the size of the obtained contrast effects *increased* with participants' increasing car expertise.

In general terms, expertise bearing on the *context stimulus* is likely to increase the size of subsequent context effects because exposure to the context stimulus will render more information accessible for experts than for novices. That is, expertise bearing on the context stimulus is functionally equivalent with providing more context information.

Expertise May Decrease Context Effects. On the other hand, expertise bearing on the *target stimulus* should attenuate the size of context effects. In this case, experts have a larger amount of other information about the target that is always accessible, which attenuates the impact of a given piece of context information. Hence, expertise bearing on the target should be functionally equivalent to the priming of additional prime ministers in the Bless et al. (2000) scandal study, reviewed previously. Several studies support this prediction.

PRODUCT LINE EXTENSIONS. In one series of studies, Wänke, Bless, and Schwarz (1998) investigated the role of expertise in the context of brand or product line extensions. Participants first received descriptions

TABLE 9.2. *Average Evaluation of the Target Car as a Function of Name Continuation and Participants' Expertise*

Expertise	Name		
	Continuation	Control	Discontinuation
Nonexperts	2.8[a]	2.5[a]	1.2[b]
Experts	1.6[a]	1.9[a]	2.2[ab]

Note: The scores reflect a compound measure of nine ratings that were all assessed on a scale ranging from −5 to +5. Higher scores reflect a more active, young, etc. evaluation. Different superscripts represent differences of $p < .05$.
Source: After Wänke, Bless, and Schwarz (1998).

of several sports cars of one brand to establish a brand image. Subsequently, they were presented with an allegedly newly launched compact car. In contrast to other available research, we varied neither the product categories used nor the central features of the extension. In fact, we presented an *identical extension* and an *identical core brand* and merely varied whether the model name suggested continuation or discontinuation of the product line of a sports car brand. Name continuation should facilitate the inclusion of the brand's sporty image in the representation of the new compact car, resulting in an assimilation effect that makes the compact car look "sporty." Conversely, name discontinuation should facilitate the exclusion of the sportive brand image from the representation formed of the compact car, resulting in a contrast effect. As shown in the top row of Table 9.2, participants' evaluations of the compact car assimilated toward the trendy brand image when the name suggested continuation (inclusion), whereas a contrast effect emerged when the name suggested discontinuation (exclusion).

As shown in the bottom row of Table 9.2, these effects were obtained only for novices' evaluations of the compact car. In contrast, experts' evaluations were not influenced by the context and categorization manipulations, consistent with other findings in the consumer literature (e.g., Bettman & Sujan, 1987; Bickart, 1992; Rao & Monroe, 1988). This presumably reflects the fact that experts can draw on a larger amount of chronically accessible information when constructing representations of the target and standard, thus diluting the impact of the temporarily accessible contextual information.

As a caveat, we add that experts may also be able to detect commonalities that are not obvious to novices. We therefore agree with Muthukrishnan and Weitz (1991) that knowledge differences may result in different categorizations. Note, however, that differential categorization influences the direction of context effects, not their size. To safeguard against this complication, it is important to manipulate categorization operations directly, as done in the Wänke et al. (1998) studies.

ORDER EFFECTS IN PUBLIC OPINION SURVEYS. Numerous studies demonstrated question order effects in survey research: Answering a preceding question may bring information to mind that is subsequently used in answering related questions, resulting in assimilation or contrast effects as a function of the inclusion/exclusion operations discussed previously (for reviews see Schwarz, 1999; Sudman, Bradburn, & Schwarz, 1996). Such question order effects should again be less pronounced for individuals with high rather than low expertise in the respective domain. To test this possibility, Weller, Bless, and Schwarz (1994) examined data from the Eurobarometer, a public opinion survey conducted in all nations of the European Community (EC). Drawing on data from multiple years, we first identified cases in which two identical questions were presented in different orders. For example, in one condition, respondents first reported their general approval of their nation's membership in the EC and subsequently reported their perception of the unanimity among the EC nations. In another condition, these questions were asked in the reverse order.

Not surprisingly, individuals who perceived low unanimity were less supportive of their nation's membership in the EC than were individuals who perceived high unanimity. As expected, this relationship was more pronounced when the unanimity question preceded rather than followed the membership question, reflecting a conditional question order effect (see Schwarz et al., 1991). Presumably, the unanimity question brought positive or negative aspects to mind, which were subsequently used to answer the membership question. More important, the size of this context effect was less pronounced for individuals with a higher level of education. Given that highly educated individuals are reliably more knowledgeable about the EC, this observation is consistent with the set-size logic: Adding the information brought to mind by the unanimity question to these respondents' larger knowledge base about the EC exerted less influence than adding the same information to the smaller knowledge base of less educated respondents.

Summary and Implications

In sum, the available evidence suggests that expertise may increase as well as decrease the size of context effects, consistent with the mental construal logic of the inclusion/exclusion model. First, expertise bearing on the *context stimulus* brings a richer set of context information to mind for experts than for novices. Accordingly, it *increases* the size of context effects (e.g., Herr, 1989). Second, expertise bearing on the *target stimulus* entails that a given piece of context information is added to a larger knowledge structure. Accordingly, it *decreases* the size of context effects. Finally, expertise may often bear on *both* the context stimulus and the target stimulus. In this case, the emerging context effect should be a function of the relative size of the two opposing influences, which may cancel one another out. Data bearing on this possibility, however, are not available.

It is informative to contrast this set-size analysis of the attenuating influence of target expertise with competing accounts. One account suggests that experts are less likely to be influenced by context information because they may be able to retrieve a previously formed judgment from memory, thus obliterating the need to form a judgment in the context given. As a result, their judgment would be unaffected by the present context. Note that this is possible only when the previously formed judgment bears directly on the question asked. In most cases, however, the question asked is unlikely to match the specifics of a previously formed judgment and some adjustment will be required, giving rise to context effects (see Schwarz & Strack, 1991; Strack & Martin, 1987, for a discussion). More important, this possibility cannot account for the observation that experts showed attenuated context effects on judgments pertaining to new and fictitious targets, such as the cars used in the Wänke et al. (1998) studies, for which participants cannot rely on previously formed judgments.

An alternative account traces experts' greater immunity to context effects on differences in attitude strength (for a discussion see Converse, 1964; Krosnick & Abelson, 1992). Presumably, experts hold attitudes in their domain of expertise with greater strength and conviction and hence are less likely to be influenced by contextual variables. Although intuitively appealing, studies that directly tested the role of attitude strength (rather than expertise) in the emergence of context effects provided no support for this prediction (Krosnick & Schuman, 1988). Accordingly, Krosnick and Abelson (1992, p. 193) concluded that the hypothesis that context effects in attitude measurement "are greater in the case of weaker attitudes has clearly been disconfirmed." We therefore conclude that differential attitude strength is unlikely to be at the heart of the observed difference in novices' and experts' susceptibility to context effects. Instead, this phenomenon is most likely driven by the differential amount of chronically accessible information that experts and novices can bring to bear on the mental representation of the target, consistent with the set-size principle.

THE COMBINED IMPACT OF ASSIMILATION AND CONTRAST

So far, we have discussed how the amount of either temporarily or chronically accessible information influences the size of assimilation and contrast effects. We implicitly assumed that a given piece of context information may change either the representation of the target or the representation of the standard. Under certain conditions, however, context information may influence both representations. In these cases, the net effect on the observed judgment is a function of the relative size of the assimilation and contrast effects. In the following section, we will briefly outline this possibility and report some supporting evidence.

The inclusion/exclusion model holds that when a judgment pertains to a target category that is *superordinate* to the context information, the context information is likely to be included into the representation of the target. This results in assimilation effects, as the preceding examples illustrate. When the judgment pertains to a target category that is *lateral* to the context information, the context information is used in constructing a standard of comparison, resulting in contrast effects. In addition to these *direct* assimilation and contrast effects, context information may also exert an *indirect* influence. Suppose that a context exemplar elicits an assimilation effect on the evaluation of a superordinate target category. If features of the superordinate category are subsequently included in the representation formed of another exemplar that is a member of this category, the initial assimilation effect on the superordinate category may carry over to the exemplar evaluation, resulting in an *indirect* assimilation effect on a target that is lateral to the initial context information. Conversely, suppose that a context exemplar elicits a contrast effect on a lateral target. If this lateral target is subsequently included in the representation formed of the superordinate category, it may result in an *indirect* contrast effect on a target that is superordinate to the initial context information.

Support for these considerations is reported by Wänke, Bless, and Igou (2001), who presented participants with an extreme product (exemplar), namely, a top-of-the-line model of a toaster of the fictitious brand "Logan," a moderately priced model of the brand "Logan," and a moderately priced model of a fictitious competing brand, "Wellington." In one condition, the salience of the common category for the two Logan products was increased (e.g., information about all models of the same brand was printed on paper of the same color), thus providing a cue that emphasized the models' joint membership in the same superordinate category (brand). In another condition, information about the same models was printed on paper of different colors, thus deemphasizing their joint membership in the same superordinate category. Following a perusal of the product information, participants evaluated a moderately priced model of the brand, the brand itself, and the top-of-the-line model, as well as models of other brands (evaluations were assessed in various orders, and order cannot account for the effects to be described; see Wänke et al., 2001).

When the common category for the two Logan products was less salient (i.e., paper of *different* colors was used to describe them), the results showed the familiar pattern. Introducing the top-of-the-line model resulted in less favorable ratings of the moderately priced models of the same as well as different brands, indicating that the top-of-the-line model served as a standard of comparison in evaluating the lateral targets. In addition, the top-of-the line model increased the favorability of the brand, indicating an assimilation effect on judgments of the superordinate category. When the salience of the common category was increased (e.g., models of the same brand were described on paper of the *same* color), however, an additional effect emerged. In this case, the positive *direct* effect of the top-of-the-line model on the evaluation of the brand resulted in *indirect* assimilation effects on moderately priced models of the same brand. This indirect effect attenuated the otherwise observed contrast effect elicited by a comparison with the lateral top-of-the-line model. Importantly, the indirect effect was observed only when the membership of all models in the same superordinate category was highly salient, that is, when all models belonged to the same brand and were described on paper of the same color. Mediational analyses confirmed that the observed judgment was the net effect of a direct contrast effect, based on a comparison with the top-of-the-line model, and an indirect assimilation effect, mediated through the positive influence of the top-of-the-line model on the brand evaluation.

The Influence of Timing

Theoretically, indirect context effects on the evaluation of an exemplar, mediated through the exemplar's category membership, should be more pronounced, the less other information is accessible about the exemplar. The temporal distance between information acquisition and judgment is likely to influence this variable. Shortly after exposure to an extreme and a moderate exemplar, relevant details are highly accessible in memory and the two exemplars can be compared, giving rise to (direct) contrast effects. After a delay, however, the relevant details fade from memory and individuals are more likely to draw on general information about the exemplars, such as their category membership. If the extreme exemplar influenced judgments of the superordinate category (brand), the indirect assimilation effect, mediated through category membership, should eventually overpower the direct contrast effect.

Bless, Wänke, and Lickes (2002) tested this prediction with the product and brand information used in the Wänke et al. (2001) study reviewed previously. Without delay, exposure to the top-of-the-line model resulted in a contrast effect on evaluations of moderately priced models and an assimilation effect on evaluations of the brand. This replicates earlier findings. Introducing a delay, however, eliminated the contrast effect and resulted in a more positive evaluation of the moderately priced products, which was mediated by their membership in the brand category. By the same token, we may expect that any other variable that increases reliance on category membership information increases the size of *indirect* context effects. Such variables include decreased processing capacity – for example, due to distractor tasks or time pressure – and decreased processing motivation (for a discussion see Brewer, this volume; Kruglanski et al., this volume). This possibility awaits further research.

CONCLUSIONS

Many researchers assume that the emergence of a context effect indicates that individuals formed a judgment on the spot, whereas the absence of a context effect indicates that they reported a stable, preexisting attitude (for a discussion see Tourangeau & Rasinski, 1988, and the contributions in Petty & Krosnick, 1995). In contrast, the inclusion/exclusion model (Schwarz & Bless, 1992a) assumes that judgments are always formed on the spot and traces the context dependency as well as the apparent stability of judgments to the same mental construal processes. From this perspective, "stability" is merely the result of conditions that elicit small context effects (for a discussion see Schwarz & Bohner, 2001). Accordingly, it is of crucial importance to understand the variables that determine the size of context effects. The reviewed research contributes to this understanding by highlighting the operation of the set-size principle and the combined influence of direct and indirect context effects.

First, the size of assimilation effects increases with the amount and extremity of contextual information that is included in the representation of the target. Thus, adding three crooks to the representation of "American politicians" has a more negative impact on judgments of trustworthiness than adding only a single crook. All models of social judgment share this information integration prediction.

Second, by the same token, including a given piece of extreme context information in the representation of the target exerts less influence the more other, moderate information is used in forming this representation (e.g., Bless et al., 2000).

Third, and more important, the same set-size principle holds for the construction of mental representations of a standard and governs the size of contrast effects (e.g., Bless et al., 2000). This prediction is unique to the inclusion/exclusion model and has not previously been tested.

Fourth, the model assumes that temporarily and chronically accessible information is functionally equivalent. This assumption has been supported by the reviewed research and provides the basis for a set-size analysis of the role of expertise. As seen, expertise bearing on the context stimulus results in larger context effects. This is the case because the context stimulus brings more information to mind for experts than for novices, thus increasing the amount of context information that enters the respective representation (e.g., Herr, 1989). Conversely, expertise bearing on the target stimulus results in attenuated context effects. This is the case because a given piece of context information exerts less influence when added to the larger knowledge base of experts than of novices (e.g., Wänke et al.,

1998). Finally, these effects may cancel one another out when the expertise bears on both the context and the target stimulus, a possibility that awaits further research.

Fifth, when a given piece of context information influences the evaluation of a superordinate category, this influence can carry over to evaluations of lateral targets that are members of this category. Conversely, when a given piece of context information influences the evaluation of an exemplar, this influence can carry over to evaluations of a superordinate category of which the exemplar is a member. These *indirect* effects combine with *direct* effects, and the size of the resulting net effect is a function of their relative impact.

As this discussion of the size of context effects indicates, a mental construal logic can account for the context dependency as well as the apparent stability of social judgment based on the same theoretical principles. Hence, the absence of a context effect provides neither any evidence for the presence of a previously formed judgment or attitude nor any evidence that the reported judgment was not based on a temporary construal. Instead, it may simply indicate that the amount and extremity of the context information were insufficient to change the evaluation in competition with other information used in forming a representation of the target or the standard (see Schwarz & Bohner, 2001). By the same token, the observation that expertise bearing on the target attenuates context effects is not necessarily a function of experts' higher attitude strength. Instead, it may merely reflect the operation of the set-size principle, as suggested by the parallel effects of chronically (Wänke et al., 1998) and temporarily (Bless et al., 2000) accessible information. Hence, the set-size principle provides a parsimonious account for the operation of situational as well as individual differences and traces their influence to the size of the accessible knowledge structure.

References

Alba, J., & Hutchinson, J. (1987). Dimensions of consumer expertise. *Journal of Consumer Research, 13,* 411–454.

Anderson, N. H. (1981). *The foundations of information integration theory.* New York: Academic Press.

Barsalou, L. W. (1987). The instability of graded structure: Implications for the nature of concepts. In U. Neisser (Ed.), *Concepts and conceptual development: Ecological and intellectual factors in categorization* (pp. 101–140). Cambridge: Cambridge University Press.

Bettman, J., & Sujan, M. (1987). Effects of framing on evaluation of comparable and non-comparable alternatives by expert and novice consumers. *Journal of Consumer Research, 14,* 141–154.

Bickart, B. (1992). Question-order effects and brand evaluations: The moderating role of consumer knowledge. In N. Schwarz & S. Sudman (Eds.), *Context effects in social and psychological research* (pp. 63–80). New York: Springer-Verlag.

Bless, H., Igou, E., Schwarz, N., & Wänke, M. (2000). Reducing context effects by adding context information: The direction and size of context effects in political judgment. *Personality and Social Psychology Bulletin, 26*, 1036–1045.

Bless, H., & Schwarz, N. (1998). Context effects in political judgment: Assimilation and contrast as a function of categorization processes. *European Journal of Social Psychology, 28*, 159–172.

Bless, H., Schwarz, N., Bodenhausen, G. V., & Thiel, L. (2001). Personalized versus generalized benefits of stereotype disconfirmation: Tradeoffs in the evaluation of atypical exemplars and their social groups. *Journal of Experimental Social Psychology, 37*, 386–397.

Bless, H., & Wänke, M. (2000). Can the same information be typical and atypical? How perceived typicality moderates assimilation and contrast in evaluative judgments. *Personality and Social Psychology Bulletin, 26*, 306–314.

Bless, H., Wänke, M., & Lickes, K. (2002). *Determinants of assimilation and contrast in consumer judgments.* Unpublished manuscript, University of Mannheim.

Converse, P. E. (1964). The nature of belief systems in mass publics. In D. E. Apter (Ed.), *Ideology and discontent* (pp. 202–261). New York: Free Press.

Helson, H. (1964). *Adaptation-level theory.* New York: Harper & Row.

Herr, P. M. (1989). Priming price: Prior knowledge and context effects. *Journal of Consumer Research, 16*, 67–75.

Herr, P. M., Sherman, S. J., & Fazio, R. H. (1983). On the consequences of priming: Assimilation and contrast effects. *Journal of Experimental Social Psychology, 19*, 323–340.

Kahneman, D., & Miller, D. (1986). Norm theory: Comparing reality to its alternatives. *Psychological Review, 93*, 136–153.

Krosnick, J. A., & Abelson, R. P. (1992). The case for measuring attitude strength. In J. M. Tanur (Ed.), *Questions about questions* (pp. 177–203). New York: Russell Sage.

Krosnick, J. A., & Schuman, H. (1988). Attitude intensity, importance, and certainty and susceptibility to response effects. *Journal of Personality and Social Psychology, 54*, 940–952.

Lombardi, W., Higgins, E., & Bargh, J. (1987). The role of consciousness in priming effects on categorization: Assimilation and contrast as a function of awareness of the priming task. *Personality and Social Psychology Bulletin, 13*, 411–429.

Martin, L. L. (1986). Set/reset: Use and disuse of concepts in impression formation. *Journal of Personality and Social Psychology, 51*, 493–504.

Martin, L. L., Strack, F., & Stapel, D. A. (2001). How the mind moves: Knowledge accessibility and the fine-tuning of the cognitive system. In A. Tesser & N. Schwarz (Eds.), *Blackwell handbook of social psychology: Intraindividual processes* (Vol. 1, pp. 236–256). London: Blackwell.

Muthukrishnan, A. V., & Weitz, B. A. (1991). Role of product knowledge in evaluation of brand extension. *Advances in Consumer Research, 18*, 407–413.

Ostrom, T. M., & Upshaw, H. S. (1968). Psychological perspective and attitude change. In A. C. Greenwald, T. C. Brock, & T. M. Ostrom (Eds.), *Psychological foundations of attitudes* (pp. 217–242). New York: Academic Press.

Parducci, A. (1965). Category judgments: A range-frequency model. *Psychological Review, 72*, 407–418.

Petty, R. E., & Krosnick, J. A. (Eds.) (1995). *Attitude strength: Antecedents and consequences.* Mahwah, NJ: Erlbaum.

Rao, A., & Monroe, K. (1988). The moderating effect of prior knowledge on cue utilization in product evaluations. *Journal of Consumer Research, 15,* 253–264.

Schwarz, N. (1996). *Cognition and communication: Judgmental biases, research methods and the logic of conversation.* Hillsdale, NJ: Erlbaum.

Schwarz, N. (1999). Self-reports: How the questions shape the answers. *American Psychologist, 54,* 93–105.

Schwarz, N., & Bless, H. (1992a). Constructing reality and its alternatives: Assimilation and contrast effects in social judgment. In L. L. Martin & A. Tesser (Eds.), *The construction of social judgment* (pp. 217–245). Hillsdale, NJ: Erlbaum.

Schwarz, N., & Bless, H. (1992b). Scandals and the public's trust in politicians: Assimilation and contrast effects. *Personality and Social Psychology Bulletin, 18,* 574–579.

Schwarz, N., Bless, H., Wänke, M., & Winkielman (in press). Accessibility revisited. In G. V. Bodenhausen & A. J. Lambert (Eds.), *Foundations of social cognition: A Festschrift in honor of Robert S. Wyer, Jr.* Mahwah, NJ: Erlbaum.

Schwarz, N., & Bohner, G. (2001). The construction of attitudes. In A. Tesser & N. Schwarz (Eds.), *Blackwell handbook of social psychology: Intraindividual processes* (Vol. 1, pp. 436–457). Oxford: Blackwell.

Schwarz, N., & Clore, G. L. (1996). Feelings and phenomenal experiences. In E. T. Higgins & A. Kruglanski (Eds.), *Social psychology: A handbook of basic principles* (pp. 433–465). New York: Guilford Press.

Schwarz, N., & Strack, F. (1991). Context effects in attitude surveys: Applying cognitive theory to social research. In W. Stroebe & M. Hewstone (Eds.), *European review of social psychology* (Vol. 2, pp. 31–50). Chichester, UK: Wiley.

Schwarz, N., Strack, F., & Mai, H. P. (1991). Assimilation and contrast effects in part–whole question sequences: A conversational logic analysis. *Public Opinion Quarterly, 55,* 3–23.

Stapel, D. A., & Schwarz, N. (1998). The Republican who did not want to become President: Colin Powell's impact on evaluations of the Republican Party and Bob Dole. *Personality and Social Psychology Bulletin, 24,* 690–698.

Strack, F., & Martin, L. L. (1987). Thinking, judging, and communicating: A process account of context effects in attitude surveys. In H. J. Hippler, N. Schwarz, & S. Sudman (Eds.), *Social information processing and survey methodology* (pp. 123–148). New York: Springer-Verlag.

Strack, F., Schwarz, N., Bless, H., Kübler, A., & Wänke, M. (1993). Awareness of the influence as a determinant of assimilation versus contrast. *European Journal of Social Psychology, 23,* 53–62.

Sudman, S., Bradburn, N., & Schwarz, N. (1996). *Thinking about answers: The application of cognitive processes to survey methodology.* San Francisco: Jossey-Bass.

Tajfel, H. (1981). *Human groups and social categories.* Cambridge: Cambridge University Press.

Thibaut, J. W., & Kelley, H. H. (1959). *The social psychology of groups.* New York: Wiley.

Tourangeau, R., & Rasinski, K. (1988). Cognitive processes underlying context effects in attitude measurement. *Psychological Bulletin, 103,* 299–314.

Turner, J. C. (1987). *Rediscovering the social group: A self-categorization theory.* Oxford: Blackwell.

Wänke, M., Bless, H., & Igou, E. (2001). Next to a star: Paling, shining, or both? Turning inter-exemplar contrast into inter-exemplar assimilation. *Personality and Social Psychology, 27,* 14–29.

Wänke, M., Bless, H., & Schwarz, N. (1998). Contrast and assimilation in product line extensions: Context is not destiny. *Journal of Consumer Psychology, 7,* 299–322.

Weller, I. M., Bless, H., & Schwarz, N. (1994, May). *Context effects in standardized surveys.* Boston: American Association for Public Opinion Research.

Wyer, R. S., & Srull, T. K. (1989). *Memory and cognition in its social context.* Hillsdale, NJ: Erlbaum.

10

Affective Influences on Social Judgments and Decisions

Implicit and Explicit Processes

Joseph P. Forgas and Rebekah East

CONTENTS

INTRODUCTION

Imagine that as you are leaving a movie theater having just seen a very funny film, you are approached on the street by a person collecting responses to a public opinion survey. You are asked to make a number of judgments indicating your evaluation of the current prime minister, the performance of the main political parties, your views on various topical issues, your satisfaction with your life, and your expectations about the future. As you ponder your judgments, would your responses be influenced by the fact that you happen to be in a good mood after seeing the entertaining film? Would your judgments have been different if the film was a depressing war drama? After some reflection, most people would admit to the unexpected possibility that temporary affect could indeed bias

This work was supported by a Special Investigator award from the Australian Research Council and by the Research Prize from the Alexander von Humboldt Foundation to Joseph P. Forgas. The contribution of Stephanie Moylan, Joseph Ciarrochi, Patrick Vargas, and Joan Webb to this project is gratefully acknowledged. Please address all correspondence in connection with this chapter to Joseph P. Forgas, School of Psychology, University of New South Wales, Sydney 2052, Australia; e-mail: jp.forgas@unsw.edu.au. For further information on this research project, see also the website at www.psy.unsw.edu.au/~joef/jforgas.htm

their judgments. And they would be right. We carried out this experiment some years ago with almost 1,000 moviegoers as respondents and found a highly significant mood effect on the judgments people made (Forgas & Moylan, 1987). But do we know how, when, and why affective states can impact on our social judgments and decisions? What are the implicit and explicit psychological mechanisms responsible for such affect infusion phenomena?

This chapter will discuss recent evidence and theorizing about the nature and causes of affect infusion into social judgments. A number of empirical studies illustrating these phenomena from our laboratory will be reviewed, with particular focus on the differences between implicit and explicit processes that can promote or inhibit affect infusion. We have recently defined *affect infusion* as the process whereby affectively loaded information exerts an influence on, and becomes incorporated into, a person's cognitive and behavioral processes, entering into his or her constructive deliberations and eventually coloring the outcome in a mood-congruent direction (Forgas, 1995a, 2002). Affect infusion occurs because paying attention to, learning, encoding, and interpreting social information necessarily require high-level constructive processing that forces judges to go beyond the information given. Affect can have both an indirect, *implicit* influence on judgments by impacting on the way past knowledge is accessed and used when constructing a judgment (Forgas, 2002) and a direct, *explicit* influence when judges simply infer a response based on their current affective state (Clore, Gasper, & Garvin, 2001).

Of course, the subtle influence of feelings on thinking and judgments has long been of interest to philosophers including Plato, Aristotle, Epicurus, Descartes, Pascal, Kant, and others. Many of these theorists saw affect as a potentially dangerous, invasive force that tends to subvert rational judgment, an idea that was to reemerge in Freud's psychodynamic theories. However, during the past few decades, important advances in neuroanatomy, psychophysiology, and social cognition produced a radically different view. Rather than being viewed as a dangerous and disruptive influence on our rational judgments, affect is increasingly seen as a useful and even essential component of adaptive responding to social situations (Adolphs & Damasio, 2001; Ito & Cacioppo, 2001). For example, individuals who suffer brain damage in the areas responsible for affective reactions in the prefrontal cortex often make disastrous social decisions, even though their intellectual abilities remain unaffected (Adolphs & Damasio, 2001).

Although most of us are intuitively aware that feelings can have a profound influence on our thoughts and judgments, we do not yet fully understand how and why these influences occur. The challenge for researchers has been to understand and specify why affect sometimes influences judgments, whereas other times the effects are weak, absent, or even reversed (Martin, 2000). This chapter will argue that the key to understanding this puzzle lies in the different processing strategies individuals employ when making different kinds of social judgments. Whereas some processing strategies allow affective states to exert an implicit or explicit influence on judgments, others reduce or even reverse this effect. Before looking at contemporary research in detail, a brief overview of early research on affect and judgments will help to provide the necessary background.

AFFECT AND JUDGMENTS: THE BACKGROUND

The Importance of Affect

Research on social judgments has traditionally emphasized the rational, logical processes involved in combining external stimulus information with internal knowledge structures in producing a response (Wyer & Srull, 1989). Just how important is affect as a component of and as a determinant of judgments? In an influential article, Zajonc (1980) argued that affective reactions often constitute the primary response to social stimuli, a point he reiterated more recently (Zajonc, 2000). Supporting evidence comes from studies showing that people often display an affective preference toward stimuli long before they have a chance to process it properly and even when they have no awareness of having encountered it before (Zajonc, 1980, 2000). Affect also plays a crucial role in implicit cognitive representations about common recurring social experiences (Forgas, 1979). Feelings such as anxiety, confidence, intimacy, pleasure, or discomfort seem to determine how individuals represent various social episodes (Forgas, 1982). As Niedenthal and Halberstadt (2000) showed more recently, "stimuli can cohere as a category even when they have nothing in common other than the emotional responses they elicit" (p. 381). Similar conclusions were reached by Pervin (1976), who wrote that "what is striking is the extent to which situations are described in terms of affects (e.g., threatening, warm, interesting, dull, tense, calm, rejecting) and organized in terms of similarity of affects aroused by them" (p. 471). Thus, affect seems to play a predominant role in cognitive representations and judgments about the social world.

The Nature of Social Judgments

Why are social judgments so sensitive to affective influences? More than four decades ago, Bruner (1957) argued that social judgments involve a constructive act of categorization, in which the expectations and states of the perceiver can play a major role. Many social judgments require high-level cognitive processes to infer characteristics that are not directly observable (Heider, 1958). Affect can play an important dual role in social judgments by influencing both (a) the information processing strategy adopted by judges (Forgas, 1995a, 2002) and (b) the information people attend to, and how they interpret, learn, remember, and evaluate this information (Bower, 1981; Fiedler, 1990; Forgas, 2001; Forgas & Bower, 1987). In essence, it is the constructive, inferential nature of social judgments that makes affective influences possible.

Constructivist versus Mechanistic Approaches

The constructive nature of social judgments has been clearly recognized by theorists such as Heider (1958), Bruner (1957), and Asch (1946), who maintained that even the simplest social stimuli may be subject to constructive biases as the perceiver seeks to categorize the information and attempts to impose form or *Gestalt* on a complex and often indeterminate stimulus (Asch, 1946). The tradition of constructivism in judgmental research was counterbalanced by a second, more atomistic and mechanistic approach. *Cognitive algebra*, a field pioneered by Anderson (1974), was based on the psychophysical measurement tradition and conceptualized social judgments as the predictable outcome of simple, arithmetically derived information integration processes. The individual states and constructions of the perceiver were of little interest within this paradigm. This approach assumed that social information has permanent, enduring meanings. However, in most social judgments the information is not given but has to be selected or inferred, and its meaning is not constant but also subject to the constructions of the perceiver (Forgas, 1981). It seems then that the information integration approach and its metaphor of the social judge as a passive processor of stable information may at best be an incomplete account of social judgments.

The Social Cognition Approach

The conflicting assumptions of the constructivist and the mechanistic views of social judgments were ultimately reconciled within the current social cognition paradigm. This approach focuses on the role of information processing strategies and memory processes involved in the translation of information into semantic representations and the integration of past experiences with new information (Wyer & Srull, 1989). In line with Bruner's (1957) suggestions, it is the process of "going beyond the information given" that makes judgments open to affect infusion. Principles of semantic and evaluative priming can play an important role in influencing information availability in judgments (Bower & Forgas, 2001; Stapel, this volume). However, the social cognitive approach to judgments has traditionally also assumed "cold" cognition on the part of the perceiver, in which feelings, emotions, and preferences were relatively neglected (Forgas, 1981, 1983). The model's focus on the isolated and affectless perceiver, separated from the social, cultural, and emotional context in which judgments are usually made, has been a recurrent point of criticism (Argyle, 1991; Forgas, 1981).

Early Evidence for Affect Infusion into Judgments

Several early experiments suggested that affect does play a dynamic role in social judgments. Early accounts of such affect infusion emphasized either psychodynamic or conditioning principles. The *psychoanalytic account* suggested that affect has a dynamic, invasive quality and can "take over" judgments unless adequate resources are deployed to control these impulses. Feshbach and Singer (1957), in an early study, tested the psychoanalytic prediction that attempts to suppress affect should increase the "pressure" for affect to infuse unrelated judgments. They induced fear in their subjects through electric shocks and then instructed some of them to suppress their fear. Fearful subjects were more likely to judge "another person as fearful and anxious" (p. 286), and this effect was greater when judges were instructed to suppress their fear. Feshbach and Singer explained this in terms of the hydraulic principle: Attempts to suppress affect increase the pressure for it to be infused into unrelated judgments. Thus, "suppression of fear facilitates the tendency to project fear onto another social object" (p. 286).

An alternative account of affect infusion was offered by *conditioning theories*. Although radical behaviorists denied the value of studying internal constructs such as affect, Watson's classic little Albert studies were among the first to show that judgments of a previously neutral stimulus, such as a furry rabbit, could be influenced by associating fear-arousing stimuli, such as a loud noise, with this target. According to Watson, all of our complex affective judgments throughout life are conditioned by such patterns of complex and cumulative associations. An early study by Razran (1940) seemed to support this view. Razran made people feel bad or good (by exposing them to aversive smells or giving them a free lunch) and then asked them to make judgments about persuasive messages presented to them. Judges spontaneously reported significantly more negative or positive attitudes toward persuasive messages, depending on whether they had been made to feel bad or good previously.

The conditioning framework was later extended by Byrne and Clore (1970) and Clore and Byrne (1974) to study affective influences on interpersonal judgments. They argued that affective reactions to a neutral target (such as a previously unknown person) could be conditioned by associating them with positive or negative affect-eliciting situations. In other words, simple temporal and spatial contiguity will be enough to link an affective state to an incidentally encountered person. Several experiments demonstrated just such a conditioning effect, showing that people will be judged more positively when encountered in a pleasant situation and more negatively in an aversive environment (Gouaux, 1971; Gouaux & Summers, 1973; Griffitt, 1970). More recently, Berkowitz and his colleagues (Berkowitz, Jaffee, Jo, & Troccoli, 2000) also proposed a neoassociationist account of affective influences on judgments.

Ultimately, neither the conditioning nor the psychoanalytic theories could provide a convincing explanation for when, how, and why affect will infuse social judgments. It was only with the recent emergence of the social cognitive paradigm (Forgas, 1981) and the growing attention paid to information processing mechanisms that more comprehensive explanations of affect infusion began to emerge. Some of these models emphasized *implicit*, automatic cognitive processes as the main source of affect infusion (such as the affect priming model), whereas others proposed a more *explicit* mechanism to explain affect congruence, such as the affect-as-information model (Clore et al., 2001). We shall now briefly consider the role of different processing strategies in producing affect infusion effects.

IMPLICIT AND EXPLICIT MECHANISMS OF AFFECT INFUSION
INTO JUDGMENTS

Implicit Processes of Affect Infusion: The Affect-Priming Model

It was the affect-priming model developed by Bower (1981) that first highlighted the implicit role of affect in social cognition and judgments. Implicit affect infusion occurs, according to Bower (1981; Bower & Forgas, 2001), because affective states are directly linked to cognitions within a single associative network of memory representations. Affect may thus influence judgments through the automatic priming of associated constructs, as "activation of an emotion node also spreads activation throughout the memory structures to which it is connected" (Bower, 1981, p. 135). Affect priming has several important consequences: Affect should facilitate the learning of mood-congruent information because of the greater availability of an affect-congruent associative base. Affect should also facilitate the recall of information encountered in a matching rather than a nonmatching mood state (mood-dependent memory; Eich & Forgas, in press). Due to the greater availability of affect-consistent associations, judges should evaluate and interpret current social stimuli in an affect-congruent manner in their judgments (but see Stapel, this volume, for an alternative view).

The affect-priming model received strong initial support in studies of social judgments (Bower & Forgas, 2001; Forgas & Bower, 1987; Forgas, Bower, & Krantz, 1984), although paradoxically, the evidence for the basic memory effects remained less than clear-cut (Eich & Forgas, in press; Eich & Macauley, 2000). It turns out, however, that implicit affect infusion in judgments is most likely when people engage in genuinely open, constructive processing strategies that require the use of memory-based information to construct a judgment. We may define as *constructive* those cognitive tasks that involve the active elaboration and transformation of the available stimulus information, require the activation and use of previous knowledge structures, and result in the creation of new knowledge from the combination of stored information and new stimulus details.

Judgments that do not rely on memory-based information cannot be influenced by affect; it is probably for this reason that mood-state dependence has been difficult to demonstrate with abstract and uninvolving stimulus materials, such as the word lists typically preferred by cognitive researchers (Eich & Macauley, 2000). In contrast, affective influences on judgments are reliably found in experiments where the stimulus information to be judged is complex, realistic, and involving (Forgas, 1994; Forgas & Bower, 1987; Sedikides, 1995).

The Explicit Route to Affect Infusion: Misattribution Models

An alternative model predicting explicit affective influences on judgments was proposed by Schwarz and Clore (1983). These authors argued that "rather than computing a judgment on the basis of recalled features of a target, individuals may ... ask themselves: 'How do I feel about it?' [and] in doing so, they may mistake feelings due to a pre-existing state as a reaction to the target" (Schwarz, 1990, p. 529). This "how-do-I-feel-about-it?" heuristic assumes that affect influences judgments mainly because of an inferential error: People misread their prevailing affective states as indicative of their evaluation of a judgmental target. The origins of this theory can be traced to earlier conditioning research (Clore & Byrne, 1974), as well as misattribution research and work on judgmental heuristics (Clore et al., 2001). Whereas conditioning accounts emphasized blind temporal and spatial contingencies that link affect to judgments, the affect-as-information model – rather less parsimoniously – posits a more explicit inferential process (cf. Berkowitz et al., 2000). Like misattribution theories, the affect-as-information model also predicts that only previously unattributed affective states can (mis)inform subsequent judgments.

Again, affect-as-information effects occur only in some conditions. Typically, people rely on their affective state as a heuristic cue only when they lack motivation and/or cognitive resources to compute a more thorough response. For example, in the original experiment by Schwarz and Clore (1983), judges received an unannounced phone call asking them unexpected and unfamiliar questions. In such a situation, they presumably had little personal involvement and motivation in responding to a stranger, and had little time or few cognitive resources to engage in extensive processing. Relying on their prevailing mood as a shortcut to infer a response appears a reasonable strategy in such circumstances. Other studies confirm this pattern. For example, in the study alluded to in the Introduction, we asked almost 1,000 people who were feeling good or bad after seeing happy or sad films to complete an attitude survey on the street after leaving the movie theater (Forgas & Moylan, 1987). As they presumably had little time and little capacity to engage in elaborate processing before producing a response, they may well have relied on their temporary affect as a heuristic cue to infer a reaction.

There are several issues that limit the validity of this theory. It is sometimes claimed that the model is falsifiable because it predicts the *absence* of affect congruence when the affective state is already attributed. However, the fact that affect congruence can be eliminated by calling subjects' attention to the correct source of their affect does not logically support the model. In fact, Berkowitz et al. (2000) showed that affect congruence in judgments can always be reversed by instructing subjects to focus on the source of their moods, irrespective of how congruence was produced in the first place. A further issue is that the informational value of affective states is not given, as the model assumes, but depends on the particular situational context (Martin, 2000). Thus, the same affective state may mean very different things in different settings: Feeling good does not have the same informational value in a cabaret as at a funeral, for example.

Probably the most serious problem with the affect-as-information model is that the model has little to say about how sources of information other than affect and internal knowledge structures are combined in producing a response. In that sense, this is really a theory of nonjudgment or aborted judgment rather than a theory of judgment. On balance, it now appears that this simple and explicit process of affect infusion is of little relevance in most judgments that do require some degree of elaboration and processing. Under any but the most simple conditions, the implicit process of affect priming is far more likely to produce affect infusion.

Affective Influences on the Processing of Social Judgments

The implicit, affect-priming and the explicit, affect-as-information mechanisms both focus on the informational role of affect as it impacts on the content and valence of judgments. In addition to influencing *what* people think, affect may influence the *process* of cognition, that is, *how* people think (Fiedler, 2001; Fiedler & Forgas, 1988; Forgas, 2000). Early experiments suggested that people experiencing positive affect seem to complete judgments faster, employ less effortful and more superficial processing strategies, use less information, avoid demanding, systematic thinking, and are more confident about their judgments. In contrast, negative affect seems to trigger a more effortful, systematic, analytic, and vigilant processing style (Clark & Isen, 1982; Mackie & Worth, 1989). More recent work, however, showed that positive affect can also produce distinct processing advantages. Happy people are more likely to adopt more creative, open, and inclusive thinking styles, use broader categories, show greater mental flexibility, and perform more effectively on secondary tasks (Bless, 2000; Fiedler, 2000, 2001). How can we explain these affect-induced processing differences?

Some theorists suggested that both negative (Ellis & Ashbrook, 1988) and positive affect (Mackie & Worth, 1989) may impair processing capacity. However, as the processing consequences of affect are clearly asymmetrical – positive and negative affect clearly promote very different thinking styles – it is unlikely that these explanations could both be correct. According to other theorists (Clark & Isen, 1982), positive affect may motivate people to maintain this pleasant state by refraining from effortful information processing, whereas negative affect should motivate people to engage in vigilant, systematic processing as an adaptive response to improving an aversive state. A slightly different version of this theory, the *cognitive tuning* theory, was proposed by Schwarz (1990). Schwarz argued that positive and negative affect have a signaling/tuning function, and their evolutionary role is to inform the person automatically of whether a relaxed, effort-minimizing (in positive affect) or a vigilant, effortful (negative affect) processing style is appropriate. A shared problem with these explanations is that they all assume that the main consequence of positive and negative affect is an increase or decrease in processing effort and vigilance. In contrast, theorists such as Bless (2000) and Fiedler (2000; Fiedler & Bless, 2001) suggested that the basic evolutionary function of positive and negative affect is not simply to influence processing effort, but also to trigger equally effortful but qualitatively different processing styles. Thus, positive affect should promote a top-down, assimilative, schema-based processing style in which preexisting ideas, attitudes, and representations dominate information processing. Negative affect, by contrast, produces a more bottom-up, accommodative, and externally focused processing strategy in which attention to situational information dominates thinking (Bless, 2000; Fiedler, 2000; Higgins, 2001).

TOWARD AN INTEGRATION OF THE ROLE OF DIFFERENT PROCESSING STRATEGIES IN AFFECT INFUSION: THE AFFECT INFUSION MODEL

Although affect clearly has an impact on social judgments and reasoning, these effects are neither simple nor straightforward. Both affect congruence and affect incongruence have been demonstrated, and at times mood seems to have no effect at all on judgments. An integrative theory, the Affect Infusion Model (AIM; Forgas, 1995a, 2002), was developed as a multiprocess framework to explain how different explicit and implicit processing strategies adopted by people in response to different circumstances can produce affect congruence, incongruence, or no infusion in judgments.

Unlike other models, the AIM recognizes that people may rely on a number of processing strategies when dealing with a judgmental task. A combination of situational and contextual influences ultimately determines what kind of processing strategy is used and, thus, the kind of effect that affect has on judgments. The AIM predicts that affect infusion is most likely under conditions that promote elaborative, constructive information processing (Fiedler, 2001; Forgas, 1995a, 2002). In contrast, there should be less affect infusion under conditions that inhibit open, constructive thinking.

The AIM identifies four distinct processing strategies: direct access, motivated, heuristic, and substantive processing. Direct access and motivated processing involve relatively closed, predetermined, and directed information search and selection strategies that allow little scope for constructive elaboration. Thus, there is little opportunity for affect infusion. In contrast, heuristic and substantive processing are more open-ended and constructive processing styles that require more open and generative information search and selection strategies, and thus allow for greater affect infusion.

The direct access strategy is based on the direct retrieval of a preexisting response. Most people possess a rich store of such crystallized, preformed judgments. Such stored judgments are most likely to be used when the target is well known or familiar and when there are no strong cognitive, affective, situational, or motivational cues mandating more elaborate processing. Direct access is usually an implicit strategy, and precludes affect infusion because there is little cognitive elaboration involved and thus no opportunity for affectively primed information to be incorporated in a judgment. Several studies reported an absence of affect infusion precisely under conditions favoring the direct access of stored judgments (Salovey & Birnbaum, 1989).

The motivated processing strategy tends to be used when there are motivational pressures for a particular outcome to be achieved. As motivated processing involves highly selective and targeted information search strategies, affect infusion is again unlikely. Indeed, motivated processing guided by objectives such as affect maintenance or affect improvement is the key mechanism for producing affect-incongruent judgmental outcomes (Berkowitz et al., 2000; Clark & Isen, 1982; Forgas, 2001). A number of goals can trigger motivated processing, such as affect repair, affect maintenance, self-evaluation maintenance, ego enhancement, achievement motivation, affiliation, and in-group favoritism (Forgas, 1991a, 1991b; Forgas & Fiedler, 1996; Forgas, Bower, & Moylan, 1990; Sedikides, 1994). Normative pressures arising within a group were also found to produce motivated processing and the elimination of affect infusion (Forgas, 1990).

The heuristic processing strategy should be adopted when judges seek to compute a judgment with minimal effort and rely on cognitive shortcuts or heuristics in order to avoid more elaborate or substantive processing.

Heuristic thinking is very common in making judgments. In terms of the AIM, heuristic processing is most likely when the target is simple or highly typical, personal relevance is low, there are no motivational objectives, there is limited cognitive capacity, and the situation does not demand accuracy. Heuristic judgments may be based on erroneous inferences made from a prevailing affective state (Clore et al., 2001). This represents an explicit route of affect infusion.

It is the fourth, *substantive processing strategy* that most closely resembles normal thinking, when judges actually select, learn, and interpret novel information and relate this information to their preexisting knowledge structures in producing a response. Substantive processing is more likely when the target is complex or atypical, the judge has no specific motivation to pursue, has adequate cognitive capacity, or there are explicit or implicit situational demands for extensive processing. Substantive processing can facilitate implicit affect infusion, as affect may selectively prime the ideas, memories, and interpretations used by a judge, thus influencing the way complex and often ambiguous social stimuli are interpreted and judged (Bower, 1981; Bower & Forgas, 2001).

Specific evidence linking substantive processing to affect infusion comes from processing latency and memory data (Forgas & Bower, 1987). Consistent with the affect priming principle, people seem to pay selective attention to affect-congruent information and produce mood-congruent judgments more rapidly (Forgas & Bower, 1987). Affect was found to have a significant congruent influence on a variety of judgments that require substantive processing, including behavior interpretations (Forgas et al., 1984), person perception (Baron, 1987; Forgas & Bower, 1987), perceptions of health and illness (Salovey & Birnbaum, 1989), self-judgments (Sedikides, 1995), reactions to persuasion, and stereotypic judgments (Forgas, 1990; Forgas & Fiedler, 1996) as well as causal attributions (Forgas et al., 1990).

The AIM also makes the counterintuitive prediction that implicit affect infusion in the course of substantive processing should be enhanced when more extensive processing is required to deal with a more complex and demanding judgment. In fact, targets that are atypical, unusual, or complex tend to recruit longer and more substantive processing and produce greater affect infusion effects. Such a link between extended processing and greater implicit affect infusion has been demonstrated in several recent studies using more or less complex and atypical people (Forgas, 1992a, 1992b), relationships (Forgas, 1993), situations (Forgas, 1998a, 1998b, 1999a, 1999b), and conflict episodes (Forgas, 1994) as stimuli. These results confirm that processing differences indeed mediate differential levels of affect infusion.

The variables determining processing choices are an integral part of the AIM. Features of the *target*, the *judge*, and the *situation* are the main variables of interest. Important *target* features include familiarity, complexity, and typicality. Important *judge* features include personal relevance, motivational goals, cognitive capacity, and affective state. Important *situational* features include perceived need for accuracy, social desirability expectations, and the availability of objective criteria against which a judgment can be checked.

THE EMPIRICAL EVIDENCE

As the previous discussion suggests, affective states can influence our thoughts, memories, and responses to social stimuli, as well as the information processing styles we adopt. The following section briefly reviews evidence for the process dependence of affect infusion and demonstrates affect infusion in several substantive areas, including (a) self-judgments, (b) person perception judgments, (c) stereotyping and prejudice, and (d) judgmental biases and errors.

Evidence for the Process Dependence of Affect Infusion into Judgments

By varying the extent to which social perceivers need to engage in substantive processing, we demonstrated that longer processing produces greater mood infusion, as predicted by the AIM. In one such study, participants were asked to make judgments about typical and atypical persons (the *strange people* experiments). Atypical targets should recruit more extensive processing and thus be more subject to affect infusion. After watching mood-inducing films, participants read about and formed impressions of typical and atypical students (Forgas, 1992b, Exp. 1). Impressions of the atypical target showed greater affect infusion than did impressions of the typical target. Recall data offered further evidence for the affect-priming hypothesis: Recall was better about atypical than typical targets, consistent with the presumably more extensive processing these stimuli received (Forgas, 1992b, Exp. 2).

In a third study, reaction times were also recorded (Forgas, 1992b, Exp. 3). Consistent with the AIM, participants took significantly longer to make judgments about atypical compared to typical targets, and there was a correspondingly greater affect infusion into these more elaborately processed judgments. In a conceptually similar set of studies, we used nonverbal stimuli to control for possible semantic priming effects. Images of well-matched or badly matched couples were used to create targets that required more or less elaborate processing (the *strange couples* studies). Incidentally, the idea for this experiment came to the first author during a visit to a restaurant as attention was attracted to the obviously romantic interaction between an apparently ill-matched couple – a very attractive young woman and

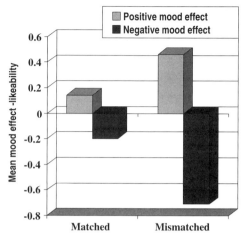

Figure 10.1. The effects of positive and negative mood on judgments about typical, well-matched and atypical, badly matched couples. Positive mood produced more positive judgments and negative mood produced more negative judgments, and these effects were significantly greater when the couples were badly matched and atypical, so that judgments required more elaborate and substantive processing. (Data based on Forgas, 1995b.)

a rather unattractive older man. Observing this scene, it became obvious that observers need to do much more cognitive work to make sense of this couple than if they were well matched, and so the chances of implicit affect infusion should also be greater. To test this prediction, in the first of these studies (Forgas, 1995b) happy, neutral, or sad people judged pictures of couples designed to be either typical (well matched for physical attractiveness) or atypical (mismatched for physical attractiveness). Again, consistent with the AIM, judgments of atypical couples produced greater affect infusion (Figure 10.1). A second study showed that recall was also better about mismatched couples, suggesting that they recruited greater information processing effort, as expected. In a third study, images of couples were created that could differ in terms of both physical attractiveness and race, allowing for three degrees of match/mismatch to be manipulated (fully matched, partly matched, fully mismatched).

As predicted by the AIM, the degree of atypicality was directly related to the size of the mood effect on judgments. In a fourth study, a mediational analysis of processing latencies confirmed that the time taken to process information about more or less well-matched couples significantly mediated the relationship between mood and judgments. That is, longer processing latencies increased and shorter processing latencies decreased the extent of mood congruence and affect infusion. Although consistent with the AIM, this is nevertheless a surprising and paradoxical effect, because intuitively one would expect longer and more systematic processing to reduce rather than increase affective biases in social judgments and decisions.

Interestingly, social judgments about highly familiar real-life events such as relationship conflicts show similar affect sensitivity (see also Shaver & Mikulincer, this volume). In the first of three experiments (Forgas, 1994), subjects feeling happy or sad after reading affectively laden literary passages were asked to make causal attributions for happy or conflict episodes in their current *intimate relationship*. Sad mood produced more internal, self-blaming attributions for conflicts and more external attributions for happy events in a pattern of mood-congruent, self-deprecating judgments. In contrast, happy subjects were more likely to blame external factors for conflicts but took greater credit for happy events (Figure 10.2). Additional studies showed that these mood effects on attributions were consistently greater when more extensive, constructive processing was required to deal with more complex, serious events. The possibility that mood effects on judgments may be particularly marked when serious and personally involving issues are at stake is, of course, of considerable practical relevance to areas of clinical and relationship research. The general principle predicted by the AIM, and supported in these studies, is that the effects of mood on social judgments tend to be most robust when perceivers are encouraged to think substantively and constructively about social judgments.

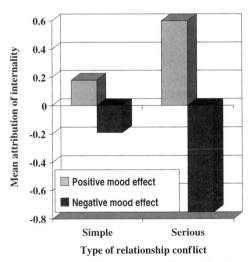

Figure 10.2. Mood-congruent effects of positive and negative mood on attributions for conflicts in real-life intimate relationships. Conflicts were less likely to be attributed internally in a positive than in a negative mood, and these effects were significantly greater when the conflicts were serious rather than simple. (After Forgas 1994.)

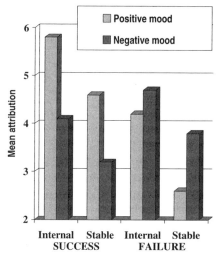

Figure 10.3. Mood-congruent effects of positive and negative mood on attributions for success and failure on an exam. Happy persons claim credit for success (make more internal and stable attributions) but reject blame for failure (make more external and unstable attributions). Unhappy persons take less credit for success and blame themselves more for failure. (Data based on Forgas, Bower, & Moylan, 1990.)

Affect and Self-Judgments

Affect seems to have a particularly strong influence on self-related judgments (Sedikides, 1995; see also Shaver & Mikulincer, this volume). Positive affect improves and negative affect impairs the valence of the self-concept (Nasby, 1994). For example, when we asked students to make judgments about their success or failure on a recent exam, induced positive or negative mood had a significant mood-congruent influence. Those in a negative mood blamed themselves more when failing and took less credit for their successes, whereas those in a positive mood claimed credit for success but refused to accept responsibility for their failures (Forgas et al., 1990; Figure 10.3). As suggested by the AIM, however, such effects are highly dependent on the nature of the task and the kind of processing strategies used.

For example, Nasby (1994) asked happy, neutral, and sad subjects to make affirmative (yes) or nonaffirmative (no) judgments about whether a variety of traits applied to them. Later, happy persons remembered more positive self-traits and sad persons remembered more negative self-traits – but only when prior ratings required an affirmative format. It seems that rejecting a trait as not applicable to the self may be a short, direct process that requires little elaborate processing, and affectively primed information is thus less likely to be relevant. In contrast, affirming that a trait applies to the self invites more elaborate thinking and should produce greater affect infusion, as was indeed found.

Mood effects on self-judgments also seem to depend on which aspect of the self is being judged. It appears that central and peripheral self-conceptions may be differentially sensitive to affect infusion (Sedikides, 1995). Because central self-conceptions are well rehearsed and stable, judgments about the central self require less online elaboration, and there should be less scope for affect to infuse these judgments. Sedikides (1995) found that affect had no influence on judgments related to central traits but had a significant mood-congruent influence on judgments related to peripheral traits. The process mediation of this effect was further confirmed when it was found that encouraging people to think more extensively about peripheral self-conceptions – paradoxically – further increased the influence of mood on these judgments. Traits such as self-esteem may also mediate mood effects on self-judgments. Low self-esteem persons generally have less certain and stable self-conceptions, and affect may thus have a greater influence on their self-judgments.

This prediction was confirmed in a study by Brown and Mankowski (1993), who found that induced mood had a clear mood-congruent influence on the self-judgments of low self-esteem persons but not on the self-rating by high self-esteem individuals. Smith and Petty (1995) found a similar pattern. They induced happy and sad moods in high and low self-esteem participants, who were then asked to report on three memories from their school years. Mood had a significant influence on the quantity and quality of responses by the low but not by the high self-esteem group. It seems, then, that low self-esteem people may need to engage in more open and elaborate processing when thinking about themselves, and their current mood may thus have a greater influence on the outcome (Sedikides, 1995).

There is also good evidence that motivated processing can eliminate or reverse affect infusion into self-judgments, as predicted by the AIM. Sometimes the reversal of affect infusion is a spontaneous phenomenon, as people automatically switch from affect-congruent to affect-incongruent judgments in an effort to maintain a reasonable affective equilibrium. This *mood management* hypothesis was investigated in a recent series of experiments (Forgas & Ciarrochi, 2002). We found that negative mood effects on self-descriptions were spontaneously reversed over time. These motivated mood management processes seem to be closely linked to individual differences such as self-esteem. People who scored high on self-esteem were able to eliminate the negativity of their self-judgments very rapidly, whereas low self-esteem individuals continued to persevere with negative self descriptions to the end of the task.

In summary, the evidence suggests that affect seems to have a strong mood-congruent influence on many self-related judgments, but only when some degree of open and constructive processing is required and there are no motivational forces to override affect congruence. Low self-esteem, judgments related to peripheral rather than central self-conceptions, and ratings that require elaborate rather than simple processing all seem to promote affect infusion into self-judgments.

Affective Influences on Judgments about Others

Some of the earliest demonstrations of affect infusion involved person perception judgments (Clore & Byrne, 1974; Feshbach & Singer, 1957). Indeed, perhaps the most fundamental judgment we make about others in everyday life occurs when we observe ongoing social behaviors. In one experiment, we induced happy or sad affect in participants, who were then shown a videotape of their own social interactions with a partner from the previous day (Forgas et al., 1984). Participants were asked to make a series of rapid online judgments evaluating the observed behaviors of themselves as well as their partners. Happy people saw significantly more positive, skilled and fewer negative, unskilled behaviors both in themselves and in their partners than did sad subjects (Figure 10.4). It is almost as if the same smile that was seen as friendly in a good mood was evaluated as awkward or condescending when the observer experienced negative affect. These effects seem to occur because affect priming implicitly

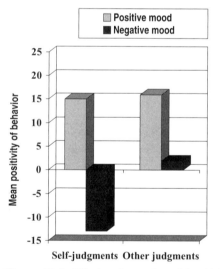

Figure 10.4. Effects of mood on identifying positive and negative behaviors in a videotaped interaction. Happy persons see more positive and fewer negative behaviors than do sad persons, both in their own and in their partner's recorded interactions. (After Forgas, Bower, & Krantz, 1984.)

influences the kinds of interpretations, constructs, and associations that people rely on as they form judgments about complex and indeterminate behaviors.

Memory mechanisms and affect priming appear to be largely responsible for these affect infusion effects, according to compelling evidence from subsequent experiments. Happy or sad people were asked to make judgments about persons described in terms of a number of positive and negative features on a computer screen (Forgas & Bower, 1987). Happy judges formed more positive judgments, and sad judges did the opposite. Crucially, reaction time data showed that people spent more time reading and thinking about affect-congruent information but were faster in producing an affect-congruent judgment, as implied by affect-priming theories. These results suggest that affective states can infuse social judgments because of the disproportionate influence that affectively primed information plays in the way social stimuli are learned, interpreted, and remembered.

Suprisingly, as we have seen, several experiments found that the more people need to think in order to produce a judgment, the greater the likelihood of affect infusion (Forgas, 1993, 1994, 1995b). We are currently seeking to extend this finding by exploring the influence of affective states on suspiciousness (East & Forgas, 2002). Given that people experiencing positive affect should have more positive ideas and memories activated, these ideas should be more available for use when evaluating ambiguous or suspicious information (Bower & Forgas, 2001). As a result, happy people should be more likely to accept ambiguous behaviors at face value and be relatively less suspicious than people in a sad mood, who should be more likely to form more negative impressions about an ambiguous target person. Again, we expect these affect-priming effects to occur only when people have to form a judgment about complex, ambiguous, or indeterminate information, thus increasing their need to engage in more constructive processing and rely more on their stored knowledge about the world to make sense of the stimulus. Affectively primed associations should thus have a greater chance to infuse social judgments whenever the people, couples, or situation judged are complex and unusual rather than simple and predictable (Forgas, 1992b, 1994).

Another field study investigated affective influences on judgments about and responses to a person who unexpectedly approached participants with an impromptu request (Forgas, 1998b). The scene of the study was a university library. Affect was induced by leaving folders containing pretested pictures (or text) designed to induce positive or negative mood on some unoccupied library desks with the instruction "Please open and consider this." Students occupying the desks were surreptitiously observed to ensure that they exposed themselves fully to the mood induction. Soon afterward they were approached by another student (in fact, a confederate) and received an unexpected polite or impolite request for several sheets

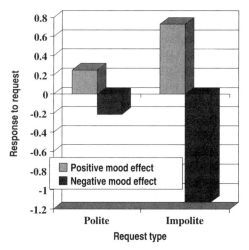

Figure 10.5. The effects of happy, control, and sad mood on judgments about an impromptu request received in a public setting (higher values indicate more positive evaluations). Positive mood produced more positive judgments, and these mood effects on request evaluation were greater when the request was impolite and atypical, and thus required more substantive processing. (Data based on Forgas, 1998b.)

of paper needed to complete an essay. Their responses were noted, and a short time later they were asked to complete a brief questionnaire assessing their attitudes toward and evaluation of the request and the requester.

There was a clear mood-congruent pattern in judgments of the requester. Negative mood resulted in more critical, negative judgments and less compliance than did positive mood. In an interesting pattern, these mood effects were greater when the request was impolite rather than polite, presumably because impolite, unconventional requests are likely to require more elaborate and substantive processing that facilitates affect infusion (Figure 10.5). This explanation was supported by evidence of better recall memory for these messages. More routine, polite, and conventional requests, on the other hand, were processed less substantively, were less influenced by mood, and were also remembered less accurately later on. These findings confirm that affect infusion can have a significant effect on determining attitudes and responses to people encountered in realistic everyday situations.

Affective Influences on Bargaining Decisions

Judgments about how to conduct a negotiating session may also be open to affect infusion (Forgas, 1998a). In several studies, mood was induced before

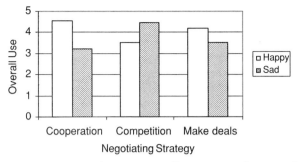

Figure 10.6. Mood-congruent influences on judgments about preferred negotiating strategies. Happy persons plan and use more cooperative and less competitive bargaining strategies, and are more likely to make and honor deals than negotiators experiencing negative affect. (Data based on Forgas, 1998a.)

participants engaged in highly realistic interpersonal and intergroup negotiation in what they believed was a separate experiment. Results showed that happy participants were more confident, formed higher expectations about their success, and formulated specific action plans that were more optimistic and cooperative than did control or unhappy participants. Further, happy participants behaved more cooperatively, were more willing to use integrative strategies, and were more willing to make and reciprocate deals than unhappy participants (Figure 10.6). These mood effects on bargaining behavior produced significantly better outcomes for happy participants. Further experiments showed that participants who scored low on measures such as Machiavellianism and need for approval were more influenced by mood in formulating their plans and behaviors than were high scorers on these measures. Theoretically, as implied by the AIM, affect infusion should be constrained for individuals who habitually approach interpersonal tasks such as bargaining from a highly motivated, predetermined perspective that limits the degree of open, constructive thinking they employ.

It seems that affect infusion is partly determined by such individual differences between people (Ciarrochi, Forgas, & Mayer, 2001). For example, we found that people who score high on traits such as Openness to Feelings seem more likely to be influenced by affect in how they evaluate and judge various consumer items they own, or want to own, than do low scorers on this measure (Ciarrochi & Forgas, 2000; Figure 10.7). Trait anxiety can also moderate affect infusion (Ciarrocchi & Forgas, 1999). These findings support the general principle that mood effects on social responses are significantly moderated by different processing strategies linked to enduring personality traits.

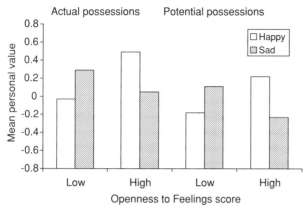

Figure 10.7. Mood-congruent influences on evaluations of consumer items already owned or desired. Positive mood increases the evaluation placed on consumer possessions; however, this effect is limited to individuals who score high on measures of openness to feelings. Low scorers on this measure show the opposite pattern. (Data based on Ciarrochi & Forgas, 2000.)

Affective Influences on Stereotyping

It has long been assumed that affect also plays a key role in stereotyping and intergroup judgments. After all, contact with an out-group may produce feelings of anxiety, uncertainty, and insecurity that could influence subsequent judgments. The experience of anxiety may also reduce information processing capacity and increase reliance on stereotypes. In recent experiments, we found that trait anxiety significantly moderates the influence of negative affect on intergroup judgments (Ciarrochi & Forgas, 1999). Low-trait-anxious Whites in the United States reacted more negatively to a threatening Black out-group when experiencing negative affect. Surprisingly, high-trait-anxious individuals showed the opposite pattern: They went out of their way to control their negative tendencies when feeling bad and produced more positive judgments. It appears that low-trait-anxious people processed automatically and allowed affect to influence their judgments, whereas high-trait anxiety combined with aversive mood triggered a more controlled, motivated processing strategy designed to eliminate socially undesirable intergroup judgments (see also Galinsky, Martorana, & Ku, this volume, for a discussion of the implicit and explicit cognitive processes that may be activated when people attempt to control stereotypic thoughts).

On the other hand, positive affect may often promote a schema-driven, top-down information processing strategy (Bless, 2000; Fiedler, 2001). This may facilitate reliance on group stereotypes when responding to others as long as there are no other demands for more elaborate processing (Forgas

& Fiedler, 1996, Exp. 1). For example, when allocating rewards to members of in-groups and out-groups, positive mood increased reliance on simple group stereotype information (Forgas & Fiedler, 1996). In these experiments, we found that the personal relevance of category membership was critically important. Positive affect promoted greater discrimination but only when group membership was of low relevance. When group membership was personally relevant, judges who experienced negative mood were more likely to discriminate against out-groups, consistent with an affect repair strategy.

Other experiments also showed that affect congruence in stereotype judgments can be easily eliminated when judges have reason to engage in motivated, rather than open, substantive processing. One influence likely to trigger motivated thinking is participation in a group when one is exposed to normative influences from other group members (Forgas, 1990). In one relevant experiment, we asked judges induced to feel happy or sad to make a series of judgments about groups such as Catholics, Jews, Communists, Italians, Asians, and so on. Judgments were made first as individuals, and 2 weeks later, the same individuals again underwent a mood induction and made the same judgments as a group. We found a clear mood-congruent pattern on judgments by individuals. The group interaction, however, had a surprising effect: Those in a positive mood made even more positive judgments in groups than as individuals, and negative mood effects were reduced as a result of the group discussion. It seems that normative and social desirability pressures within the group acted to magnify positive mood effects and eliminate negative mood effects by inducing more motivated judgmental strategies.

The Processing Consequences of Affect for Judgmental Errors and Biases

The processing consequences of affect may also influence the likelihood that people succumb to various judgmental errors and biases. As feeling good seems to produce a thinking style that relies more heavily on internal thoughts, dispositions, and ideas than on external stimulus information, in this mode of thinking individuals tend to pay less attention to external information, and tend to assimilate external details into their preexisting knowledge about the world (Bless, 2000; Fiedler, 2001). There is some experimental evidence, for example, suggesting that negative mood may help us to avoid certain judgmental mistakes, such as the *fundamental attribution error* (but see Haselton & Buss, this volume, for an analysis of whether such biases are in fact errors in judgment). The FAE occurs because people mistakenly assume that most actions are internally caused and ignore external influences on behavior. In several studies, we asked happy or sad people to judge others based on an essay written by them that advocated either desirable or undesirable attitudes on topical issues such as student fees. Judges were also told that this topic was either freely chosen or was assigned to the writer (Forgas, 1998c). Happy persons largely ignored this information and assumed that the essay reflected the writer's attitudes, thus committing the FAE. Negative mood reduced this bias. Those feeling bad paid more attention to the available information and tended to discount coerced essays as indicative of the writer's real views. Many decisions in everyday life – including important personal, clinical, and organizational decisions – are made in very similar circumstances. It is obviously important to understand how affect can influence many everyday judgments.

More generally, mood may also influence the way people use various judgmental heuristics, such as anchoring, availability, and representativeness. In a recent experiment on anchoring, we found some initial support for this idea (Chan & Forgas, 2002). After a mood induction, participants answered general knowledge questions, half of which included externally provided anchors and the other half featured anchors that were generated by the participants themselves. Negative mood increased the influence of anchoring information but only when the anchor value was externally provided. This result provides further support for the notion that negative affect increases attention to external information.

Eyewitness judgments represent another example of how affective states may influence processing strategies and thus judgmental errors. To evaluate the role of affect in eyewitness judgments, we asked people to witness complex social events presented on videotapes (such as a wedding scene or a robbery). A week later, we used films to induce a good or bad mood and then questioned subjects about what they saw; the questions either included or excluded "planted" misleading information about the scenes (Forgas, 2001). When memory for the incidents was tested later, misleading information was more likely to be mistaken for a real experience by those who were in a positive mood when the information was presented. Negative mood reduced this memory distortion. The same effects were also observed in a field study in which students were asked to observe and later recall a staged incident during a lecture (Forgas, 2001; Figure 10.8).

Low-intensity mood states can also have significant effect on judgments and behavior in organizations (Forgas & George, 2001). For example, in a series of recent studies, Stephanie Moylan (2000) showed that positive mood tends to increase and negative mood tends to decrease the incidence of a variety of errors and distortions in performance assessment judgments.

SUMMARY AND CONCLUSIONS

We have seen that mild everyday affective states can have a highly significant affect-congruent influence on a variety of social judgments. These affect infusion effects may occur due to *implicit* mechanisms, such as the

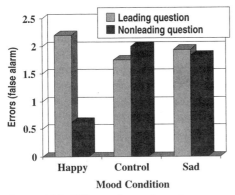

Figure 10.8. Effects of mood on the accuracy of eyewitness judgments. Leading questions containing misleading information are more likely to be incorporated into eyewitness judgments by persons experiencing positive rather than negative mood when exposed to the information. (Unpublished data.)

automatic priming and greater use of affect-congruent information in judgments, or as a result of *explicit* mechanisms, such as reliance on the "how-do-I-feel-about-it?" heuristic. Further, a number of the experiments discussed here show that different information processing strategies play a key role in facilitating or inhibiting affect infusion. The multiprocess AIM (Forgas, 1995a), in particular, offers a simple and parsimonious explanation of when, how, and why affect infusion into judgments is likely to occur. A number of studies found support for the counterintuitive prediction derived from the AIM that more extensive, substantive processing enhances implicit affect infusion effects (Forgas, 1992b, 1994, 1995b, 1999a, 1999b; Nasby, 1994; Sedikides, 1995).

We have also seen, however, that affect infusion is absent whenever a judgmental task could be performed using a simple, well-rehearsed, direct-access strategy or a highly motivated strategy. In these conditions, there is little need and little opportunity for incidentally primed mood-congruent information to infuse information processing (Fiedler, 1991; Forgas, 1995a). Several of these experiments also demonstrated that affect infusion occurs not only in the laboratory but also in many real-life situations. Even such highly involved and personal judgments as explaining intimate relationship conflicts can be subject to a mood-congruent bias (Forgas, 1994). In summary, this chapter emphasized the closely interactive relationship between affective states and different information processing strategies as the key to understanding affective influences on attitudes, judgments, social cognition, and interpersonal behavior. The real-life consequences of affect infusion in applied domains such as clinical, organizational, health, and consumer psychology deserve serious attention (Forgas & Ciarrochi, 2002; Forgas & George, 2001).

References

Adolphs, R., & Damasio, A. (2001). The interaction of affect and cognition: A neurobiological perspective. In J. P. Forgas (Ed.), *The handbook of affect and social cognition* (pp. 27–49). Mahwah, NJ: Erlbaum.

Anderson, N. H. (1974). Cognitive algebra: Integration theory applied to social attribution. In L. Berkowitz (Ed.), *Advances in experimental social psychology* (Vol. 7, pp. 1–101). New York: Academic Press.

Argyle, M. (1991). A critique of cognitive approaches to social judgments and social behaviour. In J. P. Forgas (Ed.), *Emotion and social judgments* (pp. 161–180). Oxford: Pergamon Press.

Asch, S. E. (1946). Forming impressions of personality. *Journal of Abnormal and Social Psychology, 41*, 258–290.

Baron, R. (1987). Interviewers' moods and reactions to job applicants: The influence of affective states on applied social judgments. *Journal of Applied Social Psychology, 16*, 16–28.

Berkowitz, L. Jaffee, S., Jo, E., & Troccoli, B. T. (2000). On the correction of feeling-induced judgmental biases. In J. P. Forgas (Ed.), *Feeling and thinking: The role of affect in social cognition* (pp. 131–152). New York: Cambridge University Press.

Bless, H. (2000). The interplay of affect and cognition: The mediating role of general knowledge structures. In J. P. Forgas (Ed.), *Feeling and thinking: The role of affect in social cognition* (pp. 201–222). New York: Cambridge University Press.

Bower, G. H. (1981). Mood and memory. *American Psychologist, 36*, 129–148.

Bower, G. H., & Forgas, J. P. (2001). Mood and social memory. In J. P. Forgas (Ed.), *The handbook of affect and social cognition* (pp. 95–120). Mahwah, NJ: Erlbaum.

Brown, J. D., & Mankowski, T. A. (1993). Self-esteem, mood, and self-evaluation: Changes in mood and the way you see you. *Journal of Personality and Social Psychology, 64*, 421–430.

Bruner, J. S. (1957). On perceptual readiness. *Psychological Review, 64*, 123–152.

Byrne, D., & Clore, G. L. (1970). A reinforcement model of evaluation responses. *Personality: An International Journal, 1*, 103–128.

Chan, N. Y. M., & Forgas, J. P. (2002). *Affective influences on the use of judgmental heuristics in social judgments*. Manuscript, University of New South Wales, Sydney.

Ciarrochi, J. V., & Forgas, J. P. (1999). On being tense yet tolerant: The paradoxical effects of trait anxiety and aversive mood on intergroup judgments. *Group Dynamics: Theory, Research and Practice, 3*, 227–238.

Ciarrochi, J. V., & Forgas, J. P. (2000). The pleasure of possessions: The interactive effects of mood and personality on evaluation of consumer items. *European Journal of Social Psychology, 30*, 631–649.

Ciarrochi, J. V., Forgas, J. P., & Mayer, J. D. (Eds.). (2001). *Emotional intelligence in everyday life*. Philadelphia: Psychology Press.

Clark, M. S., & Isen, A. M. (1982). Towards understanding the relationship between feeling states and social behavior. In A. H. Hastorf & A. M. Isen (Eds.), *Cognitive social psychology* (pp. 73–108). New York: Elsevier-North Holland.

Clore, G. L., & Byrne, D. (1974). The reinforcement affect model of attraction. In T. L. Huston (Ed.), *Foundations of interpersonal attraction* (pp. 143–170). New York: Academic Press.

Clore, G. L., Gasper, K., & Garvin, E. (2001). Affect as information. In J. P. Forgas (Ed.), *The handbook of affect and social cognition* (pp. 121–144). Mahwah, NJ: Erlbaum.

East, R., & Forgas, J. P. (2002). *The effects of mood on suspiciousness in interpersonal judgments.* Manuscript, University of New South Wales, Sydney.

Eich, E., & Forgas, J. P. (in press). Mood congruence and mood dependence in cognition and memory. In I. B. Weiner (Ed.), *Comprehensive handbook of psychology: Volume 3. Experimental psychology* (A. F. Healy & R. W. Proctor, Eds.). New York: Wiley.

Eich, E., & Macauley, D. (2000). Fundamental factors in mood-dependent memory. In J. P. Forgas (Ed.), *Feeling and thinking: The role of affect in social cognition* (pp. 109–130). New York: Cambridge University Press.

Ellis, H. C., & Ashbrook, T. W. (1988). Resource allocation model of the effects of depressed mood state on memory. In K. Fiedler & J. P. Forgas (Eds.), *Affect, cognition and social behaviour* (pp. 25–43). Toronto: Hogrefe.

Feshbach, S., & Singer, R. D. (1957). The effects of fear arousal and suppression of fear upon social perception. *Journal of Abnormal and Social Psychology, 55,* 283–288.

Fiedler, K. (1990). Mood-dependent selectivity in social cognition. In W. Stroebe & M. Hewstone (Eds.), *European review of social psychology* (Vol. 1, pp. 1–32). New York: Wiley.

Fiedler, K. (1991). On the task, the measures and the mood in research on affect and social cognition. In J. P. Forgas (Ed.), *Emotion and social judgments* (pp. 83–104). Oxford: Pergamon Press.

Fiedler, K. (2000). Towards an integrative account of affect and cognition phenomena using the BIAS computer algorithm. In J. P. Forgas (Ed.), *Feeling and thinking: The role of affect in social cognition* (pp. 223–252). New York: Cambridge University Press.

Fiedler, K. (2001). Affective influences on social information processing. In J. P. Forgas (Ed.), *The handbook of affect and social cognition* (pp. 163–181). Mahwah, NJ: Erlbaum.

Fiedler, K., & Bless, H. (2001). The formation of beliefs in the interface of affective and cognitive processes. In N. Frijda, A. Manstead, & S. Bem (Eds.), *The influence of emotions on beliefs* (pp. 112–139). New York: Cambridge University Press.

Fiedler, K., & Forgas, J. P. (Eds.) (1988). *Affect, cognition, and social behavior: New evidence and integrative attempts* (pp. 44–62). Toronto: Hogrefe.

Forgas, J. P. (1979). *Social episodes: The study of interaction routines.* London: Academic Press.

Forgas, J. P. (Ed.). (1981). *Social cognition: Perspectives on everyday understanding.* London: Academic Press.

Forgas, J. P. (1982). Episode cognition: Internal representations of interaction routines. In L. Berkowitz (Ed.), *Advances in experimental social psychology* (pp. 59–104). New York: Academic Press.

Forgas, J. P. (1983). What is social about social cognition? *British Journal of Social Psychology, 22,* 129–144.

Forgas, J. P. (1990). Affective influences on individual and group judgments. *European Journal of Social Psychology, 20,* 441–453.

Forgas, J. P. (1991a). Mood effects on partner choice: Role of affect in social decisions. *Journal of Personality and Social Psychology, 61*, 708–720.

Forgas, J. P. (Ed.). (1991b). *Emotion and social judgments.* Oxford: Pergamon Press.

Forgas, J. P. (1992a). Affect in social judgments and decisions: A multi-process model. In M. Zanna (Ed.), *Advances in experimental social psychology* (Vol. 25, pp. 227–275). New York: Academic Press.

Forgas, J. P. (1992b). On bad mood and peculiar people: Affect and person typicality in impression formation. *Journal of Personality and Social Psychology, 62*, 863–875.

Forgas, J. P. (1993). On making sense of odd couples: Mood effects on the perception of mismatched relationships. *Personality and Social Psychology Bulletin, 19*, 59–71.

Forgas, J. P. (1994). Sad and guilty? Affective influences on the explanation of conflict episodes. *Journal of Personality and Social Psychology, 66*, 56–68.

Forgas, J. P. (1995a). Mood and judgment: The Affect Infusion Model (AIM). *Psychological Bulletin, 117*(1), 39–66.

Forgas, J. P. (1995b). Strange couples: Mood effects on judgments and memory about prototypical and atypical targets. *Personality and Social Psychology Bulletin, 21*, 747–765.

Forgas, J. P. (1998a). On feeling good and getting your way: Mood effects on negotiation strategies and outcomes. *Journal of Personality and Social Psychology, 74*, 565–577.

Forgas, J. P. (1998b). Asking nicely? Mood effects on responding to more or less polite requests. *Personality and Social Psychology Bulletin, 24*, 173–185.

Forgas, J. P. (1998c). Happy and mistaken? Mood effects on the fundamental attribution error. *Journal of Personality and Social Psychology, 75*, 318–331.

Forgas, J. P. (1999a). On feeling good and being rude: Affective influences on language use and request formulations. *Journal of Personality and Social Psychology, 76*, 928–939.

Forgas, J. P. (1999b). Feeling and speaking: Mood effects on verbal communication strategies. *Personality and Social Psychology Bulletin, 25*, 850–863.

Forgas, J. P. (Ed.). (2000). *Feeling and thinking: The role of affect in social cognition.* New York: Cambridge University Press.

Forgas, J. P. (Ed.). (2001). *Handbook of affect and social cognition.* Mahwah, NJ: Erlbaum.

Forgas, J. P. (2002). Feeling and doing: Affective influences on social behaviour. *Psychological Inquiry, 13*, 1–28.

Forgas, J. P., & Bower, G. H. (1987). Mood effects on person perception judgements. *Journal of Personality and Social Psychology, 53*, 53–60.

Forgas, J. P., Bower, G. H., & Krantz, S. (1984). The influence of mood on perceptions of social interactions. *Journal of Experimental Social Psychology, 20*, 497–513.

Forgas, J. P., Bower, G. H., & Moylan, S. J. (1990). Praise or blame? Affective influences on attributions for achievement. *Journal of Personality and Social Psychology, 59*, 809–818.

Forgas, J. P., & Ciarrochi, J. V. (2002). On managing moods: Evidence for the role of homeostatic cognitive strategies in affect regulation. *Personality and Social Psychology Bulletin, 28*, 336–345.

Forgas, J. P., & Fiedler, K. (1996). Us and them: Mood effects on intergroup discrimination. *Journal of Personality and Social Psychology, 70*, 36–52.

Forgas, J. P., & George, J. M. (2001). Affective influences on judgments and behavior in organizations: An information processing perspective. *Organizational Behavior and Human Decision Processes, 86,* 3–34.

Forgas, J. P., & Moylan, S. J. (1987). After the movies: The effects of transient mood states on social judgments. *Personality and Social Psychology Bulletin, 13,* 478–489.

Gouaux, C. (1971). Induced affective states and interpersonal attraction. *Journal of Personality and Social Psychology, 20,* 37–43.

Gouaux, C., & Summers, K. (1973). Interpersonal attraction as a function of affective states and affective change. *Journal of Research in Personality, 7,* 254–260.

Griffitt, W. (1970). Environmental effects on interpersonal behavior: Ambient effective temperature and attraction. *Journal of Personality and Social Psychology, 15,* 240–244.

Heider, F. (1958). *The psychology of interpersonal relations.* New York: Wiley.

Higgins, E. T. (2001). Promotion and prevention experiences: Relating emotions to non-emotional motivational states. In J. P. Forgas (Ed.), *The handbook of affect and social cognition* (pp. 186–211). Mahwah, NJ: Erlbaum.

Ito, T., & Cacioppo, J. (2001). Affect and attitudes: A social neuroscience approach. In J. P. Forgas (Ed.), *The handbook of affect and social cognition* (pp. 50–74). Mahwah, NJ: Erlbaum.

Mackie, D. M., & Worth, L. T. (1989). Processing deficits and the mediation of positive affect in persuasion. *Journal of Personality and Social Psychology, 57,* 27–40.

Martin, L. (2000). Moods don't convey information: Moods in context do. In J. P. Forgas (Ed.), *Feeling and thinking: The role of affect in social cognition* (pp. 153–177). New York: Cambridge University Press.

Moylan, S. (2000). *Affective influence on performance appraisal judgments.* Unpublished Ph.D. thesis, University of New South Wales.

Nasby, W. (1994). Moderators of mood-congruent encoding: Self-/other-reference and affirmative/nonaffirmative judgement. *Cognition and Emotion, 8,* 259–278.

Niedenthal, P., & Halberstadt, J. (2000). Grounding categories in emotional response. In J. P. Forgas (Ed.), *Feeling and thinking: The role of affect in social cognition* (pp. 357–386). New York: Cambridge University Press.

Pervin, L. A. (1976). A free-response description approach to the analysis of person–situation interaction. *Journal of Personality and Social Psychology, 34,* 465–474.

Razran, G. H. S. (1940). Conditioned response changes in rating and appraising sociopolitical slogans. *Psychological Bulletin, 37,* 481.

Salovey, P., & Birnbaum, D. (1989). Influence of mood on health-relevant cognitions. *Journal of Personality and Social Psychology, 57,* 539–551.

Schwarz, N. (1990). Feelings as information: Informational and motivational functions of affective states. In E. T. Higgins & R. Sorrentino (Eds.), *Handbook of motivation and cognition: Foundations of social behaviour* (Vol. 2, pp. 527–561). New York: Guilford Press.

Schwarz, N., & Clore, G. L. (1983). Mood, misattribution and judgments of well being: Informative and directive functions of affective states. *Journal of Personality and Social Psychology, 45,* 513–523.

Sedikides, C. (1994). Incongruent effects of sad mood on self-conception valence: It's a matter of time. *European Journal of Social Psychology, 24,* 161–172.

Sedikides, C. (1995). Central and peripheral self-conceptions are differentially influenced by mood: Tests of the differential sensitivity hypothesis. *Journal of Personality and Social Psychology, 69*(4), 759–777.

Smith, S. M., & Petty, R. E. (1995). Personality moderators of mood congruency effects on cognition: The role of self-esteem and negative mood regulation. *Journal of Personality and Social Psychology, 68*, 1092–1107.

Wyer, R. S., & Srull, T. K. (1989). *Memory and cognition in its social context*. Hillsdale, NJ: Erlbaum.

Zajonc, R. B. (1980). Feeling and thinking: Preferences need no inferences. *American Psychologist, 35*, 151–175.

Zajonc, R. B. (2000). Feeling and thinking: Closing the debate over the independence of affect. In J. P. Forgas (Ed.), *Feeling and thinking: The role of affect in social cognition* (pp. 31–58). New York: Cambridge University Press.

11

Hot Cognition and Social Judgments

When and Why Do Descriptions Influence Our Feelings?

Diederik A. Stapel

CONTENTS

> I always heard
> I could get hurt
> I knew that from the start.
>
> Break my face, my back
> My arms, my neck
> But please, do not break my heart.
>
> K's Choice "My heart"

INTRODUCTION

Affect plays a pivotal role in our mental and social lives, in what we think and in what we do. Whether a stimulus elicits a positive reaction ("I like

Please address correspondence to Diederik A. Stapel, Heymans Institute, Department of Behavioral and Social Sciences, University of Groningen, Grote Kruisstraat 2/1, 9712 TS Groningen, the Netherlands; e-mail: d.a.staple@ppsw.rug.nl this") or a negative reaction ("I hate this") or puts us in a positive affective state ("I feel good") or a negative affective state ("I feel bad") is a determining force in whether we act or do not act, whether we remember or forget, and whether we approach or avoid. The affect-laden features of stimuli help us to discriminate between what matters and what does not. Affect infuses our thoughts with meaning and fuels our actions with purpose (see also Forgas & East, this volume). In fact, in most if not all major psychological processes, affect plays an important role, for a world bereft of affect cannot exist. In such a world, there would be no evaluations, no feelings, no preferences, no moods, and no emotions, and therefore no affiliation, friendship, solidarity, mating, love, or hate, and hence no life (Zajonc, 1998). In other words, not only does affect make our heart beat quicker (or slower), it makes the world go round. Affect goes at our hearts and makes or breaks us.

AFFECT AND SURVIVAL

Affect not only plays a prominent role in our daily lives, it also is important when we consider our evolutionary past. The evolutionary advantage of affect-based discrimination is obvious: Evolutionary forces do not value knowledge or truth per se, but rather a species' survival (see also Haselton & Buss, this volume). For a species to survive, affect-based processing is essential because it helps to differentiate between hospitable (good) and hostile (bad) stimuli. In other words, affective categorizations, such as good–bad or positive–negative discriminations, allow organisms to avoid becoming a meal. As Hunt and Campbell (1997) argue, the human brain and body have been shaped by natural selection to perform affective categorizations quickly and effectively and to respond accordingly. Affective categorizations and responses are so critical for survival that humans have rudimentary reflexes for such categorizing ("Is this good or bad?"), as well as for approaching or withdrawing from certain classes of stimuli and for providing metabolic support for such actions (Cacioppo & Gardner, 1999).

The importance of affective processing is also immediately clear if one considers its role in classical conditioning, that is, in the emergence and sustainability of learning and performance. After all, for conditioning to occur, a response must previously be succeeded by a reinforcing event. And an event is reinforcing only if the organism can discriminate it as a positive or a negative event. Put differently, an organism that could not discriminate between the positive and negative consequences of its actions could not acquire stable response dispositions and therefore could not survive (Tesser, 1993).

AFFECT'S ADVANTAGE

On an empirical level, the importance of affective processing, of quickly detecting and reacting adequately to the affective features of stimuli, is probably illustrated most convincingly by studies on Zajonc's (1980) *theory of affective primacy*. This theory holds that affective reactions are basic, automatic, and autonomous, occurring prior to and separately from cognitive responses. Zajonc has typically been quite vague about what he means exactly by *cognitive responses*, and has been and still is heavily criticized for attacking a straw person by (either implicitly or explicitly) assuming that *cognition* is by definition conscious, verbal, and controllable (Stapel, Koomen, & Ruijs, 2002). However, if we repackage Zajonc's theory of affective primacy in terms of the present analysis, it is clear that there is strong empirical support for (at least components) of his central thesis.

One important aspect of the theory of affective primacy is that the affective system, concerned with the processing of affective stimulus features (e.g., "Is this positive or negative?"), is separate from and partially independent of the nonaffective (in Zajonc's terms, cognitive) system, concerned with the processing of stimulus description (e.g., "Is this a woman or a man?"). This independence hypothesis is now supported by psychological as well as neuropsychological evidence (Zajonc, 1998).

Another aspect of the theory of affective primacy is the hypothesis that affective reactions (e.g., positive–negative classifications) occur *prior* to nonaffective reactions (or more descriptive responses, such as big–small classifications). And indeed, several lines of research indicate that mere detection of a stimulus by the perceiver's sensory apparatus is sufficient to classify this stimulus as positive or as negative, whereas nonevaluative classifications need longer exposure times. For example, in a series of studies Murphy and Zajonc (1993) found that very brief exposure to smiling (positive) versus frowning (negative) faces influenced participants' subsequent evaluations of novel ambiguous stimuli (Chinese ideographs), whereas very brief exposure to geometric shapes (e.g., circles) varying on nonevaluative, more descriptive dimensions (e.g., size) had no impact on participants' judgments. However, at longer (optimal, supraliminal) exposure times, these nonevaluative primes did influence participants' judgments.

These and other studies (for a review, see Stapel et al., 2002) support Zajonc's (1980, 1998) hypothesis that the affective qualities of stimuli are processed more readily than their nonaffective attributes.

IS A DIET OF AFFECTIVE PROCESSING ENOUGH TO SURVIVE?

Quick detection of affective stimulus features is important for survival. Therefore, the processing of affective features occurs quickly, automatically, and prior to the processing of their nonaffective counterparts. That is what the studies of the theory of affective primacy (see earlier) have shown. Affect precedes cognition because affect is more important, because affect has more survival value. Taken to its extreme, this line of reasoning seems to suggest that affect is enough to survive. If one knows whether an environment or a stimulus is hostile or hospitable, then one has sufficient knowledge to avoid becoming a meal. The question is, of course, whether this is true. Is the (quick and automatic) detection of affective features enough to postpone death? Is knowing that something is positive or negative enough to prepare for proper action? Is assessment of the valence of things enough to respond adequately and efficiently to the diverse and ever-changing stimuli and events in the world? I do not think so.

The stimuli in the world are complex and multidimensional, seemingly incomparable. Our perceptual system has evolved to be tuned to specific features, resulting in the expression on common metrics (Cosmides & Tooby, 2000). But what are the features our system tunes to spontaneously and automatically? Are translations of multidimensional stimuli to relatively gross and nonspecific dimensions such as positive–negative, good–bad, or hospitable–hostile sufficient to regulate our feelings, thoughts, and actions successfully? Some have argued that gross, nonspecific, valence-based classifications are indeed sufficient to prepare us for proper responses to affect-laden stimuli (Bargh, 1997; Kahneman, 1998; Zajonc, 1998). I disagree.

Although valence detection is necessary, I posit that it probably is not always sufficient for successful adaptation in a complex social environment. Following and extending Scherer's (e.g., 1984) as well as Öhman's theorizing on the function of emotions (see also Öhman & Mineka, 2001), I propose that to function successfully, people need to be flexible in their (automatic) reactions and behavioral adaptations to their environment and that *descriptive* (nonaffective) processing allows for such flexibility.

In terms of evolutionary history, the flexibility of the behavioral adaptation of organisms to their environment is largely due to the ability to make *descriptive* rather than *affective* classifications. Attending and reacting solely to the affective tone of things is not enough. Descriptive classifications *decouple* the behavioral reaction from an affect-infused stimulus event by replacing rigid reflex-like stimulus–response patterns or instinctive innate releasing mechanisms. As higher species evolve, they develop a need for increasingly complex information processing together with greater flexibility and variability of behavioral inventories. To accomplish this, the organism requires a mechanism to allow for the quick, efficient, and adequate adaptation of its behavior to changing external and internal stimuli (Cacioppo & Gardner, 1999). Such a mechanism makes possible the constant evaluation and reevaluation of complex stimuli, situations, and events without much time delay. The quick and efficient detection of not only affective but also nonaffective (i.e., descriptive) stimulus features is such a mechanism.

Description adds specificity to affective processing. Description shapes affective processing by making it specific, and specificity is essential to obtain flexibility in processing and variability in responding. Without the processing of its descriptive features, an affect-laden stimulus is classified only in terms of its valence (i.e., on a positive–negative dimension), and knowing only that something is positive or negative is hardly enough to prepare for proper action (Robinson, 1996). To give an example from the domain of emotions: To react quickly but properly to someone expressing fear, it is important to detect the valence of this emotion (negative), as well as its descriptive meaning. Only then can we react appropriately and distinctively. After all, seeing fear demands a different reaction than seeing disgust, sadness, or anger. And often, this reaction needs to be quick and effective. If one is not capable of quickly determining whether a person (or an animal) expresses anger, disgust, or fear, one may get hurt (Forgas, 2001; Zajonc, 1998). To react quickly and properly to changes in the environment, it is important to detect automatically affective as well as nonaffective features of the stimuli inhabiting that environment.

I thus argue that even though affective (i.e., diffuse, nondescriptive) stimulus components constitute the main (and relatively early) input of our feelings, emotions, evaluations, and behaviors, affect seldom is the only input. The meaning of an affective reaction changes when it is enriched by particular descriptive inferences. Being in a good mood is pleasant, but being in a good mood after a hard day's work feels different from being in a good mood after winning the lottery. Similarly, noticing a colleague smile at you while you leave the building is likely to be different when you have just been fired than when you have just become a parent.

Descriptive inferences that accompany affective reactions thus constitute an important determinant of the content of affect-infused feelings, thoughts, and actions. Moreover, because descriptive processing is essential for adequate maneuvering through our complex social world (i.e., has survival value), it is likely to occur in the earliest stages of the information processing chain. If it is so important, descriptive processing should be quick. In other words, descriptive processing of affect-laden information is likely to occur automatically, without awareness, intention, or control (cf. Bargh, 1997).

VARIETIES OF AUTOMATICITY: AUTOMATIC EVALUATION AND DESCRIPTION EFFECTS

If we consider what the human mind is designed for, it is only logical to assume that the information processing system is designed in such a manner that both affective and nonaffective appraisals of affect-laden stimuli can occur in the earliest stages of the processing chain, that is, spontaneously and automatically. Because early detection of affective as well as nonaffective stimulus features is essential for survival, there is no a priori reason to assume that the domain of automaticity should be reserved for the processing of affective stimulus properties.

Surprisingly, to date, studies on automaticity and affective processing have been concerned mainly with demonstrating that the evaluative or *affective* meaning of affect-laden stimuli can be processed without awareness. There is now a small cottage industry of studies showing this *automatic evaluation effect* (Bargh, 1997; Fazio, 2001; Glaser & Banaji, 2001), but there is hardly any research demonstrating the automatic detection of nonaffective features of affect-tinged stimuli. Reviews of automaticity research (Bargh, 1997; Bargh & Ferguson, 2001) and affect priming studies (Fazio, 2001; Glaser & Banaji, 2001; Zajonc, 1998) tend to equate automatic processing with affective processing. I posit that in the processing of affect-laden stimuli, nonaffective as well as affective features can be processed automatically.

Even though there is a large number of studies corroborating Zajonc's idea that affective information is picked up prior to nonaffective information, there is no reason to conclude from such affect-precedes-cognition findings that only affective and information can be perceived without awareness. In fact, in both the cognitive psychology and social psychology literatures, there is ample evidence that nonaffective, descriptive, denotative meaning can be picked up without awareness. A number of studies have demonstrated that people may process the meaning of *neutral* words, such as *table*, *cat*, or *building*, without awareness (e.g., Greenwald, Draine, & Abrams, 1996), and several investigations have shown effectively the impact of suboptimally presented, *neutral* (nonaffective) information on judgment and behavior (Stapel & Koomen, 2000). However, even though the notion that descriptive meaning can be processed automatically can hardly be called new, the possibility that the descriptive processing of *affect-laden* stimuli could occur automatically is typically overlooked and under-researched in the relevant literature (Bargh, 1997; Forgas, 2001; Zajonc, 1998).

EARLY AND LATE AFFECT

A functionalist perspective on affective processing that focuses on what kind of processing is needed to survive suggests that there may be varieties of unconscious affect. Previous studies on automaticity and affective priming have shown that the detection of affective stimulus features may occur without awareness and has a stable processing advantage over the detection of nonaffective features. It is logical to assume, however, that because crude affective (e.g., positive–negative) classifications will seldom be sufficient to adapt adequately in a complex social environment, nonaffective (e.g., big–small) classifications should also occur quickly and automatically. In Zajonc's terminology: Affect may precede cognition, but both affective and cognitive reactions may occur without awareness.

a   b

Figure 11.1. What we see when we see without awareness. When exposed to a smiling, young, dark-haired female face (a), exposure time may be an important determinant of what one actually perceives. At very short subliminal exposure, only affect (the valence of the facial expression) should be detected (b). At slightly longer subliminal exposure, however, information about other features of the picture, such as hair color or gender, will become available (e.g., a smiling dark-haired woman), filling in one's initial affective reaction with more descriptive appraisals, resulting in a representation that is akin to what is actually presented (a).

This suggests that what we see when we see without awareness depends (at least in part) on the *exposure duration* of the presented information. At very short exposures, affective influences might take place, giving rise to gross affective classifications (positive–negative). These early affective reactions will be unencumbered by more descriptive, nonevaluative reactions that may require fuller access if the stimuli are to be fully encoded. At longer exposures, stimuli also are likely to activate more complex networks of associations allowing for feature identification and recognition (Bargh, Litt, Pratto, & Spielman, 1989; Murphy & Zajonc, 1993). Thus, when one is exposed to a smiling, young, dark-haired female face (Figure 11.1a), exposure time may be an important determinant of what one actually perceives. At very short exposures, only the valence of the facial expression should be detected (e.g., positive; Figure 11.1b). At longer exposure, however, information about other features of the picture, such as hair color or gender, will become available (e.g., a smiling, dark-haired woman), filling in the initial affective reaction with more descriptive appraisals.

An important difference between early and late reactions to stimuli possessing affective as well as nonaffective features is that, by definition, affective information that is activated early is more simple, gross, or *diffuse* (e.g., positive versus negative) than affective information that is activated late (e.g., "happy dark-haired woman" versus "angry blond man"). Early affective reactions are, by definition, diffuse and unspecified because they are cognitively unappraised. Early affect is "free-floating" and "undedicated" (Murphy & Zajonc, 1993, p. 591). Later in the information processing chain (but still without awareness), these diffuse, gross, affective appraisals may become enriched by descriptive (cognitive) appraisals. In other words, even within the domain of affect-infused reactions to suboptimally presented stimuli, one may distinguish early affect-only (Figure 11.1b) reactions that are relatively gross and *diffuse* and late affect-plus-cognition

(Figure 11.1a) reactions that may result in the activation of affect-infused exemplar information that is relatively specific and *distinct*.

THE CONSEQUENCES OF EARLY (DIFFUSE) AND LATE (DISTINCT) AFFECT

This distinction between early and late affective reactions in terms of the distinctiveness of the activated representations may have important implications for affect's effects. That is, the distinction between *diffuse affect* and *distinct affect* is essential when it concerns the consequences of affect-laden stimuli on subsequent evaluations and actions. Why should distinctness matter for the impact of suboptimally activated information? In earlier studies, my colleagues and I tested the hypothesis that distinctness is important for the direction of *supraliminal* priming effects. The reasoning behind these investigations was as follows: Many impression formation models assume (either implicitly or explicitly) a direct relation between the *direction* of the impact of activated information on judgment (assimilation or contrast) and the *component* of the impression formation process on which such information mainly exerts its influence (interpretation or judgment) (for extensive reviews, see Stapel & Koomen, 2001a, 2001b). That is, activated information should be more likely to yield assimilation when it is used during encoding or interpretation, whereas contrast is more likely when this information serves as a comparison standard during judgment (see also Bless, Schwarz, & Wänke, this volume; McClure, Sutton, & Hilton, this volume). But what determines whether accessible knowledge will serve predominantly as an interpretation frame or as a comparison standard?

In a number of studies, we showed that one important determinant of the direction of accessibility effects is the distinctness of the activated information. Whereas diffuse information is more likely to be used as an interpretation frame during the encoding of a stimulus and result in assimilation, distinct information is more likely to be used as a comparison standard in the judgment stage and result in contrast (Stapel & Koomen, 2001a). Distinct information constitutes a separate entity with clear object boundaries (e.g., a person exemplar, "a sad, dark-haired woman") and is therefore more likely to be used as a specific comparison standard in the construction of judgments than diffuse information (e.g., an abstract construct, positive). When information is diffuse, assimilation is likely to occur. As Murphy and Zajonc (1993, p. 736) put it in their discussion of the impact of diffuse affect, such affect "can 'spill over' onto unrelated stimuli" (for a similar line of reasoning, see Forgas & East, this volume; Schwarz & Clore, 1996). Or as Zajonc (1998, p. 54) wrote when summing up some of the features of diffuse affect, "It is more like moisture, it is like odor, like heat. It can disperse, displace, scatter, permeate, float, combine, fuse, blend, spill over, and become attached to any stimulus, even one totally unrelated to its origins."

There are now several empirical studies that support the distinctness hypothesis in domains as diverse as person perception, self-perception, advertising effects, and organizational decision making (Stapel & Koomen, 2001a). For example, we found that when the task is to judge a target person, priming diffuse trait information ("hostile" versus "friendly") before a target person (vaguely hostile Mike) has to be judged results in assimilative interpretation effects, whereas priming distinct person information ("Dracula" versus "Mandela") yields contrastive comparison effects.

The present functionalist analysis of the processing of affect-laden stimuli suggests that my previous research on the impact of supraliminally presented context information could be taken one important step further. That is, the preceding analysis of the differences between early and late affective reactions implies that distinctness may be an important determinant not only of the impact of optimally presented stimuli, but also of the effect of suboptimally exposed stimuli. In the impression formation chain, one can distinguish between the early, diffuse activation of affective information and the later, distinct activation. We also know that diffuse information is more likely to yield assimilation, whereas distinct information is more likely to lead to contrast. Combining these two principles suggests that automatic effects of (affect-laden) information may be assimilative and diametrically opposed to the effects of later, distinct information that is more likely to produce contrast effects. Whether assimilation or contrast is observed should thus depend on the latency of the response. Following Zajonc's affect-precedes-cognition logic and recent research on the role of information distinctness in determining the direction of context effects, it could be assumed that the impact of suboptimally presented affective stimuli (e.g., positive versus negative faces) may be contrastive as well as evaluative on evaluative judgments of neutral target stimuli. Specifically, subliminal exposure to a distinct, specific emotion face (e.g., Figure 11.1a) should result in assimilation when this face is flashed very briefly, such that affective features only can be detected, and diffuse information is activated (e.g., Figure 11.1b). Contrast should occur when this emotion face is flashed somewhat longer, such that affective as well as nonaffective features can be detected, and a distinct face exemplar may be activated (e.g., Figure 11.1a).

Very Short versus Moderately Short Priming

In a first study, we (Stapel et al., 2002) tested this line of thinking, and this was precisely what we found. In this study, we used an unrelated-task subliminal priming paradigm. Participants were told that they would participate in a number of ostensibly unrelated tasks. First, participants performed a parafoveal vigilance task in which line drawings of

Figure 11.2. Priming and target stimuli used in the first study. In a vigilance task, participants were first primed subliminally (very short or moderately short) with positive (happy) or negative (sad) male faces. After having completed the vigilance task, participants were presented with a drawing of the neutral male face and were asked to rate this face on a sad–happy dimension.

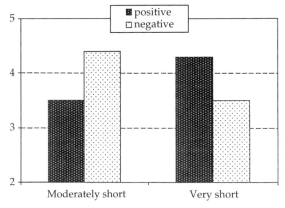

Figure 11.3. Mean sad–happy (1–7) ratings of a neutral male target face drawing as a function of prime exposure (moderately short, extremely short) and prime valence (positive, negative) using male faces as priming stimuli.

positive (happy) or negative (sad) facial expressions of a male person (see Figure 11.2) were presented outside of awareness. In the *very short* exposure conditions, these pictures were primed suboptimally, but for a very short time (30 ms). In the *moderately short* exposure condition, the drawings were also primed suboptimally (for relevant tests, see Stapel et al., 2002), but for a slightly longer time (100 ms). Participants were told that their task was to decide as quickly and accurately as possible whether the flash appeared on the left or right side of the screen. After having completed the vigilance task, participants were presented with a drawing of a neutral male face (see Figure 11.2) and were asked to rate this face on a sad–happy dimension.

As can be seen in Figure 11.3, the impact of subliminally primed positive versus negative emotion faces on judgments of a neutral target face is a function of prime exposure. In the *extremely short* exposure conditions, exposure to positive male faces yielded more positive target judgments than exposure to negative male faces, an assimilation effect. In the moderately short exposure conditions, however, this pattern was reversed. Exposure to a positive male face yielded less positive target judgments than exposure to a negative male face, a contrast effect.

These findings corroborate the present perspective on (automatic) affective processing effects. They suggest that even though affective stimulus features are picked up earlier than their nonaffective counterparts, both affective and nonaffective stimulus features may be picked up outside of conscious awareness. They also demonstrate that exposure time is an important determinant of whether subliminal priming of affect-laden stimuli results in assimilation or contrast, which is in line with the hypothesis that early affect is diffuse, whereas late affect can be distinct.

Affect Only versus Affect and Cognition

To test the robustness of these first findings, we performed a second experiment in which we expanded the design of our first study in a way that allowed us to test more directly the early-diffuse-assimilation versus late-distinct-contrast logic that constitutes the cornerstone of the current argument (Stapel et al., 2002). That is, in a second study, we not only primed participants with faces that possessed affective features (valence-related cues, e.g., a smiling mouth) as well as nonaffective cues (valence-unrelated cues, e.g., a male hairdo), but also added a condition in which participants were exposed to an emotion face that is "pure affect," which possesses no nonaffective features (no hair, no moustache, no necklace, no earrings, no tie, no eyebrows).

If the distinctness argument is correct, then exposure time should becomes less of an issue when participants are exposed to affect-only stimuli. When the priming stimulus itself is relatively diffuse, longer exposure time is unlikely to make it a distinct, specific entity that could serve as a comparison standard when judging a particular target stimulus. Thus, similar to the way in which priming diffuse trait information ("intelligent") yields assimilation, whereas priming distinct person information ("Einstein") yields contrast (Stapel & Koomen, 2000), presenting participants with happy emotion faces that are diffuse "by nature" should produce assimilation, independent of exposure time.

Using the same parafoveal priming paradigm as before, this is exactly what we found. As can be seen in Figure 11.4, when the same distinct *affect-and-cognition* primes as in our first study were used, the results of that study were replicated. In the *extremely short* exposure conditions assimilation occurred, whereas in the moderately short exposure conditions contrast occurred. However, when diffuse affect-only primes were flashed, exposure time had no effect. In both the very short and the moderately short exposure conditions, exposure to positive male faces yielded more

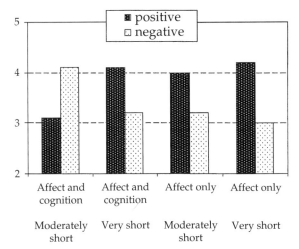

Figure 11.4. Mean sad–happy (1–7) ratings of a neutral male target face drawing as a function of prime type (affect, no cognition or affect and cognition), prime exposure (moderately short, extremely short), and prime valence (positive, negative).

positive target judgments than exposure to negative male faces, an assimilation effect. This finding further supports the early-diffuse-assimilation versus late-distinct-contrast logic: Priming diffuse, affect-no-cognition faces yields assimilation, independent of exposure time. Priming affect-and-cognition faces also yields assimilation, but only when exposure time is sufficiently short to avoid the detection of the cognitive features of these stimuli. At longer exposure, contrast occurs, suggesting that cognitive features were picked up and a more distinct representation of the face was activated.

Not Drawings But Real Faces

In the studies just reported, we (Stapel et al., 2002) used drawings of happy, sad, and neutral facial expressions that consisted of more or less gender-specific features to provide empirical evidence for the early-diffuse late-distinct affect hypothesis. Using face drawings allowed us to control and manipulate systematically both the evaluative and nonevaluative features of our priming and target stimuli. To ensure that the effects we found in the previous studies were not an artifact of the fact that we used drawings instead of facial expressions of real people, we decided to replicate the design of the first study described. Instead of face drawings we used photographs of real facial expressions as priming and target stimuli (see Figure 11.5).

In line with the findings of our first study, we found that the impact of suboptimally exposed positive and negative male faces on the perception

Figure 11.5. Priming and target stimuli used in the real human faces study. Participants were first primed subliminally (very short or moderately short) with positive (happy) or negative (sad) male faces. After having completed the vigilance task, participants were presented with a picture of a neutral male face and were asked to rate it on a sad–happy dimension.

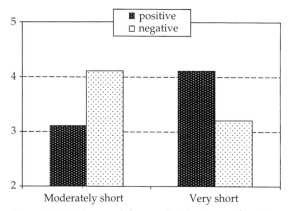

Figure 11.6. Mean sad–happy (1–7) ratings of a picture of a neutral male target face drawing as a function of prime exposure (moderately short, extremely short) and prime valence (positive, negative) using pictures of male faces as priming stimuli.

of a neutral male face would switch from assimilation to contrast, depending on whether these primes were flashed for an extremely short or a moderately short time. As can be seen in Figure 11.6, the impact of subliminally primed positive versus negative real emotion faces on judgments of a neutral target face is a function of prime exposure. In the *extremely short* exposure conditions, exposure to positive male faces yielded more positive target judgments than exposure to negative male faces. In the moderately short exposure conditions, however, this assimilative pattern was reversed. Exposure to a positive male face yielded less positive target judgments than exposure to a negative male face.

WHAT ABOUT THE MURPHY–ZAJONC STUDIES?

It is interesting to compare and contrast these findings to the famous, fre-quently cited study on the consequences of subliminal affect by Murphy and Zajonc (1993). These investigators *did* vary the exposure time of their priming stimuli, emotion faces. And indeed, they found that at very short exposures (e.g., 10 ms), priming emotion faces resulted in assimilation – as the present analysis suggests. However, contrary to the present anal-ysis, Murphy and Zajonc found that at longer exposures (e.g., 1000 ms), priming emotion faces did not yield contrast. At such exposures, priming had no effect at all. How can we explain the discrepancy between these Murphy–Zajonc findings and the findings presented earlier?

The Problem of Comparing Supraliminal and Subliminal Priming

One way to answer this question is by pointing to the fact that, strictly speaking, the Murphy–Zajonc studies are irrelevant to the present pro-posal. In those studies, the difference between short and long exposure conditions was such that the impact of subliminal stimulus exposures (be-low individuals' conscious thresholds) was compared to that of supra-liminal exposures (above individuals' conscious thresholds). The present proposal concerns the impact of *subliminal* exposure to affect-laden stim-uli. I posit that even *within* the category of subliminal presentation, one can distinguish (early) diffuse and (late) distinct affective reactions that may have diametrically opposite effects on subsequent judgments.

   The problem with supraliminal priming is that this technique may in-troduce ambiguity as to what may have caused its effects (Martin, 1986; Schwarz & Bless, 1992; Wegener & Petty, 1995; Wilson & Brekke, 1994). Priming emotion faces above people's conscious threshold may not only lead to more descriptively appraised, more distinct affective reactions (Stapel & Koomen, 2001a, 2001b), it may also make participants aware of the potentially contaminating impact of the primed faces on judgment. As Petty and Wegener (1998, p. 338) contend when discussing Murphy and Zajonc's (1993) finding that affective priming led to assimilation when primes were presented outside of conscious awareness but not when primes were presented visibly: "One possible reason for such an effect might be that visibly presented priming stimuli are noticed as obviously irrelevant to perceptions of the targets. Therefore, this 'blatant priming' might instigate an avoidance of the perceived effects of the emotional primes." In fact, the typical explanation of the findings of the Murphy–Zajonc studies is in terms of the extent to which their participants were aware of the influence of the emotion faces rather than in terms of the distinctness of the information these faces activated (Bargh, 1997, p. 25; Chaiken, Wood, & Eagly, 1996, p. 719; Schwarz & Clore, 1996, p. 440). In the study presented earlier, we avoided the ambiguity surrounding the interpretation of contrast effects after optimal or supraliminal exposure (Is it correction contrast? Is it comparison contrast?) by examining the impact of early-diffuse and late-distinct affect *within* a suboptimal priming paradigm.

The Problem of Comparing Apples and Oranges

A second explanation of the lack of comparison contrast findings in previous studies of affect priming effects may be that for primed information to result in contrastive comparison effects, distinctness is not the only criterion. A distinct prime will yield comparison contrast, given that there is categorical overlap between the prime and target stimuli. Stimuli that belong to the same category (two persons, two apples) more readily invite comparison processes than stimuli that belong to dissimilar categories (persons and animals, apples and oranges). In recent empirical tests of this similarity criterion, my colleagues and I found that primed friendly or hostile *animals* (e.g., "puppy" versus "shark") are not used as a comparison standard when judging an ambiguous (friendly/hostile) human target stimulus, whereas primed friendly or hostile *persons* (e.g., "Gandhi" versus "Hitler") do result in contrastive comparison effects (see further Stapel & Koomen, 2001a; see also Bless et al., this volume; McClure et al., this volume).

In previous studies of affect priming, the categorical overlap between priming and target stimuli was typically quite low. For example, Murphy and Zajonc (1993) examined the impact of priming specific emotion faces on the perception of Chinese ideographs. Because a human face is unlikely to be used as a comparison standard when constructing a judgment of a Chinese ideograph, it is perhaps not surprising that Murphy and Zajonc (1993) did not find contrast.

Following earlier studies investigating the impact of supraliminally primed stimuli (Stapel & Koomen, 2000), it could be argued that subliminal exposure to an emotion face is most likely to yield contrast when such a facial expression is perceived as distinct (i.e., prime exposure is sufficiently long) *and* when prime and target stimuli belong to the same category: The prime is a face and the target is a face, not a Chinese ideograph. Therefore, we (Stapel et al., 2002) performed a study on the impact of subliminally primed (positive versus negative) emotion faces on judgments of a Chinese ideograph (no prime–target overlap), using the same very/moderately short priming paradigm we used in the studies described earlier (for details, see Stapel et al., 2002). The findings were as expected: The pattern of the famous Murphy–Zajonc studies was replicated. Similar to the Murphy–Zajonc studies, in the moderately short exposure conditions, affect priming had no impact on evaluative judgments of the

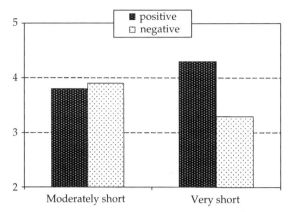

Figure 11.7. Mean sad–happy (1–7) ratings of a Chinese ideograph as a function of prime exposure (moderately short, extremely short) and prime valence (positive, negative) using female faces as priming stimuli.

Chinese ideograph. In the extremely short conditions, however, an assimilation effect was found. The ideograph was evaluated more positively when positive emotion faces were flashed than when negative faces were flashed (Figure 11.7).

This replication of the Murphy–Zajonc findings points to the importance of the categorical relation between priming and target stimuli, particularly when prime exposure is sufficiently long for affective as well as nonaffective features to be activated. Furthermore, the importance of prime–target overlap attests to the importance of using *socially* meaningful stimuli when investigating the impact of primed affect on *social* perception. Although it may be convenient to use meaningless nonsense stimuli in experimental affect priming studies, the similarity criterion implies that the findings of such studies are not as easily generalized to social psychological phenomena, as is often assumed (Bargh, 1997; Glaser & Banaji, 1999; Robinson, 1996; Zajonc, 1998).

When seen in this light, the Chinese ideograph study attests to the importance of prime–target relations when explaining the impact of suboptimal affect priming stimuli on judgment. The impact of what is primed is dependent not only on what is primed (diffuse affect, distinct affect) but also on what is measured, because the extent to which there is prime–target overlap (or not) is a crucial determinant of priming effects. As our Chinese ideograph study suggests, primed emotion faces will be used differently in constructing judgments of unfamiliar words, geometric shapes, or Chinese ideographs (Zajonc, 2000) than in forming an impression of a neutral facial expression. It is stating the obvious, but even when it concerns the effects of subliminally primed information, a Chinese ideograph is not a human face.

EVALUATIVE PRIMING VERSUS AFFECTIVE PRIMING

One criticism that is sometimes voiced against the kinds of affect-priming studies reported earlier is that they are more relevant to the nonaffective priming literature than to studies of affect, mood, or emotion effects. In other words, for a study showing the automatic impact of affect-laden primes (such as emotion faces) to be defined as a study of the impact of affective reactions, the influence of these primes on actual affective experiences should be demonstrated. As Schwarz and Clore (1996, p. 440) conclude after reviewing the affect-priming literature to date, "In the absence of experienced feelings, affective priming studies may indeed be better conceptualized as reflecting automatic evaluation processes (...), which have been observed with materials unlikely to elicit any feelings (e.g., Bargh et al., 1989), rather than feeling-based inferences."

To assess whether the priming paradigm used in the studies reported in this chapter may influence not only evaluations of a neutral target stimulus but also participants' conscious affective experiences, we again reran our first study, but now replaced the face evaluation task with a mood measure. After the vigilance task, we instructed participants to indicate their immediate affective feelings on a scale ranging from 1 (negative) to 7 (positive) on "how positive or negative your mood is at this moment." The findings of this study showed that the affect-priming methodology we employed influences people's conscious mood judgments (Figure 11.8). In the extremely as well as the moderately short conditions, priming positive emotion faces resulted in more positive affective experiences than priming negative emotion faces. This gives extra credence to the claim that the priming methodology, as employed in this paradigm, indeed elicits "felt"

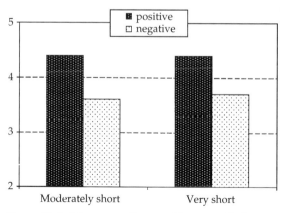

Figure 11.8. Mean negative–positive mood judgments (1–7) as a function of prime exposure (moderately short, extremely short) and prime valence (positive, negative) using male faces as priming stimuli.

rather than "unfelt" affective experiences and is thus relevant to the affective priming as well as to the automatic evaluation literature (cf. Schwarz & Clore, 1996). In other words, our (Stapel et al., 2002) affect-priming method should not be portrayed as solely activating "unfelt evaluations or meaning appraisals."

This demonstration that subliminal exposure to affect-laden stimuli may affect conscious judgments of affective experiences is important for at least two reasons. First, it suggests that whether an affect-laden stimulus activates diffuse or distinct affect does not influence the intensity or valence of felt affective experiences. Thus, although the perceived distinctness of activated affect-laden information is important for the occurrence of assimilation versus contrast when judging a specific neutral target stimulus (see earlier), whether elicited affect is diffuse or distinct does not change the affective feeling it elicits. In other words, affect's distinctness is important for its impact on how we judge stimuli but not for how we feel (cf. Schwarz & Clore, 1996).

Second, the demonstration that subliminal exposure to affect-laden stimuli may affect conscious judgments of affective experiences is important because, in previous affect-priming studies (e.g., Edwards, 1990; Krosnick, Betz, Jussim, & Lynn, 1992; Winkielman, Zajonc, & Schwarz, 1997), no such effects were found. I think that this discrepancy between the effect-on-mood study and previous investigations may be explained as follows: Mood measures should be less easily affected when using a priming methodology in which primes are presented and each priming trial is followed immediately by a target that needs to be responded to. In such a paradigm, the activation potential of single priming trials may be nullified by the target presentation and judgment that immediately follow (Edwards, 1990; Krosnick et al., 1992; Murphy & Zajonc, 1993; Winkielman, Zajonc, & Schwarz, 1997). Mood measures may be affected more easily when a methodology similar to the unrelated task paradigm is used, as in the studies described here. In such a paradigm, priming and target stimuli are presented in separate tasks. In the first task, primes (and masks) are flashed but *not* evaluated. Next, in an ostensibly unrelated task, the target stimuli are presented and evaluated (Chartrand & Bargh, 1996; Erdley & D'Agostino, 1988; Stapel & Koomen, 2001b).

CONCLUSIONS AND CONJECTURES

Environmental stimuli processed outside of awareness can have important consequences for a person's understanding of his or her world. That is what this age of automaticity research keeps reminding us of (Bargh & Ferguson, 2001). Emotions, attitudes, stereotypes, prejudices, dispositional inferences, self-views, and social comparisons: Each of these may be activated and may operate outside of conscious awareness (for reviews, see

Bargh, 1997). It is not entirely clear, however, what are the contents of automatic perception and, perhaps more important, how these contents may shape subsequent cognition and behavior. That is, *what do we see when we see without awareness?* And what features determine the consequences of this type of seeing?

In this chapter, I have tried to defend and corroborate the claim that when we see without awareness, we first see diffuse affect. However, these early affective reactions may not become cognitively appraised and thus may not become attached to a distinct stimulus (such as a facial expression). The studies described here thus support the theory of affective primacy (Zajonc, 1980, 2000) and corroborate earlier tests of this theory (Edwards, 1990; Murphy & Zajonc, 1993; Niedenthal, 1990; Winkielman et al., 1997). More important, the findings of the Stapel et al. (2002) studies also provide empirical support for an aspect of the theory of affective primacy that to date has received little or no attention.

The theory of affective primacy suggests that because early affective reactions to a priming stimulus are by definition cognitively unappraised, the kind of information these reactions activate is diffuse (undedicated, free-floating). The longer exposure time to an affect-laden stimulus becomes, the more affect will become enriched with cognitive appraisals, and the more distinct and specific the information becomes that is activated.

One of the novel aspects of the studies presented in this chapter is that they demonstrate that the distinction between early/diffuse and late/distinct affect has important implications for the impact of these reactions on subsequent judgments. In fact, our findings suggest that the impact of unaware exposure to a picture of a happy or sad person may be diametrically opposite, depending on whether exposure of this (parafoveally primed) picture was extremely short (30 ms) or moderately short (100 ms). What we see when we see without awareness may thus depend in an important sense on the time we are exposed to what we see.

Together, these findings are in line with the *interpretation/comparison* model of knowledge accessibility effects (Stapel & Koomen, 2001a, 2001b). One of this model's main hypotheses is that whereas diffuse information is more likely to be used as an interpretation frame during the encoding of a stimulus and results in assimilation, distinct information is more likely to be used as a comparison standard and results in contrast (see Stapel & Koomen, 2001a). To date, empirical support for the interpretation/comparison model has been based mainly on studies of the effects of *supraliminally* presented information on subsequent judgment and behavior. Furthermore, the hypothesis that diffuse information should yield assimilative interpretation effects, whereas distinct information may yield contrastive comparison effects, was tested mainly by varying the priming stimuli (e.g., diffuse-trait versus distinct-person information), thus introducing a variety of alternative explanations (person information is more vivid, memorable, and extreme than trait information). The early-diffuse-assimilation versus late-distinct-contrast logic of the studies discussed here reveals that one can distinguish early-diffuse and late-distinct reactions to the same affect-laden stimulus. This also allowed us to test the distinctness hypothesis, not by varying the types of priming stimuli participants were exposed to but by manipulating the exposure duration of such stimuli.

As I noted before, Murphy and Zajonc (1993) found that affect primes led to assimilation effects only when prime exposure was extremely short. This has led some to conclude that it is impossible for affect-driven assimilation to obtain when prime exposure is not extremely short (Zajonc, 1998). What the results discussed here clearly suggest is that assimilation may occur independent of prime exposure, given that priming stimuli have mainly nonspecific, affective features. Nonaffective features increase the likelihood that a distinct representation is activated when prime exposure is sufficiently long. If an affect-laden stimulus is pure affect, and thus diffuse and nonspecific by nature, then longer prime exposure times are unlikely to make this stimulus distinct.

Furthermore, it is important to note that because, in the Stapel et al. (2002) studies, a subliminal rather than a supraliminal priming paradigm was used to test the early-diffuse/late-distinct hypothesis, models that explain the impact of affect priming in terms of the extent to which individuals are aware (of the source) of the primed information are difficult to apply to the present findings. Such models are typically used to understand previous affect priming studies (Bargh, 1997; Chaiken et al., 1996; Schwarz & Clore, 1996; Zajonc, 2000). However, it is difficult to use constructs as conscious recall, source recognition, misattribution, or correction to explain the impact of suboptimal priming (cf. Martin, 1986; Murphy & Zajonc, 1993; Schwarz & Bless, 1992; Schwarz & Clore, 1996), explanations that have been suggested to understand previous affect priming studies. The empirical findings discussed here thus indicate that the cognitive appraisal of primed information should not be equated with becoming aware of its (potentially contaminating) influence on cognition and judgment, as some have suggested (Chaiken et al., 1996; Murphy & Zajonc, 1993; Schwarz & Clore, 1996; Zajonc, 1998). The Stapel et al. (2002) findings are also difficult to reconcile with perspectives that concur that differences between assimilation and contrast effects arise because assimilation is governed by a relatively "automatic," "affective," and "unintentional" processing mode, whereas contrast effects are governed by an "effortful," "intentional," and "conscious" processing mode (Ford & Thompson, 2000, pp. 332–333; Smith & DeCoster, 2000, pp. 112–113). Both assimilation and contrast can occur without awareness, even when it concerns the processing of affect-laden stimuli (see also Fiedler, 2000; Glaser & Banaji, 1999).

CODA: A FRESH NEW LOOK AT HOT COGNITION

The emprirical work and theoretical arguments presented here were inspired by the functionalist argument that affective as well as descriptive processing will often (if not always) be needed to respond flexibly and adaptively to affect-laden stimuli. I hope that this functionalist perspective on the interplay between affect and cognition will provide a new look at the cognitive principles underlying people's reactions to affect-laden stimuli above and beyond the paradigm-dependent investigations discussed in this chapter. In my opinion, this approach to understanding the specifics of affective processing may be a useful step forward (or sideward) in a research tradition that started with the New Look.

The New Look, a set of closely related programs of psychological research in the later 1940s and 1950s, was represented by a number of researchers who argued that the emotional meaning of a stimulus could be responded to before the stimulus was consciously perceived (Stapel & Koomen, 1997). At the time, the ideas of the New Look in perception were thought to be intriguing and clearly important, but theoretical and empirical problems prevented the work conducted during the New Look from having a significant impact on psychology.

The New Look of the 1950s was lost in the subsequent *cognitive revolution*, which embraced the metaphor of the person as computer-like and emphasized the rational, systematic, or logically permissible computations that constitute cognitive processing. During the heyday of the cognitive era in psychology, affect and emotion were regarded as epiphenomena that inflate the variance in virtually every dependent measure, ranging from simple motor response to complex learning, and were therefore to be carefully controlled or otherwise to be partialed out of the resulting data (for potent examples, see Niedenthal & Kitayama, 1994). This enthusiasm for explaining seemingly emotional effects as a somewhat convoluted or otherwise trivial consequence or concomitant of systematic cognitive information processing was especially evident in social psychology. It was fashionable during the cognitive revolution to attribute evidently affect-driven effects such as self-serving biases to cognitive factors (e.g., Miller & Ross, 1975). Although this Zeitgeist produced a number of fruitful insights and important empirical findings (Nisbett & Ross, 1980), it also effectively masked potentially powerful contributions of affect and emotion to the psychology of everyday life.

Fortunately, times have changed. Affect and emotion have come back to the forefront of psychological inquiry. And, analyses of the interplay between affect and cognition are especially in vogue in many subbranches of psychology (Forgas, 2001; Forgas & East, this volume). Most if not all these analyses of the affect–cognition interface investigate the ways in which affect shapes cognition. Their emphasis is on how moods, feelings, and emotions influence our thought, judgments, and actions.

In a sense, then, the current perspective – with its focus on the role of cognition in shaping affective processing and effects – presents a fresh (perhaps even a new) look at the interplay between affect and cognition. Similar to previous studies of the affect–cognition interface, the present perspective is concerned with the antecedents and consequences of *hot cognition* (cf. Abelson, 1963). Thus, its focus is on those mental processes that are driven by moods, feelings, and emotions, preferences, and attitudes. However, whereas previous hot cognition research was concerned primarily with demonstrating how affect influences memory, judgment, decisions, and behavior (Forgas, 2001; Forgas & East, this volume), the research discussed in this chaper emphasized the ways in which affective processing is shaped by cognition rather than how cognitive processing is shaped by affect. The emphasis was not on assessing how *warmth* (affect) influences *cold* phenomena (memory, judgment), as were previous studies of hot cognition. Rather, the focus was on the role of *cold* (i.e., nonaffective) features in *hot* (i.e., the effects of affect) mental phenomena. Hopefully, the reader of this chapter is now convinced that this focus on the impact of cold features on hot phenomena was worth the effort.

References

Abelson, R. P. (1963). Computer simulation of "hot cognitions." In S. Tomkins & S. Mednick (Eds.), *Computer simulation of personality* (pp. 34–75). New York: Wiley.
Bargh, J. A. (1997). The automaticity of everyday life. In R. S. Wyer (Ed.), *Advances in social cognition* (Vol. 10, pp. 1–61). Mahwah, NJ: Erlbaum.
Bargh, J. A., & Ferguson, M. J. (2001). Beyond behaviorism: On the automaticity of higher mental processes. *Psychological Bulletin, 126*, 925–945.
Bargh, J. A., Litt, J., Pratto, F., & Spielman, L. A. (1989). On the preconscious evaluation of social stimuli. In A. F. Bennett & K. M. McConkey (Eds.), *Cognition in individual and social contexts: Proceedings of the XXV International Congress of Psychology* (Vol. 3, pp. 357–370). Amsterdam: Elsevier/North-Holland.
Cacioppo, J. T., & Gardner, W. L. (1999). Emotion. *Annual Review of Psychology, 50*, 191–214.
Chaiken, S., Wood, W., & Eagly, A. H. (1996). Principles of persuasion. In E. T. Higgins & A. W. Kruglanski (Eds.), *Social psychology: Handbook of basic principles* (pp. 702–742). New York: Guilford Press.
Chartrand, T. L., & Bargh, J. A. (1999). The chameleon effect: The perception–behavior link in social interaction. *Journal of Personality and Social Psychology, 76*, 893–910.
Cosmides, L., & Tooby, J. (2000). Evolutionary psychology and the emotions. In M. Lewis & J. M. Haviland-Jones (Eds.), *Handbook of emotions* (2nd ed., pp. 91–115). New York: Guilford Press.
Edwards, K. (1990). The interplay of affect and cognition on attitude formation and change. *Journal of Personality and Social Psychology, 59*, 202–216.

Erdley, C. A., & D'Agostino, P. R. (1988). Cognitive and affective components of automatic priming effects. *Journal of Personality and Social Psychology, 54,* 741–747.

Fazio, R. H. (2001). On the automatic activation of associated evaluations: An overview. *Cognition and Emotion, 15,* 115–141.

Fiedler, K. (2000). *The hidden vicissitudes of the priming paradigm in evaluative judgment research.* Manuscript under review.

Ford, T. E., & Thompson, E. P. (2000). Preconscious and postconscious processes underlying construct accessibility effects: An extended search model. *Personality and Social Psychology Review, 4,* 317–336.

Forgas, J. P. (Ed.). (2001). *Handbook of affect and social cognition.* Mahwah, NJ: Erlbaum.

Glaser, J., & Banaji, M. R. (1999). When foul is fair and foul is fair: Reverse priming in automatic evaluation. *Journal of Personality and Social Psychology, 77,* 669–687.

Glaser, J., & Banaji, M. R. (2001). *The relation between stereotypes and prejudice. A brief history and evidence from newly formed automatic associations.* Unpublished manuscript.

Greenwald, A. G., Draine, S. C., & Abrams, D. T. (1996). Three cognitive markers of unconscious semantic activation. *Science, 273,* 1699–1702.

Hunt, P. S., & Campbell, B. A. (1997). Autonomic and behavioral correlates of appetitive conditioning in rats. *Behavioral Neuroscience, 111,* 494–502.

Kahneman, D. (1998). Objective happiness. In D. Kahneman, E. Diener, & N. Schwarz (Eds.), *Well-being: The foundations of hedonic psychology* (pp. 34–56). New York: Russell Sage.

Krosnick, J. A., Betz, A. L., Jussim, L. J., & Lynn, A. R. (1992). Subliminal conditioning of attitudes. *Personality and Social Psychology Bulletin, 18,* 152–162.

Martin, L. L. (1986). Set/reset: Use and disuse of concepts in impression formation. *Journal of Personality and Social Psychology, 51,* 493–504.

Miller, D. T., & Ross, L. (1975). Self-serving attributional bias: Fact or fiction? *Psychological Bulletin, 82,* 213–225.

Murphy, S. T., & Zajonc, R. B. (1993). Affect, cognition, and awareness: Affective priming with optimal and suboptimal stimulus exposures. *Journal of Personality and Social Psychology, 64,* 723–739.

Niedenthal, P. M. (1990). Implicit perception of affective information. *Journal of Experimental Social Psychology, 26,* 505–527.

Niedenthal, P. M., & Kitayama, S. (Eds.). (1994). *The heart's eye.* San Diego, CA: Academic Press.

Nisbett, R. E., & Ross, L. (1980). *Human inference: Strategies and shortcomings in social judgment.* Englewood Cliffs, NJ: Prentice-Hall.

Öhman, A., & Mineka, S. (2001). Fears, phobias, and preparedness: Toward an evolved module of fear and fear learning. *Psychological Review, 108,* 483–522.

Petty, R. E., & Wegener, D. T. (1998). Attitude change: Multiple roles for persuasion variables. In D. T. Gilbert & S. T. Fiske (Eds.), *The handbook of social psychology* (Vol. 1, 4th ed., pp. 323–390). Boston: McGraw-Hill.

Robinson, M. D. (1996). Running from William James' bear: A review of preattentive mechanisms and their contribution to emotional experience. *Cognition & Emotion, 12,* 667–696.

Scherer, K. R. (1984). On the nature and function of emotion: A component process approach. In K. R. Scherer & P. Ekman (Eds.), *Approaches to emotion* (pp. 293–318). Hillsdale, NJ: Erlbaum.

Schwarz, N., & Bless, H. (1992). Constructing reality and its alternatives: An inclusion/exclusion model of assimilation and contrast effects in social judgment. In L. L. Martin & A. Tesser (Eds.), *The construction of social judgments* (pp. 217–245). Hillsdale, NJ: Erlbaum.

Schwarz, N., & Clore, G. (1996). Feelings and phenomenal experiences. In E. T. Higgins & A. W. Kruglanski (Eds.), *Social psychology: Handbook of basic principles* (pp. 433–465). New York: Guilford Press.

Smith, E. R., & DeCoster, J. (2000). Dual-process models in social and cognitive psychology: Conceptual integration and links to underlying memory systems. *Personality and Social Psychology Review, 4,* 108–134.

Stapel, D. A., & Koomen, W. (1997). Social categorization and perceptual judgment of size: When perception is social. *Journal of Personality and Social Psychology, 73,* 1177–1190.

Stapel, D. A., & Koomen, W. (2000). How far do we go beyond the information given? The impact of knowledge activation on interpretation and inference. *Journal of Personality and Social Psychology, 78,* 19–37.

Stapel, D. A., & Koomen, W. (2001a). Let's not forget the past when we go to the future: On our knowledge of knowledge accessibility effects. In G. B. Moskowitz (Ed.), *Cognitive social psychology* (pp. 226–246). Mahwah, NJ: Erlbaum.

Stapel, D. A., & Koomen, W. (2001b). The impact of interpretation versus comparison goals on knowledge accessibility effects. *Journal of Experimental Social Psychology, 37,* 134–149.

Stapel, D. A., Koomen, W., & Ruijs, K. (2002). The effects of diffuse and distinct affect. *Journal of Personality and Social Psychology, 83,* 60–74.

Tesser, A. (1993). The importance of heritability in psychological research: The case of attitudes. *Psychological Review, 100,* 129–142.

Wegener, D. T., & Petty, R. E. (1995). Flexible correction processes in social judgment: The role of naive theories in corrections for perceived bias. *Journal of Personality and Social Psychology, 68,* 36–51.

Wilson, T. D., & Brekke, N. (1994). Mental contamination and mental correction: Unwanted influences on judgments and evaluations. *Psychological Bulletin, 116,* 117–142.

Winkielman, P., Zajonc, R. B., & Schwarz, N. (1997). Subliminal affective priming resists attributional intervention. *Cognition and Emotion, 11,* 433–465.

Zajonc, R. B. (1980). Feeling and thinking: Preferences need no inferences. *American Psychologist, 35,* 151–175.

Zajonc, R. B. (1998). Emotions. In D. T. Gilbert, D. T. Fiske, & G. Lindzey (Eds.), *Handbook of social psychology* (4th ed., pp. 591–632). New York: McGraw-Hill.

12

Attitudinal Process versus Content

The Role of Information Processing Biases in Social Judgment and Behavior

William von Hippel, Patrick Vargas, and
Denise Sekaquaptewa

CONTENTS

INTRODUCTION

Is Yasser Arafat a freedom fighter or a terrorist? Is abortion murder? Is gun control a good idea? Is capital punishment immoral? Despite the fact that many people have the exact same information at their disposal concerning these questions, there is a great deal of disagreement about the answers. Why is it that different people respond to identical objects or events in such divergent ways? Social psychology provides two answers to this question. First, and most obviously, different people have different preferences. For example, one person strongly favors the Palestinians, whereas another favors the Israelis, and these preferences might lead them to regard a person like Arafat in very different terms. The possibility that people have different attitudes, and that their attitudes drive judgment and behavior, has received enormous empirical support (for reviews, see Eagly &

We thank Markus Brauer for helpful comments on an earlier draft of this chapter, and the Social Cognition Research Group and social psychology faculty at Ohio State University for many useful discussions. Address correspondence to William von Hippel, School of Psychology, University of New South Wales, Sydney 2052, Australia; e-mail: w.vonhippel@unsw.edu.au

Chaiken, 1993, 1998) and is consistent with commonsense understanding as well.

There is also a second answer to this question: the idea that even people with the same attitude might interpret a situation differently, causing them to respond differently. For example, although two people might have identical attitudes regarding violence and the situation in the Middle East, they might nevertheless disagree about whether Arafat is a terrorist. One person might see Arafat as *unable* to stop the violence toward Israelis, whereas another might feel that he is simply *unwilling* to do so (later in this chapter, we address the issue of why such interpretive differences might emerge). This difference in the interpretation of his behavior will have a sizable impact on perceptions of Arafat, behavior toward him and his compatriots, and judgments about the best way to achieve peace. The impact of this difference in interpretation should be substantial, even between two people with identical preferences regarding the actors and the situation in the Middle East.

This example suggests that how people make social judgments and decisions, and how they behave in relevant circumstances, are determined not only by their preferences or attitudes, but also by how they interpret attitude-relevant information. Because biases in information processing change both the amount and meaning of information that an individual collects from the environment (Ditto & Lopez, 1993; Fazio, 1990; Hilton & von Hippel, 1990), the biases themselves have the potential to directly influence responses to the environment. Indeed, it is often biases in information processing that enable the individual's preferred response to an attitude object (Chatman & von Hippel, 2001; Karpinski & von Hippel, 1996; Kunda, 1990). Thus, biases in information processing can be just as important as the attitudes themselves in determining behavior and judgment (von Hippel, Sekaquaptewa, & Vargas, 1995).[1]

Social psychology has a long history of the study of attitudes, and much of this work has focused on how and when attitudes predict behavior and judgment. The predictive power of preferences is thus well established. In contrast, the predictive role of biases in information processing has been largely ignored. Social psychologists have been aware for some time that attitudes have the potential to bias information processing (e.g., Hammond, 1948; Lord, Ross, & Lepper, 1979; Proshansky, 1943; Sherif & Hovland, 1961). These biases in information processing are widely regarded as an

---

[1] Because *bias* means different things to different people (implying concepts such as inaccuracy, motivation, etc.), it is important to define what we mean by it. Our use of the term is borrowed from Fiske and Taylor (1991), who define bias as systematic distortion (overuse or underuse) of otherwise accurate or appropriate cognitive processes (p. 66). Biases can be either cognitive or motivational in origin, and they may or may not lead to error (see also Fiedler & Freytag, this volume; Haselton & Buss, this volume).

attitudinal outcome, however, and thus have been examined almost exclusively in terms of their antecedents rather than their consequences (see Fazio, 1990, for an important exception). As suggested previously, biases in information processing are more than just an outcome of an attitude: They change the way the environment is understood and thereby exert an independent influence on how people respond to that environment. To return to our earlier example, Arafat the peacemaker is likely to engender a very different response than Arafat the terrorist, independent of one's attitudes toward the actors and the situation in the Middle East.

In this chapter, we explore the possibility that attitudes might be thought of in terms of the *content* of people's preferences versus the *processes* in which they engage when they encounter attitude-relevant information. *Attitudinal content* is our label for the traditional approach to the study of attitudes, whereby the attitude is considered the evaluative beliefs that people hold about an object, person, or event (Eagly & Chaiken, 1998). In contrast, *attitudinal process* is the idea that the way people process attitude-relevant information has an important impact on their eventual representation of the attitude object, thereby influencing behavior and judgment with regard to that object (Figure 12.1). In other words, persons' attitudes might be considered not just their evaluative beliefs, but also the ways that they process attitude-relevant information.

CLASSIFICATION OF ATTITUDINAL PROCESS

Although there are probably global differences in processing styles across individuals (e.g., individual differences in authoritarianism), the process component of an attitude is likely to be largely specific to individual attitude objects. In this regard, we view individual differences in attitudinal process in a manner analogous to Bandura's (1977) conception of self-efficacy. Much in the same way that self-efficacy is domain specific, attitudinal process is likely to be attitude object specific. Most people are likely to show biased information processing with regard to at least some attitude objects, but most people are also likely not to show biased information processing with regard to all attitude objects. Rather, one person might show biased interpretation of racial information, whereas another might show bias with regard to religion or politics, and still another might show bias primarily when evaluations involve the self.

The possibility that people show object-specific biases that play an important role in behavior and judgment leads to the question of how one might measure such biases. The answer to this question lies in the voluminous research in social cognition establishing the circumstances that lead to biased processing. As Markus and Zajonc (1985) wrote in their authoritative *Handbook* chapter, "If we were to compare the contributions to the product of a cognitive process made by the target and the cognizer, then in

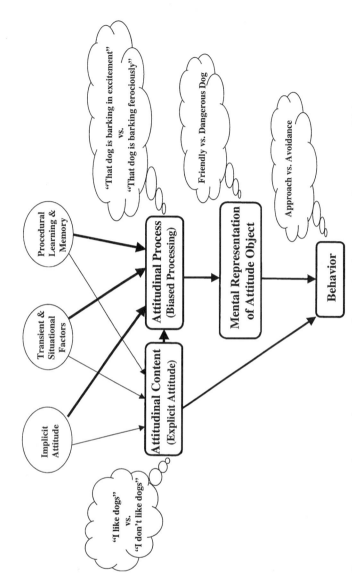

Figure 12.1. Antecedents and consequences of attitudinal content and process. Bold lines represent a relatively strong influence, and narrow lines represent a relatively weak influence. Callout bubbles are an illustration of the variables depicted in the model.

the case of social cognition the cognizer would generally play a more significant role than in the case of nonsocial cognition. There is indeed greater between-subject variance in social cognition, and the sources of this variance are nontrivial. They are not caused by random error and need to be systematically explored" (p. 211).

This view of social cognition suggests that bias is likely to be both prevalent and important in social perception, and indeed, social cognitive research has focused to a substantial degree on documenting and classifying biases in information processing. It is our view that with regard to attitudinal process, most of these biases are largely interchangeable to the degree that they are relevant to the situation at hand. That is, people are likely to show any of a variety of biases with regard to certain attitude objects, and which of these biases is shown is just as likely to be determined by their applicability to the situation as by the experiences or habits of the perceiver. Thus, attentional biases are likely to emerge when people are encoding events (e.g., Hilton, Klein, & von Hippel, 1991; Roskos-Ewoldson & Fazio, 1992), attributional biases are likely to emerge when people are interpreting events (e.g., Chatman & von Hippel, 2001), memorial biases are likely to emerge when people are recalling events (Klein, Cosmides, Tooby, & Chance, 2002), and linguistic biases are likely to emerge when people are describing events (e.g., Karpinski & von Hippel, 1996; Wigboldus, Semin, & Spears, 2000). All of these biases, and many others, have been theorized to play an important role in expectancy maintenance, belief perseverance, and so on. Thus, the specific bias under study is probably important only to the degree that it is relevant to the information processing demands and opportunities provided by the situation. Consistent with this possibility, research in stereotyping and prejudice suggests that people who show an attributional bias with regard to a particular group are likely to show a linguistic bias toward that group as well (von Hippel, Sekaquaptewa, & Vargas, 1997, Exp. 3). For this reason, the study of attitudinal process can, and probably should, involve any of a large number of biases in information processing that have been documented in social psychology.

DISSOCIATION BETWEEN PROCESS AND CONTENT

In the example at the beginning of this chapter, we proposed that two people with the same attitudinal content might show different attitudinal process, but we have yet to explain why process and content might be dissociated. There are four broad classes of reasons why attitudinal process and content might be dissociated (see Figure 12.1). First, both explicit and implicit attitudes are likely to bias information processing. When explicit and implicit attitudes overlap substantially, these sources of bias can be considered essentially isomorphic. For example, a religious person may hold similarly positive conscious and unconscious attitudes toward religion. Often, however, explicit and implicit attitudes will diverge from one another (Wilson, Lindsey, & Schooler, 2000). For example, a religious person who holds a favorable conscious attitude toward religion might have consciously inaccessible memories of punitive instructors in religious schools, or tedious religious classes and events, that contribute to a more negative unconscious attitude toward religion. Under the latter circumstances, explicit and implicit attitudes can be considered important alternative sources of bias, and accurate prediction of bias will depend on knowledge of both conscious and unconscious attitudes. Furthermore, the stronger these attitudes are, the more likely they are to bias information processing (Petty & Krosnick, 1996). Thus, attitudinal content will largely reflect information that is available to consciousness, whereas attitudinal process should be sensitive to both conscious and unconscious evaluations.

Second, transient and situational factors such as mood and threats to self-esteem have been shown to influence information processing in a manner that is distinct from their influence on attitudinal content (e.g., Fein & Spencer, 1997; Forgas & East, this volume). In Fein and Spencer's research (Fein & Spencer, 1997; Spencer, Fein, Wolfe, Fong, & Dunn, 1998), for example, people who experienced a threat to their self-esteem showed automatic activation of out-group stereotypes under circumstances in which their nonthreatened counterparts did not show automatic stereotype activation. These data suggest that threatened individuals change the way they process information about out-group members in a fashion that allows them to restore a more favorable image of themselves. Interestingly, these changes in information did not occur with regard to all attitude objects, but only with regard to out-group members. In our terms, attitudinal process was affected even though information processing did not show an overall change with regard to understanding people in general. To the degree that a variety of transient factors influence attitudinal processes in a manner that is distinct from their impact on attitudinal content, one would expect dissociation between process and content.

Third, it seems likely that people can learn attitudinal process in a manner that is largely independent of the learning of attitudinal content. For example, imagine a family in which the parents espouse egalitarian attitudes toward women and never endorse gender-stereotypic roles. With a little help from the environment, such parents may successfully raise their children to be unprejudiced, in the attitudinal content sense of the word, toward women. On the other hand, by virtue of their early socialization of gender stereotypes, these parents might nevertheless retain a variety of biases in the way they process information about women (e.g.,

Dunning & Sherman, 1997). Perhaps these parents provide explanations whenever they witness a woman behaving in a counterstereotypic manner, but not when a woman behaves in a stereotypic fashion (von Hippel et al., 1997). This pattern of information processing renders counterstereotypic information less potent than stereotypic information in its ability to influence dispositional judgments. If children show incidental learning of this attributional style, they could begin to show a prejudiced process in the absence of any prejudicial content. In support of this general possibility, Squire, Knowlton, and Musen (1993) write that "Under some circumstances, skills and habits can be acquired in the absence of awareness of what has been learned and independently of long-term declarative memory for the specific episodes in which learning occurred" (p. 471).

The process outlined by Squire et al. leads to the fourth way that attitudinal process might become dissociated from attitudinal content. That is, because mental habits can become proceduralized, and thereby largely autonomous from conscious processes, it is possible that an attitudinal process that was originally initiated by attitudinal content might persist long after the attitudinal content has changed (see also Wilson et al., 2000). To the degree that the attitudinal process is automatically engaged whenever the relevant environmental stimuli are encountered (see Chartrand & Jefferis, this volume), people might show a bias in information processing that is in direct opposition to their attitudinal content. In support of such a possibility, Dunning and Sherman (1997) demonstrated that people tended to make tacit gender-stereotypic inferences upon encountering inference-inviting behaviors, and that this tendency was unrelated to conscious attitudes about gender roles and gender stereotypes. Because people are thought to develop automatic gender stereotypes at an early age, and only later reject them if they develop conscious attitudes regarding gender egalitarianism (cf. Devine, 1989), Dunning and Sherman's (1997) findings suggest that people's tacit inference process is driven by their earlier acquired automatic stereotypes, and not by their later acquired egalitarian attitudes.

Finally, it is likely to be the case that attitudinal processes are not only influenced by these four factors in a manner often independent of attitudinal content, but also in a manner that is often the product of an (undoubtedly dynamic) interaction among these factors. As a consequence, dissociations between process and content are likely to be commonplace rather than the exception. Furthermore, even if one could reliably predict process from content, attitudinal content would still be a relatively poor predictor of the outcome of attitudinal processes because, as suggested at the outset of this chapter, attitudinal processes are likely to have emergent properties of their own. For these reasons, we propose that the study of attitudinal process is a worthwhile endeavor that will not simply be redundant with the study of attitudinal content, and that should facilitate the prediction of judgment and behavior.

EMPIRICAL WORK ON ATTITUDINAL PROCESS

The remainder of this chapter is divided into three sections. The goal of the first section is to establish the validity of the concept of attitudinal process. In the service of this goal, we introduce an attitudinal process measure that taps differences in the way people interpret internally inconsistent, attitude-relevant information. We then report a series of studies that assess whether attitudinal process predicts unique variance in behavior beyond that predicted by attitudinal content.

In the second section we address the issue of social desirability. If attitudinal process predicts behavior and judgment because it changes the meaning of the information an individual encounters, then it should have predictive validity independent of a person's willingness or ability to report his or her attitudes accurately. One important domain in which social desirability is a chronic concern is that of stereotyping and prejudice. Indeed, a number of theories of prejudice are based on the premise that individuals do not want to admit even to themselves that they rely on stereotypes and are prejudiced, and thus people are thought to suppress their prejudiced attitudes (e.g., aversive racism: Gaertner & Dovidio, 1986) or to rationalize them by linking them to other issues (e.g., symbolic and modern racism: Kinder & Sears, 1981; McConahay, Hardee, & Batts, 1981). Because stereotypes are conceived as beliefs about a group that an individual is often unwilling to admit even to himself or herself, they would seem to be an important and fruitful domain in which to extend our research on the ability of attitudinal process measures to predict socially undesirable judgments and behaviors. Assessment of such socially undesirable beliefs is unlikely to be successful with a measure of attitudinal process that is not implicit, and thus we introduce a new class of measures in this section that tap biases in information processing in a manner that is largely outside of awareness.

Finally, the self-concept also provides a useful domain for the study of the impact of attitudinal process on behavior and judgment, because self-relevant biases are often so important and pervasive. Indeed, most people show a number of self-serving biases, and many of these biases are thought to be necessary for the maintenance of good mental health (Taylor & Brown, 1988). Thus, it seems likely that biased processing should be particularly evident with regard to the self-concept, and should thereby be an important determinant of self-relevant behavior. The secondary goal in this section is to examine the role of ambiguity in determining when attitudinal process will play a greater or lesser role in predicting behavior. If attitudinal processes influence behavior and judgment because they change the meaning of information that is encountered (see Figure 12.1), then attitudinal process should be a better predictor of behavior when the situation is ambiguous (and more open to different interpretations) than when it is unambiguous. The experiments on self-relevant attitudinal processes provide an initial test of this idea.

ATTITUDINAL PROCESS: THE CASE OF CONTRAST

Of the variety of methods that can be used to study attitudinal process, we chose to rely on biases in the interpretation of inconsistent or ambiguous information. Our measure is derived from the theoretical position articulated by Cook and Selltiz (1964), who referred to this type of measure as *interpretation of partially structured stimuli*. According to Cook and Selltiz, the goal of such measures is to solicit the participants' reaction to attitude-relevant information that is at least somewhat ambiguous with regard to its meaning. To the degree that participants show attitudinal process, they should interpret the information differently from those who do not show such biases in information processing.

In order to test this possibility, three studies were conducted using biased interpretation of vignettes as our measure of attitudinal process (for a more complete description, see Vargas, von Hippel, & Petty, 2002). The first experiment examined attitudes toward religion under the assumption that religious attitudes would be relatively free of social desirability concerns, and thus would allow a test of whether attitudinal process predicts independent variance in behavior even in domains in which social desirability concerns do not disrupt the report of attitudinal content. In order to measure attitudinal process, participants were presented with a series of vignettes, an example of which follows:

Mary didn't go to church once the whole time she was in college, but she claimed that she was still a very religious person. She said that she prayed occasionally, and that she believed in Christian ideals. Sometimes she watched religious programs on TV like the 700 Club or the Billy Graham Crusade.

Following each vignette, respondents were asked to rate how religious the target is. According to the logic behind this measure, different people should encode these scenarios in different ways. Because Mary behaves in both religious (occasional prayer, watching religious TV programs) and nonreligious (skipping church for years) ways, her behavior should be discrepant for religious and nonreligious people alike. Thus, her behaviors should lie in both religious and nonreligious people's latitudes of rejection (Sherif & Hovland, 1961). As a consequence, to the extent that participants demonstrate religious or nonreligious processing biases, these behaviors should be contrasted away by people with both types of attitudes.

Evaluations of the target as highly religious thereby reveal a nonreligious processing bias, evaluations of the target as highly nonreligious reveal a religious processing bias, and evaluations of the target as near the midpoint of the scale reveal an absence of a religious processing bias. In addition to this measure of attitudinal process, attitudinal content was measured with the Religious Attitude Scale (RAS; Poppleton & Pilkington, 1963). Participants also completed the Balanced Inventory of Desirable Responding (BIDR; Paulhus, 1991) and a comprehensive behavioral index of self-reported religious behaviors (Fishbein & Ajzen, 1974). All of the measures were counterbalanced and given to participants in a single packet.

The first step in the analysis was to assess whether attitudinal process was correlated with attitudinal content. Consistent with the idea that attitudinal process and content are often dissociated, a correlational analysis revealed no reliable relationship between process and content measures. Indeed, in all but a few of the experiments we have conducted across the domains of attitudes, stereotyping and prejudice, and the self, content and process measures have been uncorrelated. In the few studies in which a reliable relationship did emerge, it was small in magnitude. One consequence of this dissociation is that although we present a number of multiple regressions throughout this chapter, the bivariate relationships are very similar to the multivariate ones, given the lack of a relationship between process and content.

With this in mind, the next step in our analysis was to assess whether attitudinal process could predict the index of self-reported religious behavior. In order to test this possibility, a hierarchical multiple regression equation was estimated, and the measure of attitudinal process was entered after the impression management scale and the RAS. This analysis revealed that although the RAS was a strong predictor of religious behavior, the measure of attitudinal process predicted unique variance in behavior beyond that predicted by the measure of attitudinal content. Inconsistent with expectations, however, religious attitudes proved to be somewhat related to impression management, and as a consequence, this experiment did not provide a strong test of the idea that attitudinal process can predict unique variance in behavior independent of social desirability concerns.

Because religious attitudes and behaviors were related to impression management, our next experiment examined attitudes toward politics (pretesting revealed that political behaviors and attitudes were unrelated to social desirability concerns). As in the first experiment, participants were given a counterbalanced set of paper-and-pencil measures of attitudinal process and content regarding political conservatism. Two attitudinal content measures were used: a series of semantic differential items measuring attitudes toward "being politically conservative" and a revised version of the Wilson Conservatism Scale (rWCS; Wilson, 1985). The process measure of political conservatism was similar to that of the first experiment, in that participants read a series of vignettes, each of which described an individual expressing ambiguously conflicting statements about current political issues. A self-report index of political behavior was included, as in the first experiment, and an actual political behavior was included at the end of the study by providing participants the opportunity to request a flier to join one of the political clubs on campus.

As in the first experiment, the semantic differential, rWCS, and attitudinal process measure were entered into hierarchical multiple regression equations. For the equation predicting self-reported political behavior, the regression revealed that the semantic differential and the rWCS were strong predictors and the process measure was a marginal predictor. For the equation predicting actual political behavior, the regression revealed that the semantic differential was a significant predictor, the rWCS was a marginal predictor, and the process measure was a significant predictor. Thus, individuals who showed a conservative processing bias (i.e., perceiving the targets as more liberal) tended to request information about joining the college Republicans, whereas individuals who showed a liberal processing bias (i.e., perceiving the targets as more conservative) tended to request information about joining the college Democrats. This experiment suggests that even in the case of attitudes that are unrelated to social desirability concerns, attitudinal process can predict unique variance in behavior beyond that predicted by attitudinal content.

Although the first two experiments provide evidence for the effectiveness of measures of attitudinal process in predicting unique variance in behavior, it could be argued that the measures are effective not because they tap processing biases, but because they are indirect and thus tap implicit attitudes. In order to address this possibility, we replicated the experiment on religious attitudes but added a religious version of the Implicit Association Test (IAT; Greenwald, McGhee, & Schwartz, 1998). According to our proposal that the vignette measure is an indicator of attitudinal process, the process measure should be largely independent of the IAT and should predict independent variance beyond that predicted by both the IAT and the explicit attitude measure. Consistent with this possibility, the process measure again predicted unique variance in self-reported religious behavior beyond that predicted by both implicit and explicit measures. An interesting finding in this experiment was that the implicit and explicit measures were both correlated with the behavioral index and also with each other. When they were added to the same multiple regression equation, the explicit measure remained a reliable predictor of behavior, but the IAT was no longer a reliable predictor.

In sum, these studies provide initial evidence that attitudinal process is largely independent of attitudinal content and that attitudinal process predicts unique variance in behavior beyond that predicted by attitudinal content. These findings emerged with both self-report and actual behaviors, and in the domains of both religion and politics.

STEREOTYPIC PROCESS: THE CASE OF
SPONTANEOUS EXPLANATION

Our initial work on stereotypic process was based on the Linguistic Intergroup Bias (LIB; Maass, Salvi, Arcuri, & Semin, 1989), wherein we found that people who preferred abstract descriptions of stereotype-congruent behaviors over abstract descriptions of stereotype-incongruent behaviors (i.e., showed the LIB) also made stereotypic implicit and explicit evaluations of out-group members (von Hippel et al., 1997, Exps. 1 and 2). We then developed an additional measure of stereotypic process that was adapted from an attributional measure designed by Hastie (1984) and found that it was correlated with the tendency to show the LIB (von Hippel et al., 1997, Exp. 3). The measure of attributional bias involves presenting people with a series of sentence stems and asking them to complete them in any way they like, so long as they are grammatically correct. Hastie found that people tended to spontaneously explain behaviors that were inconsistent with their prior expectations. In our adaptation of this procedure, we presented people with sentence stems that were stereotype-congruent (e.g., "Mary asked for help getting home") or incongruent (e.g., "Mary read the engineering manual") and assessed the differential explanations of these two types of sentences. If people are more likely to spontaneously explain stereotype-incongruent rather than stereotype-congruent behaviors, then they are showing a stereotypic attributional bias, as they are explaining away behaviors that are inconsistent with their stereotype-based expectancies but not behaviors that are consistent with these expectancies (we refer to this process as the *stereotypic explanatory bias,* or SEB). The SEB has the potential to play an important role in stereotype maintenance, as it renders the incongruent information less relevant to dispositions of the actors than the congruent information. The consequence of this process should thereby be stereotype maintenance even in the face of incongruence.

In order to examine the role of the stereotypic process in behavior and judgment, we conducted a series of studies in which SEB toward women and African Americans was examined (for a more complete description of these studies, see Sekaquaptewa, Espinoza, Thompson, Vargas, & von Hippel, 2003; Sekaquaptewa, Vargas, & von Hippel, 1997). The SEB was assessed in all of these experiments by presenting people with sentence beginnings that were either irrelevant, congruent, or incongruent with stereotype-based expectancies and then coding their completions of these sentences by whether they provided an explanation for the behavior. SEB is indicated when the number of completions that explain stereotype inconsistency is greater than the number of explanations that explain stereotype consistency.

In our first experiment, male participants interviewed either a male or female confederate. As in Rudman and Borgida (1995), they were given pairs of questions and told to ask one of each pair. Some of the pairs represented a choice between mildly sexist or nonsexist versions of the question. Consistent with predictions, participants who showed the SEB with regard to women were more likely than participants who did not show the SEB to choose the sexist phrasing of the question to ask the female but not the male confederate. The Attitudes Toward Women Scale (Spence, Helmreich, & Stapp, 1973) did not predict question choice. A similar study with Blacks and Whites showed the same basic effect: White participants who showed the SEB with regard to African Americans were more likely than White participants who did not show the SEB to choose slightly racist questions to ask of a Black confederate but not of a White confederate. The Modern Racism Scale (MRS; McConahay et al., 1981) did not predict question choice. In a follow-up study using the race version of the SEB scale, Black but not White confederates rated their interaction with White participants more negatively when White participants showed the SEB than when they did not. In this experiment, neither the IAT nor the MRS interacted with race of confederate to predict ratings of the White participant.

If the SEB taps stereotypic process, as we propose, then it should be sensitive to situational factors that influence the degree to which people show stereotyping and prejudice. One such situational factor is threat to the self; people tend to stereotype more when they are threatened than when they are not (Fein & Spencer, 1997; Spencer et al., 1998). In order to test this possibility, we conducted an experiment (Carlisle & von Hippel, 2000) in which White participants were told that the university was changing its admissions standards. Half of the participants were then told that one consequence of this change was that Asian American students would soon be in the majority on campus. After this manipulation, participants completed a version of the SEB that tapped stereotypic processing of Asian Americans and African Americans. Consistent with predictions, participants showed greater SEB toward Asian Americans but not African Americans if they believed that Asian Americans would soon be in the majority on their campus. Conceptually similar results have been reported by Schimel et al. (1999), who found greater stereotyping on a gender version of the SEB when people had been led to think about their own death than when they had not. Chartrand and Jefferis (this volume) have also shown situational effects on the SEB, demonstrating that failure at automatic goal pursuit can lead to increased stereotyping on a gender version of the SEB (see also Johnston & Miles, this volume).

Finally, Sekaquaptewa and Kiefer (2002) have recently extended research on the SEB to perceptions of stereotype-relevant behaviors performed by the self. In their experiment, female participants who showed the SEB when presented with gender-stereotype-consistent and -inconsistent behaviors that were imagined to have been performed by the self (e.g., I read the engineering manual ...) were particularly susceptible to stereotype threat. That is, when told that a difficult math test showed gender differences (Spencer, Steele, & Quinn, 1999), the women who showed the SEB with regard to the self performed poorer on the math test than the women who did not.

In sum, these studies suggest that much like attitudinal process, stereotypic process predicts relevant behaviors toward members of stereotyped groups. People who showed evidence of stereotypic process were more likely to treat out-group members in stereotypic and unfriendly ways. Additionally, stereotypic process was exacerbated under conditions that typically facilitate stereotyping. Furthermore, women who showed stereotypic process with regard to themselves were also more likely to behave in stereotypic ways when they were the targets of stereotypes.

SELF-SERVING PROCESS: THE CASE OF AGGRANDIZING
SUCCESS AND DOWNPLAYING FAILURE

Recall that the goal of our research on the self-concept was to demonstrate that self-serving biases in information processing should predict self-relevant behavior in much the same way that attitudinal and stereotypic processes predicted associated behavior. Of the many measures of self-serving bias, we chose to focus on a measure that does not rely on a comparison of the individual to the population mean, as it is difficult to know whether any single person is really better than average in any particular domain. Such comparison measures reliably demonstrate self-serving biases in the aggregate, as not everyone can be better than average, but they are not well designed for showing that a particular person is being self-serving. For this reason, in the current experiments we relied on a type of self-serving bias whereby people claim that tasks at which they have succeeded are inherently more important than tasks at which they have failed (Tesser & Paulhus, 1983). This measure does not involve claiming to be better than one is, but rather involves minimizing one's faults and maximizing one's strengths (for a more complete description of this work, see von Hippel, Shakarchi, & Lakin, 2002).

In order to create an individual difference measure that relies on this type of self-serving bias, we presented people with two novel tasks and gave them success feedback on one and failure feedback on the other. One task involved differentiating real from fake suicide notes (Ross,

Lepper, & Hubbard, 1975), and the other task involved differentiating mildly schizophrenic word definitions from word definitions that were just somewhat unusual (Manis & Paskewitz, 1984). The novelty of the tasks was important for two reasons: (1) it increased the likelihood that participants would believe the false feedback, and (2) it ensured that they would have no basis for knowing whether the tasks were important or trivial. Self-serving bias was idiographically measured in this procedure as the degree to which people claimed (or did not claim) that the task at which they had succeeded involved more important qualities than the task at which they had failed. Thus, self-serving bias was a difference score, representing the rated importance of the task at which they ostensibly failed subtracted from the rated importance of the task at which they ostensibly succeeded. According to predictions, self-serving bias in information processing should predict self-serving behavior. As noted previously, however, this effect should be particularly likely to emerge when the situation is ambiguous, as self-serving biases in information processing have greater potential to influence encoding of a situation when that situation is itself ambiguous. Thus, it was predicted that self-serving biases would predict self-serving behavior when the meaning of the behavior was open to different interpretations but not when the behavior was unambiguous.

In order to measure ambiguous self-serving behavior, we developed a technique that allows people to cheat in a manner that is ostensibly outside of the experimenter's awareness and also ostensibly accidental. Specifically, we presented people with two series of math problems that were designed to be onerous but solvable. In both series of problems, people were told that there was a "bug" in the computer software, and that they would have to hit the space bar as soon as each problem appeared on the screen in order to prevent the answer from being unintentionally displayed. It was stressed to participants that hitting the space bar in a timely fashion was important, as we would not know when they saw the answers and when they did not, and thus we would have no way of knowing if the experiment was conducted properly.

Participants were further told that in the first series of problems it would be easy to hit the space bar in time, and in fact they had 10 sec to do so. For the second series of problems, however, participants were warned that it would be difficult to hit the space bar in time and that they would have to react as fast as they could. In this series of trials they had only 1 sec to hit the space bar, which is a sufficient amount of time for a task like hitting a computer key (e.g., see Greenwald et al., 1998) but was designed to be a short enough interval to give participants an excuse for not hitting the key in time. It is important to remember that participants were told that the experimenter would not know whether they had hit the key in time. Thus, this excuse was intended primarily to increase the ambiguity of the meaning of their behavior, and not to provide justification to the experimenter.

When cheating involved waiting 10 sec to hit the space bar, it would be engaged in only by people who intended to cheat and were willing to do so whether the task was ambiguous or not. In contrast, when cheating involved waiting only 1 sec to hit the space bar, it would likely be engaged in by a mix of people – some who were intentionally cheating and some who were cheating only under a mask of ambiguity. Because our prediction is that self-serving processes predict self-serving behavior primarily when the latter is ambiguous, it was necessary to remove the self-aware cheating from the mix of behavior in the fast-response task. In order to isolate ambiguous self-serving behavior in this task, the goal of the analyses was thus to predict residual cheating on the fast-response task after variance predicted by cheating on the slow-response task was removed. Once the variance in the fast-response task that is accounted for by variance in the slow-response task was removed, only error variance and ambiguous self-serving behavior should remain. Thus, the self-serving process measure should predict residual variance in the fast-response task after variance predicted by the slow-response task is removed, but not residual variance in the slow-response task after variance predicted by the fast-response task is removed.

Across three experiments, the self-serving process measure predicted residual variance on the fast-response task but not on the slow-response task, and the self-deception subscale of the BIDR was unrelated to responses on either task. Furthermore, when the design was reversed, and participants were told that if they did not hit the space bar rapidly enough the math problems would become more difficult, self-serving process was unrelated to the speed with which they hit the space bar even though the timing parameters were identical. Thus, it seems that when participants could interpret a beneficial behavioral response in more than one way, they frequently failed to hit the space bar within 1 sec, thereby causing the answers to the math problems to appear on the screen. Participants with a self-serving process bias were particularly likely to show this effect. In contrast, when failure to hit the space bar within 1 sec made the math problems more difficult, not only did participants suddenly discover abilities that they apparently did not know they had, but the speed with which they hit the space bar was now unrelated to self-serving processing.

In sum, these studies suggest that in a manner similar to attitudinal and stereotypic process, self-serving process predicted behaviors that have a self-serving function. Furthermore, this effect emerged primarily when the situation was ambiguous and self-serving process thereby had potential to influence how the situation was interpreted.

CONCLUSION

In this chapter we have described the role of information processing biases in determining behavior and judgment. This perspective provides a different viewpoint than is provided by the prevalent focus on implicit versus explicit attitudes. We are not suggesting that the implicit–explicit distinction is unimportant, but rather that there are a variety of dimensions on which attitudes vary, of which implicit–explicit is only one. As the current work demonstrates, the consideration of attitudinal process facilitates the prediction of behavior and judgment beyond that gained by consideration of implicit and explicit attitudes. Across the domains of politics and religion, stereotypes of women and Blacks, and of the self, measures of attitudinal process predicted unique variance in behavior unaccounted for by standard implicit and explicit attitude measures.

Finally, it is worth noting that our emphasis on attitudinal process represents in some ways a return to earlier work on attitudes, in which the construct was defined very broadly to include what would now be called *information processing components* (e.g., Allport, 1935). As Ostrom (1988) observed, these early conceptions of attitudes were too broad to be captured adequately by the methods of the day, and thus Thurstone's (1928) research on attitude measurement necessarily narrowed how attitudes have since been conceived and operationalized. Because modern research has dramatically expanded the list of available methods for attitude measurement, it may be time to reconsider old definitions of attitudes that incorporated elements of information processing. The findings from the current research suggest that consideration of attitudinal process may enable a more complete understanding of what it means to hold an attitude. By shifting the study of attitudes away from an examination of a static collection of feelings and beliefs, and toward a set of active processing strategies or styles, this approach to attitudes emphasizes that *how* we think can be just as important as *what* we think.

References

Allport, G. W. (1935). Attitudes. In C. Murchison (Ed.), *Handbook of social psychology* (pp. 133–175). Worcester, MA: Clark University Press.

Bandura, A. (1977). Self-efficacy: Toward a unifying theory of behavioral change. *Psychological Review, 84,* 191–215.

Carlisle, K., & von Hippel, W. (2000). *Threat to collective self-esteem and implicit stereotyping.* Paper presented at the annual meeting of the Midwestern Psychological Association, Chicago.

Chatman, C., & von Hippel, W. (2001). Attributional mediation of ingroup bias. *Journal of Experimental Social Psychology, 37,* 267–272.

Cook, S. W., & Selltiz, C. (1964). A multiple-indicator approach to attitude measurement. *Psychological Bulletin, 62,* 36–55.

Devine, P. G. (1989). Stereotypes and prejudice: Their automatic and controlled components. *Journal of Personality and Social Psychology, 56,* 5–18.

Ditto, P. H., & Lopez, D. A. (1993). Motivated skepticism: Use of differential decision criteria for preferred and nonpreferred conclusions. *Journal of Personality and Social Psychology, 63,* 568–584.

Dunning, D., & Sherman, D. A. (1997). Stereotypes and tacit inference. *Journal of Personality and Social Psychology, 73,* 459–471.

Eagly, A. H., & Chaiken, S. (1993). *The psychology of attitudes.* Fort Worth: Harcourt Brace Jovanovich.

Eagly, A. H., & Chaiken, S. (1998). Attitude structure and function. In D. T. Gilbert, S. T. Fiske, & G. Lindzey (Eds.), *Handbook of social psychology* (4th ed., pp. 269–322). New York: McGraw-Hill.

Fazio, R. H. (1990). Multiple processes by which attitudes guide behavior: The MODE model as an integrative framework. In M. P. Zanna (Ed.), *Advances in experimental social psychology* (Vol. 23, pp. 75–109). San Diego, CA: Academic Press.

Fein, S., & Spencer, S. J. (1997). Prejudice as self-image maintenance: Affirming the self through derogating others. *Journal of Personality and Social Psychology, 73,* 31–44.

Fishbein, M., & Ajzen, I. (1974). Attitudes towards objects as predictors of single and multiple behavioral criteria. *Psychological Review, 81,* 59–74.

Fiske, S. T., & Taylor, S. E. (1991). *Social cognition.* New York: McGraw Hill.

Gaertner, S. L., & Dovidio, J. F. (1986). The aversive form of racism. In J. F. Dovidio & S. L. Gaertner (Eds.), *Prejudice, discrimination, and racism* (pp. 61–89). Orlando, FL: Academic Press.

Greenwald, A. G., McGhee, D. E., & Schwartz, J. L. K. (1998). Measuring individual differences in implicit cognition: The implicit association test. *Journal of Personality and Social Psychology, 74,* 1464–1480.

Hammond, K. R. (1948). Measuring attitudes by error choice: An indirect method. *Journal of Abnormal and Social Psychology, 43,* 38–48.

Hastie, R. (1984). Causes and effects of causal attribution. *Journal of Personality and Social Psychology, 46,* 44–56.

Hilton, J. L., Klein, J. G., & von Hippel, W. (1991). Attention allocation and impression formation. *Personality and Social Psychology Bulletin, 17,* 548–559.

Hilton, J. L., & von Hippel, W. (1990). The role of consistency in the judgment of stereotype-relevant behaviors. *Personality and Social Psychology Bulletin, 16,* 430–448.

Karpinski, A. T., & von Hippel, W. (1996). The role of the Linguistic Intergroup Bias in expectancy maintenance. *Social Cognition, 14,* 141–163.

Kinder, D. R., & Sears, D. O. (1981). Prejudice and politics: Symbolic racial threats to the good life. *Journal of Personality and Social Psychology, 40,* 414–431.

Klein, S., Cosmides, L., Tooby, J., & Chance, S. (2002). Decisions and the evolution of memory: Multiple systems, multiple functions. *Psychological Review, 109*(2), 306–329.

Kunda, Z. (1990). The case for motivated reasoning. *Psychological Bulletin, 108,* 480–498.

Lord, C. G., Ross, L., & Lepper, M. (1979). Biased assimilation and attitude polariza-tion: The effects of prior theories on subsequently considered evidence. *Journal of Personality and Social Psychology, 37,* 2098–2109.

Maass, A., Salvi, D., Arcuri, L., & Semin, G. (1989). Language use in intergroup contexts: The linguistic intergroup bias. *Journal of Personality and Social Psychology, 57,* 981–993.

Manis, M., & Paskewitz, J. (1984). Judging psychopathology: Expectation and con-trast. *Journal of Experimental Social Psychology, 20,* 363–381.

Markus, H., & Zajonc, R. B. (1985). The cognitive perspective in social psychology. In G. Lindzey & E. Aronson (Eds.), *Handbook of social psychology* (Vol. 3, pp. 137–230). Hillsdale, NJ: Erlbaum.

McConahay, J. B., Hardee, B. B., & Batts, V. (1981). Has racism declined? It depends upon who's asking and what is asked. *Journal of Conflict Resolution, 25,* 563–579.

Ostrom, T. M. (1988). Interdependence of attitude theory and measurement. In A. R. Pratkanis, S. J. Breckler, & A. G. Greenwald (Eds.), *Attitude structure and function* (pp. 11–36). Hillsdale, NJ: Erlbaum.

Paulhus, D. L. (1991). Measurement and control of response bias. In J. P. Robinson, P. R. Shaver, & L. S. Wrightsman (Eds.), *Measures of personality and social psycho-logical attitudes* (pp. 17–59). San Diego, CA: Academic Press.

Petty, R. E., & Krosnick, J. A. (1996). *Attitude strength: Antecedents and consequences.* Hillsdale, NJ: Erlbaum.

Poppleton, P., & Pilkington, G. (1963). The measurement of religious attitudes in a university population. *British Journal of Social and Clinical Psychology, 2,* 20–36.

Proshansky, H. M. (1943). A projective method for the study of attitudes. *Journal of Abnormal and Social Psychology, 38,* 393–395.

Roskos-Ewoldson, D. R., & Fazio, R. H. (1992). On the orienting value of attitudes: Attitude accessibility as a determinant of an object's attraction of visual attention. *Journal of Personality and Social Psychology, 63,* 198–211.

Ross, L., Lepper, M. R., & Hubbard, M. (1975). Perseverance in self-perception and social perception: Biased attributional processes in the debriefing paradigm. *Journal of Personality and Social Psychology, 32,* 880–892.

Rudman, L. A., & Borgida, E. (1995). The afterglow of construct accessibility: The behavioral consequences of priming men to view women as sexual objects. *Journal of Experimental Social Psychology, 31,* 493–517.

Schimel, J., Simon, L., Greenberg, J., Pyszczynski, T., Solomon, S., Waxmonsky, J., & Arndt, J. (1999). Stereotypes and terror management: Evidence that mortality salience enhances stereotypic thinking and preferences. *Journal of Personality and Social Psychology, 77,* 905–926.

Sekaquaptewa, D., Espinoza, P., Thompson, M., Vargas, P., & von Hippel, W. (2003). Stereotypic explanatory bias: Implicit stereotyping as a predictor of discrimina-tion. *Journal of Experimental Social Psychology, 39,* 75–82.

Sekaquaptewa, D., & Kiefer, A. (2002). Unpublished raw data.

Sekaquaptewa, D., Vargas, P., & von Hippel, W. (1997). *Explanatory bias as an implicit indicator of prejudice.* Paper presented at the annual meeting of the New England Social Psychological Association, Williamstown, MA.

Sherif, M., & Hovland, C. T. (1961). *Social judgment: Assimilation and contrast effects in communication and attitude change.* New Haven, CT: Yale University Press.

Spence, J., Helmreich, R., & Stapp, J. (1973). A short version of the Attitudes Toward Women Scale. *Bulletin of the Psychonomic Society, 2,* 219–220.

Spencer, S. J., Fein, S., Wolfe, C. T., Fong, C., & Dunn, M. A. (1998). Automatic activation of stereotypes: The role of self-image threat. *Personality and Social Psychology Bulletin, 24,* 1139–1152.

Spencer, S., Steele, C. M., & Quinn, D. (1999). Stereotype threat and women's math performance. *Journal of Experimental Social Psychology, 35,* 4–28.

Squire, L. R., Knowlton, B., & Musen, G. (1993). The structure and organization of memory. In J. T. Spence, J. M. Darley, & D. J. Foss (Eds.), *Annual review of psychology* (Vol. 43, pp. 453–495). Palo Alto, CA: Annual Reviews.

Taylor, S. E., & Brown, J. D. (1988). Illusion and well-being: A social psychological perspective on mental health. *Psychological Bulletin, 103,* 193–210.

Tesser, A., & Paulhus, D. (1983). The definition of self: Private and public self-evaluation management strategies. *Journal of Personality and Social Psychology, 44,* 672–682.

Thurstone, L. L. (1928). Attitudes can be measured. *American Journal of Sociology, 33,* 529–554.

Vargas, P. T., von Hippel, W., & Petty, R. E. (2002). *Using "partially structured" attitude measures to enhance the attitude-behavior relationship.* Manuscript under review.

von Hippel, W., Sekaquaptewa, D., & Vargas, P. (1995). On the role of encoding processes in stereotype maintenance. In M. P. Zanna (Ed.), *Advances in experimental social psychology* (Vol. 27, pp. 177–254). San Diego, CA: Academic Press.

von Hippel, W., Sekaquaptewa, D., & Vargas, P. (1997). The Linguistic Intergroup Bias as an implicit indicator of prejudice. *Journal of Experimental Social Psychology, 33,* 490–509.

von Hippel, W., Shakarchi, R. J., & Lakin, J. (2002). *Self-deception and self-serving bias.* Manuscript under review.

Wigboldus, D. H. J., Semin, G. R., & Spears, R. (2000). How do we communicate stereotypes? Linguistic bases and inferential consequences. *Journal of Personality and Social Psychology, 78,* 5–18.

Wilson, G. D. (1985). The "catchphrase" approach to attitude measurement. *Personality and Individual Differences, 6,* 31–37.

Wilson, T. D., Lindsey, S., & Schooler, T. Y. (2000). A model of dual attitudes. *Psychological Review, 107,* 101–126.

PART III

INTERPERSONAL AND SOCIAL INFLUENCES ON
SOCIAL JUDGMENTS

13

The Importance of the Question in the Judgment of Abilities and Opinions via Social Comparison

Jerry Suls, René Martin, and Ladd Wheeler

CONTENTS

INTRODUCTION

The guiding premise of Festinger's (1954a, 1954b) theory of social comparison is that people compare themselves with others to learn what they are capable of doing and to hold correct opinions about the world (i.e., the *self-evaluation motive*). In recent years, however, more attention has focused on how comparisons are used to cope with threats to bolster self-esteem or feel better (Buunk & Gibbons, 1997; Taylor & Lobel, 1989; Wills, 1981; Wood, 1989). The present authors have returned to the original aim in the Proxy ability (Martin, 2000; Wheeler, Martin, & Suls, 1997) and Triadic opinion comparison models (Suls, Martin, & Wheeler, 2000) because in some cases people want veridical information. Both models build on attributional concepts introduced to the area by Goethals and Darley (1977) but add an emphasis on the self-evaluative question with which the comparer is concerned. This chapter presents the Proxy and Triadic models and reviews recent empirical evidence from our lab. On the explicit-to-implicit processing continuum that is considered in this

Jerry Suls and René Martin, Department of Psychology, University of Iowa, Iowa City, Iowa 52245. Ladd Wheeler, School of Psychology, Macquarie University. Research reported in this chapter was supported by National Science Foundation Grants SBR-96-31808 and BCS-99-10592. Please address correspondence to Jerry Suls, Department of Psychology, University of Iowa, Iowa City, IA 52245; e-mail: Jerry-suls@uiowa.edu; telephone: 319-335-0569; fax: 319-335-0191.

volume, the models focus on conscious, deliberative processing of social information.

EVALUATING ABILITY

Before setting a goal or starting a difficult, even dangerous task, the performer might need to evaluate personal ability. Social comparisons can provide information to make such predictions when objective standards are unavailable or too risky to be utilized effectively. Festinger (1954a) predicted that comparing oneself with "similar others" would be maximally informative, but he was ambiguous about which dimensions of similarity might be important in evaluating personal ability. In one passage, Festinger (1954a, Hypothesis III) emphasized similarity on performance outcomes (e.g., a comparison other who received the same score on an examination). However, he emphasized similarity on dimensions related to performance (e.g., practice or resources) at another point in his theory (1954a, Hypothesis VIII).

Early research that operationalized similarity in terms of performance outcomes found that subjects often sought information about individuals with extreme scores rather than information from similar others (Thornton & Arrowood, 1966; Wheeler et al., 1969). Defining the similar comparison other on the basis of performance outcomes also presented researchers with a logical conundrum. To know whether a potential comparison other might in fact have a similar performance outcome is impossible without first engaging in some sort of (perhaps implicit) comparison process (Jones & Regan, 1974).

The ambiguities associated with performance-based similarity were effectively resolved in Goethals and Darley's (1977) integration of Festinger's eighth hypothesis (1954a) with ideas drawn from attribution theory (Kelley, 1967; see also McClure, Sutton, & Hilton, this volume). In their reformulation, people prefer to compare themselves with others who are similar on the basis of characteristics or attributes related to the performance outcome rather than the performance itself. The rationale for related attribute similarity hinges on the attributional principle of discounting – that is, attribution to any single cause, in this case ability, is problematic whenever two or more plausible causes are present. For example, if one of the authors runs fewer laps than a college athlete, she should not infer that her own athletic ability is poor. Further, she should not conclude that her athletic ability is superior if she runs more laps than a 10-year-old child. Comparison with others who are dissimilar on related attributes (whether they be advantaged or disadvantaged) yields ambiguous information. Different standing on related attributes provides just as plausible an explanation for the relative performances of the child, athlete, and author as any fundamental differences in physical ability. In contrast, comparison with a person who is similar on related attributes leads to a straightforward conclusion, because any performance disparity can be reliably attributed to differences in ability. Experimental evidence supporting Goethals and Darley's related attributes hypothesis comes from several sources (Gastorf & Suls, 1978; Suls, Gastorf, & Lawhon, 1978; Wheeler, Koestner, & Driver, 1982; Zanna, Goethals, & Hill, 1975).

In Goethals and Darley's (1977) approach, the focus is the use of social comparison in answering the question "How well have I done relative to others?" (or "Am I as good as I ought to be?"). The individual who learns that he ran faster (or slower) than someone similar on related attributes should feel good (or bad), because this information provides an indication of whether he has fulfilled his potential (Wheeler et al., 1982). However, this comparison outcome is *not* informative about the probability of success or failure for any specific performance situation. For example, if that same individual is considering running a marathon, it is doubtful that he would be comfortable starting the marathon with only the knowledge that he is more fit that someone possessing similar related attributes. The attributional reformulation of social comparison speaks to a general self-assessment question (Kruglanski & Mayseless, 1990; Smith, 1981). However, it does not capture the sorts of social comparison processes likely to be used in answering realistic questions about personal ability for some novel undertaking (i.e., the "Can I do X?" question).

The Proxy Comparison Model

The Proxy Comparison Model (Martin, 2000; Martin, Suls, & Wheeler, 2002; Wheeler et al., 1997) builds on the attributional reformulation but focuses on the use of comparison information in answering the question "Can I do X?" The model is most germane to situations where someone must decide whether to undertake a novel and consequential task (i.e., failure would have costs). Because there can be serious consequences if people miscalculate about their capabilities in attempting a novel task, the model assumes conscious, explicit processing. Under certain circumstances, unconscious goals primed by situational variables may circumvent this conscious deliberative process (see Chartrand & Jefferis, this volume).

According to the Proxy Model, a comparison other who already has undertaken the unfamiliar task may serve as a proxy for the self in predicting one's own likely outcome. Not every potential comparison other will represent an informative proxy, however. The model specifies that the relevance of any given proxy depends on the configuration of variables such as similarity to the self, effort exerted, and related attributes.

The model has three main premises. First, a proxy's success on some novel task (X) should be a good indicator of one's likely future performance on X if both self and proxy performed similarly on a prior related task and the proxy is known to have exerted maximal effort on that occasion. If it is unclear, however, that the proxy exerted maximum effort on the initial task, then that proxy may not provide an appropriate comparison. For example, if the proxy was fatigued when he or she performed similarly to the self, then the proxy's prior performance might be an underestimate of his or her ability. This means that the proxy's performance on X might be a poor prognosticator for personal success on that task.

Second, the model posits, in the absence of information about maximum effort, that the proxy may still be useful if the individual and proxy share related attributes (i.e., characteristics that are predictive of performance). Thus, in the absence of information about maximum effort, related attribute standing can serve as a substitute.

Third, we propose that information about related attributes is irrelevant if the proxy is known to have performed at maximum effort. In other words, related attribute information is useful only when the proxy's level of effort does not permit a clear inference regarding that proxy's ability level. However, when a proxy is known to have performed at maximal effort, that proxy's performance provides a reliable basis for personal performance prediction – irrespective of the proxy's standing on related attributes. For example, if an individual knows that both he and a proxy ran 25 laps and he was confident that 25 laps represented the proxy's best or maximal effort, then it would be reasonable to infer that he will be able to match the proxy's subsequent performance in a marathon. Learning that the proxy practices several times a week (i.e., a related attribute) does not inform or change the individual's expectation of matching the proxy's performance on the new task. Thus, the Proxy Model predicts that related attribute information should be disregarded in the context of information that the proxy has performed at maximal effort.

In support of this approach, Jones and Regan (1974) showed that people most preferred a discussion partner who had performed similarly to them on a first test of ability and who had already attempted the task at issue. Smith and Sachs (1997) also theorized about proxies and performance prediction and found that confidence in predictions was highest when the proxy's score was similar. These findings generally are consistent with the Proxy Model, but prior studies have not examined the specific role of maximum effort or manipulated related attributes to assess their effects.

Empirical Evidence for the Proxy Model

Martin et al. (2002) conducted several lab studies to test key premises of the Proxy Model. In some experiments, a physical strength paradigm was used. Research subjects began by squeezing a handgrip as many times as possible in 30 sec (Task 1). They then predicted (i.e., the dependent variable) how many kilograms/force they would exert in gripping a hand dynamometer (Task 2). Prior to making their Task 2 predictions, subjects

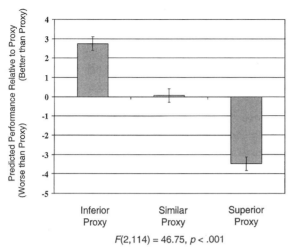

Figure 13.1. Task 2 predictions as a function of the proxy's Task 1 performance. (Adapted from Martin, Suls, & Wheeler, 2002.)

were given social comparison information about a proxy who previously had completed both tasks.

In an initial study, we tested the model's proposition that a proxy's success on a novel task (Task 2) should be a good indicator of one's future performance on that undertaking if both proxy and self performed similarly on a prior related task (Task 1) and the proxy is known to have exerted maximal effort on that occasion. Task 1 performance similarity was manipulated; subjects learned that the proxy's Task 1 score was similar, better, or worse than their own. Consistent with the model, subjects used the proxy's relative standing on Task 1 and the proxy's Task 2 performance score to predict their own Task 2 outcomes (Figure 13.1).

The model also proposes that in the absence of information about maximum effort, a proxy may still be useful if self and proxy share related attributes; this proposition was tested in a second study. All subjects learned that the proxy might not have performed at maximum capacity on Task 1. Hand size (a related attribute for grip strength) provided a basis for comparison. Subjects learned that the proxy's hand size was similar, larger, or smaller than their own; control subjects did not receive this information. In the context of ambiguous information about the proxy's Task 1 effort, participants used related attribute information about hand width to formulate rational performance predictions (Figure 13.2).

Most interestingly, the model posits that information about related attributes is irrelevant if the proxy is known to have performed at maximum effort on Task 1. Study 3 was constructed to test this prediction by manipulating effort (maximum vs. ambiguous) and related attributes (hand size: similar vs. larger vs. smaller vs. no information) in a between-subjects

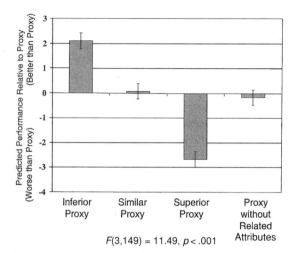

Figure 13.2. Task 2 predictions as a function of the proxy's related attributes. (Adapted from Martin, Suls, & Wheeler, 2002.)

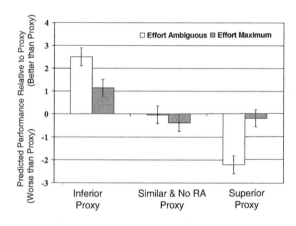

Figure 13.3. Task 2 predictions as a function of the proxy's related attributes and effort. (Adapted from Martin, Suls, & Wheeler, 2002.)

design. Subjects responded to the related attribute information in formulating their performance predictions when the proxy's effort was ambiguous (Figure 13.3).[1] However, when participants knew that the proxy had

---

[1] Because predictions did not differ between the similar related attribute and no related attribute conditions and did not vary as a function of information about the proxy's Task 1 effort, the means for similar and no related attribute information cells were collapsed in the subsequent analyses.

exerted maximal effort on the tasks, participants expected to perform approximately at the level of the proxy, regardless of the related attribute information received. Similar results were also found in a paradigm that involved an intellectual task (Study 4). In summary, several experiments support the three major predictions made by the Proxy Model.

Implications of the Proxy Model

Festinger (1954b) observed that someone who knows his score on an intelligence test does not know what he is capable of accomplishing in the real world, but he is in a position to compare himself with others. If the comparison other's intelligence score is substantially different from his own, he only knows that what he can accomplish probably will be different – but he does not learn what level of performance he is likely to attain. Alternatively, if he compares to someone possessing a similar score, he can infer that his own probable outcome will be identical or at least very similar to that of the comparison other. "This gives him the subjective feeling of knowing what he can or cannot do" (Festinger, 1954b, p. 197).

This is what Festinger probably meant when he wrote that a comparison other needs to be similar to the self. The comparison other needs to be similar *on the ability* (or some performance manifestation of that ability) in order for the comparer to determine what he *can do*. This perspective guided the development of the proxy comparison model of ability self-evaluation and the experiments described previously.

We perceive our approach to have strong connections to cognitive psychological theories of behavior. For example, Anderson's (1990) *if-then* rules provide an effective characterization of how our participants responded to information about a proxy. The formulation of a Task 2 performance prediction (the "then" component) was shaped by subjects' cognitive representations of the situation (the "if" component). For example, *if* he squeezed the grip exerciser 15 times more than I did, *then* I should expect to exert fewer kilograms/force than he did with the hand dynamometer. *If* she was ill when she performed Task 1, *then* I don't have clear information about what she might really be capable of doing. However, *if* her hand was smaller than mine, *then* I can expect that I probably am stronger than she was. In predicting Task 2 performances, participants used informational cues, such as effort and related attributes, that seemed relevant to the evaluative question. If-then rules provided the link between how participants understood the social comparison situation and their subsequent performance expectations. This conceptualization places the Proxy Model in a broader context by highlighting the fact that people reason about social comparison information and ability self-evaluation very much as they process information in other domains (Kruglanski & Mayseless, 1990; Stapel & Koomen, 2000; Wills & Suls, 1991; also see Kruglanski et al., this volume).

We, however, do not assume that individuals always are consciously aware of the *if-then* rules they are using.

These results complement and supplement earlier findings. Kulik, Mahler, and Moore (1996) found that patients awaiting open heart surgery sought information and adapted more effectively when they had a room-mate who already had undergone the same surgical procedure. In other words, surgery patients benefited from exposure to a similar proxy.

We did not mention earlier that the presence/absence of a substantial monetary incentive (i.e., $10) for accurate predictions was manipulated in some of the grip strength studies. The incentive had no effects on predictions, however. Participants seemingly were motivated to generate rational performance predictions even in the absence of a monetary incentive. People prefer diagnostic information about their abilities, at least under certain conditions (Trope, 1983). Because the participants anticipated an imminent task, which was to be performed in the presence of an experimenter, perhaps it is not surprising that even the no-incentive participants generated thoughtful performance predictions.

The fact that the participants in the experiments showed no evidence of self-enhancement in formulating their Task 2 performance predictions seems to conflict with research demonstrating that social comparisons are frequently selected or construed in ways to make oneself look or feel good (e.g., Wood, 1989). In our studies, however, participants expected to outperform the proxy only when it was rational to do so (i.e., when they compared themselves with a proxy who was inferior in terms of Task 1 performance or related attributes). Actually, our finding no evidence of self-enhancement is consistent with reports that positive illusions are reduced when people must make a decision about a course of action (Taylor & Gollwitzer, 1995). The adaptive consequences of self-evaluative accuracy seem to outweigh the potential affective benefits of self-enhancement, at least when trying to predict important outcomes.

EVALUATING OPINIONS

The Triadic Model also emphasizes the evaluative question under consideration, but for different types of opinions. Festinger (1954a,b) thought that people obtain certainty about their opinions by finding agreement with others (i.e., similar others). Goethals and Darley (1977) recognized that Festinger's view of attitudes was too limited, leading them to distinguish between beliefs and values. The Triadic Model (Suls et al., 2000) extended this view to posit three types of opinions: current preferences, beliefs, and future preferences. Current preferences ("Do I like X?") are personally relevant value-type opinions (e.g., "Do I hate mimes?"). The model proposes that people sharing similar related attributes (e.g., background, general worldview) will be seen as personally relevant and therefore most influential for preference evaluation. Similar others further elucidate which preferences will be accepted by one's reference group. (Note that the individual, in some cases, might ask "Do I really like/dislike X?" because he or she is surprised by the immediate positive/negative response; see Forgas and East, this volume, for an explanation about why this might happen.)

Belief evaluation ("Is X correct?") pertains to verifiable facts (e.g., "Am I correct in expecting terrorists to attack again?"). Others possessing expertise (i.e., superior on related attributes) can answer such questions. An expert's response on this issue is likely to be rejected, however, unless that person shares one's fundamental religious, political, and social values. Thus, the model assigns considerable importance to the role of the *similar expert* (someone who is similar in values but different in knowledge) in belief evaluation (Hains, Hogg, & Duck, 1997; Turner, 1991).

The third type of opinion question concerns predictions about future preferences ("Will I like X?"). Knowing that a proxy enjoyed a particular book does not allow someone to anticipate his or her own response *unless* the pattern of the proxy's past preferences, relative to the self, is known. In other words, laypeople intuitively use a strategy formally implemented by marketers called *collaborative filtering*. For example, Amazon.com uses shared shopping patterns as a basis for formulating customer recommendations. Along similar lines, knowing whether self and proxy have agreed about books in the past adds informational utility to the proxy's feedback about the book currently in question. In the absence of information about the proxy's past relative preferences, related attributes can provide a basis for comparison. The model does not argue that only a proxy with similar past preferences can be informative. For example, a proxy's reaction to a new novel also will be informative if the proxy had a consistently dissimilar pattern: If Al dislikes all of the novels that you have liked, then Al's enjoyment of the new novel suggests that you probably will not enjoy it. What is essential is that the proxy has a *consistent history* of past preferences relative to the self. Then the proxy's response to the new stimulus can be informative about one's own future response.

Empirical Evidence for the Triadic Model

Belief versus Current Preference Assessment. The Triadic Model predicts that similar others (on related attributes) are most important for current preferences but that experts play a greater role in belief judgments. The prediction regarding current preferences is supported by past studies conducted for different purposes. For example, people were more likely to choose or be persuaded by similar others when making a decision in which subjectivity was emphasized (Goethals & Nelson, 1973; Gorenflo & Crano, 1989; Reckman & Goethals, 1973). Stotland and Patchen (1961) found that subjects became more prejudiced (toward African Americans) if they received a case history of a prejudiced authoritarian other who shared the subject's background and objective characteristics. The case history was unpersuasive when it described someone with a different background and objective characteristics. Evidence for the special role of advantaged or expert others for belief comparison can be found in the persuasion literature, with high-status ("more expert") sources or sources with more ability producing more attitude change (e.g., Aronson, Turner, & Carlsmith, 1963; Hovland, Janis, & Kelley, 1953) and conformity (e.g., Asch, 1956; Kidd & Campbell, 1955; Mausner, 1953; Strodtbeck, James, & Hawkins, 1958).

We also have conducted experiments in which the same attitudinal stimuli were used but the nature of the judgment – belief versus preference – was manipulated (a procedure adapted from Goethals & Nelson, 1973). Sophomore college students were asked to decide which of two students they liked more (*current preference*) or had a superior academic record (*belief*). All subjects received information about the two students, formulated their opinions, and then were offered the opportunity to sample another research participant's opinion about the two targets prior to making a final decision. There were four comparison alternatives: a same-sex student who had scored similarly to the subject on a personality inventory administered earlier in the semester (similar other), a same-sex student who had scored very differently on the personality test (dissimilar other), a senior who worked in the college admissions office (more expert), and a high school graduate who worked in a local convenience store (less expert). Participants rated their level of interest in each comparison source, which comprised the dependent variable.

As shown in Figure 13.4, subjects in the belief condition tended to choose the expert, whereas subjects in the current preference condition selected

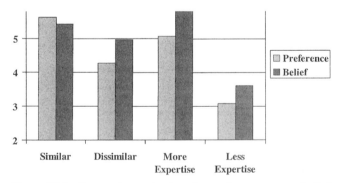

Figure 13.4. Comparison selections for preference versus belief assessment. Ratings were made on 7-point scales ranging from 1 (no interest) to 7 (very interested). (Adapted from Suls, Martin, & Wheeler, 2000.)

the person with a personality similar to their own (similar on related attributes). The results for the belief condition also illustrate an important aspect of the model. When evaluating a belief, participants were especially interested in the opinion of a more advantaged student. However, the greater expertise consisted only of having worked in the registrar's office. Here is a case where the expertise was only modestly greater than the subject's but was perceived as useful. This indicates that even a little more expertise is important for belief-type opinions. This situation actually is quite common. For example, people experiencing novel physical symptoms tend to first consult with other laypeople who, while lacking formal medical expertise, have somewhat more experience than they do (Friedson, 1961; Sanders, 1981; Suls, Martin, & Leventhal, 1997).

The "Similar Expert." Ryan and Gross's (1943) classic study of diffusion of the innovation of growing hybrid corn in Iowa in the 1920s and 1930s provides evidence for the similar expert hypothesis. They found that although hybrid corn was highly effective, the average farmer moved slowly from awareness of the innovation to adoption. When farmers made the change, it resulted not from communication with representatives of the agricultural extension office (i.e., persons who were presumably highly expert), but from neighbors who were early adopters. These innovators tended to have larger farms, higher incomes, more years of formal education, and more sophistication. They were more influential because they were perceived as somewhat more knowledgeable persons who also shared a fundamental background with the late adopters – in other words, a similar expert (see also Coleman, Katz, & Menzel, 1957; Katz & Lazarsfeld, 1955; Rogers, 1983).

Suls et al. (2002) surveyed college students about whether they had talked with others about their feelings and opinions concerning the massacre of the students at Columbine High School. People were more likely to talk to someone who shared their basic values but had more expertise when the opinion had an important belief component. In an experimental study involving the effectiveness of an alternative medicine cure (belief), participants chose a physician (expert) who matched their personal orientation about being traditional or unconventional (value).

Future Preferences. The model also proposes that preference prediction ("Will I like X?") is facilitated by learning about the response of a proxy who already experienced X and exhibited consistency in past preferences or related attributes. In the context of fiction selections, research subjects showed more interest in learning the responses of a proxy who either had similar past preferences regarding literature *or* similar related attributes (Suls et al., 2000, Studies 2A and 2B).

In another experiment, we tested whether personal preference predictions will be based on a proxy's reaction if he or she exhibits a consistent set of prior preferences. College students were asked to generate lists of their five favorite and five least favorite movies. Then we prepared fictitious movie lists supposedly completed by other students. For a third of the subjects, the bogus list was created to have a profile similar to that of the subject, that is, with similar liked and disliked films. For another third, lists were created to be mirror images of the subject's lists – with the proxy listing the subject's least favorite movies as his or her most favorite films and the subject's favorites as the proxy's least favorites. The final third received a list of random or inconsistent patterns of movie preferences, that is, the proxy's list indicated no consistent pattern of agreement or disagreement with the subject.

The following week, each subject received the "other participant's" preference list and also learned that he or she had seen a recently released film and either liked or disliked it. Participants were asked to predict their response to the film and whether they would try to attend. As Figure 13.5 shows, subjects predicted that they would have the same response to X, the new film, as a proxy with a similar history of preferences and the opposite response of a proxy with a dissimilar history. A neutral response was predicted if the proxy exhibited an inconsistent pattern of past preferences.

Thus, people appear to use a dissimilar proxy's reactions as a gauge to predict their own, as long as there is consistency in the proxy's preference pattern. The patterning or alignment of the proxy's preferences or past behaviors is more critical than his or her similarity.

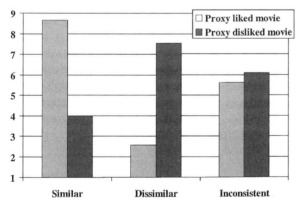

Figure 13.5. Predicted reaction to a new stimulus as a function of the proxy's past preference pattern and reaction to a new stimulus. Ratings were made on 11-point scales ranging from 1 (not at all) to 11 (enjoyed film very much). (Adapted from Suls, Martin, & Wheeler, 2000.)

In sum, although related attributes appear to be important for all three kinds of opinions, the patterning of attributes plays different roles. For current preferences, similarity is important, but for beliefs, someone who is similar in some ways but different in others – the similar expert – plays the decisive role. In making judgments about future preferences, related attributes or past preferences provide helpful information to assess whether a proxy's response is an appropriate guide for oneself. Further, similarity/ dissimilarity per se is not as critical as the consistency of the proxy's attributes or past reactions.

GENERAL IMPLICATIONS

The main premise of both the Proxy and Triadic models is that identification of the evaluative question is the first step in understanding the direction that the social comparison process takes and the type of referent who provides the most useful information. An answer to the evaluative question requires the person to apply attributional principles (e.g., Heider, 1958; Kelley, 1967), if-then rules (Anderson, 1990), and implicit constructs about abilities and opinions. Discounting and augmentation rules are important for answering the question "Am I as good as I ought to be?" (Goethals & Darley, 1977). These principles also operate on cognitive representations of the situation (the "if" component) to formulate predictions (the "then" component) ("Can I do X?") and future preferences ("Will I like X?"). Both the selection and outcomes of social comparison depend on the explicit and implicit theories about the domains under evaluation (e.g., preferences vs. beliefs). Knowledge about the nature of these implicit theories for specific domains is still limited, although research on explanatory models in concept formation (Murphy & Medin, 1985) and motivation (Dweck, 1999) offer direction.

The present approach also offers a new perspective on the decades-long debate about whether the similar other has a special status in social comparison. Sharing attributes may render another person more appropriate for testing certain types of opinions; dissimilarity (particularly superiority on background factors) actually can be an asset for other types. Similarity in attributes or past history is less important than the consistency a proxy exhibits for preference prediction. There are situations in which opposites can be as informative about what one will enjoy as are similars. Increased recognition of the role of underlying patterns, rather than feature matching per se, draws connections from social comparison to research on analogy and structural alignment in cognitive psychology (Markman & Gentner, 1993). People learn about their abilities and opinions by comparing themselves with others who are analogous. This means that just as similarity based on underlying patterns of relations among elements can lead people to form analogies among objects that are superficially quite different from each other (Holyoak & Thagard, 1995), seemingly irrelevant persons may be influential if they exhibit alignment in underlying patterns (Lockwood, 2002; Lockwood & Kunda, 1997).

Most important, the current models draw several connections to general cognitive processes involved in comparison and judgment (see Stapel, this volume). Just as social comparison research in the 1970s and 1980s advanced by importing concepts from attribution and self theories, the present work has drawn from insights about adaptive cognitive systems (Anderson, 1990) and implicit theories and analogy (Markman & Gentner, 1993). (For a different approach to comparison utilizing concepts from cognitive psychology, see Bless, Schwarz, & Wänke, this volume.) These applications from cognitive psychology and social cognition seem quite appropriate when we appreciate that social comparison is a variant of the more general human capacity to compare objects and symbols.

References

Anderson, J. R. (1990). *The adaptive character of thought*. Hillsdale, NJ: Erlbaum.

Aronson, E., Turner, J., & Carlsmith, M. (1963). Communicator credibility and communicator discrepancy as determinants of opinion change. *Journal of Abnormal and Social Psychology, 67*, 31–36.

Asch, S. (1956). Studies of independence and conformity: I. A minority of one against a unanimous majority. *Psychological Monographs, 70*, No. 9 (whole No. 416).

Buunk, B., & Gibbons, F. X. (Eds.). (1997). *Health and coping: Perspectives from social comparison theory*. Mahwah, NJ: Erlbaum.

Coleman, J. S., Katz, E., & Menzel, H. (1957). The diffusion of innovation among physicians. *Sociometry, 20*, 253–270.

Dweck, C. (1999). *Self theories*. Philadelphia: Psychology Press.

Festinger, L. (1954a). A theory of social comparison processes. *Human Relations, 7*, 117–140.

Festinger, L. (1954b). Motivation leading to social behavior. In M. R. Jones (Ed.), *Nebraska symposium on motivation* (Vol. 2, pp. 191–218). Lincoln: University of Nebraska Press.

Friedson, E. (1961). *Patients' views of medical practice*. New York: Russell Sage.

Gastorf, J. W., & Suls, J. (1978). Performance evaluation via social comparison: Performance similarity versus related attribute similarity. *Social Psychology, 41*, 297–305.

Goethals, G. R., & Darley, J. (1977). Social comparison theory: An attributional approach. In J. Suls & R. L. Miller (Eds.), *Social comparison processes: Theoretical and empirical perspectives* (pp. 259–278). Washington, DC: Hemisphere.

Goethals, G. R., & Nelson, R. E. (1973). Similarity in the influence process: The belief–value distinction. *Journal of Personality and Social Psychology, 25*, 117–122.

Gorenflo, D. W., & Crano, W. D. (1989). Judgmental subjectivity/objectivity and locus of choice in social comparison. *Journal of Personality and Social Psychology, 57*, 605–614.

Hains, S. C., Hogg, M. A., & Duck, J. M. (1997). Self-categorization and leadership: Effects of prototypicality and leader stereotypicality. *Personality and Social Psychology Bulletin, 23,* 1087–1199.

Heider, F. (1958). *The psychology of interpersonal relations.* New York: Wiley.

Holyoak, K., & Thagard, P. (1995). *Mental leaps: Analogy in creative thought.* Cambridge, MA: MIT Press/Bradford Books.

Hovland, C., Janis, I., & Kelley, H. H. (1953). *Communication and persuasion.* New Haven, CT: Yale University Press.

Jones, S. C., & Regan, D. (1974). Ability evaluation through social comparison. *Journal of Experimental Social Psychology, 10,* 133–146.

Katz, E., & Lazarsfeld, P. F. (1955). *Personal influence: The part played by people in the flow of mass communications.* Glencoe, IL: Free Press.

Kelley, H. L. (1967). Attribution theory in social psychology. In D. L. Levine (Ed.), *Nebraska symposium on motivation* (pp. 192–241). Lincoln: University of Nebraska Press.

Kidd, J. S., & Campbell, D. T. (1955). Conformity to groups as a function of group success. *Journal of Abnormal and Social Psychology, 51,* 390–393.

Kruglanski, A., & Mayseless, O. (1990). Classic and current social comparison research: Expanding the perspective. *Psychological Bulletin, 108,* 195–208.

Kulik, J. A., Mahler, H. I. M., & Moore, P. J. (1996). Social comparison and affiliation under threat: Effects on recovery from major surgery. *Journal of Personality and Social Psychology, 71,* 967–979.

Lockwood, P. (2002). Could it happen to you? Predicting the impact of downward comparisons on the self. *Journal of Personality and Social Psychology, 82,* 343–358.

Lockwood, P., & Kunda, Z. (1997). Superstars and me: Predicting the impact of role models on the self. *Journal of Personality and Social Psychology, 73,* 91–103.

Markman, A., & Gentner, D. (1993). Structural alignment during similarity comparison. *Cognitive Psychology, 25,* 431–467.

Martin, R. (2000). "Can I do X?" Using the Proxy Comparison Model to predict performance. In J. Suls & L. Wheeler (Eds.), *Handbook of social comparison: Theory and research* (pp. 67–80). New York: Kluwer Academic/Plenum.

Martin, R., Suls, J., & Wheeler, L. (2002). Ability evaluation by proxy: Role of maximum performance and related attributes. *Journal of Personality and Social Psychology: Interpersonal Relations and Group Processes, 82,* 781–791.

Mausner, B. (1953). Studies in social interaction: III. Effect of variation in one partner's prestige on the interaction of observer pairs. *Journal of Applied Psychology, 37,* 391–393.

Murphy, G., & Medin, D. (1985). The role of theories in conceptual coherence. *Psychological Review, 92,* 289–316.

Reckman, R. F., & Goethals, G. R. (1973). Deviancy and group-orientation as determinants of group composition preferences. *Sociometry, 36,* 419–423.

Rogers, E. M. (1983). *Diffusion of innovations.* New York: Free Press.

Ryan, B., & Gross, N. C. (1943). The diffusion of seed corn in two Iowa communities. *Rural Sociology, 8,* 15–24.

Sanders, G. S. (1981). The interactive effect of social comparison and objective information on the decision to see a doctor. *Journal of Applied Social Psychology, 11,* 390–400.

Smith, W. P. (1981). On the nature of the question in social comparison. In J. Harvey (Ed.), *Cognition, social behavior and the environment* (pp. 225–239). Hillsdale, NJ: Erlbaum.

Smith, W. P., & Sachs, P. (1997). Social comparison and task prediction: Ability similarity and the use of a proxy. *British Journal of Social Psychology, 36,* 587–602.

Stapel, D., & Koomen, W. (2000). Distinctness of others, mutability of selves: Their impact on self-evaluations. *Journal of Personality and Social Psychology, 79,* 1068–1087.

Stotland, E., & Patchen, M. (1961). Identification and changes in prejudice and in authoritarianism. *Journal of Abnormal and Social Psychology, 62,* 265–274.

Strodtbeck, F. L., James, R. M., & Hawkins, C. (1958). Social status in jury deliberations. In E. E. Maccoby, T. M. Newcomb, & E. L. Hartley (Eds.), *Readings in social psychology* (3rd ed., pp. 379–388). New York: Holt, Rinehart, & Winston.

Suls, J., Gastorf, J., & Lawhon, J. (1978). Social comparison choices for evaluating a sex- and age-related ability. *Personality and Social Psychology Bulletin, 4,* 102–105.

Suls, J., Martin, R., & Leventhal, H. (1997). Social comparison, lay referral, and the decision to seek medical care. In B. Buunk & F. Gibbons (Eds.), *Health and coping: Perspectives from social comparison theory* (pp. 195–226). Mahwah, NJ: Erlbaum.

Suls, J., Martin, R., & Wheeler, L. (2000). Three kinds of opinion comparison: The Triadic Model. *Personality and Social Psychology Review, 4,* 219–237.

Suls, J., Martin, R., Wheeler, L., Wallio, S., Bobier, D., & Lemos, K. (2002). *The similar expert: Two tests of the Triadic opinion comparison model.* Poster presented at the third annual Society of Personality and Social Psychology meetings, Savannah, GA.

Taylor, S. E., & Gollwitzer, P. M. (1995). Effects of mindset on positive illusions. *Journal of Personality and Social Psychology, 69,* 213–226.

Taylor, S. E., & Lobel, M. (1989). Social comparison activity under threat: Downward evaluation and upward contacts. *Psychological Review, 96,* 569–575.

Thornton, D., & Arrowood, A. J. (1966). Self-evaluation, self-enhancement, and the locus of social comparison. *Journal of Experimental Social Psychology, 2*(Suppl. 1), 40–48.

Trope, Y. (1983). Self-assessment in achievement behavior. In J. Suls & A. G. Greenwald (Eds.), *Psychological perspectives on the self* (Vol. 2, pp. 93–121). Hillsdale, NJ: Erlbaum.

Turner, J. C. (1991). *Social influence.* Pacific Grove, CA: Brooks/Cole.

Wheeler, L. (1966). Motivation as a determinant of upward comparison. *Journal of Experimental Social Psychology, 2*(Suppl. 1), 27–31.

Wheeler, L., Koestner, R., & Driver, R. E. (1982). Related attributes in choice of comparison others. *Journal of Experimental Social Psychology, 20,* 263–271.

Wheeler, L., Martin, R., & Suls, J. (1997). The Proxy social comparison model for self-assessment of ability. *Personality and Social Psychology Review, 1,* 54–61.

Wheeler, L., Shaver, K. G., Jones, R. A., Goethals, G. R., Cooper, J., Robinson, J. E., Gruder, C. L., & Butzine, K. W. (1969). Factors determining choice of a comparison other. *Journal of Experimental Social Psychology, 5,* 219–232.

Wills, T. A. (1981). Downward comparison principles in social psychology. *Psychological Bulletin, 90,* 245–271.

Wills, T. A., & Suls, J. (1991). Commentary: Neo-social comparison theory and beyond. In J. Suls & T. A. Wills (Eds.), *Social comparison: Contemporary theory and research* (pp. 395–412). Hillsdale, NJ: Erlbaum.

Wood, J. V. (1989). Theory and research concerning social comparisons of personal attributes. *Psychological Bulletin, 22,* 520–537.

Zanna, M. P., Goethals, G. R., & Hill, J. F. (1975). Evaluating a sex related ability: Social comparison with similar others and standard setters. *Journal of Experimental Social Psychology, 11,* 86–93.

14

Consequences of Automatic Goal Pursuit and the Case of Nonconscious Mimicry

Tanya L. Chartrand and Valerie E. Jefferis

CONTENTS

INTRODUCTION

What sets goal pursuit in motion? Perhaps the most intuitively appealing and compelling answer is that we do. We deliberate among our various desires and decide to pursue a particular goal in a particular social situation. We determine which strategies will best serve us in attaining the goal, engage in goal-directed behavior and plans of action, and evaluate our progress made toward the goal (Gollwitzer, 1990; Heckhausen, 1991). Thus, intuition tells us that goal pursuit is put in motion by our conscious will and that it is a deliberate, intentional process. Reflecting this, most models of self-regulation posit continuous, conscious choice and guidance as a central feature, if not the core foundation, of goal pursuit (Bandura, 1986, 1997; Cantor & Kihlstrom, 1987; Carver & Scheier, 1981; Deci & Ryan, 1985; Dweck, 1996; Locke & Latham, 1990; Mischel, Cantor, & Feldman, 1996).

However, goal pursuit does not always involve deliberate direction of goal-driven behavior. Like other automatic processes discussed in this volume (Brewer; Forgas & East; Galinsky, Martorana, & Ku; Haselton & Buss;

The preparation of this manuscript was partially supported by a grant from the National Institute for Mental Health (R03 MH65250-01) to the first author. Please address correspondence to Tanya L. Chartrand or Valerie E. Jefferis, Department of Psychology, Ohio State University, 1885 Neil Avenue Mall, Columbus, OH, 43210; e-mail: chartrand.2@osu.edu or jefferis.6@osu.edu

McClure, Sutton, & Hilton; von Hippel, Vargas, & Sekaquaptewa; Williams, Case, & Govan, all this volume), sometimes goal pursuit occurs outside of one's awareness, intent, and even control. Social environments automatically activate goals frequently associated with them in the past, and these goals then operate to guide information processing and behavior without conscious intervention (Chartrand & Bargh, 2002). Theoretical interest in nonconscious goal pursuit began more than a decade ago (Bargh, 1990), and supporting research soon followed.

A THREE-STAGE MODEL OF NONCONSCIOUS GOAL PURSUIT

In this chapter, we propose that nonconscious goal pursuit can be divided at both the conceptual and empirical levels into three stages: (a) the environment automatically *activates* associated goals and motives, (b) individuals *pursue* goals they are not aware of having, and (c) individuals succeed and fail at nonconsciously pursued goals, and this has downstream *consequences*.

Stage 1: Direct Situation–Goal Linkages

The first proposed stage assumes that goals are mentally represented in memory just as schemas, attitudes, stereotypes, and other social constructs are (Bargh, 1990). Previous research has demonstrated that constructs represented in memory can become automatically activated by stimuli that have been associated with them in the past, and thus goal representations should also be capable of this automatic activation. If one frequently and consistently chooses a certain goal whenever one is in a certain situation, then eventually the goal representation and the representation of the triggering situation become linked in memory. Once this association is formed, then merely being in that situation will nonconsciously and automatically activate the associated goal, regardless of any conscious intentions the individual may have at the time.

This first stage has received empirical support. In a recent study by Spencer, Fein, Wolfe, Fong, and Dunn (1998, Exp. 3), participants were given either positive or negative feedback on a bogus intelligence test and then, while under a cognitive load, were subliminally primed with drawings of either African American or European American faces. The researchers found that participants who were given a blow to their self-esteem via the negative feedback were more likely to have stereotypes automatically activated if they had been primed with African American faces. These results are particularly interesting given that cognitive load has been shown in past research to inhibit stereotype activation (Gilbert & Hixon, 1991; Spencer et al., 1998, Exp. 2). Importantly for the present discussion, the results suggest that a threat to one's self-image (triggering situation) can automatically activate an associated goal to restore self-esteem.

There has been other research showing that individuals in certain sub-populations can have goals activated by various situations. For instance, among individuals who have a chronic egalitarian goal, the presence of a minority group member can automatically activate the goal to be fair (Moskowitz, Gollwitzer, Wasel, & Schaal, 1999). Moreover, for men high in the tendency to sexually harass, being in a situation of relative power can trigger sex-related goals (Bargh, Raymond, Pryor, & Strack, 1995). The same situation of power can furthermore activate social responsibility goals for individuals with communal orientations and power-abuse goals for those with exchange orientations (Chen, Lee-Chai, & Bargh, 2001; Lee-Chai, Chen, & Chartrand, 2001). In sum, there is substantial evidence for the idea that social environments can automatically activate associated goals in memory.

Stage 2: Pursuit of Goals without Awareness

There is also evidence supporting the second proposed stage of noncon-scious goal pursuit – that nonconscious goals, once activated, guide sub-sequent cognition and behavior just like their conscious counterparts. Individuals are aware neither of the goal activation itself nor of the goal's subsequent guiding role. In a direct investigation of nonconscious goal pursuit, Chartrand and Bargh (1996, Study 1) replicated a study in which participants were given conscious goals to either memorize information or form an impression of a target, and were then exposed to sentence pred-icates that fell into four trait categories (Hamilton, Katz, & Leirer, 1980). In the original study, participants were given a surprise free recall test, and results revealed that those given the goal of forming an impression recalled more of the predicates and clustered them more by trait category. Chartrand and Bargh replicated this test but gave participants no conscious goals. Instead, they primed participants with either an impression forma-tion goal or a memorization goal, asked them to read the series of behavioral predicates, and then gave them a surprise free recall test. Replicating the results of the original study, Chartrand and Bargh (1996) found that par-ticipants who were primed with an impression formation goal were more likely to (a) recall more behaviors and (b) organize the behaviors accord-ing to trait category compared to those primed with a memorization goal. Importantly, none of the participants were aware during the study of hav-ing a goal to memorize information or to form an impression. Thus, they pursued these goals nonconsciously (see also Séquin & Pelletier, 2002).

Bargh, Gollwitzer, Lee-Chai, Barndollar, and Trötschel (2001) recently conducted a series of studies that tested for the presence of motivational states during nonconscious goal pursuit. Specifically, there are unique mo-tivational qualities that have previously been reserved to describe con-scious goal pursuit (e.g., Atkinson & Birch, 1970; Bandura, 1986; Gollwitzer,

1990; Lewin, 1951). Bargh et al. (2001) found that, like conscious goals, nonconscious goals increase in strength over time, lead to persistence when participants encounter obstacles during their goal pursuit, and lead to resumption of goal-directed behaviors following interruptions. In fact, there is now neurophysiological evidence that the pursuit of conscious and nonconscious evaluative goals invokes extremely similar brain patterns (Gardner, Bargh, Shellman, & Bessenoff, 2002), suggesting that once activated, people can pursue nonconscious goals as they do conscious goals.

Stage 3: Consequences of Success and Failure at Nonconscious Goal Pursuit

The third proposed stage of nonconscious goal pursuit concerns the consequences that it can engender. Once goals have been put in motion, people succeed or fail at them, just as they do at consciously activated goals. Evidence suggests that success or failure at nonconscious goals can have important downstream consequences, including effects on mood and self-enhancement.

Consequences for Mood. Chartrand (2002) explored the effects of succeeding and failing at nonconscious goals for mood. In the first experiment, participants completed a scrambled sentence task, which served as an achievement prime for half of the participants and a neutral prime for the other half. This was followed by a set of anagram puzzles that was described as a "fun filler task." The puzzles were accompanied by information concerning their "average" completion time, and the puzzles were either very easy or very difficult to complete in this amount of time. This manipulation led participants to either succeed or fail at the achievement goal without being given explicit feedback, which would have brought their performance to their conscious attention. Participants were then asked to report their current mood. The results indicated that those who were given the easy anagram task reported a more positive mood than those who were given the difficult version, but only when they had been primed with an achievement goal. When participants had completed the neutral version of the scrambled sentence task and thus did not have an achievement goal, no mood differences were found between participants who completed the easy anagram task and those who completed the difficult version. Importantly, postexperimental interviews confirmed that participants were not aware of having a conscious achievement goal during the study, and thus the goal was indeed nonconscious.

The second experiment (Chartrand, 2002) replicated these mood effects using a subliminal rather than a supraliminal priming technique as well as a different goal – impression formation. A conscious goal condition was also included to compare the consequences of conscious and nonconscious goal pursuit. Specifically, participants completed a parafoveal vigilance task in which words related to impression formation (or neutral words in the control conditions) were presented subliminally. Participants in the conscious goal condition received additional explicit instructions to form an impression of the target person. All participants then listened to a recording of a description of the target person, which would allow participants to act on their impression formation goal if they in fact had such a goal. Success or failure at this goal was manipulated by the description. The target person was described as performing either consistent or inconsistent behaviors, making it either easy or difficult to form a coherent impression of the target. Results indicated that participants who had an impression formation goal, regardless of whether it was given through explicit instruction or subliminal priming, reported being in a better mood when they had received the consistent description (and had presumably succeeded at their impression formation goal) than when they received the inconsistent description (and had presumably failed). Mood did not vary as a result of the description when participants did not have a goal of forming an impression. Importantly, postexperimental interviews indicated that participants who were primed with the goal did not have a conscious goal to form an impression.

Thus, success and failure at nonconscious goals can affect mood in much the same way that success and failure at conscious goals do. However, unlike conscious goal pursuit, one cannot link the consequences of success and failure with a consciously experienced goal. These "mystery moods" that result from nonconscious goal pursuit may be qualitatively different from moods that result from conscious goal pursuit. Recent findings suggest that negative mystery moods do indeed have consequences different from those of negative understood moods.

Consequences for Self-Enhancement: Conscious versus Nonconscious Goal Pursuit. Tesser and his colleagues (Tesser, 2000, 2001; Tesser, Crepaz, Collins, Cornell, & Beach, 2000; Tesser, Martin, & Cornell, 1996) have argued that self-enhancement strategies are invoked when a negative mood of unknown origin is experienced. A series of studies by Chartrand, Cheng, and Tesser (2002) examined the relationship between mystery moods and self-enhancement.

The first study measured self-enhancement by assessing the extent to which participants created self-serving definitions of success (Dunning, Leuenberger, & Sherman, 1995). Participants were given an achievement goal either through a scrambled sentence task (nonconscious goal condition) or through explicit instructions (conscious goal condition), or they were given no goal. They then completed a fun filler task of anagrams, during which the experimenter casually mentioned the "average" completion time. The time that the experimenter mentioned was in fact an underestimate of the time the task would take, thus leading the participants to fail at the achievement goal. Participants then read a description of a target person who had been in a successful marriage for 25 years. The description included various attributes of the person, and participants rated the contribution of each attribute to the person's success. They then completed a survey that asked them about their own attributes, which included the attributes of the target person. The results indicated that those who failed at a nonconscious goal were the most likely to create self-serving definitions of success, as measured by rating the qualities that they shared with the successful target person as more important than the qualities that they did not share. Those who failed at a conscious goal created moderately self-serving definitions of success, and those who had no goal created the least self-serving definitions.

This first study supported the hypothesis that mystery moods lead to self-enhancement. It also supported the notion that the consequences of nonconscious goal pursuit are not always the same as the consequences of conscious goal pursuit. However, because all of the participants in the study failed to meet their achievement goal, the possibility remained that mystery moods in general, rather than only negative mystery moods, led to the increased self-enhancement. Thus, a conceptual replication of Study 1 was done to examine whether it is the mysteriousness of the mood or the valence of the mood that leads to self-enhancement. Participants were once again given a conscious goal, a nonconscious goal, or no goal. This was followed by information that led them to either succeed or fail at the goal if they had one. Self-enhancement was again measured by examining self-serving biases. The results indicated that only those who failed engaged in self-enhancement.

Two additional studies by Chartrand et al. (2002) concerned potential moderating factors of the link between negative mystery moods and self-enhancement. Study 3 examined the effect of expressing the negative mood and thus being made aware of it. A different measure of self-enhancement was also used. Recent research suggests that stereotyping may function as a self-enhancement technique (e.g., Fein & Spencer, 1997). Thus, Study 3 measured self-enhancement using the Stereotypic Explanatory Bias scale, *an implicit measure of stereotyping* (von Hippel, Sekaquaptewa, & Vargas, 1997). Participants were led to fail at a conscious goal, a nonconscious goal, or no goal to achieve. Half of the participants then completed a questionnaire that instructed them to think about the experiment and indicate how the different tasks made them feel, whereas the other half of the participants completed a filler task. The questionnaire presumably allowed participants to express their mood and led them to consider the reasons for it. Lastly, the implicit stereotyping measure was administered. The results replicated Studies 1 and 2, in that failing at a nonconscious goal, as opposed to a conscious goal or no goal, led to greater self-enhancement, in this case evidenced by greater stereotyping. This replicated the findings from Study 1 that suggest that there are different downstream consequences of failing at conscious versus nonconscious goals. Importantly, however, this effect was eliminated when participants understood the source of their mood. Participants who completed the questionnaire concerning their mood and its source did not stereotype more than participants who had a conscious goal or no goal. Furthermore, there were no significant differences in stereotyping as a result of the mood questionnaire for participants who had a conscious goal or no goal.

Study 4 (Chartrand et al., 2002) sought to examine the mechanism through which the mood awareness manipulation in Study 3 attenuated the self-enhancement effect. Participants in that study were able to both express their mood and explore its source. It was therefore unclear whether it is the presence of an attribution or the expression of the mood that is most crucial. Participants in Study 4 either failed at a nonconscious goal or were given no goal. During half of the experimental sessions, the experimenter casually said to the group after the failure manipulation, "You guys look dull. For some reason, everybody's in a bad mood after this task. It must be that long computer task," and then proceeded with instructions for the next task. In the other half of the sessions, the group only received instructions for the next task. The experimenter's comment served to provide the participants with an attribution for their mood without allowing them to express it. Participants then completed a self-enhancement measure. The results indicated that those who failed at a nonconscious goal were more likely to self-enhance only when they were not provided with an attribution for their mood. The attribution attenuated self-enhancement in the nonconscious goal failure conditions but had no effect when participants did not have a goal. Thus, the results indicate that understanding the source of a negative mystery mood, rather than expressing it, leads to less self-enhancement.

The results of Chartrand et al.'s (2002) studies support the notion that success and failure at nonconscious goals can have consequences, and these consequences can sometimes be different from those that result from conscious goal pursuit. Understanding the source of one's moods appears to play an important role in shaping the consequences of those moods. Because nonconscious goal pursuit can lead to moods for which the source is unknown, nonconscious goals may be involved in processes that are important determinants of our behavior, including self-enhancement. On the other hand, because conscious goal pursuit usually leads to moods for which the source is known, distinct processes take place, which may lead to different behaviors, including less self-enhancement.

NONCONSCIOUS GOAL PURSUIT: A CASE STUDY INVOLVING
BEHAVIORAL MIMICRY

Thus far, we have discussed nonconscious goal pursuit and the three proposed stages that it involves. It might be helpful at this point to examine one example of nonconscious goal pursuit in some depth. There has been quite a bit of recent research on the goal to affiliate and how that goal can be (a) automatically activated by certain social environments, (b) nonconsciously pursued in the form of unintentional mimicry of others, and (c) succeeded and failed at, leading to various consequences. The evidence for each of these stages will be reviewed in the hope that it will give a richer understanding of nonconscious goal pursuit and the way it occurs in everyday life.

A Brief Background on Mimicry and Affiliation

Individuals nonconsciously mimic the postures, gestures, mannerisms, and behaviors of others (Bavelas, Black, Chovil, Lemery, & Mullett, 1988; Bernieri, 1988; Chartrand & Bargh, 1999). Why? Individuals have an enormously strong need to belong and affiliate (Baumeister & Leary, 1995; Brewer, 1991). Given the ubiquitous need to belong and be accepted, mimicry is very important in everyday life (Chartrand, Maddux, & Lakin, in press). If one looks, talks, and acts like somebody else, that might mean that both persons have something in common or are "on the same wavelength." This in turn might lead to greater empathy, liking, and smoother interactions. In fact, there is now substantial evidence that mimicry and affiliation are correlated (e.g., Bernieri, 1988; La France, 1979; La France & Broadbent, 1976).

Chartrand and Bargh (1999, Study 2) wanted to take this theory one step further and test whether mimicry can actually *cause* greater rapport and liking between people. In this study, participants took turns describing various photographs with a confederate. Throughout the interaction, the confederate either mimicked the posture, gestures, and mannerisms of the participant (with a 2-sec lag, and with the behaviors not always matching exactly so that participants would not notice the mimicry) or used neutral, nondescript posture, gestures, and mannerisms. It was expected that participants who were mimicked by the confederate would later report liking the confederate more, and would report that the interaction had been more smooth and harmonious, compared to those who were not mimicked. Results were as predicted, suggesting that one function that behavioral mimicry serves is to increase liking between interactants. This study also provides the first experimental demonstration that behavioral mimicry *causes* an increase in rapport between two interactants.

The Moderating Role of an Affiliation Goal

Thus, mimicry and affiliation are clearly related, and mimicry can cause greater affiliation between interactants. However, what if there is no existing rapport but individuals want to create that rapport? Can the mere *goal* to affiliate with someone else lead to greater mimicry of that person? If so, it suggests that on some level we recognize the powerful effect that mimicry has on fostering liking and affiliation between people, and that we use this knowledge implicitly to get other people to like us when we have a goal to affiliate with them. Thus, when we have a goal to affiliate with someone or be liked by that person, we will nonconsciously start to mimic the person more than usual. Thus, mimicry is a strategy in our repertoire of behaviors that help us affiliate with other people. Importantly, we are not aware of this strategy. Consistent with this lack of awareness, recent research by Aarts and Dijksterhuis (2000) suggests that higher-order goals automatically activate the associated behavioral strategies commonly used to achieve those goals. Perhaps we are not consciously aware of some of these plans of action, including the mimicry that automatically is triggered when one has an affiliation goal.

Thus, the plan of action often nonconsciously used to satisfy an affiliation goal may be the subtle mimicry of others' postures, gestures, and mannerisms. But can affiliation goals become automatically activated by the environment? And if so, do they lead to the automatic activation of the associated behavioral plan of nonconscious mimicry? And finally, does succeeding and failing at an affiliation goal have downstream consequences? These are questions that we have been exploring recently in our lab.

Stage 1 of Nonconscious Goal Pursuit: Situations Can Automatically Activate an Affiliation Goal. A number of recent studies have put individuals in situations that are presumed to activate an affiliation goal. The presence of such a goal was tested by measuring the subsequent amount of mimicry. For example, Cheng and Chartrand (2002) explored various conditions in which people might be motivated to affiliate with one another. For one study, it was assumed that college students would have a goal to affiliate with a fellow attractive undergraduate student, whereas they would not be as motivated to affiliate with someone of a different age group – either a high school student or a graduate student. It was further hypothesized that high self-monitors would be more aware of differences in age and what that meant for them, and would be more attuned to situations where they might gain a friend (the undergraduate) versus situations where they would not (the high school or graduate student). We thus predicted that high self-monitors would more readily pick up on the affiliation cues in the environment and be more successful at using nonconscious mimicry as a strategy for getting people to like them.

Participants interacted with a female confederate who was supposedly either a high school student, an undergraduate student, or a graduate student. The confederate was always the same individual. They engaged in the same photo description task from Chartrand and Bargh (1999), and the confederate subtly touched her face throughout the interaction. The results supported the hypothesis: Low self-monitors did not differentially mimic the confederate based on her supposed age. However, high self-monitors mimicked the fellow undergraduate student more than they did either the high school student or the graduate student. This suggests that, relative to the low self-monitors, the high self-monitors realized that the undergraduate confederate was someone with whom they could potentially become friends. They therefore had an affiliation goal activated in this condition, and they pursued this goal by nonconsciously mimicking the confederate more than did high self-monitors who interacted with the high school or graduate student. High self-monitors have been called *social chameleons*. The results of this study suggest that this is true: When it suits them and might be advantageous for them, they act as chameleons and change their own behavior to match that of their current environment. Importantly, this all takes place on a nonconscious level and is a somewhat different way of conceptualizing the way high self-monitors navigate their environment.

In a second study (Cheng & Chartrand, 2002, Study 2), participants were told that they were randomly assigned to be either the "leader" or "worker" during an interaction with another participant (actually a confederate). It was predicted that high self-monitors would have an affiliation goal automatically activated when the situational cues indicated that it might be useful for them (i.e., when they were the worker and the other person had the relative power). This was consistent with what was found: High self-monitors mimicked the confederate more when that confederate was the leader than when she was the worker, whereas low self-monitors did not differentially mimic the confederate based on their relative power in the experimental situation.

In another study examining situations in which individuals might have an affiliation goal, Uldall, Hall, and Chartrand (2002) gave participants false feedback on a bogus personality inventory. The feedback took the form of being placed in one of four personality categories. One category was the most common one, and the majority of undergraduates supposedly fell into it. Another category was rare, and only a small percentage of undergraduates fell into it. The other two categories were neither very common nor very rare. Participants were told that they were either in the common category, the rare category, or one of the other categories. It was assumed, based on optimal distinctiveness theory (e.g., Brewer, 1991), that those who were told they were in effect just like everyone else would feel common and have a need for distinctiveness, and those who were told they were in the rare personality category would feel different from everyone else and would therefore have a need for assimilation. This should take the form of wanting to affiliate with others and be more like them, and thus we predicted that it would lead to greater mimicry of others. After they received the bogus feedback, they engaged in a photo description task with a confederate who shook her foot throughout the interaction. As expected, participants who were made to feel distinct mimicked the confederate more than those who were made to feel common, with those in the control condition falling in the middle. Thus, those who were put in a situation that would lead to an affiliation goal – being made to feel different from others – engaged in more mimicry.

Finally, van Baaren, Maddux, Chartrand, de Bouter, and van Knippenberg (in press, Study 3) examined the relationship between self-construal and mimicry. In general, members of Western cultures tend to focus on maintaining independence from others and expressing their own uniqueness. In contrast, members of Asian cultures tend to focus on harmonious interdependence with others (Markus & Kitayama, 1991). Because behavior mimicry leads to smoother interactions and greater rapport between individuals, it may serve as a nonconscious strategy for maintaining harmonious relationships. Participants in the van Baaren et al. studies were native-born Americans (of European American descent) and recent Japanese immigrants. Participants completed a neutral task similar to that used by Chartrand and Bargh (1999) in the presence of a European American confederate and again in the presence of a native-born Japanese confederate (with the order of the confederates being counterbalanced). Both confederates engaged in constant, subtle face touching, and the amount of face touching that the participants engaged in during the two tasks was measured. The results indicated that the Japanese participants engaged in significantly more mimicry than the American participants. Interestingly, the same pattern of results was found with both the Japanese confederate and the American confederate, with no effect found for confederate ethnicity. Thus, the Japanese participants did not mimic the Japanese confederate more (or less) than the American confederate, and the American participants did not mimic the American confederate more (or less) than the Japanese confederate. This speaks to the nonconscious nature of the mimicry and supports the notion that individuals from more interdependent cultures, where greater weight is placed on harmonious and smooth interactions, mimic more than individuals from more independent cultures, where being unique is more heavily emphasized.

Stage 2 of Nonconscious Goal Pursuit: Direct Activation of an Affiliation Goal Leads to Greater Mimicry. The studies we have presented thus far offer some support for behavioral mimicry as a strategy for affiliation. We assumed that the affiliation goal was automatically activated by the environment in the studies, and that this goal is what led to greater nonconscious mimicry. However, it is possible that some other factor is the cause of the greater mimicry. One would need to manipulate the goal directly in order to identify it definitively as the cause. In a study that did exactly this, Lakin and Chartrand (in press, Study 1) induced a goal to affiliate in some participants. Participants were subliminally flashed either neutral words or words related to affiliation (e.g., *friend, together, affiliate*). They then watched a videotape of a person who was ostensibly another participant in the next room. The video was described as a memory task, and participants were told to memorize the clerical tasks that she performed. While she completed the tasks she touched her face continually, and the participants' behavior was recorded and later coded for mimicry of the face-touching behavior. In addition, a conscious goal condition was added in which, rather than being subliminally primed with an affiliation goal, the experimenter told participants that they would be interacting later with the person as part of a cooperative task in which it was important to get along and work well together. The results indicated that having a goal to affiliate, whether it is conscious or nonconscious, increases behavior mimicry. In this study, no differences in mimicry were found between the conscious and nonconscious conditions.

Stage 3 of Nonconscious Goal Pursuit: Consequences of Succeeding and Failing at a Nonconscious Affiliation Goal. Earlier, we reviewed the evidence that succeeding and failing at nonconscious goals has important consequences. What happens when one succeeds or fails at a goal to affiliate with another person? In a second study, Lakin and Chartrand (in press, Study 2) explored this question. It was predicted that failing at a nonconscious affiliation goal would increase subsequent affiliation goal-directed behaviors, including unintentional mimicry of another's mannerisms. To test this, participants who had earlier been subliminally primed with an affiliation goal or not conducted two interviews with other students (actually confederates). The first interview was conducted "online," and the confederate (who was actually in the next room typing out scripted answers to the questions) responded in either a friendly or an unfriendly way, thereby manipulating success and failure at the affiliation goal (if one existed). Participants then completed a second face-to-face interview with a confederate who gave neutral answers and shook her foot throughout the interaction.

The main hypothesis was that participants who were primed with an affiliation goal, and who experienced failure in the online interaction, would display the most mimicry of the confederate's behavior during the face-to-face interaction. Videotapes were coded for the amount of time participants spent shaking their feet while interacting with the second confederate. A composite measure of liking for the second confederate was also created. Reliable interactions were uncovered on both measures. In the no-goal condition, percentage of time mimicking and liking for the confederate did not vary differentially according to the success/failure condition. However, in the affiliation-goal condition, percentage of time mimicking and liking for the confederate was greater in the failure condition than in the success condition. The next question becomes, does the increased mimicry pay off for the participants in the failure condition? The answer seems to be yes. Analyses of the confederate's ratings of the participants revealed a marginally significant interaction: She most liked participants who were primed with an affiliation goal and failed. Thus, these results suggest that initially failing at an affiliation goal leads to increased efforts to affiliate with a new interaction partner. This, in turn, leads to greater mimicry of that person's mannerisms, which is effective in increasing overall liking by both persons. Importantly, the results of the Lakin et al. studies provide further evidence that we are able to use nonconscious mimicry to our advantage.

CONCLUSION

In this chapter, we have argued for a three-stage model of nonconscious goal pursuit. First, we reviewed the literature supporting the various stages. Next, we presented in detail one particular nonconscious goal that has received much attention in our lab recently: the goal to affiliate. This goal has been shown to be automatically activated by various social environments (Stage 1), nonconsciously pursued in the form of greater behavioral mimicry (Stage 2), and capable of producing consequences upon success and failure at meeting the goal (Stage 3). Yet the goal to affiliate is but one of many potential nonconscious goals that we pursue in everyday life. Other nonconscious goals, such as the goals to achieve or form an impression or restore self-esteem, have also received empirical support, usually providing evidence for one stage of our model. In this chapter we have argued that one can look at a single goal and examine the mechanisms involved during all stages of the nonconscious goal pursuit process. It is our hope that other goals can be examined in a similar fashion, and that this will lead to a richer, more sophisticated understanding of the role that nonconscious goals play in our daily lives.

References

Aarts, H., & Dijksterhuis, A. (2000). The automatic activation of goal-directed behaviour: The case of travel habit. *Journal of Environmental Psychology, 20,* 75–82.
Atkinson, J. W., & Birch, D. (1970). *A dynamic theory of action.* New York: Wiley.
Bandura, A. (1986). *Social foundations of thought and action: A social cognitive theory.* Englewood Cliffs, NJ: Prentice-Hall.

Bandura, A. (1997). *Self-efficacy*. New York: W. H. Freeman.

Bargh, J. A. (1990). Auto-motives: Preconscious determinants of social interaction. In E. T. Higgins & R. M. Sorrentino (Eds.), *Handbook of motivation and cognition* (Vol. 2, pp. 93–132). New York: Guilford Press.

Bargh, J. A., Gollwitzer, P. M., Lee-Chai, A. Y., Barndollar, K., & Trötschel, R. (2001). The automated will: Nonconscious activation and pursuit of behavioral goals. *Journal of Personality and Social Psychology, 81*(6), 1014–1027.

Bargh, J. A., Raymond, P., Pryor, J., & Strack, F. (1995). Attractiveness of the underling: An automatic power–sex association and its consequences for sexual harassment and aggression. *Journal of Personality and Social Psychology, 68*, 768–781.

Baumeister, R. F., & Leary, M. R. (1995). The need to belong: Desire for interpersonal attachments as a fundamental human motivation. *Psychological Bulletin, 117*, 497–529.

Bavelas, J. B., Black, A., Chovil, N., Lemery, C. R., & Mullett, J. (1988). Form and function in motor mimicry: Topographic evidence that the primary function is communication. *Human Communication Research, 14*, 275–299.

Bernieri, F. J. (1988). Coordinated movement and rapport in teacher–student interactions. *Journal of Nonverbal Behavior, 12*, 120–138.

Brewer, M. B. (1991). The social self: On being the same and different at the same time. *Personality and Social Psychology, Bulletin, 17*, 475–482.

Cantor, N., & Kihlstrom, J. F. (1987). *Personality and social intelligence*. Englewood Cliffs, NJ: Prentice-Hall.

Carver, C. S., & Scheier, M. F. (1981). *Attention and self-regulation: A control theory approach to human behaviors*. New York: Springer.

Chartrand, T. L. (2002). *Mystery moods and perplexing performance: Consequences of succeeding or failing at a nonconscious goal*. Manuscript submitted for publication.

Chartrand, T. L., & Bargh, J. A. (1996). Automatic activation of impression formation and memorization goals: Nonconscious goal priming reproduces effects of explicit task instructions. *Journal of Personality and Social Psychology, 71*, 464–478.

Chartrand, T. L., & Bargh, J. A. (1999). The chameleon effect: The perception–behavior link and social interaction. *Journal of Personality and Social Psychology, 76*, 893–910.

Chartrand, T. L., & Bargh, J. A. (2002). Nonconscious motivations: Their activation, operation, and consequences. In A. Tesser, D. Stapel, & J. Wood (Eds.), *Self and motivation: Emerging psychological perspectives* (pp. 13–41). Washington, D.C.: American Psychological Association Press.

Chartrand, T. L., Cheng, C. M., & Tesser, A. (2002). *Consequences of failing at nonconscious goals for self-enhancement and stereotyping*. Manuscript submitted for publication.

Chartrand, T. L., Maddux, W., & Lakin, J. (in press). Beyond the perception-behavior link: The ubiquitous utility and motivational moderators of nonconscious mimicry. In R. Hassin, J. Uleman, & J. A. Bargh (Eds.), *Unintended thought II: The new unconscious*. New York: Guilford Press.

Chen, S., Lee-Chai, A. Y., & Bargh, J. A. (2001). Relationship orientation as a moderator of the effects of social power. *Journal of Personality and Social Psychology, 80*(2), 173–187.

Cheng, C. M., & Chartrand, T. L. (2002). *Self-monitoring, power, and nonconscious mimicry.* Manuscript submitted for publication.

Deci, E. L., & Ryan, R. M. (1985). *Intrinsic motivation and self-determination in human behavior.* New York: Plenum.

Dunning, D., Leuenberger, A., & Sherman, D. A. (1995). A new look at motivated inference: Are self-serving theories of success a product of motivational forces? *Journal of Personality and Social Psychology, 69,* 58–68.

Dweck, C. S. (1996). Implicit theories and organizers of goals and behaviors. In P. M. Gollwitzer & J. A. Bargh (Eds.), *The psychology of action* (pp. 69–90). New York: Guilford Press.

Fein, S., & Spencer, S. J. (1997). Prejudice as self-image maintenance: Affirming the self through derogating others. *Journal of Personality and Social Psychology, 73,* 31–44.

Gardner, W. L., Bargh, J. A., Shellman, A., & Bessenoff, G. (2002). *This is your brain on primes: Explicit and implicit evaluation goals induce similar lateralized event-related brain potentials.* Manuscript under review.

Gilbert, D. T., & Hixon, J. G. (1991). The trouble of thinking: Activation and application of stereotypic beliefs. *Journal of Personality and Social Psychology, 60,* 509–517.

Gollwitzer, P. M. (1990). Action phases and mind-sets. In E. T. Higgins & R. M. Sorrentino (Eds.), *Handbook of motivation and cognition* (pp. 53–92). New York: Guilford Press.

Hamilton, D. L., Katz, L. B., & Leirer, V. O. (1980). Organizational processes in impression formation. In R. Hastie, T. M. Ostrom, E. B. Ebbesen, R. S. Wyer, Jr., D. L. Hamilton, & D. E. Carlston (Eds.), *Person memory: The cognitive basis of social perception* (pp. 121–153). Hillsdale, NJ: Erlbaum.

Heckhausen, H. (1991). *Motivation and action.* Berlin, Heidelberg, New York: Springer-Verlag.

La France, M. (1979). Nonverbal synchrony and rapport: Analysis by the cross-lag panel technique. *Social Psychology Quarterly, 42,* 66–70.

La France, M., & Broadbent, M. (1976). Group rapport: Posture sharing as a non-verbal indicator. *Group and Organization Studies, 1,* 328–333.

Lakin, J., & Chartrand, T. L. (in press). Increasing nonconscious mimicry to achieve rapport. *Psychological Science.*

Lee-Chai, A. Y., Chen, S., & Chartrand, T. L. (2001). From Moses to Marcos: Individual differences in the use and abuse of power. In A. Y. Lee-Chai & J. A. Bargh (Eds.), *The use and abuse of power: Multiple perspectives on the causes of corruption* (pp. 57–74). Philadelphia: Psychology Press.

Lewin, K. (1951). *Field theory in social science.* Chicago: University of Chicago Press.

Locke, E. A., & Latham, G. P. (1990). *A theory of goal setting and task performance.* Englewood Cliffs, NJ: Prentice-Hall.

Markus, H. R., & Kitayama, S. (1991). Culture and the self: Implications for cognition, emotion, and motivation. *Psychological Review, 98,* 224–253.

Mischel, W., Cantor, N., & Feldman, S. (1996). Principles of self-regulation: The nature of willpower and self-control. In E. T. Higgins & A. W. Kruglanski (Eds.), *Social psychology: Handbook of basic principles* (pp. 329–360). New York: Guilford Press.

Moskowitz, G. B., Gollwitzer, P. M., Wasel, W., & Schaal, B. (1999). Preconscious control of stereotype activation through chronic egalitarian goals. *Journal of Personality and Social Psychology, 77*, 167–184.

Séquin, C., & Pelletier, L. G. (2002). *Automatic activation of intrinsic and extrinsic motivation.* Manuscript under review.

Spencer, S. J., Fein, S., Wolfe, C. T., Fong, C., & Dunn, M. (1998). Automatic activation of stereotypes: The role of self-image threat. *Personality and Social Psychology Bulletin, 11*, 1139–1152.

Tesser, A. (2000). On the confluence of self-esteem maintenance mechanisms. *Personality and Social Psychology Review, 4*, 290–299.

Tesser, A. (2001). On the plasticity of self-defense. *Current Directions in Psychological Science, 10*, 66–69.

Tesser, A., Crepaz, N., Collins, J. C., Cornell, D., & Beach, S. R. H. (2000). Confluence of self-esteem regulation mechanisms: On integrating the self-zoo. *Personality and Social Psychology Bulletin, 26*, 1476–1489.

Tesser, A., Martin, L. L., & Cornell, D. P. (1996). On the substitutability of self-protective mechanisms. In P. M. Gollwitzer & J. A. Bargh (Eds.), *The psychology of action* (pp. 48–68). New York: Guilford Press.

Uldall, B., Hall, C., & Chartrand, T. L. (2002). *Optimal distinctiveness theory and mimicry: When being distinct leads to an affiliation goal and greater nonconscious mimicry.* Manuscript in preparation.

van Baaren, R., Maddux, W. W., Chartrand, T. L., de Bouter, C., & van Knippenberg, A. (in press). Moderators of nonconscious mimicry: The implicit behavioral consequences of self-construal. *Journal of Personality and Social Psychology.*

von Hippel, W., Sekaquaptewa, D., & Vargas, P. (1997). The linguistic intergroup bias as an implicit indicator of prejudice. *Journal of Experimental Social Psychology, 33*, 490–509.

15

Implicit and Explicit Processes in Social Judgments
The Role of Goal-Based Explanations

John L. McClure, Robbie M. Sutton, and Denis J. Hilton

CONTENTS

IMPLICIT JUDGMENTS IN GOAL-BASED EXPLANATIONS

What processes govern people's explanations of actions? Consider the following simple action: "Mary crossed the quadrangle and bought lunch costing $3 at the local restaurant." People may explain this action in a number of different ways. They may offer explanations such as "She wanted a meal" or "she wanted to impress friends" that focus on the agent's goals or intentions. Alternatively they may explain the action by saying that "The café was open" or "She had enough money in her wallet," focusing on conditions that enable actions to occur. Research shows that in different conditions one of these two types of explanation is usually preferred and the other is discounted, or "left out" of the explanation (Leddo, Abelson, & Gross, 1984).

We thank Todd Jones, John McDowall, and Frank van Overwalle for valuable comments on an earlier draft of this chapter. Research for this chapter was supported by a Science Faculty grant from the Victoria University of Wellington. Address correspondence about this chapter to John McClure, School of Psychology, Victoria University of Wellington, New Zealand; e-mail: john.mcclure@vuw.ac.nz

This chapter outlines factors influencing people's goal-based explanations and examines whether judgments about explanations relate to the distinction in social cognition between implicit and explicit processing. The concept of *implicit processing* has been used in various ways in regard to explanations and social perception. The most common use of the concept in social cognition applies to automatic judgments about actions and traits, judgments that are unaffected by cognitive load and that are unavailable to introspection. Applied to dispositional inferences, researchers suggest that these inferences involve a two-stage process, in which the first stage is automatic (implicit) and involves categorizing a person's behavior, as when an observer categorizes an actor's hitting a person as an aggressive behavior (e.g., Gilbert & Malone, 1995). The second stage involves controlled (explicit) processing that takes account of situational factors and may correct the initial automatic inference. It is at this second controlled stage that causal reasoning comes into play. After seeing the hitting action, an observer may reason that the act was self-defense because the person was being attacked.

Researchers have applied this model to the *correspondence bias* (sometimes called the *fundamental attribution error* [FAE]) wherein observers show a bias toward dispositional attributions and downplay situational factors (e.g., Gilbert & Malone, 1995). The implicit processing explanation suggests that people make an initial automatic categorization of the actor that corresponds to the action, which is followed by controlled judgments that only partially correct the initial judgment. This underadjustment in the second controlled stage suggests that the initial automatic categorization exerts a strong influence that is overcome only with partial success. This account is supported by research showing that the correspondence bias is accentuated when people are cognitively busy or overloaded (Gilbert, Pelham, & Krull, 1988; but see Krull, 1993, for evidence suggesting that people anchor on situational attributions when oriented to do so and fail to correct for dispositional factors when cognitively busy). Other work also suggests (see Forgas & East, this volume) that mood also influences the FAE, as negative affect increases attention to situational details.

Several aspects of this model have been questioned (Trope & Alfieri, 1997; Trope & Gaunt, 2000); however, research suggests clear links between dispositional inferences and implicit processing. By contrast, few researchers have explored the links between implicit processing and other components of the attribution process. This chapter examines connections between implicit processing and research on goal-based explanations.

Researchers who write about attributions often use the term *implicit* in a different sense than that described previously (e.g., McCarthur, 1972). The concept of *implicit judgment* has been applied to people's lay theories and social representations (Wegner & Vallacher, 1977b). In other research on social judgment, *implicit* often is used either without precise definition or in ways very different from the social cognition meaning of the term described here. For example, Dweck and colleagues refer to incremental and entity theories as *implicit theories* (e.g., Hong, Chiu, Dweck, Lin, & Wan, 1999), although their measures require participants to explicitly endorse verbal questionnaire items such as "You can't do much to change your intelligence." In this chapter, we attempt to be clear about when the term *implicit processing* refers to the social cognition sense of automatic processing and when it refers to people's implicit theories and assumptions.

There are reasons to broaden the connections between implicit processing and attributions beyond the specific domain of dispositional inferences. Many causal explanations can be seen as examples of *content* that are produced by *processes* of causal reasoning. People can usually report content if researchers probe them for it, even if they weren't thinking of it previously (Nisbett & Wilson, 1977). The process–content distinction is an interesting one in relation to implicit processing. In general, people are usually able to report causal explanations but have much less reliable access to the cognitive processes that led them to those explanations. Arguably, attribution theory would be redundant if people had reliable introspective access to their attribution processes.

There are other a priori reasons to expect some aspects of causal reasoning and explanation to be implicit. Some findings suggest that mechanisms of covariation and abnormality detection can be implemented in ways that do not depend on explicit verbal reasoning. These include the finding that some effects in causal learning and explanation can be modeled using connectionist approaches and the Rescorla–Wagner model of animal learning (e.g., Van Overwalle, 1998). Also, in the covariational approach, calculation of Kelley's (1967) analysis of variance (ANOVA) and its even more complex reformulations (Forsterling, 1989) involves balancing a 2 (person) $\times 2$ (stimulus) $\times 2$ (time) matrix of information. People lack the working memory capacity that would be necessary to perform explicit inferences on eight cells of information (Hastie, 1988). This issue is considered in the section here on covariation information.

In real-world contexts, it is likely that causal explanation tasks are often online and need to be made very quickly. This is important, for example, in determining why a potentially threatening person is looking at you and in conversational situations with multiple demands on attention and parallel criteria to satisfy (e.g., relevance, informativeness, and truth). These tasks would be difficult to perform quickly enough if one were to rely on slow and effortful explicit processing. Theorists who apply an evolutionary argument to judgment (see, e.g., Haselton & Buss, this volume) might argue that people who are too slow in processing potentially threatening communications would be less likely to survive. So there could be powerful evolutionary pressure to automate some explanatory processes (Cummins, 2000).

This chapter reviews theories and findings in research on goal-based explanations and relates them to the research on implicit processing. First, we outline research on intentions and the knowledge structure approach to explanations. Then we review research on causal questions and the relation of covariation information to goal-based explanations. Each of these topics is discussed in terms of how it relates to implicit processing.

RESEARCH ON GOALS AND INTENTIONS

In social psychology, research suggests that people typically explain intentional actions in terms of goals or intentions. This is despite the fact that actions are influenced by other causes, including environmental factors and abilities. Heider's (1958) seminal work claimed that intentional actions reflect personal causality, allowing the inference that the person's intention leads to the action. The model implies that the best explanation of the action is the intention or goal. Heider's research is interesting in regard to implicit processing because he showed that when geometric shapes (e.g., triangles) on a movie screen moved in sequences that simulated animated action, people spontaneously attributed intentions to these shapes (Heider & Simmel, 1944). Most research on attributions after Heider's work shifted focus away from intentional actions, until goal-based theories and folk psychology recently returned to the issue.

The primacy of intentions is also suggested in theory about causation in legal contexts, where authors have demonstrated an emphasis similar to that of Heider. Hart and Honoré (1985) noted that in court cases, many explanations of events refer to both intentional and physical causes. For example, with a forest fire, an intentional explanation may be that a person lit the fire, whereas a physical explanation may be that lightning lit the fire. Hart and Honoré claimed that when explanations contain both intentional and physical causes, people see the intentional causes as a better explanation. They stated that whereas physical causes are seen as the normal order of events, intentions are seen as interventions in the natural order and hence as more informative.

The idea that people prefer goals to other causes as explanations is consistent with recent research on people's lay theories of actions (folk theories). This research shows that people see intentions as sufficient explanations for actions and see other causes as contributory (Malle, 1999, 2001; Malle & Knobe, 1997). For example, Malle and Knobe (1997) presented scenarios with different combinations of causes and asked people if an actor was likely to pursue an intentional action. If people judge that the presence of a cause is necessary for the action, then that cause is seen as integral to the concept of intention (see also Kashima, McKintyre, & Clifford, 1998). This research found two main features: the desire for the action and the belief that the action could be accomplished. Later research added two further features: an awareness of the intention and the minimum skills required for the action (Malle, 1999). As with Heider (1958) and Hart and Honoré (1985), this approach suggests the primacy of intentions in explanations. We suggest that implicit measures might also show a preference for intentional explanations, but apart from Heider's early work with geometric figures, there has been little research on the issue.

KNOWLEDGE STRUCTURES AND GOAL-BASED EXPLANATIONS

A current line of research on explanations of actions is the knowledge structure approach, which draws on artificial intelligence and relates explanations to general cognitive structures (e.g., Abelson & Lalljee, 1988; Kruglanski, 1996; Lalljee & Abelson, 1983; Read, 1987; Read & Marcus-Newhall, 1993; Schank & Abelson, 1977; Wilensky, 1983; see also Kruglanski et al., this volume). This approach models people's thinking about scenarios in the context of scripts instead of snapshot explanations, and uses the concept of goals instead of intentions, though it assumes that goals express intentions. Although the knowledge structure approach treats goals as central to actions, it recognizes the role of other causes, particularly the preconditions that enable actions to occur, such as having money when hiring a taxi. The distinction between goals and preconditions differs from the taxonomy of internal and external causes that has dominated research on attributions, in that some preconditions, such as abilities, are internal to the person. The knowledge structure approach provides a framework in this chapter for examining the relation between explanations and implicit processing.

A prototypical example of the knowledge structure approach as applied to explanations of actions is Leddo et al.'s (1984) research. These studies present scenarios describing scripted actions that are either completed or not completed and then present a range of explanations of the action (or nonaction). For example, one scenario describes a character, John, driving along the freeway, who sees a restaurant ahead and either stops or does not stop for a meal. Following each scenario is a range of explanations, including a goal (John wanted a meal), two preconditions (e.g., he had enough money for a meal), and conjunctions combining these explanations (e.g., John wanted a meal, and he had enough money for a meal). Filler explanations are included to reduce the obviousness of the manipulations.

Participants judged the probability of each explanation, and as predicted by the knowledge structure approach, they judged goals to be more probable explanations than preconditions. For completed actions, they also judged the conjunctions of goals and preconditions as more probable than the goals, whereas for noncompleted actions, the absence of either a goal or a precondition was judged to be as good an explanation as a conjunction of the two. The research suggests that for single-cause explanations of actions, people prefer goals. For completed actions, people judge a conjunction as more probable than the goal, whereas with noncompleted actions, they see a single cause as more probable.

Subsequent research has posed two qualifications to these findings. First, these findings do not generalize to competing causes. When a person does not go to a restaurant, this inaction may arise from the presence of competing causes, such as competing goals, rather than from the absence of facilitatory causes (Wilensky, 1983). When people consider competing causes, conjunctions of these causes are judged more probable as explanations for nonactions than for actions (McClure, Lalljee, Jaspars, & Abelson, 1989).

A second qualification to the preference for goals concerns extreme actions. The scenarios in the research described here describe common actions such as going to a restaurant or borrowing a book from a library. Several theories suggest that the findings with these common actions may not extend to extreme actions. Kelley's (1972) schema model suggests that for extreme events, people apply a *multiple necessary schema* and prefer conjunctive explanations that include two or more causes. Research has shown some support for this model (e.g., Cunningham & Kelley, 1975). Reeder and Brewer (1979) made the slightly different prediction that for extreme success, people apply a *hierarchically restricted schema* and perceive ability as necessary for any substantial achievement. This claim implies that with extreme success, people are more certain that ability is present than the relevant goal. Subsequent research has supported Reeder and Brewer's (1979) model (Johnson, Boyd, & Magnani, 1994; McClure, Lalljee, & Jaspars, 1991).

To examine the effect of extremity on judgments of goals and preconditions, McClure and Hilton (1997) reframed the scenarios developed by Leddo et al. (1984) to include both moderate and extreme outcomes. They replicated Leddo et al.'s finding for explanations of common actions: Participants preferred goals, regardless of whether the actions had been obstructed; and they showed that this preference extends to unobstructed extreme actions, such as a rich person buying an expensive car. For extreme actions that have been obstructed, however, such as a poor person buying an expensive car, participants judged the acquisition of a relevant enabling condition (such as money) as a more probable explanation than the relevant goal. These different preferences for extreme and common actions are mediated by people's judgments of whether the actions are controllable rather than by the actions' inherent probability (McClure, Densley, Liu, & Allen, 2001).

CONVERSATIONAL PRAGMATICS AND CAUSAL
EXPLANATION: THE ROLE OF PRESUPPOSITION AND FOCUS

We now turn to how conversational pragmatics (Grice, 1975; Levinson, 2000) can explain the kinds of findings we have discussed previously (cf. Hilton, 1990; Hilton & Slugoski, 2001; Turnbull, 1986; Turnbull & Slugoski, 1988). Conversational pragmatics starts from the assumption that in rational conversation we normally communicate not only what is true, but also what is informative and relevant given our interlocutor's state of knowledge and goals, and do so in a way that is easily understood. Because many events are the product of complex causal processes, a rational explanation in conversation will explicitly mention only those matters that are likely to be unknown to the interlocutor, leaving the other parts of the context to be inferred by the interlocutor. Relevant factors that are unknown to the interlocutor constitute new information and are communicated in explanations, whereas other factors that are also causally necessary for the production of an event, but that are already known to the interlocutor, are presupposed as background information. Good explanations must therefore not only be true, but also informative and relevant.

This approach helps explain why people sometimes prefer goals and at other times prefer preconditions, and why people sometimes prefer single causes and at other times prefer conjunctions. Changes in preferences for explanations are often determined not by changes in truth considerations (e.g., changes in the perceived probability of the explanation being true) but by pragmatic considerations (e.g., the informativeness of the explanation in the particular conversational context). The initial research on knowledge structures obtained probability judgments about explanations, asking participants to judge the probability of a goal or precondition, given a particular scenario (e.g., Leddo et al., 1984). Subsequent research suggests that pragmatic considerations such as perceived informativeness and relevance are better predictors of changes in the perceived quality of an explanation than is probability (Hilton & Erb, 1996; McClure, 1998; McGill, 1990, 1991). The perceived probability of an explanation being true seems to be closely linked to its perceived necessity for an outcome to happen, which in turn is related to the perceived probability of the counterfactual that the outcome would have occurred if the given cause was absent. In contrast, the perceived informativeness and relevance of an explanation seem to be closely related to the judged sufficiency of the cause, assessed by getting participants to rate the likelihood of the action occurring when the cause is known to be present (Hilton & Erb, 1996; McClure, 1998).

A number of studies have examined the role of pragmatic factors in determining causal explanations. The consistent finding with scenarios where several factors have to be present conjointly for an outcome to happen is that informativeness is a better predictor of the perceived goodness of an explanation than more inferential measures such as probability and necessity (McClure & Hilton, 1997, 1998; McGill, 1990). In addition, studies using free response measures of explanations show that causes judged to be informative on structured measures are usually included in unstructured explanations of the same actions, whereas causes considered only to be necessary and probable are omitted from those explanations (McClure & Hilton, 1997, 1998). With common actions, people see enabling conditions as necessary for the action but omit those causes in their unstructured explanation of the action. Even when people see goals and abilities as equally necessary for the action, they may judge that the goal on its own is a sufficient cause and a good explanation for the action. With extreme actions, this pattern is reversed and preconditions are often seen as better explanations.

The Gricean injunction to deliver explanations that are informative, relevant, and clear makes "design" sense for anyone speaking to an interlocutor who has limited short-term but unlimited long-term memory capacity (Hastie, 1988; Srull, Lichtenstein, & Rothbart, 1985; cf. Levinson, 2000). Clearly, a rational speaker should not overload short-term memory with information, but should focus on information that is relevant to the interlocutor's goals and that cannot be presupposed from the interlocutor's long-term memory.

Likewise, the fact that people have limited short-term memory but nearly unlimited long-term memory suggests that people are likely to assume (from long-term memory) that states of the world are normal (e.g., when being told about events in a restaurant, we assume the presence of chairs, tables, food, waiters and waitresses, etc.), so that attention can be freed for novel and unexpected events. Research from artificial intelligence (Schank & Abelson, 1977) and cognitive psychology (Sanford & Garrod, 1981) suggests that people do make these kinds of implicit assumptions that facilitate information processing. Against the background of implicit expectations, Black and Bower (1979) showed that unexpected events in narratives are remembered better than expected ones, just as Hastie (1984) and Weiner (1985) showed that it is unexpected events that most often trigger explanatory processes. Taken together, these findings suggest that explanatory processes tend to focus on unexpected events that do not fit within implicitly activated scripts and expectations.

Research in cognitive psychology also shows that narratives are understood through the construction of complex causal networks where the connections of events are used to form a coherent story (Trabasso & Sperry, 1985; Trabasso & van den Broek, 1985). Even when a person reading a story gives simple explanations for an event (referring to just one or two factors), often other factors have to be presumed for the explanation to make sense. For example, if we ask, "Why did Beauty go to the Beast's castle?" and we answer, "To rescue her father," we have to presuppose many things for this explanation to make sense. Furthermore, these presuppositions typically rely on scripted world knowledge (e.g., that the strength of a child's love for her parent would be sufficient for her to put herself in danger to rescue him) that is automatically activated by the mention of concepts such as *daughter* and *father*.

Given that these causes in the sense of necessary *background conditions* (Mackie, 1980) are often omitted from explanations, are they an instance of implicit processing? These causes may be implicit in the sense that the explainer is completely unaware of them, at least until a researcher or some other person asks the explainer to evaluate the cause's contribution to the outcome. But the causes may not be implicit in the stronger sense of processes that the person cannot access, and where the person is unaware of the influence the processes have on his or her judgments and behavior (e.g., Trope & Alfieri, 1997).

CAUSAL QUESTIONS AND IMPLICIT CAUSALITY

A key issue that is often overlooked in research on explanations is the nature of the question soliciting the explanation. Researchers have created a number of fine distinctions in types of explanations and in the type of event that is the target of the explanations, but they have paid less attention to the effect of different questions on explanations. Yet this issue is important because different causal questions make different implicit assumptions about which explanations are relevant, and different questions about the same event lead to different explanations.

This point has been demonstrated in research on the effect of causal questions on recall of narratives (e.g., Graesser, Robertson, & Anderson, 1981). This research presents story narratives and then asks participants a range of questions about the narratives, such as "Why did an actor do this?" and "Please explain this event." The "why" questions generated more goals in people's answers than the "explain" questions. Graesser et al. claimed that when people are asked why an actor has performed a given action, they see the question as a goal-orientation question and generate goals that explain the action (Antaki & Leudar, 1992). In contrast, explain questions elicit more causal (i.e., nonintentional) explanations of actions.

These claims have important implications for causal attributions because they suggest that attributions are influenced by the nature of the prompting question. To test this link in relation to goal-based explanations, McClure and Hilton (1998) examined the effect of why questions and explain questions on explanations of scripted actions. They adapted Leddo et al.'s (1984) scenarios describing common actions, such as going to the restaurant, and created versions in which each action was either obstructed or unobstructed. For unobstructed actions, goals were preferred as explanations for both questions. For obstructed actions, goals were preferred for the why question but preconditions were preferred for the explain question. Similar results were obtained with free-response explanations with the same why and explain prompts. Subsequent research using a wider range of causal questions, including "how" and "how come" questions, has obtained similar results (Malle, Knobe, O'Laughlin, Pearce, & Nelson, 2000; McClure, Hilton, Cowan, Ishida, & Wilson, 2001). These findings suggest that causal questions influence the type of explanation given for actions.

The reason different questions have this effect is interesting when considering the possible connections between explanations and implicit processing. Graesser and Person (1994) claimed that causal questions reflect implicit assumptions about actions and serve a pragmatic inquiring purpose that reflects those assumptions (see also Hilton, 1990; Rips, 1998; Schwarz, 1994). To take a simple example, the question "What was your reason for buying the car?" assumes that there was a reason or goal behind the action and that the agent was aware of that goal. In contrast, the question "What caused X to happen?" does not assume that an event was determined by a goal.

The idea that different questions reflect different assumptions can be tested by presenting an action to participants and asking them which causal question they would ask to get information to explain the action. McClure et al. (2001) presented participants with different scenarios and asked them what questions they would prefer to explain the actions in the scenarios. The actions were either extreme (e.g., going on a luxury round-the-world holiday) or moderate (going on a cheap local trip), and were either obstructed (the actor was poor) or unobstructed (the actor was rich). Responses showed a strong preference for why questions with unobstructed actions and for how questions with obstructed actions. These differences were sharpened with extreme actions, such as going on an expensive world holiday.

These findings suggest that different causal questions entail implicit assumptions or presuppositions about the causes that contributed to an event. When people suggest that a why question is appropriate, as when they are explaining a wealthy person's taking a world trip, they are assuming that the person has the means or preconditions to make the trip. This does not mean that people consciously think about categories like goals and preconditions. When they are asked a causal question, they may not be consciously aware of the implication of the question, although the framing of the question may make them feel uncomfortable, even though they may struggle to say why this is so. It is likely that lawyers use these effects in legal contexts, selecting those causal questions that make actions or events appear to be intentional or unintentional (Hart & Honoré, 1985). Similarly, when asking causal questions about actions, the questioners' assumptions about the actions shape the causal question that they select, although again they may be completely unaware of this. An analogy may be made to the use of linguistic grammar, which many people can use, although they are not explicitly aware of the grammatical structure and may not even be able to articulate it (Bohannon & Stanowicz, 1988).

The assumptions in causal questions are not produced by procedures such as priming, brief exposure to stimuli, or other techniques used in social cognition to generate implicit processing. However, these assumptions are implicit in a deeper sense than the necessary causes considered in the previous section. Whereas people can easily respond to questions about whether necessary causes are present for a given action, they may be totally unaware of the assumptions implicit in a given causal question, and they may struggle to articulate what those implicit assumptions are.

COVARIATION AND IMPLICIT CAUSALITY

An issue in attributions where researchers have implied that some level of implicit processing occurs concerns the covariation between causes and effects. Kelley's (1967) covariation theory proposes that people select the cause that most covaries with the effect as the explanation. McCarthur's (1972) paper is well known for giving empirical support to this model, but the paper also examines the idea that different verbs imply different patterns of covariation. Specifically, action verbs such as *gives* or *hits* imply stimulus generalization, in that if you give one person something nice, people expect you to give nice things to others. By contrast, emotion verbs such as *likes* or *hates* imply response generalization, in that if you love someone, people expect you to also praise and protect him or her.

Although McCarthur's (1972) research suggests that different verbs imply patterns of covariation, researchers have portrayed goal-based inferences and covariation information as offering different and even conflicting paths to explanations. Lalljee and Abelson's (1983) distinction between *contrastive reasoning* (covariational) and *constructive reasoning* (goal-based) illustrates this differentiation. Hilton and Knibbs (1988) showed that goal-relevant information can counteract the effect of covariation information, as reflected in slower and less confident judgments about attributions. For example, with the scenario "Jane acts coolly on a date with Justin," the goal-relevant information is "Jane knows she likes acting coyly" and the covariation information is "Almost everyone acts coolly on a date with Justin."

Hilton and Knibbs (1988) demonstrated that goal-relevant information sometimes points to the same cause as covariation information. Sutton and McClure (2001) extended this work to claim that goal-based explanations and covariation information can be integrated, in that covariation information guides the selections of goal-based explanations, and even when covariation information is absent, judgments about goals and enabling conditions reflect implicit covariation between the causes and the actions. To support this claim, Sutton and McClure took the covariational concepts of *consensus, consistency,* and *distinctiveness* that are normally applied to the person, situation, and occasion, and applied them to motivating causes (goals) and enabling causes (preconditions). The model also distinguishes between stable causes (e.g., in the case of enabling causes, she's rich) and unstable causes (e.g., she won a prize). Scenarios contained covariation information about the motivation and the enabling causes of the actor and of other persons. For example, one version of the "buying the car" scenario said that many people were *willing* to buy a car (high consensus in the motivating cause), but only the actor was *able* to buy the car (low consensus in the enabling cause). The scenarios also gave information about the actor's and other people's purchases on other occasions (i.e., combinations of consensus and distinctiveness information). Participants then judged motivating and enabling causes as explanations, and gave the pattern of attributions to motivating and enabling causes predicted by the model.

These results extend the finding described earlier in this chapter on the effects of extremity on judgments of goals and preconditions. For common actions (e.g., buying a meal at a restaurant), people normally assume high consensus about enabling causes, that is, that most people possess them, so people attribute the action to a motivating cause (e.g., she wants a meal out). In other words, motivating factors covary with unobstructed actions. By contrast, for difficult actions (e.g., buying an expensive house), people assume low consensus about enabling causes, so they attribute the action to an enabling cause (e.g., she's wealthy).

Covariation information may be explicitly presented as a full matrix of information or may be only implicitly presented. Sutton and McClure (2001) proposed that scenarios generate the same results when covariation information is explicit and implicit. This argument is supported by the fact that goal-based explanations are similar when a full matrix of covariation information is supplied (as in Sutton & McClure, 2001) and when it is absent (as in McClure & Hilton, 1997). This similarity suggests that people make implicit assumptions about the covariation between goals and actions even when no covariation information is supplied.

As we noted earlier, the calculation of Kelley's (1967) ANOVA and its more complex reformulations (Forsterling, 1989), a task that people successfully achieve, involves balancing a 2 (person) $\times 2$ (stimulus) $\times 2$ (time) matrix of information. Sutton and McClure (2001, Exp. 3) added a fourth factor, cause (goal/precondition), so people were effectively doing a $2 \times 2 \times 2 \times 2$ ANOVA. People lack the working memory capacity necessary to perform explicit inferences on 16 cells of information (e.g., Hastie, 1988). This analysis derives informal support from participants' complaints in Sutton and McClure's experiments that they were overloaded with information and were responding randomly. Despite their complaints, participants' written responses systematically conformed to the covariational hypotheses, which suggests that there is little conscious awareness of co-variational reasoning about causes.

CONCLUSIONS: GOAL-BASED EXPLANATIONS AND IMPLICIT PROCESSING

This chapter has suggested that there are at least three ways in which research on goal-based explanations can be linked to the distinction between implicit and explicit processing of social judgments.

First, the distinction between necessary causes and communicated explanations may relate to the distinction between implicit and explicit processing. Specifically, necessary causes may be more implicit, whereas good explanations or communicated explanations are more explicit (or the opposite may be the case). It is likely that necessary causes are implicit only in the weaker sense of not being in awareness when people give explanations, even though they are readily accessible. Although this is only a weaker sense of implicit reasoning, research could examine whether necessary causes have some features of implicit processing by using social cognition methods, such as testing reaction times for causes that are seen as merely necessary and causes that are judged good explanations. Content-specific explanations such as goals come from prior knowledge to a greater extent than content-free explanations (e.g., inside or outside the person). It may well be that content-rich specific explanations (such as goals) are easily retrieved from existing memory structures, even to the extent that this is automatic.

A second issue is whether different causal questions relate to the distinction between implicit and explicit processing, in that the assumption behind the choice of question may be implicit, whereas the question itself is explicit. Causal questions entail implicit presuppositions about the causes that contributed to an event. When people ask "Why did you do this action?" or, more explicitly, "For what reason did you do this action?", the question assumes that the behavior in question reflects an intention or goal and takes for granted the various conditions that enable the action. This is not to suggest that people think about categories like goals and preconditions when offering their explanations or asking causal questions. It appears that these assumptions in causal questions are implicit in a deeper sense than necessary causes. Whereas people can easily respond to questions about whether necessary causes are likely when an action occurs, they may be unaware of the assumption implicit in a particular causal question, and they may be unable to articulate that assumption.

The effects of causal questions could be examined with reaction times. Research could examine either the *inhibition* of processing or the *activation* of processing. For example, after reading a scenario and being given a why question that points to a goal explanation, participants may show slowed responses to stimulus words that relate to preconditions for the action (e.g., *time, money*) relative to a control condition without the question. Slower reaction times would suggest the role of controlled processing. Similarly, after a *how* question, we might predict slowed responses to goal-related words (e.g., *desire, hunger*). We might also expect similar responses to, say, different questioners, where experiments inhibit material that is not relevant or informative to the particular questioner. These slowed reaction times may also be one way to operationalize *causal backgrounding*, as described by Hilton and Erb (1996).

A third issue is whether the distinction between goal-based scripts and covariation information relates to the distinction between implicit and explicit processing. Specifically, the question is whether goal-based explanations relate to explicit processing and covariation information to implicit processing. Recent research shows that covariation information can apply to goal-based explanations and has the predicted effects, regardless of whether it is presented explicitly or only implied indirectly. Real-world contexts usually do not offer a full matrix of covariation information, although they often offer fragments of it. However, even when people lack covariation information about an action, their explanations suggest that they assume a matrix of that information when they choose their explanation (Sutton & McClure, 2001). Although the explanation itself is not an instance of implicit processing, the covariation information appears to be implicit at a deeper level than the necessary causes described previously. Even where a given explanation implies low consensus in an action, for example, the person giving the explanation could be unsure about the consensus information relating to the action and could even deny that his or her explanation implies low consensus. Van Overwalle, Drenth, and Marsman (1999) conducted a study showing that both scripted events (which reflect prior knowledge) and novel covariation information (about which little prior knowledge exists) jointly determined the spontaneous use of traits to describe the person and the action. This study provides a possible paradigm for studying spontaneous inferences about goal-based explanations.

Few researchers examining goal-based explanations have paid attention to the distinction between implicit and explicit processing, but there is no inherent reason why this could not be done. For example, by examining reaction times, research could examine whether a preference for goals as explanations for common actions is reflected in shorter reaction times in judging goals as explanations when people are presented with different candidate explanations. Research would need to present a range of goals and preconditions to control for the possibility that any one goal explanation could have been generated explicitly. It is possible that explanations that are judged to be sufficient on rating scales show quicker responses on reaction time measures than causes that are merely necessary.

It might also be possible to get implicit and explicit measures to show opposite results. For example, it is possible that when people judge precondition explanations to be the best explanations on explicit measures such as questionnaires, as they do with extreme actions, they may favor goals on implicit measures such as reaction time.

Research could also apply the two-stage model to judgments about actions, and see if people initially categorize actions in terms of goals and subsequently take account of enabling factors such as preconditions. This research could assist a synthesis between the classic research of Heider (1958) on spontaneous attributions of intentions and current research on spontaneous judgments about dispositions and traits. Chartrand and Jefferis's (this volume) research on automatic goal pursuit provides one potential element of this synthesis. Research could also examine whether preferences for goals as explanations are accentuated when people are cognitively busy or overloaded. This finding would suggest that at the implicit level there is a preference for goal-based explanations that may be corrected by controlled processes. Research could also examine this issue by studying interactions with causal questions: Do experiments still get effects suggesting an implicit preference for goals in the context of a how question, when goals are inappropriate explanations? A further strategy would be to examine whether priming people with different explanations before presenting them with a scenario has an effect on subsequent explanations for the scenario. If this procedure showed positive results when participants deny any awareness of the priming effect, this would suggest that explanations can be prompted at an implicit level.

An integration of research on explanations and implicit processing would be interesting, although whether researchers should maintain a strict distinction between implicit and explicit processing is a matter for debate. Different researchers disagree as to where the boundaries fall between implicit processes and explicit or controlled processes, and an alternative strategy is to apply models that apply continuous categories to judgments, such as Kruglanski et al.'s (this volume) unimodel. For example, Kruglanski's central parameter of relevance relates closely to the criteria of informativeness and relevance that researchers apply to goal-based explanations (McClure, 1998; McClure & Hilton, 1997). Explanations that are judged as informative, relevant, and good overall on goal-based measures are likely to be rated as relevant on Kruglanski et al.'s relevance parameter. In contrast, explanations that people see as necessary but not informative are likely to be rated lower on the relevance parameter. The difference between good explanations and necessary causes is likely to be reflected in Kruglanski et al.'s cognitive capacity parameter, in that causes that are judged to be relevant are more likely to be selected (and others discounted) when the cognitive capacity allocated to the explanatory task is limited. So these parameters could be applied readily to goal-based explanations.

However, it might be useful to add the parameter of awareness to those suggested by Kruglanski et al. to take account of the degree to which people are explicitly aware of an explanation as opposed to the implicit aspects of the explanations that people can comment on when asked to but are not otherwise aware of. Two examples would be covariation information as applied to goal-based explanations (Sutton & McClure, 2001) and the causal assumptions that are implicit in different causal questions.

Regardless of whether researchers adopt the implicit–explicit distinction or a parametric model, as suggested by Kruglanski et al., there are clearly several interesting possibilities for conceptual links between goal-based explanations and theories implying that some judgments are more automatic and nonconscious than others.

References

Abelson, R. P., & Lalljee, M. (1988). Knowledge structures and causal explanations. In D. J. Hilton (Ed.), *Contemporary science and natural explanation: Commonsense conceptions of causality* (pp. 175–203). Brighton: Harvester Press.

Antaki, C., & Leudar, I. (1992). Explanation in conversation: Towards an argument model. *European Journal of Social Psychology, 22*, 181–194.

Black, J. B., & Bower, G. H. (1979). Episodes as chunks in narrative memory. *Journal of Verbal Learning and Verbal Behavior, 18*, 309–318.

Bohannon, J. N., & Stanowicz, L. (1988). The issue of negative evidence: Adult responses to children's language errors. *Developmental Psychology, 24*, 684–689.

Cummins, R. (2000). "How does it work?" versus "What are the laws?": Two conceptions of psychological explanation. In F. C. Keil & R. A. Wilson (Eds.), *Explanation and cognition* (pp. 117–144). Cambridge, MA: Bradford Books.

Cunningham, J. D., & Kelley, H. H. (1975). Causal attributions for interpersonal events of varying magnitude. *Journal of Personality, 43*, 74–93.

Forsterling, F. (1989). Models of covariation and attribution: How do they relate to the analogy of analysis of variance? *Journal of Personality and Social Psychology, 57*, 615–625.

Gilbert, D. T., & Malone, P. S. (1995). The correspondence bias. *Psychological Bulletin, 117*, 21–38.

Gilbert, D. T., Pelham, B. W., & Krull, D. S. (1988). Inference and interaction: The person perceiver meets the person perceived. *Journal of Personality and Social Psychology, 55*, 685–694.

Graesser, A. C., & Person, N. K. (1994). Question asking during tutoring. *American Educational Research Journal, 31*, 104–137.

Graesser, A. C., Robertson, S. P., & Anderson, P. A. (1981). Incorporating inferences in narrative representations: A study of how and why. *Cognitive Psychology, 13*, 1–26.

Grice, H. P. (1975). Logic and conversation. In P. Cole & J. L. Morgan (Eds.), *Syntax and semantics: Volume 3. Speech acts* (pp. 41–58). New York: Academic Press.

Hart, H. L. A., & Honoré, T. (1985). *Causation in the law* (2nd ed.). Oxford: Clarendon Press.

Hastie, R. (1984). Causes and effects of causal attribution. *Journal of Personality and Social Psychology, 46*, 44–56.

Hastie, R. (1988). A computer simulation model of person memory. *Journal of Experimental Social Psychology, 24*, 423–447.

Heider, F. (1958). *The psychology of interpersonal relations.* New York: Wiley.

Heider, F., & Simmel, M. (1944). An experimental study of apparent behavior. *American Journal of Psychology, 57*, 243–259.

Hilton, D. J. (1990). Conversational processes and causal explanation. *Psychological Bulletin, 107*, 65–81.

Hilton, D. J., & Erb, H-.P. (1996). Mental models and causal explanation: Judgments of probable cause and explanatory relevance. *Thinking and Reasoning, 2*, 273–308.

Hilton, D. J., & Knibbs, C. S. (1988). The knowledge-structure and inductivist strategies in causal attribution: A direct comparison. *European Journal of Social Psychology, 18*, 79–92.

Hilton, D. J., & Slugoski, B. R. (1986). Knowledge-based causal attribution: The abnormal conditions focus model. *Psychological Review, 93*, 75–88.

Hilton, D. J., & Slugoski, B. R. (2001). The conversational perspective in reasoning and explanation. In A. Tesser & N. Schwarz (Eds.), *Blackwell handbook of social psychology: Volume 1. Intrapersonal processes* (pp. 181–206). Oxford: Blackwell.

Hong, Y., Chiu, C., Dweck, C. S., Lin, D. M., & Wan, W. (1999). Implicit theories, attributions, and coping: A meaning system approach. *Journal of Personality and Social Psychology, 77*, 588–599.

Johnson, J., Boyd, K., & Magnani, P. (1994). Causal reasoning about rare and common events. *Journal of Personality and Social Psychology, 66*, 229–242.

Kashima, Y., McKintyre, C., & Clifford, P. (1998). The category of mind: Folk psychology of belief, desire, and intention. *Asian Journal of Social Psychology, 1*, 289–313.

Kelley, H. H. (1967). Attribution theory in social psychology. *Nebraska Symposium on Motivation, 15*, 192–238.

Kelley, H. H. (1972). Causal schemata and the attribution process. In E. E. Jones, D. E. Kanouse, H. H. Kelley, R. E. Nisbett, S. Valins, & B. Weiner (Eds.), *Attribution: Perceiving the causes of behavior* (pp. 151–174). Morristown, NJ: General Learning Press.

Kruglanski, A. W. (1996). Goals as knowledge structures. In J. A. Bargh & P. Gollwitzer (Eds.), *Motivation and action* (pp. 122–148). New York: Guilford Press.

Krull, D. S. (1993). Does the grist change the mill? The effect of perceiver's inferential goal on the process of social inference. *Personality and Social Psychology Bulletin, 19*, 340–348.

Lalljee, M., & Abelson, R. P. (1983). The organization of explanations. In M. Hewstone (Ed.), *Attribution theory: Social and functional extensions* (pp. 65–80). Oxford: Basil Blackwell.

Leddo, J., Abelson, R. P., & Gross, P. H. (1984). Conjunctive explanations: When two reasons are better than one. *Journal of Personality and Social Psychology, 47*, 933–943.

Levinson, S. C. (2000). *Presumptive meanings: The theory of generalized conversational implicature.* Cambridge, MA: MIT Press.

Mackie, J. L. (1980). *The cement of the universe.* Oxford: Clarendon Press.

Malle, B. F. (1999). How people explain behavior: A new theoretical framework. *Personality and Social Psychology Review, 3*, 23–48.

Malle, B. F. (2001). Folk explanations of intentional action. In B. F. Malle, L. J. Moses, & D. A. Baldwin (Eds.), *Intentions and intentionality: Foundations of social cognition* (pp. 265–286). Cambridge, MA: MIT.

Malle, B. F., & Knobe, J. (1997). The folk concept of intentionality. *Journal of Experimental Social Psychology, 33*, 171–189.

Malle, B. F., Knobe, J., O'Laughlin, M., Pearce, G. E., & Nelson, S. E. (2000). Conceptual structure and social functions of behavior explanation: Beyond person–situation attributions. *Journal of Personality and Social Psychology, 79*, 309–326.

McCarthur, L. Z. (1972). The how and what of why: Some determinants and consequences of causal attribution. *Journal of Personality and Social Psychology, 22*, 171–193.

McClure, J. L. (1998). Discounting causes of behavior: Are two reasons better than one? *Journal of Personality and Social Psychology, 74*, 7–20.

McClure, J. L., Densley, L., Liu, J. H., & Allen, M. (2001). Constraints on equifinality: Goals are good explanations only for controllable outcomes. *British Journal of Social Psychology, 40*, 99–115.

McClure, J. L., & Hilton, D. J. (1997). For you can't always get what you want: When preconditions are better explanations than goals. *British Journal of Social Psychology, 36*, 223–240.

McClure, J. L., & Hilton, D. J. (1998). Are goals or preconditions better explanations? It depends on the question. *European Journal of Social Psychology, 28*, 897–911.

McClure, J. L., Hilton, D. J., Cowan, J., Ishida, L., & Wilson, M. (2001). When rich or poor people buy expensive objects: Is the question how or why? *Journal of Language and Social Psychology, 20*, 229–257.

McClure, J. L., Lalljee, M., & Jaspars, J. (1991). Explanations of moderate and extreme events. *Journal of Research in Personality, 25*, 146–166.

McClure, J. L., Lalljee, M., Jaspars, J., & Abelson, R. P. (1989). Conjunctive explanations of success and failure: The effect of different types of causes. *Journal of Personality and Social Psychology, 56*, 19–26.

McGill, A. L. (1990). Conjunctive explanations: The effect of comparison of the target episode to a contrasting background instance. *Social Cognition, 8*, 362–382.

McGill, A. L. (1991). The influence of the causal background on the selection of causal explanations. *British Journal of Social Psychology, 30*, 79–87.

Nisbett, R. E., & Wilson, T. D. (1977). Telling more than we can know: Verbal reports on mental processes. *Psychological Review, 84*, 231–259.

Read, S. J. (1987). Constructing causal scenarios: A knowledge structure approach to causal reasoning. *Journal of Personality and Social Psychology, 52*, 288–302.

Read, S. J., & Marcus-Newhall, A. (1993). Explanatory coherence in social explanations: A parallel distributed processing account. *Journal of Personality and Social Psychology, 65*, 429–447.

Reeder, G. D., & Brewer, M. B. (1979). A schematic model of dispositional attribution in interpersonal perception. *Psychological Review, 86*, 61–79.

Rips, L. J. (1998). Reasoning and conversation. *Psychological Review, 105*, 411–441.

Sanford, A. J., & Garrod, S. C. (1981). *Understanding written language: Explorations of comprehension beyond the sentence*. Chichester, UK: Wiley.

Schank, R. C., & Abelson, R. P. (1977). *Scripts, plans, goals, and understanding*. Hillsdale, NJ: Erlbaum.

Schwarz, N. (1994). Judgment in a social context: Biases, shortcomings and the logic of conversation. *Advances in Experimental Social Psychology, 26*, 123–162.

Srull, T. K., Lichtenstein, M., & Rothbart, M. (1985). Associative storage and retrieval models. *Journal of Experimental Psychology: Learning, Memory, and Cognition, 11*, 316–345.

Sutton, R. J., & McClure, J. L. (2001). Covariational influences on goal-based explanation: An integrative model. *Journal of Personality and Social Psychology, 80*, 222–236.

Trabasso, T., & Sperry, L. L. (1985). Causal thinking and story comprehension. The causal basis for deciding importance of story events. *Journal of Memory and Language, 24*, 595–611.

Trabasso, T., & van den Broek, P. (1985). Causal thinking and story comprehension. *Journal of Memory and Language, 24*, 612–630.

Trope, Y., & Alfieri, T. (1997). Effortfulness and flexibility of dispositional judgment processes. *Journal of Personality and Social Psychology, 73*, 662–674.

Trope, Y., & Gaunt, R. (2000). Processing alternative explanations of behavior: Correction or integration. *Journal of Personality and Social Psychology, 79*, 344–354.

Turnbull, W. M. (1986). Everyday explanation: The pragmatics of puzzle resolution. *Journal for the Theory of Social Behaviour, 16*, 141–160.

Turnbull, W. M., & Slugoski, B. R. (1988). Conversational and linguistic processes in causal attribution. In D.J. Hilton (Ed.), *Contemporary science and natural explanation: Commonsense conceptions of causality* (pp. 66–93). Brighton: Harvester Press.

Van Overwalle, F. (1998). Causal explanation as constraint satisfaction: A critique and a feedforward connectionist alternative. *Journal of Personality and Social Psychology, 74*, 312–328.

Van Overwalle, F., Drenth, T., & Marsman, G. (1999). Spontaneous trait inferences: Are they linked to the actor or to the action? *Personality and Social Psychology Bulletin, 25*, 450–462.

Wegner, D. M., & Vallacher, R. R. (1977a). *Implicit psychology: An introduction to social cognition*. New York: Oxford University Press.

Wegner, D. M., & Vallacher, R. R. (1977b). Common-sense psychology. In J. P. Forgas (Ed.), *Social cognition: Perspectives on everyday understanding* (pp. 225–246). London: Academic Press.

Weiner, B. (1985). "Spontaneous" causal thinking. *Psychological Bulletin, 97*, 74–84.

Wilensky, R. W. (1983). *Planning and understanding: A computational approach to human reasoning*. Reading, MA: Addison-Wesley.

16

Impact of Ostracism on Social Judgments and Decisions

Explicit and Implicit Responses

Kipling D. Williams, Trevor I. Case,
and Cassandra L. Govan

CONTENTS

INTRODUCTION

Imagine that your colleagues suddenly act as though you do not exist. They don't harass or belittle you, but neither do they look at you or talk to you, even if you ask them a question. When informal social groups form for work or recreation, you are excluded. How do you feel? How do you present your feelings to others? How do you behave when you know you are being evaluated, possibly by the group who ostracized you, or by another group to which you might belong? How do you behave when you are less accountable for your actions?

In this chapter, we review the recently burgeoning empirical literature on ostracism, social exclusion, and rejection, and emerge with what appear to be two sets of reliable yet opposing conclusions. On the one hand, ostracism appears to set in motion behaviors that will increase the likelihood that the individual will be reincluded in the ostracizing group or will be attractive to a new group. On the other hand, social exclusion has led individuals to react antisocially, which would almost assure them of further exclusion.

Please address all correspondence to Kipling D. Williams, Department of Psychology, Macquarie University, Sydney, NSW 2109; e-mail: kip@psy.mq.edu.au

How can we make sense of these two sets of findings? We offer two possible explanations and present some new data that shed light on the viability of these explanations. The first explanation is that two opposing forces are activated in the ostracized individual: Threats to belonging and self-esteem pull the individual toward repairing his or her inclusionary status; threats to control and recognition push the individual toward provocative behaviors that capture the attention of others. To the extent that a negative impression is easier or quicker to manage, an antisocial response will be forthcoming. Ironically, such a response may decrease the possibility of subsequent inclusion.

A second explanation is that perhaps both reactions occur in individuals, much as Wilson, Lindsey, and Schooler (2000) argued was the case with dual attitudes. One could have an explicit attitude, say tolerance and liking for a minority group, while simultaneously holding an implicit attitude of resentment and derogation for the same minority group. Depending upon which attitude was activated, the consequent expression would look like either egalitarianism or prejudice. Implicit measures, they argue, activate implicit attitudes; explicit measures activate explicit attitudes. In a similar vein, we think that individuals who suffer ostracism may implicitly be hurt, angry, and resentful. If allowed or encouraged to follow these inclinations, they will be antisocial, hostile, and competitive. At an explicit level, however, they want to manage their impressions to others so that they can be reinstated in the offending group or in a new group. Thus, they will behave in ways that appear selfless and other-oriented: conforming with group members who are clearly wrong or contributing more to a collective task than an individual task.

In this chapter, we will review research from three literatures that seem to be studying roughly the same thing. *Ostracism* refers to ignoring and excluding one or more individuals (Williams, 2001); *rejection* is the act of expelling (usually accompanied by an explicit derogation of) individuals from groups (Leary, 2000); and *social exclusion* refers specifically to exclusion without reference to being ignored (Tice, Twenge, & Schmeichel, 2002; Twenge, Baumeister, Tice, & Stucke, 2001). It may well be that differences in responses result in part because of the minor distinctions between these phenomena, and we welcome other investigations of this possibility. For our purposes, however, we will combine the research findings under the rubric of ostracism and discuss them as though they represent the same fundamental processes.

Recent examinations of ostracism, social exclusion, and rejection indicate that these are universally and powerfully aversive social behaviors. Animals use them to enhance their survival, weeding out the unfit and disruptive; tribes use them for their ultimate punishment; religions excommunicate, educational institutions practice "time-out," governments exile, and family, friends, and relationship partners use the silent treatment on one another. We also tend to be very sensitive to signs of ostracism and even err on the side of false alarms, especially in situations where there is high social risk (Haselton & Buss, this volume). For almost a century, social psychology seemed to assume its importance without really examining its causes and consequences. We assumed that people would conform so as not to be excluded and rejected by others. In fact, some variant of this explanation has been offered for such wide-ranging social behaviors as compliance, bystander apathy, obedience, cooperation, and intergroup conflict.

But in the past 10 years, experimental social psychologists have become intrigued with the mechanisms of ostracism, exclusion, and rejection and have amassed a rather sizable literature in a relatively short time.

EFFECTS ON THE TARGET

In an attempt to provide a framework from which a systematic and theory-driven investigation of the powerful phenomena of ostracism could develop, Williams (1997, 2001) proposed a temporally based need-threat model of ostracism. This model detailed the taxonomic dimensions, antecedents, moderating and mediating factors, and reactions to ostracism. Central to Williams's model of ostracism, however, was the assumption that four fundamental human needs could be individually and simultaneously affected in targets of ostracism. In particular, when targets are ignored or excluded, their basic needs for belonging, control, self-esteem, and meaningful existence are threatened.

There is ample evidence to suggest that these four needs are each fundamental to human well-being. The need to belong – the desire for frequent, positive, and stable interactions with others – is important for emotional stability and may also be evolutionarily adaptive (Baumeister & Leary, 1995; Buss, 1990). Moreover, in a review of the literature on affiliation and intimacy, Baumeister and Leary concluded that an eroded sense of belonging can lead to depression, anxiety, and mental illness. The need to belong is vulnerable to all forms of interpersonal rejection. However, unlike other forms of interpersonal rejection, in which the target continues to enjoy some form of social connection, ostracism represents a severing of social attachment. Accordingly, ostracism may have a particularly adverse impact on the need to belong.

The need for control has also been identified as a basic motivation in the psychological literature (e.g., deCharms, 1968; White, 1959). Essentially, people strive to understand, predict, and control their environments in order to maximize positive outcomes and minimize negative outcomes. Accordingly, the motivation for control has considerable adaptive value. Furthermore, heightened perceptions of control have been associated with psychological and physical well-being (Taylor & Brown, 1988), whereas perceptions of undermined control have been associated with feelings of helplessness and other negative psychological and physical consequences (Abramson, Seligman, & Teasdale, 1978; Seligman, 1975). When targets of ostracism are confronted with no response from sources, their sense of control or influence over the interaction diminishes. In this way, ostracism is imposed upon the target by the source and the target is left helpless to affect outcomes in the conflict. Additionally, targets of ostracism are often unable to be certain that they are, in fact, being ignored or excluded (Williams, 2001), which further diminishes control.

Like the needs for belonging and control, the need to maintain high self-esteem is argued to be both adaptive and important for psychological well-being (e.g., Greenberg et al., 1992; Steele, 1988; Tesser, 1988). Ostracism strikes at the heart of self-esteem because the target is rejected as being unworthy of the source's attention or acknowledgment. In addition, when the reason for ostracism is unclear, targets may generate numerous self-depreciating justifications for this treatment, further lowering their self-esteem. Interestingly, although sources behave as if the target is not even worth the effort of argument, sources actually expend considerable effort maintaining this façade (Ciarocco, Sommer, & Baumeister, 2001).

One final need that is threatened by ostracism is the need for meaningful existence. According to terror management theory (Greenberg et al., 1990), individuals have a fundamental fear of facing reminders of their mortality. Over the past decade, a great deal of empirical evidence has emerged to support the idea that people constantly attempt to buffer themselves from the terror derived from acknowledging the inherent meaninglessness of existence and their own mortality (for a review, see Greenberg, Solomon, & Pyszczynski, 1997). In terms of ostracism, the target is cut off from social interaction and, in a sense, ceases to exist as a social being. What more poignant reminder can we have of our own mortality than to be excluded from our social world, relegated to the position of impotence and invisibility. It is hardly surprising that many targets of long-term ostracism report contemplating whether they actually exist. In this way, ostracism is a powerful metaphor for social death.

Whereas Williams's (1997, 2001) model of ostracism identifies each of these four needs as important, there is evidence to suggest that at least some of these needs might be subsumed to some extent by the other. For example, self-esteem might serve as an indication – a sociometer – when the need for belonging is threatened (Leary, Tambor, Terdal, & Downs, 1995). Furthermore, self-esteem is argued to play a critical role in buffering against the terror imposed by reminders of mortality and meaningless existence (Greenberg et al., 1997). Nonetheless, whether the four needs are orthogonal or share some overlap is of little consequence to the model of ostracism. Most important, Williams's model holds that ostracism has the capacity to threaten these needs, and, once threatened, these needs have certain motivational and cognitive consequences.

Consequences of Ostracism for Judgments and Decisions

When the realization of being ignored and excluded first hits, targets experience negative affect, anger, and physiological arousal. However, after this immediate response, targets of ostracism should be motivated behaviorally, emotionally, and cognitively to regain or repair their needs. That is, the model assumes that there is a direct relationship between need deprivation and need fulfillment, a notion consistent with research on needs for belonging (Baumeister & Leary, 1995), control (Friedland, Keinan, & Regev, 1992), self-esteem (Steele, 1988), and meaningful existence (Greenberg et al., 1990). Interestingly, in the short term, attempts to fulfill threatened needs may have two conflicting motivational consequences.

Attempts to Improve the Inclusionary Status. Perhaps most obviously, targets of ostracism may be driven to improve their inclusionary status with others (including the source) in order to regain their sense of belonging, to improve their status in others' eyes (hence improving self-esteem), to effect a consequence (thus regain control), and to experience purpose or meaning. Accordingly, after experiencing the initial hurt feelings and negative affect associated with being rejected, targets of ostracism might be expected to respond by apologizing and reestablishing ties. Strategies that strengthen each need include establishing new bonds with others, conforming to group norms (Baumeister & Leary, 1995) and maximizing efforts on collective tasks (Williams & Sommer, 1997), and may even include nonconscious behavioral mimicry (Chartrand & Jefferis, this volume).

Attempts to Be Recognized That May Decrease the Inclusionary Status. Alternatively, Williams's (1997, 2001) model of ostracism predicts that attempts to regain a sense of control, self-esteem, and meaningful existence may have motivational consequences that actually decrease the inclusionary status of the target of ostracism. Specifically, targets may bolster their self-esteem by increasing their self-importance or focusing on their past achievements. The sense of control can be regained by exercising power and controlling others, and demanding attention and recognition or otherwise maintaining cultural buffers might restore meaningful existence. If needs remain unsatisfied, such reactions may result in provocative, antisocial, and even aggressive behaviors toward the source or others (Tice et al., 2002; Twenge et al., 2001; Williams, Wheeler, & Harvey, 2001).

Cognitive Consequences of Ostracism. In addition to motivational reactions, certain cognitive consequences of ostracism have been observed. A program of research using several different inductions found that higher cognitive processes appear to be depleted by exclusion, whereas lower processes remain intact (for a review see Baumeister, Twenge, & Ciarocco, 2002). Specifically, social exclusion impairs IQ test performance and reasoning ability (but not memory). Baumeister et al. have also found that social exclusion is associated with immediate, as opposed to delayed, gratification in decision tasks and that exclusion impairs the ability to self-regulate. Effortful cognitive processing and impulse control are both diminished when people self-regulate. Thus, Baumeister et al. argue that their findings might indicate that self-regulation is involved in the behavioral effects of social exclusion. Furthermore, they suggest that impaired self-regulation resulting from social exclusion may also account for the observed antisocial responses. Specifically, attempts to restrain antisocial and selfish impulses in order to perform socially desirable actions are undermined by an impaired ability to self-regulate. Consequently, social exclusion, which impairs self-regulation, leads to the emergence of such antisocial and selfish impulses.

Ostracism may also have other cognitive consequences. Gardner, Pickett, and Brewer (2000) either included participants in or excluded them from a simulated Internet chat room and then presented them with a diary containing both social and individual events. Those who were excluded selectively recalled more explicitly social events from a diary than individual events. Gardner et al. argued that just as hunger increases memory for food-relevant information, a heightened need for belonging, associated with social exclusion, results in selective memory for socially relevant information.

Emotional Consequences of Ostracism. Interestingly, although negative emotions might be aroused initially, and although there is an extensive literature to show that mood has predictable effects on a wide range of social judgments and processes (Forgas & East, this volume), the research using short-term exclusion inductions has consistently failed to demonstrate that affect has any role in mediating responses to ostracism (Baumeister et al., 2002; Twenge et al., 2001; Williams, Cheung, & Choi, 2000). Specifically, most studies have not obtained any differences in emotion between included and ostracized participants. Moreover, when differences have emerged, the effect is small and mean ratings for excluded participants typically reflect neither positivity nor negativity (the midpoint of the scale) compared to included participants, who tend to rate more positively. Nevertheless, negative emotions might play a more important role in longer-term ostracism (Williams, 1997, 2001).

In sum, ostracism leads to attempts to repair threatened needs for belonging, self-esteem, control, and meaningful existence. In addition, attempts to repair these needs have particular motivational and cognitive consequences. Motivational consequences include attempts to improve one's inclusionary status and reunite with the source, especially if what is most important to repair is self-esteem or belonging. For example, the target might feel the need to apologize to the source, even if the target has no idea why he or she is being ostracized. If successful, inclusionary reinstatement will improve the sense of belonging and of socially based self-esteem. In addition, ostracism increases the memory for socially relevant information (Gardner, Pickett, & Brewer, 2000), again consistent with a concern for belonging. Conversely, if the primary need to repair is control and/or recognition (aka meaningful existence), then targets may do so with little concern for the valence of their actions. That is, they may exert unwanted control over others, or act out in a provocative manner, simply to get attention and recognition, without worrying about whether they will be liked in the process. If this is the case, attempts to exercise control over sources or to draw attention to oneself, or even responding with frustration or anger, might prolong or ensure further ostracism. In a similar vein, ostracism is associated with impaired information processing and poor impulse control (Baumeister et al., 2002), which suggest an urgent need to control immediate gratification at the cost of social consequences. Indeed, Lawson-Williams and Williams (1998, Study 1) found that ostracized male targets, when given the opportunity and encouragement to ask a new person to turn his head as often as the target wished (under a cover story that made this demand plausibly related to the task), used this opportunity more than included individuals, especially when the other two individuals were already friends with each other. In Study 2, ostracized (vs. included) women indicated higher desire for control after being ostracized by two women who were friends with each other.

The motivational and cognitive consequences of ostracism for the target previously described are reactions to short-term ostracism. Williams's (1997, 2001) model suggests that reactions to long-term ostracism may lead to internalization or acceptance of the loss of needs, and may have such deleterious effects on the target as alienation, helplessness, despair, and depression. Because most of the research on ostracism has been concerned with short-term ostracism, this chapter maintains its focus on the short-term effects of ostracism on targets' judgments and decisions. Thus, one explanation for the two opposing sets of findings for short-term reactions to ostracism is that in some cases the prosocial forces of belonging and self-esteem (especially self-esteem, as reflected in the eyes of others) win out, but in other circumstances (or perhaps for certain types of people), the antisocial side effects of regaining control and recognition (aka meaningful existence) triumph.

Another explanation of these two opposing sets of findings is that both responses represent forces and desires within the individual, but they are located in two separate spheres: an implicit reaction and an explicit reaction.

Explicit and Implicit Reactions to Ostracism

Most studies use explicit measures (i.e., self-ratings of needs and emotions) to assess the impact of ostracism. However, some have also used less obvious, more implicit measures such as physiological responses, indirect judgments and decisions, and behaviors.

It may be that the explicit measures tap into explicit forces and desires: desires that center on managing one's impression with the goal of improving inclusionary status (see Baumeister & Leary, 1995, for a compelling argument for this desire). Thus, when one's behaviors are under the scrutiny of individuals or groups that may entertain the notion of including the individual, overt explicit actions will be aimed at ingratiating oneself into the fold.

The literature contains numerous instances consistent with this line of thought. Williams and Sommer (1997) found that women who were ostracized in a ball-toss game worked harder on a subsequent collective task (where the contributions benefited the group's evaluation) but not on a subsequent individual task (where the contributions benefited only the individual). Similarly, Ezrakhovich et al. (1998) found that when ostracized in a brainstorming "survival" task for no apparent reason, women worked harder on a subsequent collective task. (It should be noted that ostracized men in Williams and Sommer's study worked no harder than included men and showed typical social loafing tendencies. Also, in Ezrakhovich et al.'s study, if the ostracism was perceived as direct punishment for being late, then compensatory behaviors did not ensue.)

Not only do ostracized individuals try to improve their inclusionary status with the group who ostracized them, but Williams et al. (2000) found that they also ingratiate themselves with new groups. In their Study 2, individuals played a game of Cyberball (a virtual ball-toss game) with two others and then were reassigned to a new six-person group. Those who had been ostracized in Cyberball were more likely to follow the new group's (unanimous and incorrect) judgments when asked to make their own public judgments.

Whereas research on ostracism has typically included explicit measures of underlying threatened needs for belonging, self-esteem, control, and meaningful existence, there have been fewer attempts to include implicit measures. The expected effects of ostracism on need threat have been reliably detected using explicit self-report measures, despite whatever inhibitors are present to project a happy, insulated ego. However, the specific effects of such need threat on judgments and decisions involve more implicit processes and may therefore escape accurate detection with explicit self-report impact on needs measures (McClelland, Koestner, & Weinberger, 1989). That is, although the impact of ostracism may be detected in self-report measures of need threat, attempts to refortify these needs by increasing or decreasing inclusionary status and cognitive consequences of ostracism might be accessible only via more implicit measures. We expect that implicit measures will provide greater insight into the types of decisions and judgments targets of ostracism make in an attempt to refortify threatened needs.

Some studies have used indirect assessments, not easily linked to explicit reactions to ostracism. For instance, Zadro and Williams (1998) observed the predicted self-reports of lower need and mood levels of ostracized individuals following a role-play train ride in which some participants were ostracized by the two people flanking them on the train (and others were argued with). Although there were no measures for ingratiation in this study, they were asked to guess how many Australians shared their view on the republic versus monarchy issue. As predicted, those individuals who were in the minority (for college students) and voiced a preference for the monarchy overestimated support for their position only if they had been ostracized.

Zadro and Williams (2000) also found that when ostracized by Asians in a field study, European Caucasians indicated at an explicit level little or no prejudice toward Asians. Yet they indicated higher levels of prejudice toward Arabs than did included participants. This is consistent with Crandall, Eshleman, and O'Brien's (2002) research, in which they found similar examples of stifled prejudice toward one group revealing itself in heightened prejudice toward another (less obviously related to the ostracism) group.

Finally, several ingenious studies by the Case Western Reserve University group (Baumeister et al., 2002; Tice et al., 2002; Twenge et al., 2001) have found that when given the green light to aggress (under cover stories that make the aggression seem at least socially appropriate), excluded individuals will aggress at higher levels than included individuals in retaliation to the excluders and even to neutral parties. In these studies, the experimenters go to great pains to ensure that the participants are likely not to believe that their behaviors are evaluated as explicit reactions to the exclusion but instead are in the service of the research goals (e.g., in the interest of getting honest performance appraisals or to study the effects of punishment). Again, these studies may be revealing implicit reactions to social exclusion more than explicit reactions.

CURRENT STUDIES

The following studies were designed to measure both implicit and explicit responses to ostracism. The first study used the ball-toss paradigm to examine the effects of ostracism on attraction to dubious groups. In the second study, we had participants engage in a virtual ball-toss game in which they tossed a Cyberball with two other players over the Internet. This induction was used to examine the effects of ostracism on an implicit (Implicit Association Test, IAT) and explicit measure of racial prejudice.

STUDY 1: JOINING A DUBIOUS SOCIAL GROUP

Will people who have been ostracized fall victim to cults or gangs in an attempt to fulfill their needs for belonging, self-esteem, control, and meaningful existence? Study 1 was a first attempt to investigate this question. The experiment employed a 2 (ostracism vs. inclusion) × 2 (reputable vs. dubious group) between-subjects design, and the dependent measures were (a) explicit ratings of the extent to which each of the four needs were threatened and (b) ratings of attraction to the spokesperson and the group he represented.

Fifty-two female undergraduate students were recruited for a study called "Impression Formation." In the initial stage of the experiment, each participant was involved in what appeared to be a spontaneous game of catch with the other participants (who were actually confederates). However, after receiving the ball for 1 minute, those in the ostracism condition were cut out of the game by the two confederates, who proceeded to throw the ball only to each other. In addition, the confederates even ceased eye contact with ostracized participants (for a description of the ball-tossing paradigm see Williams & Sommer, 1997). In contrast, the remaining participants were included throughout the game.

After 5 minutes of ball tossing, the experimenter returned to the experimental room to begin the impression formation study. Participants were led to individual rooms and told that impressions could be influenced by temporary mood states. They were then asked to provide self-reports of their feelings over the past 10 minutes, which included 12 questions (measured on a 5-point scale ranging from 1 = not at all to 5 = very much) designed to assess the extent to which each of the four needs was threatened (3 for each need). For example, belonging was assessed by the item "I felt accepted," self-esteem by the item "I felt good about myself," control by the item "I felt like I was in control," and meaningful existence by the item "I felt like I didn't exist." This questionnaire provided an explicit measure of the effects of ostracism on the four needs.

After completing the questionnaire, participants watched a 5-minute recruitment videotape for either a reputable or a dubious group. Both videotapes displayed a spokesperson (the same male actor) giving a scripted monologue describing his student group. In the reputable condition, a smart, casually dressed spokesperson described the aims of his student group as "to help students to grow and reach their full potential." He went on to explain that "we do this by giving members the skill that can help them empower and improve both their full personal and future business lives." In addition, the spokesperson described the group activities as focusing on improving study habits, helping members to choose their best career path, and increasing communication skills.

In contrast, the dubious condition presented a spokesperson clothed in a tie-dyed poncho with beads and an African hat woven from bright multicolored thread. The aims of the group were described as "to help students move into a higher state of consciousness and cosmic awareness." The spokesperson also explained that "we do this by giving members the skills needed to access their psychic powers and engage in out-of-body experiences." Group activities centered on learning how to harness personal psychic energy in order to experience psychic phenomena.

With the exception of the information that described the aims of the groups, the scripts for the reputable and dubious groups were identical. After viewing the videotaped presentation, participants completed a questionnaire comprising eleven 5-point items ranging from 1 (not at all) to 5 (very much) designed to assess the extent to which they were attracted to the spokesperson (e.g., "How much did you like the spokesperson of the group?") and the group he represented (e.g., "How willing would you be to meet with a member of this group?"). This measure of attraction to the spokesperson was intended to provide an implicit measure of the effects of ostracism on the four needs.

Overall, we expected ostracized individuals, compared to those who were included, to report greater need threat on the explicit ratings. As both the reputable and dubious groups offered the promise or hope of refortifying threatened needs, the reputability of the group was expected to be of little concern for those who were ostracized – both groups were expected to be similarly attractive. Thus, attraction to the group served as an implicit proxy for need fortification. In contrast, those who were included had no need to refortify needs for belonging, self-esteem, control, or meaningful existence and were therefore expected to focus on reputability-relevant information rather than need-relevant information. Accordingly, for included targets who held little concern for need-relevant information, the reputable group should have been more attractive than the dubious group.

Results

Manipulation Checks. In order to verify that those who were ostracized actually perceived that they were tossed the ball less often than those who were allocated to the inclusion condition, participants estimated the percentage of ball throws they received at the end of the experiment. Ostracized targets estimated that they received the ball significantly less often than included targets, which suggests that the ostracism manipulation was successful. Likewise, the spokesperson for the reputable group was rated as significantly more reputable than the spokesperson for the dubious group. Moreover, the reputable group was rated as significantly more reputable than the dubious group, which suggests that the manipulation of the reputability of the group was also successful.

Self-Report Needs Threat. Needs for belonging, self-esteem, control, and meaningful existence were each measured by three self-report items that were combined to produce four composite scales. Ostracism, compared to inclusion, led to greater self-report need depletion for all four needs.

Attraction to the Spokesperson and the Group. The four items designed to assess attraction to the spokesperson were combined to form a composite measure: Ostracized targets were more attracted to the spokesperson than were included targets, regardless of whether they saw the reputable or the dubious videotape. Consistent with the manipulation check, the reputable spokesperson was rated as more attractive than the dubious spokesperson, regardless of whether participants were ostracized or included.

Discussion

Consistent with the predictions of Williams's (1997, 2001) model, the results of this study showed that ostracism threatens certain basic needs. In particular, participants who were ostracized, compared to those who were included, reported greater threat to their needs for belonging, self-esteem, and meaningful existence and, to a lesser extent, control. Most important, this finding supports previous research demonstrating that the effects of ostracism can be detected using explicit self-report need-threat measures (e.g., Williams et al., 2000).

In terms of the implicit measures, we expected and found that ostracized targets, compared to included targets, were more attracted to the spokesperson. This suggests that the attraction to the spokesperson served as an implicit proxy for need fortification in ostracized targets. Overall, the findings support the predictions of Williams's (1997, 2001) model that ostracized targets might attempt to refortify threatened needs by forming bonds with others. The findings are also consistent with research showing that ostracism may lead to prosocial or reparatory behaviors (e.g., Williams & Sommer, 1997) and that low self-esteem is associated with greater attraction to others (Jacobs, Berscheid, & Walster, 1971).

To summarize, this study was a first attempt to investigate whether those who have been ostracized will be attracted to dubious groups. As there were no ostracism condition by reputability condition interactions, we can only conclude that ostracized (vs. included) targets may be more attracted to any spokesperson, regardless of whether the group this spokesperson represents is reputable or dubious. As such, the findings are limited in their ability to address the question of whether those who have been ostracized are likely to fall victim to cults or gangs in an attempt to fulfill their needs. However, these findings show a convergence between the explicit self-report of threatened needs and a more implicit measure of inclination to refortify needs – attraction to another person. Study 2 pursues this relationship further.

STUDY 2: EXPLICIT AND IMPLICIT REACTIONS TOWARD A MINORITY GROUP

The previous study examined the convergence between explicit and implicit measures of need threat. In Study 2, we compare explicit and implicit measures of attitudes toward racial groups after being ostracized or included. Will people who are excluded react more negatively toward minority groups or does the experience of ostracism promote compassion for minority outsiders? Consistent with research suggesting that social exclusion is associated with cognitive impairment (e.g., Baumeister et al., 2002), we expect that ostracism-related processing limitations would lead to a reliance on stereotyping.

A computer version of the Cyberball ball-tossing paradigm described earlier was used to induce ostracism. In this task, participants played a virtual game of catch with two other online players. In fact, the two players were computer generated, and the game was fixed so that included targets received the ball throughout, but ostracized participants received it only at the beginning (see Williams, Cheung, & Choi, 2000, for details of the Cyberball paradigm). Following the game, participants completed a race IAT (to be described) and a final questionnaire including manipulation checks, impact on needs, and an explicit racism scale.

The IAT (Greenwald, McGhee, & Schwartz, 1998) has been widely used to assess implicit attitudes. For example, it has been used to assess attitudes toward race (Dasgupta, McGhee, Greenwald, & Banaji, 2000; Greenwald et al., 1998; McConnell & Leibold, 2001; von Hippel, Vargas, & Sekaquaptewa, this volume), age (Mellott & Greenwald, 1998), religious beliefs (von Hippel et al., this volume), low-calorie food (Maison, Greenwald, & Bruin, 2001), and consumer preferences (Williams, Govan, Edwardson, & Wheeler, 2001). The IAT is suggested to bypass problems of social desirability and impression management that are common in explicit measures.

Given this advantage of the IAT, we thought it would be a useful tool for examining attitudes toward racial groups following a period of ostracism. We developed a train station IAT in which the target stimulus items were Sydney area train station names of Aboriginal origin (Booragul, Ourimbah, Turella, Koolewong, and Warawee) or of European origin

(Sandgate, Cardiff, Belmore, Asquith, and Pymble). A pilot test revealed that there was no difference in familiarity ratings between the two categories of station names. The evaluative categories for this IAT were "Pleasant" (love, peace, happy, laughter, and pleasure) and "Unpleasant" (death, sickness, hatred, evil, and agony).

A measure of implicit association with each racial group is provided by the time it takes to respond to the stimuli when the concept labels "Pleasant + European" share a response key and when the concept labels "Pleasant + Aboriginal" share a response key (note that the reaction times for "Pleasant + Aboriginal" are also the reaction times for "Unpleasant + European" as the trials are combined, but for ease of reporting, we will use the single reference). Greenwald et al. (1998) found that it is easier to complete the categorization task when two closely associated categories share a response key than when two less closely associated categories share a response key.

Previous research would suggest that White participants (or any non-Aboriginal participant) in our study would be faster at completing the categorizations when "Pleasant + European" share a response key than when "Pleasant + Aboriginal" share a response key. Although we expect this general pattern overall, what we are most interested in is whether there is a difference between the ostracized and included groups in terms of their implicit racial association.

The IAT was programmed using the Farnham Implicit Association Test (FIAT; 1998). This program gives participants practice trials before they complete the recorded trials, and we counterbalanced which combination (i.e., first combined trial with "Pleasant + Aboriginal" sharing a response key or "Pleasant + European" sharing a response key) participants received.

In addition to the implicit measure, we included an explicit measure of prejudice toward Aboriginals (Pedersen & Walker, 1997). This scale can be broken into two components: *old racism* and *modern racism*. Examples of old racism items include "I would not like an Aborigine to be my boss" and "Most Aborigines are dirty and unkempt." Examples of modern racism items include "Aborigines are getting too demanding in their push for land rights" and "Aborigines have more influence on government policy than they ought to."

Results

The general overall pattern of faster reaction times when "Pleasant + European" shared a response key than when "Pleasant + Aboriginal" shared a response key in the IAT was reliable. More interestingly, differences between the ostracized and included groups also emerged. Responses to the explicit racism scale show that ostracized and included participants are equally prosocial (especially for the old racism component).

However, ostracized participants showed a greater difference between their "Pleasant + European" response times and their "Pleasant + Aboriginal" response compared to included participants. These results suggest a less positive implicit attitude toward Aboriginals from the ostracized participants compared to the included participants. Thus, we have a disparity between what ostracized participants are reporting in the explicit scale and what the implicit measure suggests.

One interpretation of the results is that ostracized targets may be engaging in facework motivated by a need to improve their inclusionary status – thus, they respond in a socially desirable way on the explicit measure of racism. However, the implicit measure (IAT) suggests that ostracism may actually increase negativity toward the minority group.

The most obvious implication is that the reactions to ostracism that people exhibit can vary greatly, depending upon whether the measure is explicit or implicit. It may well be that at the explicit level, people try to manage their impressions to increase their attractiveness to others so that they will no longer be ostracized. At an implicit level, however, ostracized individuals may harbor ill feelings not only toward the ostracizers, but also toward others who may have had nothing to do with their exclusion.

CONCLUSIONS

The experience of being ostracized is powerful and negative. However, the way people cope with its effects varies. A variety of measures have been used, from explicit to implicit. Whereas most studies show consistency between their explicit and implicit measures, some, including new results presented in this chapter, indicate intriguing inconsistencies.

It may well be that at the more explicit end of the continuum, people admit hurt but try to manage their impressions so that others will be more likely to include them. As the measures become more implicit, however, targets of ostracism show evidence of resentment, retaliation, and hostility. We suggest that this two-sided response is similar to Wilson et al.'s (2000) notion of *dual attitudes*; both exist, but one at an implicit and the other at an explicit level. Both are accurate assessments of the individual, and both predict behaviors in circumstances commensurate with the level. The hostile reactions are more likely to surface when attributions for the hostile behavior are ambiguous, that is, when there are socially acceptable explanations for the behavior. Likewise, when the behavior is disguised or hidden, it may be more likely to be antisocial. When the target's behaviors are under the scrutiny of others and are potentially used for judgments of future inclusion, they will present themselves as attractive, agreeable, and cooperative.

In common with findings obtained in the attachment literature (see Shaver & Mikulincer, this volume), many ostracism studies have found that targets will behave in ways that will improve their inclusionary status, either with the ostracizing group or with a new group, whereas other studies show retaliatory, hostile, and generally antisocial reactions. These two extreme and apparently opposing reactions are intriguing and will undoubtedly encourage more research into the conditions under which ostracism either increases or decreases desires and behaviors aimed at improving the inclusionary status. In this chapter, we considered two possible explanations. First, differing reactions could be evidence of different sets of needs being activated: The belonging/self-esteem needs may motivate prosocial behaviors; the control/recognition needs may encourage provocative and possibly antisocial behaviors. Second, and most pertinent to the aims of this book, the two seemingly opposing reactions may actually be reflecting dual forces within the individual (see Brewer, this volume): heightened impression management activity at the explicit level and deep-seated hostile reactions at the implicit level.

References

Abramson, L. Y., Seligman, M. E., & Teasdale, J. D. (1978). Learned helplessness in humans: Critique and reformulation. _Journal of Abnormal Psychology, 87_(1), 49–74.

Baumeister, R. F., & Leary, M. R. (1995). The need to belong: Desire for interpersonal attachments as a fundamental human motivation. _Psychological Bulletin, 117_(3), 497–529.

Baumeister, R. F., Twenge, J. M., & Ciarocco, N. (2002). The inner world of rejection: Effects of social exclusion on emotion, cognition, and self-regulation. In J. P. Forgas & K. D. Williams (Eds.), _The social self: Cognitive, interpersonal, and intergroup perspectives_ (pp. 161–174). Philadelphia: Psychology Press.

Buss, D. M. (1990). The evolution of anxiety and social exclusion. _Journal of Social and Clinical Psychology, 9_, 196–201.

Ciarocco, N. J., Sommer, K. L., & Baumeister, R. F. (2001). Ostracism and ego depletion: The strains of silence. _Personality and Social Psychology Bulletin, 27_(9), 1156–1163.

Crandall, C. S., Eshleman, A., & O'Brien, L. (2002). Social norms and the expression and suppression of prejudice: The struggle for internalization. In J. P. Forgas & K. D. Williams (Eds.), _The social self: Cognitive, interpersonal, and intergroup perspectives_ (pp. 293–308). Philadelphia: Psychology Press.

Dasgupta, N., McGhee, D. E., Greenwald, A. G., & Banaji, M. R. (2000). Automatic preference for White Americans: Ruling out the familiarity effect. _Journal of Experimental Social Psychology, 36_, 316–328.

deCharms, R. (1968). _Personal causation: The internal affective determinants of behavior._ New York: Academic Press.

Ezrakhovich, A., Kerr, A., Cheung, S., Elliot, K., Jerrems, A., & Williams, K. D. (1998, April). _The effects of causal clarity of ostracism on individual performance in groups._

Paper presented at the meeting of the Society for Australasian Social Psychology, Christchurch, New Zealand.

Farnham, S. (1998). *The Farnham Implicit Association Test for Windows*, Version 2.3.

Friedland, N., Keinan, G., & Regev, Y. (1992). Controlling the uncontrollable: Effects of stress on illusory perceptions of controllability. *Journal of Personality and Social Psychology, 63*(6), 923–931.

Gardner, W. L., Pickett, C. L., & Brewer, M. B. (2000). Social exclusion and selective memory: How the need to belong influences memory for social events. *Personality and Social Psychology Bulletin, 26*, 486–496.

Greenberg, J., Pyszczynski, T., Solomon, S., Rosenblatt, A., Veeder, M., Kirkland, S., & Lyon, D. (1990). Evidence for terror management theory II: The effects of mortality salience on reactions to those who threaten or bolster the cultural worldview. *Journal of Personality and Social Psychology, 58*, 308–318.

Greenberg, J., Solomon, S., & Pyszczynski, T. (1997). Terror management theory of self-esteem and cultural worldviews: Empirical assessment and conceptual refinements. *Advances in Experimental Social Psychology, 29*, 61–136.

Greenberg, J., Solomon, S., Pyszczynski, T., Rosenblatt, A., Burling, J., Lyon, D., Symon, L., & Pinel, E. (1992). Why do people need self-esteem?: Converging evidence that self-esteem serves an anxiety-buffering function. *Journal of Personality and Social Psychology, 63*, 913–922.

Greenwald, A. G., McGhee, D. E., & Schwartz, J. L. K. (1998). Measuring individual differences in implicit cognition: The implicit association test. *Journal of Personality and Social Psychology, 74*, 1022–1038.

Jacobs, L., Berscheid, E., & Walster, E. (1971). Self-esteem and attraction. *Journal of Personality and Social Psychology, 17*, 84–91.

Lawson-Williams, H., & Williams, K. D. (1998, April). *Effects of social ostracism on desire for control.* Paper presented at the meeting of the Society for Australasian Social Psychology, Christchurch, New Zealand.

Leary, M. R. (Ed.). (2000). *Interpersonal rejection.* New York: Oxford University Press.

Leary, M. R., Tambor, E. S., Terdal, S. K., & Downs, D. L. (1995). Self-esteem as an interpersonal monitor: The sociometer hypothesis. *Journal of Personality and Social Psychology, 68*(3), 518–530.

Maison, D., Greenwald, A. G., & Bruin, R. (2001). The Implicit Association Test as a measure of implicit consumer attitudes. *Polish Psychological Bulletin, 2*, 61–79.

McClelland, D. C., Koestner, R., & Weinberger, J. (1989). How do self-attributed and implicit motives differ? *Psychological Review, 96*, 690–702.

McConnell, A. R., & Leibold, J. M. (2001). Relations between the Implicit Association Test, discriminatory behavior, and explicit racial attitudes. *Journal of Experimental Social Psychology, 37*, 435–442.

Mellott, D. S., & Greenwald, A. G. (1998). *Do older adults show automatic ageism?* Poster presented at the annual meeting of the Midwestern Psychological Association, Chicago.

Pedersen, A., & Walker, I. (1997). Prejudice against Australian Aborigines: Old-fashioned and modern forms. *European Journal of Social Psychology, 27*, 561–587.

Seligman, M. (1975). *Helplessness: On depression, development, and death.* San Francisco: W. H. Freeman.

Steele, C. M. (1988). The psychology of self-affirmation: Sustaining the integrity of the self. In L. Berkowitz (Ed.), *Advances in experimental social psychology* (Vol. 21, pp. 261–302). San Diego, CA: Academic Press.

Taylor, S. E., & Brown, J. D. (1988). Illusion and well-being: A social psychological perspective on mental health. *Psychological Bulletin, 103,* 193–210.

Tesser, A. (1988). Toward a self-evaluation maintenance model of social behavior. In L. Berkowitz (Ed.), *Advances in experimental social psychology* (Vol. 21, pp. 181–227). San Diego, CA: Academic Press.

Tice, D. M., Twenge, J. M., & Schmeichel, B. J. (2002). Social exclusion and prosocial and antisocial behavior. In J. P. Forgas & K. D. Williams (Eds.), *The social self: Cognitive, interpersonal, and intergroup perspectives* (pp. 175–182). Philadelphia: Psychology Press.

Twenge, J. M., Baumeister, R. F., Tice, D. M., & Stucke, T. S. (2001). If you can't join them, beat them: Effects of social exclusion on aggressive behavior. *Journal of Personality and Social Psychology, 81,* 1058–1069.

White, R. W. (1959). Motivation reconsidered: The concept of competence. *Psychological Review, 66,* 297–333.

Williams, K. D. (1997). Social ostracism. In R. M. Kowalski (Ed.), *Aversive interpersonal behaviors: The Plenum series in social/clinical psychology* (pp. 133–170). New York: Plenum Press.

Williams, K. D. (2001). *Ostracism: The power of silence.* New York: Guilford Press.

Williams, K. D., Cheung, C. K., & Choi, W. (2000). Cyberostracism: Effects of being ignored over the Internet. *Journal of Personality and Social Psychology, 79,* 748–762.

Williams, K. D., Govan, C. L., Edwardson, M., & Wheeler, L. (2001, February). *Consumer involvement can be measured by the Implicit Association Test.* Presented at the Society of Consumer Psychology Conference, Scottsdale, AZ.

Williams, K. D., & Sommer, K. L. (1997). Social ostracism by coworkers: Does rejection lead to loafing or compensation? *Personality and Social Psychology Bulletin, 23,* 693–706.

Williams, K. D., Wheeler, L., & Harvey, J. A. (2001). Inside the social mind of the ostracizer. In J. P. Forgas & K. D. Williams (Eds.), *The social mind: Cognitive and motivational aspects of interpersonal behavior* (pp. 294–320). New York: Cambridge University Press.

Wilson, T. D., Lindsey, S., & Schooler, T. Y. (2000). A model of dual attitudes. *Psychological Review, 107,* 101–126.

Zadro, L., & Williams, K. D. (1998, April). *Riding the "O" Train: A role-play exercise to examine social ostracism.* Presented at the "Symposium on Social Psychology on the Web" at the annual meeting of the Society for Australasian Social Psychology, Christchurch, NZ.

Zadro, L., & Williams, K. D. (2000). *The effects of ostracism on prejudice.* Unpublished manuscript, University of New South Wales, Sydney, Australia.

Zadro, L., & Williams, K. D. (2001, February). *Effects of short term ostracism on sources and targets.* Poster presented at the annual meeting of the Society of Personality and Social Psychology, San Antonio, TX.

17

To Control or Not to Control Stereotypes

Separating the Implicit and Explicit Processes of Perspective-Taking and Suppression

Adam D. Galinsky, Paul V. Martorana, and Gillian Ku

CONTENTS

INTRODUCTION

Control. If only we could regulate our thoughts, our behavior, and our social interactions more effectively, we and those around us would be better off. We would eat less, exercise more, rein in our tempers, and reveal less discrimination and prejudice toward others. We are constantly attempting to exert control over the content and nature of our cognitive processes. Attempts at mental control, however, do not always meet with success. Controlling mental content and processes can have both intended (explicit) and unintended (implicit) effects on judgments and behavior. Whether mental control succeeds or fails depends largely, not only on the explicit processes that attempts at control were meant to activate, but also the often ironic implicit processes that were incidentally activated.

The motivation to control and regulate our social thoughts and behavior, especially with regard to stereotyping and prejudice, is driven by the fact that, in contemporary society, individuals are judged on the views they

Please address correspondence to Adam D. Galinsky, Department of Management and Organization, Leverone Hall, 2001 Sheridan Road, Kellogg School of Management, Northwestern University, Evanston, IL 60208; e-mail: agalinsky@nwu.edu articulate and the meanings expressed in their social behavior, all evaluated against a standard of "correctness." Any interpersonal behavior, verbal or nonverbal, that suggests discrimination is subject to condemnation, with the potential for public censorship and legal sanction, as well as internal compunction. A suffocating atmosphere is often created in which utterances and actions possess a foreboding quality and are bathed in suspicion. We take the burden and constraints of this potentially paralyzing situation as a point of departure. How do individuals navigate a social world that is increasingly multicultural without displaying attitudes that could be the fodder for accusations? What strategies are most effective in debiasing social thought, of calibrating one's actions with contemporary social mores?

In this chapter we discuss two strategies that individuals can use to reduce stereotyping, prejudice, and discrimination: perspective-taking and suppression. We explore the separation of the conscious, explicit effects from the nonconscious, implicit effects activated by each attempt at control and how the effectiveness of each strategy as a means of reducing stereotypes depends on these separate processes. With suppression, individuals attempt to actively banish stereotypic thoughts from consciousness and to replace those thoughts with more acceptable ones. Although stereotype suppression under some circumstances can reduce the accessibility and influence of stereotypic thoughts and increase the accessibility and influence of counterstereotypic thoughts, it can also, ironically and unintentionally, produce the very thoughts one is suppressing (Macrae, Bodenhausen, Milne, & Jetten, 1994a). Because of this insidious implicit process, its use as a strategy for stereotype control is suspect. Perspective-taking, on the other hand, implicitly increases the overlap between representations of the self and representations of the other; typically, the representation of the other becomes more self-like, or similar to one's own self-conception (Davis, Conklin, Smith, & Luce, 1996). This perspective-taking-induced increase in self–other overlap appears to be a crucial mechanism in controlling stereotyping and out-group evaluations. When an individual's own self-concept is positive, as is typically the case, then perspective-taking reduces stereotyping and improves the evaluations of out-groups. But when an individual's self-concept is negative, either chronically or temporarily, then perspective-taking can lead to negative evaluations of the out-group. Suppression and perspective-taking can both have positive effects on controlling the influence of stereotypes, but their effectiveness depends on which process, the explicit or the implicit, is the crucial input into a judgment or behavior. We discuss first the nature of and the relationship between implicit and explicit processes and their role in producing and reducing the effects of stereotypes on judgments and behavior before turning to the specific strategies of suppression and perspective-taking.

THE EXPLICIT AND THE IMPLICIT

The distinction between explicit and implicit processes in social judgment comes from the work on distinguishing between explicit and implicit memory (Schacter, 1994). *Explicit memory* refers to the conscious recollection of some prior event, whereas *implicit memory* refers to situations in which cognitive processes are affected by a prior event or experience, even when there is no conscious awareness of how the prior experience is affecting current cognition. Facilitation effects – increased ease in processing some stimuli – are often taken as evidence that implicit memory is at work. Research on implicit and explicit memory suggests that the two systems are functionally independent of each other; prior experiences that affect judgment may or may not be retrievable in an explicit memory test. Further evidence for their functional independence comes from research that suggests that these implicit and explicit processes emerge from distinct neurological systems (see Lieberman, this volume; Zárate & Stoever, this volume). The fact that many mental processes can be described as implicit means that we often tell more than we know (Nisbett & Wilson, 1977). Nisbett and Wilson pointed out that many judgments, even ones that rely on complex attributional logic, are produced through cognitive processes to which the individual has no introspective access. Individuals are only aware of the judgment made, not the process that produced it, and they may not even be aware that their current judgment or attitude has changed in any appreciable way. Thus, individuals are often unaware of dissonance-induced shifts in attitudes (Goethals & Reckman, 1973) or that an environmental stimulus has affected their judgments (Higgins, Rholes, & Jones, 1977). Even important goals can be implicitly activated and pursued without conscious awareness (see Chartrand & Jefferis, this volume).

Judgments often get transformed when an implicit process becomes an explicit one. For example, exposure to trait words in a prior context produces assimilation effects on later impression formation judgments, but only when those traits are no longer (explicitly) held in consciousness. However, when one is still conscious of the traits at the time of judgment – for example, when an individual is reminded of the trait words that he or she had previously seen – contrast effects result in which judgments become less consistent with the implications of the traits than if they had not been seen at all (Martin, 1986; Moskowitz & Skurnik, 1999; Stapel, Koomen, & van der Plight, 1997). When one has these trait terms in explicit memory one will explicitly attempt to remove their potential biasing influence and to reset one's judgment, thereby producing contrast effects (Martin, 1986). Judgments thus are fundamentally altered, depending on whether the primed traits are exerting an influence through an implicit or an explicit process.

Implicit and explicit processes are linked to the conceptual distinction between automatic and controlled processes (but see Kruglanski et al., this volume, for a critique of dual-process models). Bargh (1994) suggested that automatic cognitive processes possess a number of features: They tend to be unintentional, occur outside of awareness, and are uncontrollable and efficient (i.e., consume minimal attentional resources). Few mental activities, however, meet all the requirements for automaticity. For example, traits are often inferred from behavioral descriptions, and these trait inferences often occur outside of awareness and without intent, but they are not uncontrollable or entirely free from attentional limitations (Uleman & Moskowitz, 1994).

Some researchers have placed implicit and explicit processes into a temporal sequence. Gilbert (1989) suggests that when we try to understand why an event occurred, we implicitly and immediately make a dispositional attribution for that event, locating causality in some fundamental personality aspect of one of the individuals, and only later, and with effort, explicitly consider the situational forces that contributed to the event (Gilbert, Pelham, & Krull, 1988). Similarly, when encountering a proposition or statement, we implicitly and immediately believe it to be true, and only later, with great effort, do we adjust our assessment for potential duplicity (Gilbert, 1991; Gilbert, Krull, & Malone, 1990). The sequence but not the implicit–explicit order can be reversed. Thus, implicit dispositional attributions followed by situational adjustment can become implicit situational attributions that are followed by explicit attempts to adjust for dispositions when one has the processing goal of discovering the nature of the situation (Krull, 1993). Similarly, when one believes that the environment is beset on all sides by mendacity, one implicitly remembers a proposition as false, and only later, through explicit recall, takes into account its potential veracity (Skurnik, 1998). These models suggest that an initial implicit response is corrected for by an explicit process; the explicit process helps override an implicit bias.

IMPLICIT AND EXPLICIT PROCESSES IN STEREOTYPING

The literature, especially that of stereotyping and prejudice, on explicit and implicit processes tends to paint them as either/or propositions: One is activating either an implicit process or an explicit process. Not only are the processes considered distinct, but they tend to be instantiated by very different measures: The measurement of stereotyping and prejudice is often divided into implicit (e.g., reaction time) and explicit measures (e.g., scales). There is considerable debate over whether implicit and explicit measures of stereotyping and prejudice are correlated (Dovidio, Kawakami, Johnson, Johnson, & Howard, 1997; von Hippel, Sekaquaptewa, & Vargas, 1997; Wittenbrink, Judd, & Park, 1997). In some studies, the implicit prejudice measure is reliably associated with participants' scores on explicit racial attitude measures (Wittenbrink et al., 1997; von Hippel et al., 1997). In other studies, there is no relationship between the implicit and explicit measures (Fazio, Jackson, Dunton, & Williams, 1995; Karpinski & Hilton, 2001).

Given the often low correlations between implicit and explicit measures of stereotyping, these measures are often pitted against each other in predicting behavior (see von Hippel, Vargas, & Sekaquaptewa, this volume, for the importance of focusing not only on the content of stereotypes and prejudice, but also on the processes initiated by these attitudes). It should be noted that observed behavior may not always be explicit. Overt prejudicial or discriminatory behavior would, of course, be considered to be produced through an explicit process, but more ambiguous behaviors, ones that suggest interpersonal discomfort, such as avoiding eye contact, may be considered more implicit, engaged in without awareness or intent or controllability. In fact, there appears to be a relationship between the method of measurement and the prediction of subsequent behaviors that depends on the explicit–implicit distinction. Implicit attitudes tend to be better predictors of spontaneous judgments and nonverbal behaviors, whereas explicit attitude measures are a more reliable predictor of evaluative judgments and deliberative behaviors such as legal decisions (Dovidio et al., 1997). Explicit measures predict certain behavioral choices and preferences (Karpinski & Hilton, 2001). Implicit measures predict nonverbal behaviors in interracial interactions (Fazio et al., 1995). Some have suggested that the implicit measures are the more reliable measures of stereotyping and prejudice because they are nonreactive and less prone to manipulation by social desirability concerns (Fazio et al., 1995; Greenwald, McGhee, & Schwartz, 1998). Others have suggested that implicit stereotypes have functional roots in that they allow us to understand the buzzing and chaotic cauldron of complex information with relative ease and efficiency, thereby freeing up scarce cognitive resources for other concurrent tasks; stereotyping, rather than being a product of a design flaw, might actually be considered an evolutionarily produced design feature that increases cognitive efficiency (Haselton & Buss, this volume; Macrae, Milne, & Bodenhausen, 1994).

Because implicit processes are often initiated without intent, without awareness, and without control, many have suggested strategies designed to reduce stereotyping and discrimination by overriding these implicit processes through the use of explicit ones. In addition, explicit processes are thought to be required to reduce stereotyping because implicit processes are believed to be overlearned and thus resistant to change. Typically, these strategies of overriding implicit processes through the use of explicit processes involve increasing the motivation or altering the processing goals that individuals have in interactions. Making a perceiver interdependent with a stereotyped target decreases reliance on the stereotype in forming an impression of that person (Neuberg & Fiske, 1987). Processing goals focusing on content that is irrelevant to social categorization (e.g., looking for a white dot on photographs of women) do not lead to the automatic activation of stereotypes (Macrae, Bodenhausen, Milne, Thorn, & Castelli, 1997). Another approach makes the implicit explicit by alerting people to implicit processes and their connection to stereotyping and bias. In fact, this approach is very much a part of consciousness-raising efforts. Monteith, Voils, and Ashburn-Nardo (2001) have shown that making people aware of an implicit response that could belie discrimination has a dramatic effect on self-perceptions. Awareness of the biasing influence of an implicit stereotyping process produces guilt and motivates the individual to override that response through the use of an explicit process.

For an explicit process to be employed, one needs not only motivation but also cognitive capacity. When motivation is high but cognitive capacity is low, the implicit processes will dominate and evidence of stereotyping will be observed (at least on an implicit measure) (Bodenhausen, 1990). This suggests that the best way to reduce the bias of an implicit process is to change the implicit process itself. In fact, explicit processes may over time become habitualized and thus become implicit. Stereotyping itself has been likened to a habit; in the presence of a stereotyped target, a habitualized response occurs: the automatic activation of negative and potentially pernicious stereotypes. Many people have attempted to explore how one can change or alter such habits by creating different (more positive) associations that hopefully can become habitualized themselves. The link between the group representation and the stereotype can be severed by training participants to replace the stereotype with a different set of beliefs (Kawakami, Dovidio, Moll, Hermsen, & Russin, 2000; Moskowitz, Gollwitzer, Wasel, & Schaal, 1999). In the Kawakami et al. experiments, participants responded with a forceful "no" whenever a stereotype term accompanied a photograph of a member of the stereotyped group and an enthusiastic "yes" when nonstereotypic traits accompanied a photograph. This training, which required an extensive number of trials, proved successful in reducing the automatic activation of stereotypes. For those committed to the goal of egalitarianism, not only is the stereotype not activated in the presence of an African American (Moskowitz et al., 1999), but the egalitarian goal itself gets activated (Moskowitz, Salomon, & Taylor, 2000). Egalitarian goals, rather than stereotypes, can become the habitualized response that guides information processing.

These studies raise the question of where implicit and explicit processes come from. Recent work suggests that implicit attitudes are the result of environmental pairings. To alter an implicit attitude, one does not need to engage conscious attention toward replacing thoughts; one simply needs to modify the pairings found in the environment (Dasgupta & Greenwald, 2001; Karpinski & Hilton, 2001). Encountering an African American in a nonthreatening situation (e.g., at a family barbeque) activates the positive aspects of a stereotype, whereas encountering the same person in a more threatening situation (e.g., a dimly lit street) activates the negative components of the stereotype (Wittenbrink, Judd, & Park, 2001). Explicit attitudes, on the other hand, are consciously held endorsements that reflect personal values and beliefs as well as observable social norms. With explicit attitudes, it is proposed, more overt attempts at persuasion would be necessary to alter these attitudes.

Implicit and explicit processes are often described as being in opposition with each other, with one process producing a response on the opposite end of the continuum as the other response. However, implicit and explicit processes can independently produce the same judgment or they can work in concert with each other. Work on illusory correlations suggest that stereotyping and prejudice can result from a mix of implicit and explicit processes (Hamilton, Dugan, & Trolier, 1985; Hamilton & Gifford, 1976; McConnell, Sherman, & Hamilton, 1994). The co-occurrence of infrequent and thus distinctive events (a numerical minority group member performing a negative behavior) attracts attention, and more time is spent processing and considering this information. This increase in attention leads perceivers to overestimate the frequency of such co-occurrences. The infrequency of the two distinctive events implicitly attracts attention, and this leads to the greater availability of these events in explicit memory (but see Fiedler & Freytag, this volume, for a discussion of the possible pseudocontingent basis of illusory correlations).

We suggest that attempts to direct cognition toward a goal often activate implicit and explicit processes simultaneously. Rather than simply overriding an implicit process with an explicit one or making an explicit response an implicit one through practice, attempts to control will often produce simultaneous processes, some that are more explicit and others that are more implicit. In addition, the strategies that have been effective in overriding or transforming implicitly produced bias have a number of drawbacks. Focusing on nonsocial aspects of the environment (Macrae et al., 1997) may not be a practical way to interact with others. Although spending extensive amounts of time training to negate negative responses to stereotyped targets (Kawakami et al., 2000) may be an effective long-term strategy, it may not provide an individual with an immediate mechanism to deal with a current interaction. Likewise, we may not have a choice about the environment in which we encounter a stereotyped target (Wittenbrink et al., 2001) or we may not find ourselves in an interdependent situation (Neuberg & Fiske, 1987). As an alternative, the remainder of this chapter focuses on two different individual strategies, perspective-taking and stereotype suppression, that individuals may use to reduce and control stereotyping in a variety of settings, and the implicit and explicit processes associated with each strategy.

IMPLICIT AND EXPLICIT PROCESSES OF SUPPRESSION

One intuitively appealing strategy for reducing the accessibility of stereotypes and avoiding bias and prejudice is to suppress any references to stereotypes, to actively deny them entrance into consciousness. The decision to engage in suppression activates two concurrent cognitive systems: an intentional, explicit operating system and an implicit, "ironic" monitoring system (Wegner, 1994). When a particular mental state is avoided (such as when one is asked to avoid stereotypical thoughts), the operating process seeks items inconsistent with that state; these serve as distracters, attempting to make the mind full so that undesired thoughts cannot enter (Wegner & Erber, 1992). The operating system is thus an explicit process of replacement. The monitoring process, on the other hand, is tuned to detect failures of mental control and scans the mental landscape for references to the unwanted thoughts. It is the interplay of the explicit operating system and the implicit monitoring system that determines the effectiveness of suppression. The (explicit) operating system is hypothesized to depend on an abundance of cognitive resources, whereas the (implicit) monitoring system is presumed to be an efficient process that does not depend on cognitive resources to function effectively. The introduction of concurrent tasks or other drains on resource availability can reduce the effectiveness of and essentially disable the (explicit) operating system, leaving the (implicit) monitoring system running unchecked. The disabled operating system cannot prevent the monitoring system's successful searches for the unwanted thoughts from reaching consciousness. Because suppression activates both the explicit operating system and the implicit monitoring system, attempts to suppress a thought or mental state can give rise to ironic effects in which the decision to engage in suppression can lead those very thoughts to become more, rather than less, accessible.

Wegner, Erber, and Bowman (1993, cited in Wegner, 1994) demonstrated that when resource depletion is paired with the intention to suppress stereotypic thoughts, stereotypes become more accessible than when no cognitive load exists. This might imply that the ironic effects of thought suppression would emerge only when the operating system is disabled by a secondary task introducing a cognitive load. However, once the intention to suppress has been discontinued, the suppressed thoughts often become more accessible and influential in subsequent judgments and behavior, a phenomenon known as *rebound effects* (Wegner, Schneider, Carter, & White, 1987). The monitoring system, in its search for traces of the unwanted thought, serves as a subliminal priming mechanism. Macrae, Bodenhausen, Milne, and Jetten (1994), Macrae, Milne, and Bodenhausen (1994), and Galinsky and Moskowitz (2000) demonstrated that engaging in and then discontinuing the suppression of stereotypic thoughts leads to rebound effects, that is, greater accessibility of the stereotype compared to a control condition. In line with Dovidio et al.'s (1997) work, the ironic effects of suppression, caused by the implicit monitoring system, seem to have a greater impact on implicit effects (stereotype accessibility, interpersonal distancing) than on explicit effects (stereotype expression and overt discrimination) (Galinsky & Moskowitz, 2000; Monteith, Spicer, & Tooman, 1998). Whereas Galinsky (1999) found that suppressors explicitly rated a stereotype target as being more similar to themselves, Bodenhausen et al. (1994) found that suppression led to interpersonal distancing behaviors (sitting farther away from a stereotype target), behavior assumed to be implicit effects not typically under conscious control. Neither Galinsky and Moskowitz nor Monteith et al. found reliable effects of suppression on later stereotype expression. Yet, both found reliable effects of suppression on later stereotype accessibility. These results suggest that where bias is most invidious, at the implicit level, the decision to suppress ultimately leaves individuals worse off than if no attempt at suppression had occurred.

Is this really the case? Remember that as the monitoring system is scanning for references to the suppressed thought, the operating system is searching for distractors to fill the mind. In much of the research on stereotype suppression, researchers have failed to look for the accessibility and influence of these distracter thoughts. More importantly, they have failed to look at the relative accessibility of the suppressed thoughts compared to the distracters. In fact, thought suppression is most efficient when there are readily available distracters to take the place of the suppressed thought in consciousness; rebound effects can be eliminated when specific replacement thoughts are provided (Wegner et al., 1987). Kelly and Kahn (1994) suggested that individuals are able to avoid rebound effects with their own recurring, intrusive thoughts because they have developed a rich tapestry of distracters. But where do the distracters come from? How do people attempt to stay present in an interracial or intergender interaction while suppressing stereotypic thoughts?

One possible way to resolve this dilemma is to focus on counterstereotypic information. That is, when attempting to suppress the stereotype of African Americans, an individual might replace stereotypic items that spring to mind (e.g., hostile) with their antonyms (e.g., kind). The constant process of replacing stereotypic thoughts with counterstereotypic ones should serve to make the counterstereotype as accessible as or more accessible than the stereotype under conditions of suppression. Galinsky and Moskowitz (2002) investigated whether both the stereotype and the counterstereotype could become hyperaccessible following stereotype suppression. They utilized the paradigm of Macrae and colleagues (1994) and Galinsky and Moskowitz (2000) for their investigation. Participants were asked to write a "day in the life" narrative essay of a photographed African American man. In a *stereotype suppression condition*, participants were told to actively avoid thinking about the photographed target in a stereotypical manner. In a *stereotype expression condition*, participants were told to use the cultural stereotype (rather than their personal beliefs) of the group represented in the photograph when constructing their narrative essays. A no-prime control group did not write a narrative essay, nor did they even see the photograph of the African American man; they simply started with the later tasks. Following that task and a number of filler tasks, participants completed a lexical decision task that measured the relative accessibility of stereotype-consistent, stereotype-irrelevant, and counter-stereotypic words. The results demonstrated a previously undocumented effect of suppression: Suppression led both the stereotype and the counter-stereotype to be hyperaccessible (beyond levels evidenced in participants actually asked to express the stereotype and the no-prime control group). In addition, the counterstereotype was just as accessible as the stereotype for suppressors; stereotype expressers, on the other hand, showed an accessibility advantage for the stereotype over the counterstereotype.

Galinsky and Moskowitz (2002) also examined the judgmental consequences of stereotype suppression, looking at which construct, the stereotype or the counterstereotype, would dominate impressions of a later person perception target. The priming literature suggests that the more accessible a construct is, the more likely that construct will be used to categorize and make sense of a stimulus object. When two constructs are equally applicable a priori to a social object, the more accessible one will be used to categorize the object (Allport, 1954; Bruner, 1957; Higgins, 1996). Given that the accessibility of both the stereotype and the counterstereotype is increased following stereotype suppression, which construct will win the race toward categorization of a subsequent ambiguous target is an open question.

Whether the counterstereotype or the stereotype is used to categorize a race-neutral target following suppression might depend on the type of judgment participants make. Suppressors who are asked to rate the target person along a stereotype-consistent dimension might produce more extreme (and stereotypical) judgments, but suppressors asked to rate targets along a counterstereotype dimension might also produce more extreme (but less stereotypical) ratings. This is precisely what Galinsky and Moskowitz (2002) found. Participants asked to suppress the stereotype of African Americans and then evaluated a target person along a stereotype-consistent dimension (hostility) judged that person in a stereotype-consistent fashion. However, those participants asked to rate the same person performing the same behaviors along a different, applicable dimension that was counter to the stereotype (honesty), actually judged the target person in a more counterstereotypic way than a control condition.

The simultaneous accessibility of the stereotype and counterstereotype runs counter to research that has found the active inhibition of counterstereotypic traits (Dijksterhuis & van Knippenberg, 1996) and exemplars (Rothbart, Sriram, & Davis-Stitt, 1996) following stereotype activation. Macrae, Bodenhausen, and Milne (1995) asserted that categories compete to "capture" or categorize a stimulus, with active inhibition of the competing constructs. The inhibition of stereotype-inconsistent information in the face of stereotype activation promotes efficient social perception (Bodenhausen & Macrae, 1998). Suppression prevents this competitive inhibition because counterstereotypic information provides useful distracters to assist in preventing the emergence of the stereotype into consciousness. Thus, the counterstereotype is not inhibited in the context of stereotype activation. In fact, the results of Galinsky and Moskowitz (2002) suggest that stereotype-consistent and counterstereotype words serve as mutually reinforcing retrieval cues following suppression. Suppression creates a unique context in which the stereotype and counterstereotype activate, rather than inhibit, each other. Wegner (1994) has pointed out the often ironic and paradoxical effects that emerge from attempts to control the contents of consciousness. The results of Galinsky and Moskowitz (2002) add another irony of suppression – the simultaneous accessibility of the stereotype and its foe, the counterstereotype.

We have suggested that the stereotype and counterstereotype owe their increased accessibility following a suppression goal to two different cognitive systems, the implicit monitoring system and the explicit operating system, respectively. Further, these two systems are posited to depend differentially on the availability of cognitive resources (Wegner, 1994). The implicit monitoring system tends to be resource independent and continues to function regardless of whether attention is divided. The explicit operating system is more effortful and is disabled when cognitive resources are low. Although the counterstereotype is more accessible following suppression, its level of accessibility may depend on the availability of cognitive resources.

Dividing the attention of perceivers should lead the stereotype, but not the counterstereotype, to continue to show evidence of increased accessibility. Galinsky and Moskowitz (2002) tested this notion and found that for suppressors placed under conditions of cognitive resource deprivation, the stereotype still showed increased accessibility, but the counterstereotype no longer revealed higher levels of accessibility compared to stereotype expressers. These results support the notion that suppression increases the accessibility of both the stereotype and counterstereotype but through two different cognitive systems, one implicit and one explicit. The stereotype is made accessible through the more automatic and resource-independent monitoring system. The counterstereotype is made accessible through the effortful and resource-dependent operating system; consequently, its increased accessibility is vulnerable to reductions in cognitive resources. The counterstereotype can still direct judgments following suppression but only when there is an abundance of cognitive resources at the suppressor's disposal.

Overall, suppression has multifaceted effects on cognition and judgments that depend on the relationship between the implicit monitoring system and the explicit operating system. Although suppression routinely reduces the expression of stereotypes, it not only fails to reduce but can exacerbate stereotyping and bias at the implicit, nonconscious level. Ultimately, it is only under specific circumstances – when judgments are made along counterstereotypical dimensions under optimal conditions of high cognitive capacity – that suppression will lead to decreased rather than increased stereotyping.

Is there an alternative strategy that harnesses different explicit and implicit processes, one that is less vulnerable to ironic failures of control? The next section explores the role of perspective-taking in reducing stereotype accessibility and expression.

IMPLICIT AND EXPLICIT PROCESSES OF PERSPECTIVE-TAKING

The ability to entertain the perspective of another has long been recognized as a critical ingredient in proper social functioning (Batson, 1991; Davis, 1983; Kohlberg, 1976; Piaget, 1932). Perspective-taking has been shown to make the evaluations of others more positive (Davis et al., 1996), to increase sensitivity to the plight of others (Clore & Jeffery, 1972), to provide more situational attributions for another's behavior (Regan & Totten, 1975), and ultimately to increase altruistic displays (Batson, 1998) and facilitate reaching optimal negotiated settlements (Galinsky & White, 2002).

Given all the benefits that appear to result from perspective-taking, what are the mechanisms by which perspective-taking exerts its influence? Perspective-taking appears to lead to a self–other merging or overlap (Davis et al., 1996), in which the representation of the target comes to resemble the perspective-taker's own self-representation. Davis et al. found that ascription of self-descriptive traits to the target was not due to increased liking for the target, but rather to the cognitive accessibility of the self-concept. This suggests that there are two separate processes involved in perspective-taking – a conscious, explicit effect and a nonconscious, implicit effect. When perspective-takers are asked direct questions about the target person, they will presumably feel that the perspective-taking manipulation is relevant to that judgment and will consciously give responses that are consistent with that manipulation. However, during perspective-taking, the self-concept gets implicitly activated and applied the target. Further evidence for the implicit effect of self-concept activation by perspective-taking manipulations comes from the fact that the increases in self–other overlap are generally impervious to reductions in cognitive capacity (Davis et al., 1996). Cognitive load interfered with the effortful act of perspective-taking and the general ascription of traits, but left the more automatic process, the ascription of self-relevant traits, intact. Perspective-taking manipulations typically involve explicitly imagining either (1) how a target feels or is affected by his or her situation or (2) how you would feel and would be affected if you were the target (Batson, Early, & Salvarani, 1997). Increased self–target overlap occurs both when participants imagine themselves in the target's place and when they imagine what it would be like to be the target (Davis et al., 1996). Although the emotional responses do appear to be affected by the type of perspective-taking manipulation (Batson et al., 1997; Stotland, 1969), the implicit effects of perspective-taking appear to be independent of the type of manipulation.

The increased self–other overlap following perspective-taking has implications for intergroup relations because recent research has found that it is the in-group's association with the self that leads to ethnocentric responses in favor of the in-group (Cadinu & Rothbart, 1996; Smith & Henry, 1996). Galinsky and Moskowitz (2000) proposed that the increased accessibility of the self-concept following perspective-taking could result in the use of the self-concept rather than the stereotype in categorizing and evaluating a member of a stereotyped group. Although perspective-taking manipulations increase liking for the target and activate emotional responses that imply sympathy and empathy, Galinsky and Moskowitz predicted that it would be self–other overlap that would mediate the effects of perspective-taking on stereotype accessibility and application. This mediation would result because liking and emotional reactions are explicit processes activated by perspective-taking, whereas self–other overlap is an implicit process. Given that implicit processes tend to affect implicit measures (Dovidio et al., 1997) and stereotype accessibility tends to be an implicit measure, self–other overlap should mediate the effects of perspective-taking on stereotyping.

The experiments presented in Galinsky and Moskowitz (2000) support this distinction between the conscious, explicit processes and nonconscious, implicit processes associated with perspective-taking. In Experiment 1, perspective-taking decreased stereotype expression and increased positive evaluations of the target expressed in the narrative essays of a photographed elderly man. In addition, perspective-taking prevented the hyperaccessibility of the stereotype compared to stereotype suppressors and a control condition. Thus, perspective-taking decreased bias on both the conscious, explicit task (i.e., narrative essay) and the nonconscious, implicit task (i.e., a reaction time measure of stereotype accessibility). In addition, the explicit effect of expressing more positive evaluations in their narrative essays did not mediate the implicit effect of decreased stereotype accessibility. In fact, covarying the effect of the evaluations expressed in the first narrative essay increased rather than decreased the effect of the manipulations on stereotype accessibility.

Although Experiment 1 of Galinsky and Moskowitz is suggestive of the notion that the nonconscious effect of decreased stereotype accessibility is mediated by activation of the self-concept, it did not measure self-concept accessibility or self–other overlap. In a second experiment, Galinsky and Moskowitz (2000) explored whether this implicit effect of increased self–other overlap following perspective-taking was a better predictor of reduced stereotyping than the explicit effect of expressing more positive evaluations. Perspective-taking increased evaluations of the target individual in the narrative essays, increased the overlap between representations of the self and representations of the elderly man, and reduced stereotyping. Moreover, the level of overlap was a significant predictor of reductions in stereotyping, whereas evaluations expressed in the narrative essays did not reliably predict reductions in stereotyping. Thus, the implicit effect of perspective-taking (increases in self–other overlap) rather than the explicit effect (increases in evaluations of the target of perspective-taking) is the mechanism by which perspective-taking decreases stereotyping. Implicit processes, both for perspective-taking and for suppression, appear to be more important than explicit processes in reducing stereotyping.

It should be noted that increases in self–other overlap in the Davis et al. (1996) experiments occurred for a target person who did not belong to an out-group (male participants took the perspective of a male target and female participants took the perspective of a female target). Galinsky and Moskowitz showed that increases in self–other overlap caused by perspective-taking occur even if the target of perspective-taking is a member of an out-group and this self–other overlap extends to the entire out-group. These results tend to run counter to research that shows that stereotype change is difficult to elicit because people retain their stereotypes through a process of subtyping (see Johnston & Miles, this volume). That is, targets who are perceived to be counterstereotypic are deemed to be unrepresentative of other group members (i.e., subtyped), and therefore no updating of the group representation is necessary (Brewer, Dull, & Lui, 1981; Johnston & Hewstone, 1992; Kunda & Oleson, 1995, 1997). One might expect perspective-taking to increase the tendency to treat the target of perspective-taking as atypical, and therefore to subtype that person and retain the stereotypical group representation. Perspective-taking leads to a more personalized approach toward targets (Galinsky & Moskowitz,

2000), and the more personalized the approach to a target is, the less likely stereotypes will be used in categorizing and evaluating that person (Brewer, 1996). However, the more personalized the approach to a target, the more likely that person will be subtyped and excluded from the group representation. Although personalization of a target leads to less stereotyping of that target, it does not always reduce the stereotypicality of the group representation.

Why then does perspective-taking lead group representations to be transformed and become less stereotypical, rather than result in mere subtyping and the retention of stereotypic representations? Remember that it is the self's connection to the in-group that helps create in-group biases (Cadinu & Rothbart, 1996; Smith & Henry, 1996). In fact, connecting the self somehow to the out-group might be the key to reducing these biases (Galinsky, 2002). Wright, Aron, McLaughlin-Volpe, and Ropp (1997; see also Wright, Aron, & Trop, 2002), for example, found that knowledge of an in-group member's close relationship with an out-group member improved attitudes toward the out-group. Wright et al. (1997, p. 76) proposed, but did not provide evidence, that this effect is mediated by the processes of self–other overlap: "In an observed in-group/out-group friendship, the in-group member is part of the self, the out-group member is part of that in-group member's self, and hence part of myself ... then to some extent the out-group is part of myself." The self is implicitly activated during perspective-taking and becomes connected to both the target of perspective-taking and the target's group. In this way, the implicit activation of the self appears to prevent subtyping and allow instead for the representation of the out-group to become less stereotypical.

Galinsky and Ku (2003) sought further evidence that perspective-taking involves the activation and application of the self-concept and that this activation determines how out-groups are evaluated. These experiments tested the hypothesis that if perspective-taking activates the self-concept, then the positivity of one's own self-evaluation should predict how positively a perspective-taker evaluates an out-group. In one experiment, positive and negative self-evaluations were activated by providing participants with positive or negative feedback on a jury decision-making task prior to the perspective-taking manipulation. A different experiment looked at individual differences in self-evaluation, or self-esteem. In each of these experiments, participants wrote a "day in the life" essay about a photographed elderly man with either perspective-taking or control instructions and then evaluated the elderly along a number of semantic differentials. Across both experiments, positive feedback and high self-esteem led perspective-takers to evaluate the out-group more positively, than perspective-takers exposed to negative feedback or with chronic low self-esteem.

Out-group evaluations are improved only when the perspective-taker's self-concept is positive. For the perspective-taker, the self is a critical, and implicit, ingredient in shaping intergroup evaluations.

CONCLUSION

This chapter has explored the implicit and explicit processes associated with two different strategies, suppression and perspective-taking, employed to reduce stereotyping. Attempts at control, such as regulating the accessibility and expression of stereotypes and prejudice, tend to activate both implicit and explicit processes, and a comprehensive understanding of the consequences of mental control needs to take both processes into account. Suppression and perspective-taking both decrease the explicit expression of stereotypic content, and it appears that the explicit processes of each strategy are responsible for this effect. Perspective-taking accomplishes this by increasing liking, sympathy, and empathy for stereotyped targets. Suppression accomplishes this by activating an explicit operating system that fills the mind with counterstereotypic distractors. Both perspective-takers and suppressors report increased similarity with stereotype targets. On explicit measures, it appears that suppression and perspective-taking are equally suited to the task of stereotype reduction.

It is through their implicit processes and on implicit measures that the effectiveness of suppression and perspective-taking in controlling stereotyping starts to diverge. With suppression, the implicit process of monitoring the environment for references to a negative stereotype increases the accessibility of that stereotype. In addition, the explicit evoking of counterstereotypic thoughts, but not the implicit scanning for stereotypic references, is dependent on cognitive resources. Thus, under conditions of diminished cognitive capacity, the stereotype reigns supreme and suppression appears to increase rather than decrease stereotyped biases. On the other hand, perspective-taking implicitly activates and applies the self-concept to stereotypic targets and groups; it is the self-concept and not the stereotype that wins out in the categorization process. The implicit process of self–other overlap mediates the perspective-taking-induced reductions in stereotyping, whereas the implicit process of monitoring the environment for suggestive references to negative stereotypes increases stereotyping during and after suppression. However, the implicit processes involved in perspective-taking can have their drawbacks. Whereas cognitive load is the Achilles' heel of suppression, low self-esteem, either temporary or chronic, can lead perspective-takers to evaluate stereotyped groups and targets less positively. Given that most individuals in Western cultures have high self-esteem (Crocker & Bylsma, 1996) and that concurrent tasks and cognitive load pervade mental life, it appears that perspective-taking is generally more effective than suppression in reducing stereotyping.

References

Allport, G. (1954). *The nature of prejudice*. Reading, MA: Addison-Wesley.

Bargh, J. A. (1994). The four horsemen of automaticity: Awareness, intention, efficiency, and control in social cognition. In R. S. Wyer, Jr., & T. K. Srull (Eds.), *Handbook of social cognition: Volume 1. Basic processes* (pp. 1–40). Hillsdale, NJ: Erlbaum.

Batson, C. D. (1991). *The altruism question: Toward a social-psychological answer*. Hillsdale, NJ: Erlbaum.

Batson, C. D. (1998). Altruism and prosocial behavior. In D. T. Gilbert & S. T. Fiske (Eds.), *The handbook of social psychology* (Vol. 2, pp. 282–316). New York: McGraw-Hill.

Batson, C. D., Early, S., & Salvarani, G. (1997). Perspective taking: Imagining how another feels versus imagining how you would feel. *Personality and Social Psychology Bulletin, 23*, 751–758.

Bodenhausen, G. V. (1990). Stereotypes as judgmental heuristics: Evidence of circadian variations in discrimination. *Psychological Science, 1*, 319–322.

Bodenhausen, G. V., & Macrae, C. N. (1998). Stereotype activation and inhibition. In R. S. Wyer, Jr. (Ed.), *Advances in social cognition: Volume 11. Stereotype activation and inhibition* (pp. 1–52). Mahwah, NJ: Erlbaum.

Brewer, M. B. (1996).When stereotypes lead to stereotyping: The use of stereotype in person perception. In C. N. Macrae, C. Stangor, & M. Hewstone (Eds.), *Stereotypes and stereotyping* (pp. 254–275). New York: Guilford Press.

Brewer, M. B., Dull, V., & Lui, L. (1981). Perceptions of the elderly: Stereotypes as prototypes. *Journal of Personality and Social Psychology, 41*, 656–670.

Bruner, J. (1957). On perceptual readiness. *Psychological Review, 64*, 123–152.

Cadinu, M. R., & Rothbart, M. (1996). Self-anchoring and differentiation processes in the minimal group setting. *Journal of Personality and Social Psychology, 70*, 661–677.

Clore, G. L., & Jeffery, K. M. (1972). Emotional role playing, attitude change, and attraction toward a disabled person. *Journal of Personality and Social Psychology, 23*, 105–111.

Crocker, J., & Bylsma, W. H. (1996). Self-esteem. In A. S. R. Manstead & M. Hewstone (Eds.), *The Blackwell encyclopedia of social psychology* (pp. 505–509). Oxford: Blackwell.

Dasgupta, N., & Greenwald, A. G. (2001). On the malleability of automatic attitudes: Combating automatic prejudice with images of admired and disliked individuals. *Journal of Personality and Social Psychology, 81*, 800–814.

Davis, M. H. (1983). Measuring individual differences in empathy: Evidence for a multidimensional approach. *Journal of Personality and Social Psychology, 44*, 113–126.

Davis, M. H., Conklin, L., Smith, A., & Luce, C. (1996). Effect of perspective taking on the cognitive representation of persons: A merging of self and other. *Journal of Personality and Social Psychology, 70,* 713–726.

Dijksterhuis, A., & van Knippenberg, A. (1996). The knife that cuts both ways: Facilitated and inhibited access to traits as a result of stereotype activation. *Journal of Experimental Social Psychology, 32,* 271–288.

Dovidio, J. F., Kawakami, K., Johnson, C., Johnson, B., & Howard, A. (1997). On the nature of prejudice: Automatic and controlled processes. *Journal of Experimental Social Psychology, 33,* 510–540.

Fazio, R. H., Jackson, J. R., Dunton, B. C., & Williams, C. J. (1995). Variability in automatic activation as an unobtrusive measure of racial attitudes: A bona fide pipeline? *Journal of Personality and Social Psychology, 69,* 1013–1027.

Galinsky, A. D. (1999). *Perspective-taking: Debiasing social thought.* Unpublished doctoral dissertation, Princeton University.

Galinsky, A. D. (2002). The self and the group: The role of perspective-taking in improving out-group evaluations. In M. A. Neale, E. A. Mannix, & H. Sondak (Eds.), *Research on managing in teams and groups* (Vol. 4, pp. 85–113). Elsevier Science Press.

Galinsky, A. D., & Ku, G. (2003). The effects of perspective-taking on prejudice: The moderating role of self-evaluation. Manuscript submitted for publication.

Galinsky, A. D., & Moskowitz, G. B. (2000). Perspective-taking: Decreasing stereotype expression, stereotype accessibility, and in-group favoritism. *Journal of Personality and Social Psychology, 78,* 708–724.

Galinsky, A. D., & Moskowitz, G. B. (2002). Further ironies of suppression: stereotype and counterstereotype accessibility following suppression and perspective-taking. Manuscript submitted for publication.

Galinsky, A. D., & White, J. B. (2002). Appreciating differences and similarities after perspective-taking: Overcoming position-based impasses and increasing joint gain. Manuscript in preparation.

Gilbert, D. T. (1989). Thinking lightly about others: Automatic components of the social inference process. In J. S. Uleman & J. A. Bargh (Eds.), *Unintended thought* (pp. 189–211). New York: Guilford Press.

Gilbert, D. T. (1991). How mental systems believe. *American Psychologist, 46,* 107–119.

Gilbert, D. T., Krull, D. S., & Malone, P. S. (1990). Unbelieving the unbelievable: Some problems in the rejection of false information. *Journal of Personality and Social Psychology, 59,* 601–613.

Gilbert, D. T., Pelham, B. W., & Krull, D. S. (1988). On cognitive busyness: When person perceivers meet persons perceived. *Journal of Personality and Social Psychology, 54,* 733–740.

Goethals, G. R., & Reckman, R. F. (1973). The perception of consistency in attitudes. *Journal of Experimental Social Psychology, 9,* 491–501.

Greenwald, A. G., McGhee, D. E., & Schwartz, J. L. K. (1998). Measuring individual differences in implicit cognition: The implicit association test. *Journal of Personality and Social Psychology, 74,* 1464–1480.

Hamilton, D. L., Dugan, P. M., & Trolier, T. K. (1985). The formation of stereotypic beliefs: Further evidence for distinctiveness-based illusory correlations. *Journal of Personality and Social Psychology, 48,* 5–17.

Hamilton, D. L., & Gifford, R. K. (1976). Illusory correlation in interpersonal perception: A cognitive basis of stereotypic judgments. *Journal of Experimental Social Psychology, 12,* 392–407.

Higgins, E. T. (1996). Knowledge activation: Accessibility, applicability, and salience. In E. T. Higgins & A. W. Kruglanski (Eds.), *Social psychology: Handbook of basic principles* (pp. 133–168). New York: Guilford Press.

Higgins, E. T., Rholes, W. S., & Jones, C. R. (1977). Category accessibility and impression formation. *Journal of Experimental Social Psychology, 13,* 141–154.

Johnston, L., & Hewstone, M. (1992). Cognitive models of stereotype change (3): Subtyping and the perceived typicality of disconfirming group members. *Journal of Experimental Social Psychology, 28,* 360–386.

Karpinski, A., & Hilton, J. L. (2001). Attitudes and the implicit association test. *Journal of Personality and Social Psychology, 81,* 774–788.

Kawakami, K., Dovidio, J. F., Moll, J., Hermsen, S., & Russin, A. (2000). Just say no (to stereotyping): Effects of training in the negation of stereotypic associations on stereotype activation. *Journal of Personality and Social Psychology, 78,* 871–888.

Kelly, A. E., & Kahn, J. H. (1994). Effects of suppression of personal intrusive thoughts. *Journal of Personality and Social Psychology, 66,* 998–1006.

Kohlberg, L. (1976). Moral stages and moralization: The cognitive-developmental approach. In T. Lickona (Ed.), *Moral development and behavior* (pp. 31–53). New York: Holt, Rinehart & Winston.

Krull, D. S. (1993). Does the grist change the mill? The effect of the perceiver's inferential goal on the process of social inference. *Personality and Social Psychology Bulletin, 19,* 340–348.

Kunda, Z., & Oleson, K. C. (1995). Maintaining stereotypes in the face of disconfirmation: Constructing grounds for subtyping deviants. *Journal of Personality and Social Psychology, 68,* 565–579.

Kunda, Z., & Oleson, K. C. (1997). When exceptions prove the rule: How extremity of deviance determines the impact of deviant examples on stereotypes. *Journal of Personality and Social Psychology, 72,* 965–979.

Macrae, C. N., Bodenhausen, G. V., & Milne, A. B. (1995). The dissection of selection in person perception: Inhibitory processes in social stereotyping. *Journal of Personality and Social Psychology, 69*(3), 397–407.

Macrae, C. N., Bodenhausen, G. V., Milne, A. B., & Jetten, J. (1994). Out of mind but back in sight: Stereotypes on the rebound. *Journal of Personality and Social Psychology, 67,* 808–817.

Macrae, C. N., Bodenhausen, G. V., Milne, A. B., Thorn, T. M. J., & Castelli, L. (1997). On the activation of social stereotypes: The moderating role of processing objectives. *Journal of Experimental Social Psychology, 33,* 471–489.

Macrae, C. N., Milne, A. B., & Bodenhausen, G. V. (1994). Stereotypes as energy-saving devices: A peek inside the cognitive toolbox. *Journal of Personality and Social Psychology, 66,* 37–47.

Martin, L. L. (1986). Set/reset: Use and disuse of concepts in impression formation. *Journal of Personality and Social Psychology, 51,* 493–504.

McConnell, A. R., Sherman, S. J., & Hamilton, D. L. (1994). Illusory correlation in the perception of groups: An extension of the distinctiveness-based account. *Journal of Personality and Social Psychology, 67,* 414–429.

Monteith, M. J., Spicer, C. V., & Tooman, G. D. (1998). Consequences of stereotype suppression: Stereotypes on AND not on the rebound. *Journal of Experimental Social Psychology, 34*, 355–377.

Monteith, M. J., Voils, C. I., & Ashburn-Nardo, L. (2001). Taking a look underground: Detecting, interpreting, and reacting to implicit racial biases. *Social Cognition, 19*, 395–417.

Moskowitz, G. B., Gollwitzer, P. M., Wasel, W., & Schaal, B. (1999). Preconscious control of stereotype activation through chronic egalitarian goals. *Journal of Personality and Social Psychology, 77*, 167–184.

Moskowitz, G. B., Salomon, A. R., & Taylor, C. M. (2000). Preconsciously controlling stereotyping: Implicitly activated egalitarian goals prevent the activation of stereotypes. *Social Cognition, 18*, 151–177.

Moskowitz, G. B., & Skurnik, I. W. (1999). Contrast effects as determined by the type of prime: Trait versus exemplar primes initiate processing strategies that differ in how accessible constructs are used. *Journal of Personality and Social Psychology, 76*, 911–927.

Neuberg, S. L., & Fiske, S. T. (1987). Motivational influences on impression formation: Outcome dependency, accuracy-driven attention, and individuating processes. *Journal of Personality and Social Psychology, 53*, 431–444.

Nisbett, R. E., & Wilson, T. D. (1977). Telling more than we can know: Verbal reports on mental processes. *Psychological Review, 84*, 231–259.

Piaget, J. (1932). *The moral judgment of the child.* New York: Harcourt, Brace.

Regan, D. T., & Totten, J. (1975). Empathy and attribution: Turning observers into actors. *Journal of Personality and Social Psychology, 32*, 850–856.

Rothbart, M., Sriram, N., & Davis-Stitt, C. (1996). The retrieval of typical and atypical category members. *Journal of Experimental Social Psychology, 32*, 309–336.

Schacter, D. L. (1994). Priming and multiple memory system: Perceptual mechanisms of implicit memory. In D. L. Schacter & E. Tulving (Eds.), *Memory systems* (pp. 233–268). Cambridge, MA: MIT Press.

Skurnik, I. W. (1998). *Metacognition and the illusion of truth.* Unpublished doctoral dissertation, Princeton University.

Smith, E. R., & Henry, S. (1996). An in-group becomes part of the self: Response time evidence. *Personality and Social Psychology Bulletin, 22*, 635–642.

Stapel, D. A., Koomen, W., & van der Plight, J. (1997). Categories of category accessibility: The impact of trait concept versus exemplar priming on person judgments. *Journal of Experimental Social Psychology, 33*, 47–76.

Stotland, E. (1969). Exploratory studies in empathy. In L. Berkowitz (Ed.), *Advances in experimental social psychology* (Vol. 4, pp. 271–313). San Diego, CA: Academic Press.

Uleman, J. S., & Moskowitz, G. B. (1994). Unintended effects of goals on unintended inferences. *Journal of Personality and Social Psychology, 66*, 490–501.

von Hippel, W., Sekaquaptewa, D., & Vargas, P. (1997). The linguistic intergroup bias as an implicit indicator of prejudice. *Journal of Experimental Social Psychology, 33*, 490–509.

Wegner, D. M. (1994). Ironic processes of mental control. *Psychological Review, 101*, 34–52.

Wegner, D. M., & Erber, R. (1992). The hyperaccessibility of suppressed thoughts. *Journal of Personality and Social Psychology, 63,* 903–912.

Wegner, D. M., Schneider, D. J., Carter, S. R., & White, T. L. (1987). Paradoxical effects of thought suppression. *Journal of Personality and Social Psychology, 53,* 5–13.

Wittenbrink, B., Judd, C. M., & Park, B. (1997). Evidence for racial prejudice at the implicit level and its relationship with questionnaire measures. *Journal of Personality and Social Psychology, 72,* 262–274.

Wittenbrink, B., Judd, C. M., & Park, B. (2001). Spontaneous prejudice in context: Variability in automatically activated attitudes. *Journal of Personality and Social Psychology, 81*(5), 815–827.

Wright, S. C., Aron, A., McLaughlin-Volpe, T., & Ropp, S. A. (1997). The extended contact effect: Knowledge of cross-group friendships and prejudice. *Journal of Personality and Social Psychology, 73,* 73–90.

Wright, S. C., Aron, A., & Trop, L. R. (2002). Including others (and groups) in the self: Self-expansion and intergroup relations. In J. P. Forgas & K. D. Williams (Eds.), *The social self: Cognitive, interpersonal, and intergroup perspective* (pp. 343–363). Philadelphia: Psychology Press.

18

Responding to the Social World

Attributions and Stereotype-Based Judgments

Lucy Johnston and Lynden Miles

CONTENTS

INTRODUCTION

This chapter considers recent research that has investigated how social perceivers respond to stereotype-relevant information. Past research on stereotype change[1] has focused solely on stereotype-inconsistent information and the extent to which perceivers integrate such information into their preexisting beliefs about a target group. In addition to reviewing this research, this chapter describes research that has investigated the impact of stereotype-consistent information on perceptions of the target group. Indeed, a major argument put forward in the chapter is that greater attention should be paid to perceivers' responses to stereotype-consistent information as a potential means of moderating stereotype-based judgments. The presented research considered both direct and indirect measures of the impact of stereotype-relevant information. The direct measures used were stereotype-based ratings of the target group. The indirect measures used related to measurement of the attributions that perceivers offered

---

[1] Elsewhere we argue that evidence for change in stereotyping research is weak (Johnston & Macrae, 2002) and hence will refer to stereotype moderation rather than stereotype change throughout this chapter.

Please address correspondence to Lucy Johnston, Department of Psychology, University of Canterbury, Private Bag 4800, Christchurch, New Zealand; e-mail: l.johnston@psyc.canterbury.ac.nz

for stereotype-relevant information. We believe that such indirect measures provide important insight into the reaction of social perceivers to stereotype-relevant information that may not be captured by direct measures alone.

The assumption of a strong association between negative stereotypes and discrimination (Dovidio, Brigham, Johnson, & Gaertner, 1996) has led both researchers and social legislators to pursue attempts to change social stereotypes. Guided by Allport's (1954) contact hypothesis, it has been assumed that providing perceivers with additional information about target groups will increase the accuracy of their beliefs about these groups and hence reduce their reliance on inaccurate group-based stereotypes. Experimental attempts to moderate social stereotypes have, accordingly, involved presenting perceivers with information, including stereotype-inconsistent information, about the target group and then asking them to judge the group on stereotype-based dimensions. This approach has been shown to lead to stereotype moderation under certain conditions (see Hewstone, 1994, for a comprehensive review). A number of processes by which perceivers maintain their stereotypes, even in the face of inconsistent information, have also, however, been identified, suggesting that the maintenance of stereotypic beliefs is not simply a function of lack of information about a target group. Indeed, research has demonstrated that perceivers are prepared to devote cognitive resources to stereotype maintenance (Yzerbyt, Coull, & Rocher, 1999).

One prevalent means by which the impact of inconsistent information is reduced is by isolation, or exclusion, of disconfirming group exemplars. If individuals displaying stereotype-inconsistent behavior can be considered to be atypical exemplars of the target group, they are subtyped (Brewer, Dull, & Lui, 1981; Johnston & Hewstone, 1992; Kunda & Oleson, 1995, 1997). That is, they are considered to be a distinct subcategory of the superordinate target group. A link between the subordinate and superordinate groups is acknowledged, but members of the subtype are considered to possess certain stereotype-inconsistent characteristics in addition to the stereotype-consistent characteristics that they share with the superordinate group members. Although the subtyped exemplars are judged in a less stereotype-based manner as a consequence of their stereotype-inconsistent behavior, this reduction in stereotyping is not generalized beyond the subcategory to the group as a whole. Subtyping can explain why extremely disconfirming exemplars (e.g., Margaret Thatcher, Jesse Jackson) have little impact on group-based beliefs (of women and African Americans, respectively). However, many mildly disconfirming group exemplars, who cannot be readily subtyped, are encountered in everyday situations. How is it that perceivers maintain their stereotype-based beliefs in the presence of such exemplars displaying stereotype-inconsistent behaviors?

ATTRIBUTIONS AND STEREOTYPE MODERATION

One possible process through which perceivers can maintain their stereotype-based beliefs in the face of inconsistent information is through the attributions made for that information. Compared to stereotype-consistent or expected behaviors, unexpected or inconsistent behaviors are more likely to result in spontaneous attribution or explanation by perceivers (Hastie, 1984; see also von Hippel, Vargas, & Sekaquaptewa, this volume). Hewstone (1989) proposed an attributional model of stereotype change that predicted that stereotype-inconsistent information would lead to moderation of group-based beliefs only if that behavior was attributed to stable dispositional factors of a typical group exemplar. An internal stable attribution indicates that the stereotypically inconsistent act is representative of the actor's usual behavior, leading to the actor's being perceived in a nonstereotypic manner (Krueger & Rothbart, 1988; Locksley, Borgida, Brekke, & Hepburn, 1980). Because the actor is also perceived to be a typical group exemplar, his or her behavior is considered to be representative of the target group. Hence, this nonstereotypic perception of the target individual should generalize to the group as a whole, resulting in stereotype moderation. In contrast, if the target is considered to be an atypical group member, generalization would not occur, as his or her behavior is not considered to be representative of that of other group members, and hence the exemplar could be subtyped. In a similar manner, a situational attribution for inconsistent behavior also leads to the prediction of no generalization to group-based perceptions, as the behavior is not considered to be predictive of the target's usual behavior (Jackson, Sullivan, & Hodge, 1993). Wilder, Simon, and Faith (1996) provided empirical support for Hewstone's model. Participants were presented with a stereotype-inconsistent behavior for which they were provided with either a situational or a dispositional attribution. Subsequent judgments of the target group were less stereotype-based than those of control no-information participants only when the exemplar was considered to be a typical group member and the behavior had been attributed to dispositional causes. Judgments of the group did not differ from baseline when the inconsistent behavior was attributed to situational causes. Attributing stereotype-inconsistent behavior to dispositional causes can then result in moderation of stereotype-based beliefs. However, stereotype-inconsistent behavior is usually attributed to situational rather than dispositional factors (Bodenhausen & Wyer, 1985; Duncan, 1976; Evett, Devine, Hirt, & Price, 1994; Macrae & Shepherd, 1989), attributions that do not lead to revision of stereotype-based judgments (Wilder et al., 1996).

Rather than provide participants with attributions for a stereotype-inconsistent behavior, in two experiments we asked them to rate the extent to which the behavior was caused by both situational and dispositional factors. Participants then evaluated the individual target and the stereotyped group on stereotype-based dimensions (Johnston, Bristow, & Love, 2000, Exps. 2 and 3). Consistent with past research (Bodenhausen & Wyer, 1985; Duncan, 1976; Evett et al., 1994; Macrae & Shepherd, 1989), the stereotype-inconsistent behavior was attributed more strongly to situational than to dispositional factors, although some participants (approximately 30%) did show the opposite pattern, attributing the inconsistent behavior more strongly to dispositional than to situational factors. This finding is discussed in more detail later. The stereotype-inconsistent behavior resulted in the target individual being evaluated in less stereotype-based terms, but this did not generalize to the group as a whole. Consistent with the stronger attribution to situational causes, there was no reduction in stereotype-based judgments of the target group relative to control no-information participants. In order to investigate further the relationship between the attributions made for the target's behavior and stereotype-based ratings, an attribution index was calculated for each participant. Ratings for dispositional causes were subtracted from those for situational causes; a positive index indicates stronger situational than dispositional attributions and a negative index stronger dispositional than situational attributions (Wittenbrink, Gist, & Hilton, 1997). Correlations were computed between the attribution index and stereotype-based ratings of both the target individual and the group as a whole. There was only one significant correlation, between the index and ratings of the target in Experiment 3. The higher the index (relatively stronger situational ratings), the more strongly the target was evaluated in stereotype-based terms. There was no correlation between the attribution index and judgments of the group, or between judgments of the target individual and the group, however; less stereotype-based judgments of the target were not generalized to judgments of the group as a whole. Although attributing stereotype-inconsistent behavior to dispositional causes can lead to stereotype moderation (Wilder et al., 1996), such attributions, and hence stereotype moderation, are rare. Indeed, perceivers may use situational attributions to reduce the impact of stereotype-inconsistent information on preexisting group-based beliefs.

The research discussed this far, and that reviewed by Hewstone (1994), has all involved participants being presented with a prepackaged set of information, including stereotype-inconsistent information, about members of the target group. This experimental approach allows researchers to investigate the impact of inconsistent information on perceivers' judgments of the group but, at the same time, it fails to capture an important feature of the social perceiver. Social perceivers are, by nature, active gatherers, not passive recipients, of information (Yzerbyt & Leyens, 1991). Using information-seeking methods (e.g., consulting a bulletin board, asking questions) allows perceivers to control, to some extent, the nature and amount of information they receive about members of a target group while still allowing some experimental control over the information received by participants. Using such methods, we have demonstrated that perceivers show a bias toward stereotype-consistent information and avoid stereotype-inconsistent information (Johnston, 1996; Johnston & Macrae, 1994). In addition, the impact of stereotype-inconsistent information received under such situations is reduced relative to traditional information-given research. Perceivers who received stereotype-inconsistent information under information-gathering conditions did not moderate their stereotype-based judgments relative to controls. Perceivers who received the same amount of stereotype-inconsistent information under information-given conditions, however, did show stereotype moderation. Perceivers in the information-gathering conditions did attend to the inconsistent information, but its impact was reduced (Johnston, 1996). In more realistic information-gathering situations, therefore, perceivers may avoid inconsistent information, and the impact of any such information may be less than in traditional research (Hewstone, 1989). Caution needs to be exercised, then, in generalizing findings of stereotype moderation from the research laboratory.

The attention of researchers has, understandably, focused on the impact of stereotype-inconsistent information on stereotype-based beliefs. In doing so, however, we argue that an intriguing counterintuitive alternative route to stereotype moderation has been ignored. Perceivers prefer to attend to stereotype-consistent information that is easy to process and to integrate into preexisting beliefs (Johnston, 1996; Johnston & Macrae, 1994). Such behavior is typically attributed to internal, stable factors (Bodenhausen & Wyer, 1985; Duncan, 1976; Evett et al., 1994; Macrae & Shepherd, 1989), implying generalization of the behavior across both time and target group member, and hence stereotype maintenance. In the same way that inconsistent information is attributed to dispositional factors in order to moderate stereotype-based beliefs (Wilder et al., 1996), one can ask whether attributing consistent information to situational rather than dispositional factors might lead to moderation of group-based beliefs. If perceivers believe that individuals perform stereotype-consistent behaviors because of situational pressures rather than personal characteristics, they may be less likely to endorse stereotypic beliefs about the target group to which those individuals belong. Such an argument for the impact of situational factors may be easy to sustain. Consider, for example, sex-based stereotypic beliefs. Social role theory (Eagly, 1987; Eagly & Steffen, 1984) argues that sex-based stereotypes developed as a consequence of an unequal distribution of men and women in different social roles, not as a consequence of fundamental differences between men and women. That is, sex-based perceptions are argued to be the result of situational, or role, constraints rather than dispositional factors. Making perceivers aware of the situational causes of stereotypic behavior may reduce stereotype-based perceptions, just as the reversal of roles sees the disappearance of gender-based stereotypes (Eagly & Wood, 1982).

In three experiments, we investigated the relationship between attributions made for stereotype-consistent information and stereotype-based judgments (Johnston et al., 2000). In the first experiment, participants were provided with either a dispositional or a situational attribution for a target's stereotype-consistent behavior and were asked to judge both the target and the group as a whole on stereotype-based dimensions. When the stereotypic behavior was attributed to internal causes, there was no moderation of the stereotype-based judgments of either the individual target or the group relative to control participants. Those participants given a situational attribution for the target behavior, however, rated the target group in less stereotype-based terms than did the baseline participants. Hence, as predicted, making participants aware of situational constraints on the stereotypic behavior reduced the strength of stereotype-based judgments of the target group.

Experiment 1 demonstrated that situational attributions for stereotype-consistent information can lead to stereotype moderation. In two subsequent experiments, each using a different group and target behavior, participants were asked to generate attributions rather then being provided with them. Participants rated the extent to which stereotype-consistent behavior was a result of both situational and dispositional factors prior to evaluating the target and group on stereotype-based dimensions.[2] The stereotype-consistent behavior was, in both experiments, attributed more strongly to dispositional than to situational factors, a pattern of attributions consistent with past research (Bodenhausen & Wyer, 1985; Duncan, 1976; Evett et al., 1994; Macrae & Shepherd, 1989) and with stereotype maintenance. In neither study was there moderation of the group-based stereotype relative to baseline participants. These results parallel those seen for the stereotype-inconsistent behavior. Although attributing stereotype-consistent behavior to situational causes may lead to stereotype moderation, such attributions, and consequently stereotype moderation, did not occur when participants provided the attributions for the target behavior themselves. As with the inconsistent behavior, a small number of participants (approximately 10%) did show the opposite pattern, attributing the stereotype-consistent behavior more strongly to situational than dispositional factors.

As for the inconsistent behavior, an attribution index was calculated for each participant, and correlations between the attribution index and

---

[2] Experiments 2 and 3 reported here are the same as those discussed earlier in relation to the impact of stereotype-inconsistent information. In each experiment, half of the participants received a stereotype-consistent and half a stereotype-inconsistent scenario. These scenarios were analyzed together but are reported separately here for clarity.

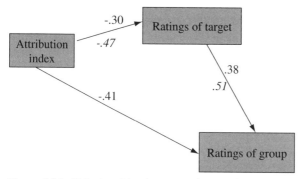

Figure 18.1. Relationships between the attribution index and ratings of the target individual and group after presentation of a stereotype-consistent scenario. Significant beta weights only are shown. Numbers in roman – Experiment 2; numbers in italics – Experiment 3. (Adapted from Johnston, Bristow, & Love, 2000.)

stereotype-based ratings of the target individual and group were computed. In contrast to the findings for the stereotype-inconsistent behavior, this analysis revealed relationships between the attribution index and stereotype-based judgments of both the target individual and the group, as shown in Figure 18.1. In Experiment 2 there were significant correlations between the attribution index and ratings of both the target individual and the group. The more strongly the behavior was attributed to situational relative to dispositional factors (higher attributional index), the less stereotypic both the individual and the group were perceived to be. In addition, there was generalization from stereotype-based ratings of the individual to those of the group. In Experiment 3 there was a significant correlation between the attribution index and ratings of the individual but not ratings of the group as a whole. There was, however, strong generalization from stereotype-based ratings of the individual to those of the group. For stereotype-consistent behavior, therefore, greater recognition of the situational constraints on stereotypic behavior (a higher attribution index) was related to less stereotype-based ratings. Stereotype moderation was not dependent on higher absolute situational than dispositional attributions. No parallel relationship between the attributional index and stereotype-based ratings was evident for the stereotype-inconsistent behavior. Hence, moderating stereotype-based beliefs through the presentation of stereotype-consistent information may be more effective than through the presentation of inconsistent information. Given perceivers' preference for stereotype-consistent information in information-gathering situations, this possible opportunity for stereotype moderation warrants further research attention.

For both stereotype-consistent and -inconsistent behaviors there was a small proportion of participants who showed the *opposite* pattern of attributions to those expected. That is, some perceivers attributed inconsistent behavior more strongly to dispositional than to situational factors or consistent behavior more strongly to situational than to dispositional factors. Although there were too few individuals in these groups to provide sufficient power for statistical analyses, two interesting trends were evident. First, a greater proportion of participants showed this opposite pattern of attributions for inconsistent than for consistent behavior. This trend is consistent with the general tendency of perceivers to attribute the behavior of others to internal causes (Ross, 1977). Second, the impact of making the opposite pattern of attributions appeared to differ for stereotype-consistent and -inconsistent behaviors. For those who made the opposite pattern of attributions for an inconsistent behavior, mean stereotype-based ratings of the target group did not show stereotype moderation relative to control participants. The impact of the attributional pattern for stereotype-inconsistent information was again minimal. For those who made the opposite pattern of attributions for a consistent behavior, however, mean ratings of the target group were less stereotype-based than those of baseline control participants. Again, the possible role of consistent information in stereotype moderation is highlighted.

PREJUDICE, ATTRIBUTIONS, AND STEREOTYPE MODERATION

The presence of individuals who made the opposite pattern of attributions for stereotype-based behavior raises the question of whether certain characteristics of the social perceiver are associated with the non-expected pattern of attributions for stereotype-relevant information and under what conditions. The remainder of this chapter describes ongoing research in our labs that addresses this question. There has been little consideration of the possible influence of individual differences on stereotype moderation. Monteith, Zuwerink, and Devine (1994) suggested that stereotype change strategies were, as a consequence, often ineffective because they were not targeted appropriately for their specific audiences. Understanding the influence of individual differences on perceivers' responses to stereotype-relevant information may enable the development of more effective stereotype-change strategies targeted at specific perceivers. An intuitively obvious individual difference factor to consider in this context is prejudice level. High- and low-prejudiced individuals differ in the extent to which they endorse and use stereotypes (e.g., Devine, 1989) and in their reactions to their own stereotype use (Devine, Monteith, Zuwerink, & Elliot, 1991). Low-prejudiced individuals strive against stereotype use and feel guilt if they do (inadvertently) use stereotypes, whereas high-prejudiced individuals do not experience negative self-focused emotions as a consequence of stereotype use (Devine et al., 1991). Low-prejudiced individuals are motivated to avoid stereotype use under all conditions.

High-prejudiced individuals, on the other hand, are happy to use stereo-types unless doing so has negative consequences such as social disap-proval (Plant & Devine, 1998). It would seem reasonable to suggest that low- and high-prejudiced individuals may display different patterns of attributions for stereotype-related behaviors. High-prejudiced individu-als are motivated to maintain stereotypes, and hence we predicted that they would display a pattern of attributions consistent with stereotype maintenance. In comparison, low-prejudiced individuals are motivated to avoid stereotype use, and hence we predicted that they would display a pattern of attributions consistent with stereotype moderation. That is, we hypothesized that those individuals making an opposite pattern of attri-butions, attributions consistent with stereotype moderation, would have lower prejudice toward the target group than those showing the usual pat-tern of attributions, attributions consistent with stereotype maintenance.

Some recent research has offered support for the prediction that high- and low-prejudiced individuals would make different attributions for stereotype-consistent and -inconsistent behavior. Sherman, Stroessner, and Azam (2002; Exp. 2) showed that high- but not low-prejudiced individu-als exhibited the usual pattern of attributions for the behaviors of a single target. High-prejudiced participants attributed stereotype-consistent be-haviors to internal causes and inconsistent behaviors to external causes, whereas low-prejudiced individuals showed no differential pattern of at-tributions for consistent and inconsistent behaviors. Low-prejudiced in-dividuals were equally likely to attribute target behaviors to internal and external causes. The stereotypicality of judgments of the target individual did not, however, differ as a function of the pattern of attributions made. Wyer (2000) similarly found differences in the attributional pattern be-tween high- and low-prejudiced individuals. Low-prejudiced individuals made relatively fewer internal attributions for consistent than inconsis-tent behaviors, which matches our opposite pattern of attributions. High-prejudiced individuals showed no differences in the attributions they made for consistent and inconsistent behaviors except under high time pressure conditions, when they did show a usual pattern of attributions consis-tent with stereotype maintenance. Wyer did not include any measures of stereotype-based judgments in her studies, so the relationship between pattern of attributions and stereotype-based judgments was not examined. Our research aimed to extend the findings of Wyer (2000) and Sherman et al. (2000). The attributions made for stereotype-consistent and -inconsistent behaviors and the stereotype-based judgments of the target group by high- and low-prejudiced individuals, as well as the relationship between the at-tributions made and the extent of the stereotype-based judgments, were examined.

The first two experiments were the same, except for the use of differ-ent attribution measures. In each experiment, participants first completed a series of affective thermometers ("very negative"–"very positive") for various social groups including, importantly, the target group for this research. Affective reaction was taken as a measure of feeling, or prejudice, toward the group, higher affective thermometer scores being indicative of lower prejudice (possible range: -100 to $+100$). Participants were then presented with a single scenario describing either a stereotype-consistent or -inconsistent behavior performed by a member of a stereotyped group. In Experiment 1, participants rated the extent to which the behavior was due to both situational and dispositional factors and rated the target group on a number of stereotype-based dimensions. As in the previous experiments, most participants showed a usual pattern of attributions, attributing stereotype-consistent behavior more strongly to dispositional factors and stereotype-inconsistent behavior more strongly to situational factors. Some participants (16%) did show the opposite pattern of attributions. To test our prediction that these participants would be lower in prejudice than those who showed the usual pattern of attributions, we compared the affective thermometer scores of those making the usual and the opposite pattern of attributions for both consistent and inconsistent information. For the inconsistent information there was no difference in affective thermometer scores as a function of attribution pattern ($M = 60.0$ and 61.0), but for the consistent behavior the affective thermometer scores of those making the opposite pattern of attributions were higher (less prejudiced) than for those making the usual pattern ($M = 71.0$ and 60.0); see Figure 18.2. Interestingly, there was no direct relationship between prejudice level (affective thermometer scores) and stereotype-based ratings (see also von Hippel et al., this volume), but there was an effect of attribution pattern on stereotypic ratings. For the inconsistent behavior, trait ratings did not differ as a function of attribution pattern ($M = 4.27$ and 4.62 for those making the usual and opposite attributions, respectively; control $= 3.96$), but for the consistent behavior the trait ratings made by those showing the opposite pattern of attributions were lower (less stereotype-based) than those made by those showing the usual pattern, and also lower than those of the control no-information group ($M = 3.50$ vs. 3.81 and 3.96). Stereotype-based judgments are shown in Figure 18.3.

Experiment 2 replaced the attributional ratings used in Experiment 1 with a sentence completion task (Hastie, 1984). For the critical scenario, participants were instructed to complete a sentence stem, beginning with the target's name, in any way they wished (see also Chartrand & Jefferis, this volume; von Hippel et al., this volume). The content of these completions was coded for the presence of internal or external attributions for the target behavior. Unlike the attribution ratings, the sentence completion task does not force participants to consider the possible impact of both situational and dispositional factors on a given behavior. Only four (6%) participants did not offer an attribution for the target behavior in their sentence completion.

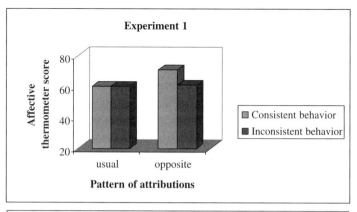

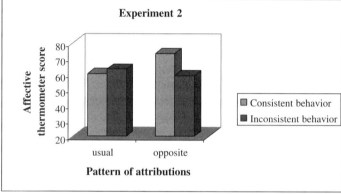

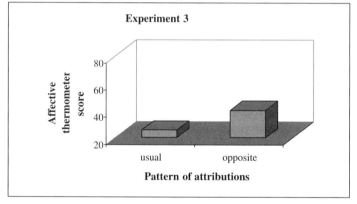

Figure 18.2. Affective thermometer scores as a function of pattern of attributions and target behavior.

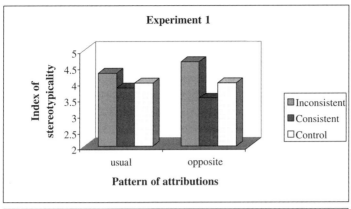

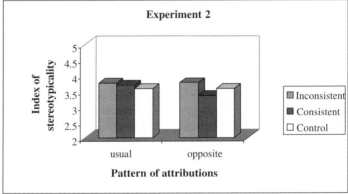

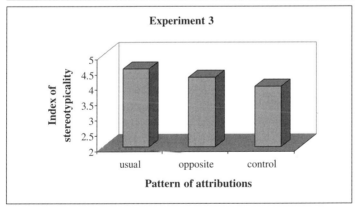

Figure 18.3. Stereotype-based ratings as a function of pattern of attributions and target behavior.

Of those who did give an explanation, three-quarters offered an internal attribution. Such a bias toward internal attributions for the behavior of others is consistent with previous research on the fundamental attribution error (Ross, 1977). The implications of internal attributions differ for consistent and inconsistent behaviors, of course; an internal attribution for a consistent behavior is consistent with stereotype maintenance, but that of an inconsistent behavior is consistent with stereotype moderation. A comparison of the affective thermometer scores as a function of attribution revealed little difference in affective scores for those making usual (external) and opposite (internal) attributions for the inconsistent behavior ($M = 63.1$ vs. 58.9). For the consistent behavior, however, those making the opposite (external) attribution felt more positively toward the group than those who offered a usual (internal) explanation ($M = 73.3$ vs. 60.2); see Figure 18.2. The prediction that those who made the opposite pattern of attributions would be less prejudiced toward the target group was supported only when attributions for a stereotype-consistent behavior were being considered, as in Experiment 1. Again as in Experiment 1, there was no direct effect of prejudice level on stereotype-based judgments of the target group, but there was an effect of attribution pattern on trait ratings. For the inconsistent behavior, there was no difference between trait ratings as a function of pattern of attributions made and no difference from control group ratings ($M = 3.77, 3.76,$ and 3.58). For the consistent behavior, however, those who made the opposite pattern of attributions again made less stereotype-based judgments of the target group than did those who made the usual attributions or than the control group ($M = 3.35$ vs. 3.69 and 3.58); see Figure 18.3.

Across both experiments there was an effect of prejudice level, or affective reaction to the target group, on the attributions made for a stereotype-consistent but not a stereotype-inconsistent behavior. There was no direct relationship between affective reaction and stereotype-based judgments, but there was an effect of attribution pattern on stereotype-based judgments, although again only for stereotype-consistent behavior. These findings offer some support for the hypothesis that those perceivers who make opposite attributions for stereotype-relevant behavior are low in prejudice toward the target group. The findings also support our previous suggestion that the possible role of reactions to stereotype-consistent information in moderating social stereotypes deserves further research attention.

Experiments 1 and 2 involved each participant considering only a single target behavior, either a stereotype-consistent or -inconsistent behavior. In the final experiment in this series, each participant was presented with both stereotype-consistent and -inconsistent scenarios such that an individual-based measure of attributional pattern could be calculated. In Experiment 3 the critical scenarios each described a different member of the same target group. Participants completed an affective thermometer measure of prejudice, a sentence completion task for each critical scenario, and rated the target group as a whole on a number of stereotype-based dimensions. An index of attributional pattern (Wyer, 2000) was calculated for each participant by subtracting the proportion of internal attributions for inconsistent items from that for consistent items. A score of zero denotes equal use of dispositional attributions for consistent and inconsistent behaviors, a positive score greater use of internal attributions for consistent behavior (i.e., the usual pattern of attributions), and a negative score greater use of internal attributions for inconsistent behavior (i.e., the opposite pattern of attributions). Comparison of the affective thermometer scores for those who made opposite and usual attributions revealed a higher score (less prejudice) for those making the opposite pattern of attributions ($M = 40.3$ vs. 25.8); see Figure 18.2. There was no direct relationship between affect scores and stereotype-based judgments of the target group. There was, however, an effect of attributional pattern on stereotype-based judgments. Those who made the opposite pattern of attributions made less stereotype-based judgments of the target group than did those who made the usual pattern of attributions ($M = 4.25$ vs. 4.52; control $= 3.96$); see Figure 18.3.

Our experiments investigating the association between attributions made for stereotype-relevant behaviors and stereotype-based judgments have revealed a number of patterns that facilitate understanding of stereotype moderation. In those experiments in which participants were asked to rate the extent to which a target's behavior was due to both dispositional and situational factors (Exp. 1; Johnston et al., 2000, Exps. 2 and 3), a pattern of attributions similar to that found in previous research was seen. Stereotype-consistent behavior was attributed more strongly to dispositional than to situational factors, and stereotype-inconsistent behavior was attributed more strongly to situational than to dispositional factors (Bodenhausen & Wyer, 1985; Duncan, 1976; Evett et al., 1994; Macrae & Shepherd, 1989). Such patterns of attribution are consistent with stereotype maintenance, which was seen. For stereotype-consistent behavior, however, there was a relationship between the relative strength of the situational and dispositional attributions and the strength of stereotype-based judgments, indicative of some moderation of stereotype-based beliefs. A small proportion of participants did show an opposite pattern of attributions. For stereotype-consistent target behaviors, there was an association between the attributions made and both prejudice level, as measured by an affective thermometer, and stereotype-based judgments. The opposite pattern of attributions was associated only with moderation of stereotype-based judgments, relative to baseline controls, after stereotype-consistent but not -inconsistent behavior was attributed to opposite causes.

When the sentence completion task (Hastie, 1984), a less directive measure of attributions that does not necessitate perceivers explicitly considering both situational and dispositional causes for an event, was used (Exps. 2

and 3), there was a strong tendency to provide dispositional explanations for all target behaviors, both stereotype-consistent and -inconsistent (Ross, 1977). It is interesting to note that the strong dominance of situational causes for inconsistent behavior is not seen using this less directive measure of attribution. When forced to consider the impact of situational factors on an inconsistent behavior, perceivers considered this to be a major influence, but when not forced to consider their influence, their impact was not highlighted. Making dispositional attributions for stereotype-inconsistent information was previously associated with stereotype moderation (Hewstone, 1989; Wilder et al., 1996). In our experiments, however, participants did not show stereotype moderation after making dispositional attributions for stereotype-inconsistent behavior. Throughout our research, the association between attributions and stereotype-based judgments has been weak or nonexistent for stereotype-inconsistent behavior but far more evident for stereotype-consistent behavior. Individuals are motivated to maintain their stereotypic beliefs and will often devote much effort to so doing (Yzerbyt et al., 1999). Accordingly, stereotype moderation will not occur readily. It is possible that the tendency to make dispositional attributions for inconsistent behavior in more naturalistic settings has weakened the relationship between this opposite attribution and stereotype moderation. Situational attributions for consistent behavior are less frequent and were shown to be associated both with lower prejudice and with stereotype moderation. Therefore, as we suggested previously, greater attention needs to be paid in the research literature to the link between stereotype-consistent information and stereotype moderation. Our research has focused on whether prejudice level influences the attributions made for stereotype-related behaviors and whether these attributions, in turn, influence stereotype-based judgments. Across a number of experiments, a link has been established between attributional judgments and stereotype-based judgments, especially when considering stereotype-consistent behaviors. Accordingly, future research needs to consider whether perceivers can be encouraged, through situational factors, to make an opposite pattern of attributions and whether this, in turn, leads to stereotype moderation.

PREJUDICE AND STEREOTYPE MODERATION

Other research in our labs has also considered the impact of stereotype-inconsistent information on stereotype-based judgments as a function of the perceiver's prejudice level, but without considering the attributions made for the inconsistent information (Johnston, 1998). The presentation of stereotype-inconsistent information can provide perceivers with information about the target group that can be integrated with preexisting beliefs to provide a more accurate perception of the target group. The presentation of inconsistent information can also provide perceivers with a cue to the social norms governing stereotype use in the present situation (Plant & Devine, 1998). Low-prejudiced individuals, motivated to avoid prejudice and the use of stereotypes (Devine et al., 1991), are likely to attend to the content of the inconsistent information presented and to devote sufficient cognitive resources to integrate that information into their beliefs about the target group and hence moderate their stereotype beliefs, possibly as a consequence of making dispositional attributions for that inconsistent behavior. High-prejudiced individuals, motivated to avoid social sanctions and negative evaluations by others, may also attend to the presence of the inconsistent information but simply as a cue to avoid stereotype use in the present situation, not as a means by which to moderate their stereotype-based beliefs. These proposed differential responses to stereotype-inconsistent information lead to different predictions for the impact of such information. We predicted that low-prejudiced individuals would integrate inconsistent information into their preexisting beliefs about the target group, that is, would internalize the information, and hence moderate their stereotype-based judgments about that group. High-prejudiced individuals, we also predicted, would moderate their stereotype-based judgments, but through compliance with the prevailing social norms regarding stereotype use rather than through internalization of the inconsistent information.

How would such differences in response to inconsistent information be manifest? Participants in this research (Johnston, 1998) were classified as high or low habitual users of stereotypes using a diary task.[3] A total of 124 participants completed diary entries for a typical Friday night for a number of individuals from a variety of stereotyped groups. These diary entries were then coded for stereotypicality. Perceivers demonstrated high consistency of stereotypicality of the diary entries across targets; individuals who used stereotypes in describing one target also tended to use stereotypes in describing other targets. Accordingly, a mean stereotypicality score across targets was used to categorize participants as high ($n = 52$) or low ($n = 72$) stereotype users.

Experimental participants were presented with information, including stereotype-inconsistent information, about members of a specific target group. Participants then evaluated both a member of the target group and a member of two other stereotyped groups about which no specific information had been presented. If, as predicted, high stereotype users' responses are primarily a function of situational norms regarding stereotype

---

[3] Although stereotype use rather than prejudice level was used to categorize participants in this research, it is assumed that high and low users of stereotypes have similar motivations toward stereotype use, or nonuse, as high- and low-prejudiced individuals, respectively. Indeed, Devine (1989) suggested that the overt use of stereotypes differentiated between high- and low-prejudiced individuals.

use, then their use of stereotypes should decrease in the experimental situation where norms against stereotype use have been activated. Accordingly, experimental participants should be less stereotypic than control participants about all targets, regardless of whether or not specific inconsistent information was presented. Low stereotype users' responses are predicted to be primarily a function of the specific information provided. Hence, presentation of stereotype-inconsistent information about a specific target group should lead low users to conclude that their perceptions of this group are inaccurate and need to be adjusted through incorporation of the presented information. Accordingly, their evaluation of a member of this group will be less stereotype-based than that of control participants. In the absence of specific information about the other target groups, no differences between experimental and control participants in evaluations of members of these groups are predicted. Although aware of salient social norms, low users' responses are unlikely to be influenced by a norm not to use stereotypes given their own high motivation to avoid stereotype use. Control participants were also categorized as high or low stereotype users; differences at baseline between high and low users would render meaningless comparisons with noncategorized control participants. Control participants completed a filler task while experimental participants read about the target group.

All participants subsequently completed the second diary task, which included three diary entries, importantly including a member of the target group about which stereotype-inconsistent information had been presented. These diary entries were also coded for stereotypicality. Analysis of the second set of diary entries revealed a condition (control/experimental) by stereotype use (high/low) by target (schizophrenic/general practitioner/homosexual) interaction; see Figure 18.4.

For the high users, there were main effects of both condition and target. The diary entries from the experimental participants were less stereotypic than those from the control participants, and the mean stereotypicality of the diaries varied across targets. There was, however, no interaction between condition and target; the difference in stereotypicality ratings between the experimental and control participants was evident for each target, not just for the target about which specific stereotype-inconsistent information had been received. For low users, in contrast, there was a significant condition by target interaction. The only difference between the control and experimental participants was for the specific target about which stereotype-inconsistent information had been presented.

These results illustrate, as predicted, a differential impact of stereotype-inconsistent information as a function of perceivers' stereotype use. Both high and low users evaluated a target from a group about which inconsistent information had been previously presented less stereotypically than did matched controls. Differences were seen, however, in the generalization

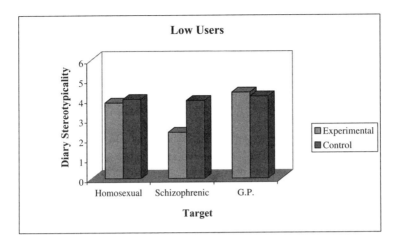

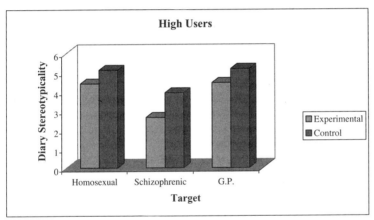

Figure 18.4. Stereotypicality of diary entries as a function of stereotype use, experimental condition, and target.

of this stereotype moderation across targets. High users showed less stereotype-based evaluations of all the targets relative to matched controls. Low users showed no differences between experimental and control participants in the reliance on stereotypes in evaluations of the additional targets from stereotyped groups about which no stereotype-inconsistent information had been presented. The differences between the high and low stereotype users are consistent with differences in the motivation of these perceivers to use, or not use, stereotypes (Plant & Devine, 1998). The reduction in stereotype-based judgments for all of the targets, relative to control participants, by the high users is consistent with compliance with external forces against stereotype use, such as a salient situational norm evoked by the experimental setup. Low users reduced their stereotype use only for the target from the group about which disconfirming information was presented, which is consistent with their being internally motivated not to use stereotypes in describing others and to be responsive to specific stereotype-relevant information. Given the motivation of low stereotype users to avoid stereotype use, it is not surprising that activation of a social norm against stereotype use had little impact on their judgments.

Neither reading time for the presented information nor a surprise recall test for the presented information differentiated between the high and low stereotype users, suggesting that the differences in judgment were not a consequence of differential processing of the stereotype-inconsistent information. Analysis of diary length did, however, differentiate between high and low users. Low users in the experimental condition wrote similar-length diary entries for those targets evaluated before and after the information was presented about one target group. High users in the experimental condition, however, wrote both shorter and less stereotypic diary entries after receiving the inconsistent information. In order to reduce their reliance on stereotypes in evaluating others after a norm against stereotype use was made salient, high users simply wrote less about the targets. If high users cannot employ stereotypes to describe others, it appears that they would rather not describe them at all. It should be noted, however, that shorter diary entries are not necessarily less stereotypic; low users in the experimental condition wrote shorter diary entries than those in the control condition, but these entries were not less stereotypic.

Both high and low stereotype users showed moderation of their stereotype-based judgments in response to the presentation of disconfirming information. The differential impact of disconfirming information on high and low users of stereotypes became apparent through the inclusion of targets from stereotyped groups other than the group about which disconfirming information had been presented. If, as in previous research, participants had only been asked to provide judgments of a target from the group about which disconfirming information had been presented, no differences between the high and low users would have been seen.

This research again demonstrated the importance of considering individual differences in the moderation of stereotype-based beliefs. It is interesting to note that these differential responses of high and low stereotype users were not due to differential processing of the presented information. High and low users attended equally to the stereotype-relevant information, but only the latter integrated this information into their group-based beliefs. However, the different processes underlying that moderation may have implications – for example, for the longevity of the moderation effects. In the present research, high users appeared to be responding under compliance with social norms, whereas low users were responding to the specific information presented. Accordingly, it would be predicted that the stereotype moderation effects reported would be longer-lasting for the low than for the high users. One consequence of our predictions would be greater perseverance of stereotype moderation across both time and situation for the low- than for the high-prejudiced individuals as a function of internalization versus compliance forces. In addition, if high users were simply suppressing stereotype use in their evaluation of others, as might be indicated by their shorter, less stereotype-based diary entries, then these individuals may be prone to rebound effects (Macrae, Bodenhausen, Milne, & Jetten, 1994) and greater use of stereotypes once the situational norms opposing stereotype use are removed.

CONCLUSIONS

The research described in this chapter has considered perceivers' responses to stereotype-relevant information as a function of both the type of information provided (stereotype-consistent versus stereotype-inconsistent) and the perceivers' affective reaction to the target group. Two general conclusions emerge from this research. The first is that stereotype-consistent information, a previously overlooked possibility for stereotype change, can in fact lead to moderation of stereotype-based beliefs. When attributing stereotypical behavior more strongly to situational rather than dispositional causes, perceivers made less stereotypical judgments of both individuals and groups. On the one hand, given that perceivers have an attentional preference for stereotypical information, this is a very promising finding with important implications for theorists, researchers, and policymakers alike. However, on the other hand, attributing stereotypical behavior to situational causes is uncommon among most perceivers giving such explanations for behavior. Further research is needed to investigate under what conditions perceivers can be induced to make such opposite attributions that facilitate the moderation of stereotype-based judgments. The second general conclusion is that perceivers' prejudice (affective reaction) toward a group affects the processing of stereotype-related information about that group, especially stereotype-consistent information. Individuals who were more highly prejudiced toward a given target group showed the usual, expected pattern of attributing stereotype-consistent behavior to dispositional causes. However, those low in prejudice showed the opposite pattern of attributions, explaining stereotypical behavior as being caused by the situation and thereby providing an avenue for stereotype moderation. Such stereotype moderation, relative to control participants, was indeed seen. This effect was not, interestingly, revealed in any direct relationship between prejudice and stereotype-based judgments, but rather was an indirect effect through the attributions made for the target behavior. Those who made situational attributions for stereotype consistent, those with the more positive affective reaction to the target group, showed moderation of their stereotype-based judgments relative to control participants. Importantly, the use of indirect measures of stereotyping (attributional judgments) enabled us to reveal this effect, whereby more traditional direct measures, we believe due to both demand characteristics of the procedures and a social desirability response bias from participants, were not sensitive to this phenomenon.

In summary, the research reviewed suggests that when attempting to moderate stereotypical beliefs, in addition to the traditional focus on disconfirming stereotypes with contrary information, it is also important to consider the role of stereotype-consistent information, particularly in concert with known effects of individual differences such as prejudice level. In turn, this will enable the development of more effective stereotype-change strategies that can be targeted at specific perceivers.

References

Allport, G. W. (1954). *The nature of prejudice*. Reading, MA: Addison-Wesley.

Bodenhausen, G. V., & Wyer, R. S., Jr. (1985). Effects of stereotypes on decision making and information processing strategies. *Journal of Personality and Social Psychology, 48*, 267–282.

Brewer, M. B., Dull, V., & Lui, L. (1981). Perceptions of the elderly: Stereotypes as prototypes. *Journal of Personality and Social Psychology, 41*, 656–670.

Devine, P. G. (1989). Stereotypes and prejudice: Their automatic and controlled components. *Journal of Personality and Social Psychology, 56*, 5–18.

Devine, P. G., Monteith, M. J., Zuwerink, J. R., & Elliot, A. J. (1991). Prejudice with and without compunction. *Journal of Personality and Social Psychology, 60*, 817–830.

Dovidio, J. F., Brigham, J. C., Johnson, B. T., & Gaertner, S. L. (1996). Stereotyping, prejudice and discrimination: Another look. In C. N. Macrae, C. Stangor, & M. Hewstone (Eds.), *Stereotypes and stereotyping* (pp. 276–322). New York: Guilford Press.

Duncan, B. L. (1976). Differential social perception and attribution of intergroup violence: Testing the lower limits of stereotyping of Blacks. *Journal of Personality and Social Psychology, 34*, 590–598.

Eagly, A. H. (1987). *Sex differences in social behavior: A social-role interpretation*. Hillsdale, NJ: Erlbaum.

Eagly, A. H., & Steffen, V. J. (1984). Gender stereotypes stem from distribution of women and men into social roles. *Journal of Personality and Social Psychology, 46*, 735–754.

Eagly, A. H., & Wood, W. (1982). Inferred sex differences in status as a determinant of gender stereotypes about social influence. *Journal of Personality and Social Psychology, 43*, 915–928.

Evett, S. R., Devine, P. G., Hirt, E. R., & Price, J. (1994). The role of the hypothesis and the evidence in the trait hypothesis testing process. *Journal of Experimental Social Psychology, 30*, 456–481.

Hastie, R. (1984). Causes and effects of causal attribution. *Journal of Personality and Social Psychology, 46*, 44–56.

Hewstone, M. (1989). *Causal attribution: From cognitive processes to collective beliefs.* Chichester, UK: Basil Blackwell.

Hewstone, M. (1994). Revision and change of stereotypic beliefs: In search of the elusive subtyping model. In W. Stroebe & M. Hewstone (Eds.), *European review of social psychology* (Vol. 5, pp. 69–109). New York: Wiley.

Jackson, L. A., Sullivan, L. A., & Hodge, C. N. (1993). Stereotype effects on attributions, predictions and evaluations: No two social judgments are quite alike. *Journal of Personality and Social Psychology, 65,* 69–84.

Johnston, L. (1996). Resisting change: Information-seeking and stereotype change. *European Journal of Social Psychology, 26,* 799–826.

Johnston, L. (1998, April). *Individual differences and stereotype change.* Presented at the fourth meeting of the Society of Australasian Social Psychologists (27th meeting of Australian Social Psychologists), Christchurch, New Zealand. Abstract published in *Australian Journal of Psychology, 50* supplement.

Johnston, L., Bristow, M., & Love, N. (2000). An investigation of the link between attributional judgments and stereotype-based judgments. *European Journal of Social Psychology, 30,* 551–568.

Johnston, L., & Hewstone, M. (1992). Cognitive models of stereotype change (3): Subtyping and the perceived typicality of disconfirming group members. *Journal of Experimental Social Psychology, 28,* 360–386.

Johnston, L., & Macrae, C. N. (1994). Changing social stereotypes: The case of the information seeker. *European Journal of Social Psychology, 24,* 581–592.

Johnston, L., & Macrae, C. N. (2002). *The case for stereotype change?* Manuscript in preparation.

Krueger, J., & Rothbart, M. (1988). Use of categorical and individuating information in making inferences about personality. *Journal of Personality and Social Psychology, 55,* 187–195.

Kunda, Z., & Oleson, K. C. (1995). Maintaining stereotypes in the face of disconfirmation: Constructing grounds for subtyping deviants. *Journal of Personality and Social Psychology, 68,* 565–579.

Kunda, Z., & Oleson, K. C. (1997). When exceptions prove the rule: How extremity of deviance determines the impact of deviant examples on stereotypes. *Journal of Personality and Social Psychology, 72,* 965–979.

Locksley, A., Borgida, E., Brekke, N., & Hepburn, C. (1980). Sex stereotypes and social judgment. *Journal of Personality and Social Psychology, 39,* 821–831.

Macrae, C. N., Bodenhausen, G. V., Milne, A. B., & Jetten, J. (1994). Out of mind but back in sight: Stereotypes on the rebound. *Journal of Personality and Social Psychology, 67,* 808–817.

Macrae, C. N., & Shepherd, J. W. (1989). Stereotypes and social judgments. *British Journal of Social Psychology, 28,* 319–325.

Monteith, M. J., Zuwerink, J. R., & Devine, P. G. (1994). Prejudice and prejudice reduction: Classic challenges, contemporary approaches. In P. G. Devine, D. L. Hamilton, & T. M. Ostrom (Eds.), *Social cognition: Impact on social psychology* (pp. 324–346). San Diego, CA: Academic Press.

Plant, E. A., & Devine, P. G. (1998). Internal and external motivation to respond without prejudice. *Journal of Personality and Social Psychology, 75,* 811–832.

Ross, L. D. (1977). The intuitive psychologist and his shortcomings: Distortions in the attribution process. In L. Berkowitz (Ed.), *Advances in experimental social psychology* (Vol. 10, pp. 174–214). New York: Academic Press.

Sherman, J. W., Stroessner, S. J., & Azam, O. (2002). *Prejudice, stereotyping, and individuation: Biased and non-biased encoding and integration processes.* Manuscript under review.

Wilder, D. A., Simon, A. F., & Faith, M. (1996). Enhancing the impact of counter-stereotypic information: Dispositional attributions for deviance. *Journal of Personality and Social Psychology, 71,* 276–287.

Wittenbrink, B., Gist, P. L., & Hilton, J. L. (1997). Structural properties of stereotypic knowledge and their influences on the construal of social situations. *Journal of Personality and Social Psychology, 72,* 526–543.

Wyer, N. A. (2000). *Strategies for stereotype inhibition.* Paper presented at the annual meeting of the Society for Personality and Social Psychology, San Antonio, TX.

Yzerbyt, V. Y., Coull, A., & Rocher, S. J. (1999). Fencing off the deviant: The role of cognitive resources in the maintenance of stereotypes. *Journal of Personality and Social Psychology, 77,* 449–462.

Yzerbyt, V. Y., & Leyens, J.-P. (1991). Requesting information to form an impression: The influence of valence and confirmatory status. *Journal of Experimental Social Psychology, 27,* 337–356.

19

Implicit and Explicit Process in Social Judgment

Deep and High

Marilynn B. Brewer

CONTENTS

INTRODUCTION

The combined themes of this volume – explicit and implicit processing, and social judgment and decision making – are readily juxtaposed, as is well illustrated by the contents of the preceding chapters. Given the pervasiveness of judgment and decision-making events in everyday life, it is not surprising to find that these processes play out at different levels of awareness and conscious effort. If many routine or recurring assessments and decisions in the social domain were not relegated to low-effort processing, social exchange would be hopelessly mired. Thus, understanding implicit, automatic, heuristic judgment processes as well as explicit, deliberative, elaborated processes, and their interplay, is essential to a full theory of social judgment and decision making.

Collectively, the chapters in this volume take on this task of explicating the roles of implicit and explicit processes across various domains of human judgment, with at least two major integrative themes that cut across the various contributions. Each of these themes takes up a particular challenge to prevailing notions in the study of human judgment and decision making. One recurring theme is a challenge to the normative view of judgment and decision making, in which heuristic strategies are labeled as

Please address correspondence to Marilynn B. Brewer, Department of Psychology, Ohio State University, 1885 Neil Avenue, Columbus, OH 43210; e-mail: brewer.64@osu.edu *errors* and *biases*, in favor of a functional, adaptive perspective in which such heuristics are viewed as goal-serving. The second challenge is that issued by Kruglanski and his colleagues (Kruglanski, Thompson, & Spiegel, 1999; Kruglanski et al., this volume) to prevailing dual-process theories of social judgment. I will use these two themes to organize my thoughts and comments on the major points represented in preceding chapters.

SOCIAL JUDGMENT: ERROR-PRONE OR FUNCTIONALLY ADAPTIVE?

The debate over the epistemological status of judgment heuristics is represented in the exchange between Kahneman and Tversky (1996) and Gigerenzer (1996), revolving around Gigerenzer's claim that it is inappropriate to judge decision making against normative statistical models. Instead, Gigerenzer (2000) has argued that the appropriate question to ask about human reasoning is, what are the organism's goals, particularly in naturalistic decision-making contexts? According to this goal-serving perspective, judgmental heuristics are not simply functional as mental shortcuts, but adaptively valid decision rules.

Several chapters in this volume take up this debate explicitly, applying an adaptive view to specific judgment phenomena. Haselton and Buss (this volume), for instance, argue from a signal detection framework that specific social judgment biases represent necessary trade-offs between the costs associated with false-positive and false-negative types of error. From a cost-analysis perspective, what appear to be judgmental flaws may represent rational design, biased toward committing the less costly error in terms of ultimate reproductive success. A similar adaptive argument is made by Fiedler and Freytag (this volume) in their analysis of judgments based on *pseudocontingencies*. Both Haselton and Buss and Fiedler and Freytag suggest that specific judgmental heuristics may be "built into" human decision making as a function of their long-run adaptive value. Consistent with this adaptive approach is Funder's (this volume) call for a renewed focus on accuracy in social perception and personality judgments. He argues that an extraordinary level of accuracy is an achievement of person perception processes, and that inaccuracies may be more a function of the information environment than of perceiver biases or inadequacies.

On the other hand, the *error* view of some aspects of human judgment is at least implicit in other chapters in this volume. For instance, Forgas and East (this volume) speak of positive mood effects as responsible for a variety of "errors and distortions" in performance assessments and false memories. Errors of judgment are also implicated in treatments of attitude-biased information processing (von Hippel, Vargas, & Sekaquaptewa, this volume) and stereotype-biased attributions (Johnston & Miles, this volume).

From the prevailing *cognitive miser* perspective on social judgment, many implicit processes are viewed as shortcuts or products of mental laziness. From this perspective, heuristics function as time- and effort-saving mechanisms, not as goal-serving devices. But further analysis may reveal an underlying adaptive logic, particularly if we shift attention to serving *social* (rather than cognitive) goals. In this vein, Shaver and Mikulincer (this volume) argue that attachment strategies may underlie certain negative mood congruence effects, and Williams, Case, and Govan (this volume) suggest that implicit prejudice may serve social inclusion needs. These analyses illustrate how a functional, social psychological perspective may illuminate the adaptive significance of many implicit judgment and decision-making phenomena.

SOCIAL JUDGMENT: UNIMODAL OR DISTINCT PROCESSES?

Parallel in many ways to the implicit–explicit distinction in the social judgment literature are the myriad *dual-process* models that postulate separate, qualitatively distinct routes to social judgments and decisions (cf. Kruglanski et al., this volume). Although the various dual-process models characterize this distinction in somewhat different ways, in most cases one processing mode is represented as quick, low-effort, relatively superficial, and heuristic-based, whereas the alternative processing mode is more deliberate, thoughtful, slow, and involves effortful processing of more information. Dual-process theories hold that these processing styles are fundamentally different in that they utilize different information and engage different underlying processing mechanisms to arrive at a judgment or decision.

Against this backdrop, Kruglanski (Kruglanski et al., 1999; this volume) has issued a challenge to the validity of most dual-process claims and poses an alternative *unimodel* theory of human judgment in which a set of judgmental parameters capture the variations in judgment styles that have been attributed to different processes. In this multidimensional (but unimodal) model, modes of judgment differ in degree rather than in kind, and most postulated dual modes can be reconceptualized in terms of the intersection of two continua of motivation and task difficulty. As Kruglanski et al. (this volume) put it, " ... the fact that some inferences may occur very quickly, outside the individual's conscious awareness and with only minimal dependence on cognitive resources ... does not imply a qualitatively separate cognitive process."

Kruglanski and his colleagues provide a convincing critique of many of the research paradigms and findings that have been garnered in support of qualitatively distinct judgment processes. Nonetheless, I believe that at least some of the phenomena that have been examined in the present volume do meet the definition of *content-free* dual processes that Kruglanski

TABLE 19.1. *Two Processing Systems*

	Deep System	High System
Locus	Subcortical	Forebrain, cerebral
Origin	Evolution (prewiring)	Explicit learning
	Early experience, conditioning	Culture (norms, rules, principles, values)
Attributes	Reflexive, rigid, mechanistic	Reflective, deliberative, constructive
	Unintentional, fast	Intentional, slow
	Associative, concrete	Rule-based, abstract
	Domain-specific	Domain-general
	Default	Override, requiring cognitive resources

challenges us to defend. The question is, what criteria can and should be proposed to assess whether processes are qualitatively different or not? I suggest that some useful answers can come from considering an analogy to the distinct subsystems that constitute human sensory processing. Although the different modalities can be viewed as parts of a single sensory system, few would deny that vision, audition, olfaction, and so on represent qualitatively distinct forms of sensory processing. Among other things, they differ in the *kind* (not simply amount) of information extracted from environmental stimuli, rely on different brain pathways, and invoke different signal transducers. Analogously, we may be able to identify distinct cognitive and affective processing subsystems that differ in parallel ways.

In Table 19.1, I have made an attempt to identify criteria for distinguishing two fundamentally different modes of information processing that may underlie social judgments and decision making. For want of a better set of terms, I have labeled these two modes *deep* and *high*, respectively.[1] In making this particular process differentiation, I am drawing heavily on the ideas presented by Lieberman (this volume; see also Lieberman, Gaunt, Gilbert, & Trope, 2002) and his distinction between *reflexive* and *reflective* judgment processes and their neurological substrates.

Deep processes reflect activity primarily at the subcortical level of the brain, perhaps involving the neural structures associated with Lieberman's *X-system* (composed of the amygdala, basal ganglia, and lateral temporal cortex). Activation of this deep system, and the environmental cues to

[1] I choose to use new labels here because I do not think that any of the existing dichotomies (e.g., implicit–explicit, automatic–controlled, conscious–subconscious) fully capture the distinction I am making. Further, the terms *high* and *deep* are evaluatively equivalent, thus avoiding the evaluative connotations implicit in comparisons such as *high level versus low level* or *shallow versus deep*.

which it responds, is either prewired (a product of our biological evolution) or set by early experience and emotional conditioning. As a repository of long-term stable knowledge, it has the properties of a "slow-learning" memory system, reflecting a large body of experiences acquired slowly and incrementally (including evolutionary time) (McClelland, McNaughton, & O'Reilly, 1995; Sherry & Schacter, 1987). As a consequence, this system operates largely by default, in a reflexive, rigid, and mechanistic manner. Deep processing is rapid, associative (Sloman, 1996; Smith & DeCoster, 2000), and probably domain-specific, and takes place automatically and unintentionally.

By contrast to deep processing, the high processing mode involves activation of the prefrontal cortex and reflects explicit learning of symbolic rules, principles, procedures, and cultural norms (Smith & DeCoster, 2000). Processing based on this system is reflective, deliberative, and constructive rather than mechanistic. It is rule-based and abstract, hence domain-general. High processing is also intentional and capable of overriding (or disrupting) deep processes (see Lieberman, this volume). Although the distinction between deep and high processing modes is not equivalent to the distinction between automatic and controlled processing, there is a contingent association in that controlled, deliberate judgments always (necessarily) involve the high processing system, but automatized, low-effort, or subconscious judgments do not always or necessarily implicate the deep processing system.

By far the greatest portion of research on social judgment and decision making has, at least historically, been devoted to studying judgments that rely on the high processing mode. Of special interest to social psychologists more recently is new evidence of how much *social* information processing takes place in the deep mode (see Haselton & Buss; Lieberman; Shaver & Mikulincer, all this volume). Amygdala activation, in particular, has been implicated in social categorization and automatic stereotyping, as well as in detection of threat cues such as fear expressions. Recently, Lieberman et al. (2002) have suggested that the automatic behavior identification stage of attribution takes place in the lateral temporal cortex, along a pathway activated by cues associated with behavior *intentionality*. In addition, short-exposure (30 ms) affective priming (Stapel, this volume) involves extraction of diffuse affective content prior to cognitive appraisal and probably reflects deep-level processing of social information. Consistent with this idea, recent experiments using event-related brain potential (ERP) measurement (Smith, Cacioppo, Larsen, & Chartrand, 2002) indicates that differential allocation of attention to negative, potentially threatening stimuli takes place well before information reaches the visual cortex for more elaborate processing. Thus, many of the fundamental components of social judgment appear to arise from processes at subcortical levels of the neurological system.

Cognitive and Motivational Outputs of the Two Systems

Although various brain imaging techniques may eventually provide direct evidence of the activation of different modes of processing, much of our knowledge of these systems will come more indirectly, from the different types of output or products of the processing modes. Thus, an important task for future research will be to identify the types of judgments, evaluations, and motivational states that arise from deep processing versus high processing. Reviewing the wide range of judgmental phenomena covered in the present volume, one realizes that we are a long way from being able to classify or explain specific effects in terms of underlying processing mode distinctions. Assimilation and contrast effects, decision heuristics, mood congruence effects, causal attributions, perceptual and conceptual judgments, impression formation, stereotyping, social comparison, goal activation – all may implicate deep or high processing systems in some way.

Daunting though the task may be to match specific judgmental outcomes to processing modes, I have made an attempt to classify some of the phenomena that have been examined in this volume in terms of the distinction between deep and high processes. Table 19.2 presents a rough classification of the types of judgments that are generated by the two processing modes, along with some specific examples. The reader will notice immediately that the table has three columns rather than two. In only some cases have I been willing to go out on a limb and classify specific judgment

TABLE 19.2. *Judgments Generated by Different Processing Systems*

Deep System Outputs	Mixed, Intermediate	High System Outputs
Identification, pattern-matching	Holistic impressions Context effects, implicit comparison	Rule-based classification Explicit comparison, analogy
Evaluative categorization (diffuse affect) Me–not me categorization Power, dominance categorization Intentionality categorization	Distinct affect Implicit beliefs, attitudes Mood priming Spontaneous inference	Emotions Explicit knowledge, attitudes Affect infusion Attribution
Domain-specific decision heuristics	Implicit biases	Rules of thumb
Self-relevance assessment Threat-security assessment	Implicit motives Implicit monitoring Implicit attachment systems Unconscious mimicry	Explicit goals Intentional suppression Explicit attachment system Social self-presentation

outputs as unequivocally representative of deep or high processing. All of the others fall into an ambiguous intermediate, or mixed category, which contains most of what has been studied in the domain of implicit judgments, evaluations, and inferences.

The most fundamental output of the deep system is object identification and classification based on pattern-matching, which is appropriately characterized by connectionist models (Smolensky, 1988). Pattern-matching takes place in the prefrontal cortex as well (Zárate & Stoever, this volume), but Lieberman et al. (2002) summarize evidence for automatic categorical pattern-matching involving activation of a pathway along the inferotemporal cortex, prior to any conscious recognition or symbolic representation. In terms of identification, there is little or no difference between judgments involving social and nonsocial objects or movements, but other primitive categorizations generated by the deep processing system are particularly relevant to social stimuli and events. These include evaluative categorization (diffuse affect, relevant to affective priming and social emotions), behavioral intentionality categorization (relevant to attribution judgments), me–not me categorization (relevant to attachment and belonging, in-group–out-group discrimination), and dominance (relevant to status and power judgments). In addition, some domain-specific decision heuristics (cf. Haselton & Buss, this volume) may reflect deep-level processing, along with automatic assessments of self-relevance and threat versus security.

Most of the judgment outcomes generated by the deep processing system have parallels in judgments and decisions resulting from high system processing. Associative, pattern-matching identification in the deep system is complemented by rule-based classification, explicit comparison, and reasoning by analogy in the high processing system. Automatic evaluative categorization is matched by explicit attitudes and preference judgments in the high system. Behavioral intentionality assessments feed into explicit attributions and personality judgments; automatic decision heuristics have their parallel in explicit "rules of thumb"; and security-threat assessments are represented in the high processing system as attachment schemas (cf. Shaver & Mikulincer, this volume) and explicit social motives and goals.

Implicit Processes: Deep or High?

In most of the chapters in this volume, high processing system outputs are discussed in comparison to related implicit, unintentional, or automatic judgments. Some of these so-called implicit phenomena may arise directly from deep system processing, as indicated previously. But the concept of implicit processing is used rather broadly in social cognition to refer to judgments that appear to occur outside of awareness and are unaffected by cognitive load (McClure, Sutton, & Hilton, this volume). Many of the social judgments and motives designated as implicit cannot be readily attributed to deep system processing because they implicate symbolic and semantic representations as well as first-order categorizations and evaluative associations. It is my hope that some heuristic value of this chapter will be derived from questions to be answered about the phenomena in this mixed category. More specifically, can implicit processes be differentiated such that some are direct products of deep processing, some are derivatives of high processing judgments that have become automatized, and some reflect more complex interactions of the outputs of both high and deep processing modes?

One example of the juxtaposition of deep and high system processing is represented in Stapel's (this volume) analysis of affective priming effects in judgments. It seems clear that the diffuse affect that gives rise to early (i.e., very short exposure duration) affective judgments is a product of deep system processing. But this is quickly supplanted by later (moderately short duration) distinct affect judgments that implicate higher-level cognitive appraisal processes. Interestingly, the consequences of affective priming (assimilation or contrast) differ dramatically, depending on which system is involved.

By contrast to Stapel's dual-system analysis of affective priming effects, Chartrand and Jefferis (this volume) discuss automatic goal activation as an automatized derivative of intentional high system processes. But their integration of automatic motives and automatic goal pursuit strategies, such as mimicry, may implicate deep system processes as well. Mimicry in particular may reflect the activation of inclusion motives derived from deep system assessments of insecurity and/or dominance. Similarly, strategies to enact or to counter prejudice/stereotyping (cf. Galinsky et al., this volume; Johnston & Miles, this volume), maintain or avoid attachment (Shaver & Mikulincer, this volume), and restore inclusion (Williams et al., this volume) may be so fundamental to survival that they are activated by assessments generated from deep system processes, rather than merely reflecting automatized high system judgments.

The interplay of implicit and explicit judgments is also represented in the discussion by McClure et al. (this volume) of the role of implicit covariation assumptions and explicit rules in goal-based explanations of social behavior, in the analysis by Bless, Schwarz, and Wänke (this volume) of the size of context effects in social judgments, in Forgas and East's (this volume) analysis of affective influences in elaborative judgments, in Suls, Martin, and Wheeler's (this volume) proxy model of the role of social comparison in self-assessment of abilities and opinions, in the analysis by Galinsky et al. (this volume) of the differential effects of implicit processes in determining the outcomes of suppression versus perspective-taking as strategies for controlling stereotype activation, and in the analysis by Johnston and

Miles (this volume) of the consequences of dispositional versus situational attributions for stereotype-consistent behaviors. In all of these domains, however, it is not clear whether the implicit aspects involve the activation of deep system processes in any way, or whether they might well be incorporated in a unimodel framework, as argued by Kruglanski et al. (this volume), or, alternatively, whether they implicate yet a third processing system that is qualitatively distinct from either deep or high systems as they have been defined here. It seems to me that this poses an interesting question for further understanding of the role of implicit judgment processes in social cognition.

IMPLICIT OR EXPLICIT: SOME FINAL THOUGHTS

The discovery that many outcomes of social judgment and decision making are influenced by processes that occur outside of awareness or conscious intention has stimulated a great deal of new and exciting research in social cognition, social motives, and social emotions. The advent of social cognitive neuroscience has produced even more intriguing suggestions about just how much social judgments are represented in the structures at primitive levels of the human brain. Nonetheless, I think it is important that we not let this fascination with subconscious and subcortical influences cause us to lose track of the primary locus of the "social brain." Though deep system judgment processes may well have been shaped by our evolution as a social species, it is the evolution of the high system, prefrontal cortex processing capacities that has most certainly been determined by the demands and complexities of social interdependence (Brewer, 1997; Caporael, 1997; Sedikides & Skowronski, 1997). For that reason, the study of conscious, deliberate, rule-based, domain-general processing that has the capability of controlling or overriding the output of deep system processes should continue to be the primary focus of social psychological theory and research on social cognition, judgment, and decision making.

References

Brewer, M. B. (1997). On the social origins of human nature. In G. McGarty & S. A. Haslam (Eds.), *The message of social psychology: Perspectives on mind and society* (pp. 54–62). Oxford: Blackwell.

Caporael, L. R. (1997). The evolution of truly social cognition: The core configuration model. *Personality and Social Psychology Review, 1*, 276–298.

Gigerenzer, G. (1996). On narrow norms and vague heuristics: A reply to Kahneman and Tversky (1996). *Psychological Review, 103*, 592–596.

Gigerenzer, G. (2000). *Adaptive thinking: Rationality in the real world.* New York: Oxford University Press.

Kahneman, D., & Tversky, A. (1996). On the reality of cognitive illusions. *Psychological Review, 103*, 582–591.

Kruglanski, A. W., Thompson, E. P., & Spiegel, S. (1999). Separate or equal: Bimodal notions of persuasion and a single-process "unimodel." In S. Chaiken & Y. Trope (Eds.), *Dual-process theories in social psychology* (pp. 293–313). New York: Guilford Press.

Lieberman, M. D., Gaunt, R., Gilbert, D. T., & Trope, Y. (2002). Reflexion and reflection: A social cognitive neuroscience approach to attributional inference. In M. Zanna (Ed.), *Advances in experimental social psychology* (Vol. 34, pp. 199–249). New York: Elsevier.

McClelland, J. L., McNaughton, B. L., & O'Reilly, R. C. (1995). Why there are complementary learning systems in the hippocampus and neocortex: Insights from the successes and failures of connectionist models of learning and memory. *Psychological Review, 102,* 419–457.

Sedikides, C., & Skowronski, J. J. (1997). The symbolic self in evolutionary context. *Personality and Social Psychology Review, 1,* 80–102.

Sherry, D. F., & Schacter, D. (1987). The evolution of multiple memory systems. *Psychological Review, 94,* 439–454.

Sloman, S. A. (1996). The empirical case for two systems of reasoning. *Psychological Bulletin, 119,* 3–22.

Smith, E. R., & DeCoster, J. (2000). Dual-process models in social and cognitive psychology: Conceptual integration and links to underlying memory systems. *Personality and Social Psychology Review, 4,* 108–131.

Smith, N. K., Cacioppo, J. T., Larsen, F. T., & Chartrand, T. L. (2002). *May I have your attention, please: Electrocortical responses to positive and negative stimuli.* Unpublished manuscript.

Smolensky, P. (1988). On the proper treatment of connectionism. *Behavioral and Brain Sciences, 11,* 1–74.

Author Index

Note: Page numbers in italics refer to citations in references.

Subject Index

Continued from page iii

SSP 3. SOCIAL INFLUENCE: DIRECT AND INDIRECT PRO-CESSES (Edited by Joseph P. Forgas and Kipling D. Williams). Contributors: Robert Cialdini (*Arizona*), Eric Knowles et al. (*Arkansas*), Bibb Latane (*Florida Atlantic*), Marty Bourgeois (*Wyoming*), Mark Schaller (*UBC*), Ap Dijksterhuis (*Nijmegen*), James Tedeschi (*SUNY*), Richard Petty (*Ohio State*), Joseph P. Forgas (*UNSW*), Herbert Bless (*Mannheim*), Fritz Strack (*Wurzburg*), Sik Hung Ng (*Hong Kong*), Thomas Mussweiler (*Wurzburg*), Kip Williams (*Macquarie*), Chuck Stangor and Gretchen Sechrist (*Maryland*), John Jost (*Stanford*), Debbie Terry and Michael Hogg (*Queensland*), Stephen Harkins (*Northeastern*), Barbara David and John Turner (*Australian National*), Robin Martin (*Queensland*), Miles Hewstone (*Cardiff*), Russell Spears and Tom Postmes (*Amsterdam*), Martin Lea (*Manchester*), Susan Watt (*Amsterdam*). Psychology Press, New York, 2002; ISBN 1-84169-038-4 (hardback), 1-84169-039-2 (paperback).

SSP 4. THE SOCIAL SELF: COGNITIVE, INTERPERSONAL AND INTERGROUP PERSPECTIVES (Edited by Joseph P. Forgas, Kipling D. Williams, and William von Hippel). Contributors: Herbert Bless (*Mannheim*), Marilynn Brewer (*OSU*), Tanya Chartrand (*OSU*), Klaus Fiedler (*Heidelberg*), Joseph P. Forgas (*UNSW*), Dave Funder (*UC Riverside*), Adam Galinsky (*Utah*), Martie G. Haselton (*UCLA*), David Buss (*Texas*), Lucy Johnston (*Canterbury, NZ*), Arie Kruglanski (*Maryland*), Matt Lieberman (*UCLA*), Phil Shaver (*UC Davis*), Mario Mikulincer (*Bar-Ilan*), Diederik Stapel (*Groningen*), Jerry Suls (*Iowa*), Bill von Hippel (*UNSW*), Kip Williams (*Macquarie*), Michael Zarate (*Texas*). Psychology Press, New York, 2002; ISBN 1-84169-062-7 (hardback).